British Social Attitudes

Attitudes The 17th REPORT

The **National Centre for Social Research** is an independent, non-profit social research institute. It has a large professional staff together with its own interviewing and coding resources. Some of the *National Centre*'s work – such as the survey reported in this book – is initiated by the institute itself and grant-funded by research councils or foundations. Other work is initiated by government departments, local authorities or quasi-government organisations to provide information on aspects of social or economic policy. The *National Centre* also works frequently with other institutes and academics. Founded in 1969 and now Britain's largest social research institute, the *National Centre* has a high reputation for the standard of its work in both qualitative and quantitative research. The *National Centre* has a Survey Methods Centre and, with the Department of Sociology, University of Oxford, houses the Centre for Research into Elections and Social Trends (CREST), which is an ESRC Research Centre. It also houses, with Southampton University, the Centre for Applied Social Surveys (CASS), an ESRC Resource Centre, two main functions of which are to run courses in survey methods and to establish and administer an electronic social survey question bank.

The contributors

Michael Adler
Professor of Socio-Legal Studies in the Department of Social Policy, University of Edinburgh.

Catherine Bromley
Researcher at the *National Centre for Social Research* and Co-director of the *British Social Attitudes* survey series

Caroline Bryson
Research Director at the *National Centre for Social Research*.

Ian Christie
Associate Director of the consultancy The Local Futures Group and an associate of Forum for the Future.

John Curtice
Deputy Director of the ESRC Centre for Research into Elections and Social Trends (CREST), and Professor of Politics and Director of the Social Statistics Laboratory at Strathclyde University

Nan Dirk De Graaf
Reader at the Department of Sociology, Nijmegen University, the Netherlands.

Geoffrey Evans
Official Fellow in Politics, Nuffield College Oxford and University Reader in the Sociology of Politics.

Anthony Heath
Professor of Sociology at the University of Oxford, and Co-director of the ESRC Centre for Research into Elections and Social Trends based at the National Centre and Department of Sociology, Oxford.

Annette Hill
Reader in Communication at the Centre for Communication and Information Studies, University of Westminster.

Kerstin Hinds
Senior Researcher at the *National Centre for Social Research* Scotland.

Lindsey Jarvis
Senior Researcher at the *National Centre for Social Research* and Co-director of the *British Social Attitudes* survey series.

Roger Jowell
Director of the *National Centre for Social Research* and Co-director of the *British Social Attitudes* survey series; Visiting Professor at the London School of Economics and Political Science

Peter Kemp
Professor of Housing and Social Policy at the University of Glasgow.

Ariana Need
Reader at the Department of Sociology, Amsterdam University, the Netherlands.

Bill New
Independent health policy analyst.

Alison Park
Director of the *National Centre for Social Research* Scotland and Co-director of the *British Social Attitudes* Series.

Michael Rosie
Research Associate in the Governance of Scotland Forum, University of Edinburgh.

Nina Stratford
Senior Researcher at the *National Centre for Social Research* and Co-director of the *British Social Attitudes* survey series.

Katarina Thomson
Research Director at the *National Centre for Social Research* and Co-director of the *British Social Attitudes* survey series

British Social Attitudes

Attitudes The 17th REPORT

Focusing on Diversity

EDITORS

Roger Jowell
John Curtice
Alison Park
Katarina Thomson
Lindsey Jarvis
Catherine Bromley
Nina Stratford

SAGE Publications
London · Thousand Oaks · New Delhi

National Centre *for*
Social Research

SAGE Publications Ltd
6 Bonhill Street
London EC2A 4PU

SAGE Publications Inc
2455 Teller Road
Thousand Oaks, California 91320

SAGE Publications India Pvt Ltd
32, M-Block Market
Greater Kailash – I
New Delhi 110 048

British Library Cataloguing in Publication data

A catalogue record for this book is available from the British Library

ISSN 0267 6869

ISBN 0 7619 7045 2

Library of Congress catalog record available

Printed in Great Britain by The Cromwell Press, Ltd, Trowbridge, Wiltshire

Contents

List of tables and figures

Chapter 1

Chapter 2

Chapter 3

Chapter 4

Chapter 5

Chapter 6

Chapter 7

Chapter 8

Chapter 9

Chapter 10

Introduction

This volume, like each of its annual predecessors, presents results, analyses and interpretations of the latest *British Social Attitudes* survey – the 17th in the series of reports on the studies designed and carried out by the *National Centre for Social Research*.

The primary focus of this volume is on diversity within Britain. Most of the chapters examine the extent to which various sub-groups in society differ from one another in their attitudes, values and perspectives. Chapter 1, for instance, exposes the different vantage points from which younger and older people view the world and themselves, while chapter 5 looks at women's and men's different perceptions of their society and their lives. Chapter 3 looks at the age-old class divide in Britain and examines how much and in what ways the gap is narrowing, and chapter 9 looks at the contrasting priorities and preferences of urban and rural dwellers. Chapter 6 explores cross-national differences between countries with and without a strong religious faith, and chapter 8 probes into the rather more subtle and elusive variations in national sentiment between the English, Scottish and Welsh as devolution takes root in Britain. Meanwhile, chapter 7 investigates the changing landscape of council tenants *versus* home owners, housing association and private tenants.

Some differences we uncover in this volume are surprisingly large and others remarkably small. Overall, they underline the fact that although British society enjoys a wide range of shared values, the picture is far from homogeneous. Different sub-groups have different interests (in both senses of the word), which translate themselves into different viewpoints and judgements on many issues. The resulting picture is of a healthy civil society containing many different and sometimes persistent shades of opinion, none of which seem to presage serious conflict.

The robustness of the *British Social Attitudes* series owes a great deal to its many generous funders. We are particularly grateful to our core funders – the Gatsby Charitable Foundation (one of the Sainsbury Family Charitable Trusts) – whose continuous support of the series from the start has given it security and independence. But other funders too have made long-term commitments to supporting particular modules and we are ever grateful to them too – notably the

Department for Education and Employment, and the Departments of Health, Social Security, and the Environment, Transport and the Regions.

The series also receives support for particular modules of questions from a number of funding agencies – among them the Economic and Social Research Council (ESRC), the Leverhulme Trust, the Wellcome Trust and the Nuffield Foundation – and from independent bodies such as the Countryside Agency.

Last year we were once again grateful to have support for a special module of questions on issues of 'taste and decency' in television programmes, videos, cinemas and the internet. The results are reported on in chapter 4. Funding for this module came from a consortium of bodies including the British Board of Film Classification, the Broadcasting Standards Council, the Independent Television Commission, the BBC, and Flextech Television.

Two new modules of questions are reported here for the first time. Funding from the King's Fund enabled us to include a module on attitudes to health care rationing (see chapter 2). And a grant from the ESRC provided support for a fascinating series of questions on public responses to begging, as reported in chapter 10.

In collaboration with a number of eminent academics in Scotland, we launched a new *Scottish Social Attitudes* survey series in 1999, supported in the first instance by the ESRC. It is closely associated with its British counterpart and incorporates many of the same questions to enable comparison, while also providing a detailed examination of attitudes to particular issues within Scotland. The first book on this series will be published in the spring of 2001 by Edinburgh University Press and will report on social and political attitudes at the time of the first Scottish parliamentary election.

The ESRC also continues to finance two other pieces of the jigsaw. First, it supports the *National Centre*'s participation in the International Social Survey Programme (ISSP), which now comprises 37 nations, each of whom help to design and then field a set of equivalent questions every year on a rotating set of issues. Findings from this survey on variations in religiosity across cultures and countries are included in this volume in chapter 6.

Secondly, the ESRC continues to fund the *Centre for Research into Elections and Social Trends* (*CREST*) – an ESRC Research Centre that links the *National Centre* with the Department of Sociology at Oxford University – whose purpose is to uncover and investigate long-run changes in Britain's social and political complexion.

The *British Social Attitudes* series is, of course, a team effort. The researchers who design, direct and report on the study are supported by complementary teams who implement the sampling strategy and carry out data processing. They in turn depend on fieldwork controllers, area managers and field interviewers who are responsible for getting all the interviewing done, and on administrative staff to compile, organise and distribute the survey's extensive documentation. The questions have to be translated into a computer-assisted questionnaire, a task that is expertly performed by Sue Corbett and her colleagues in the *National Centre*'s computing department. Meanwhile, the raw data have to be transformed into a workable SPSS system file – a task that has for many years been performed with great care and efficiency by Ann Mair at the Social

Statistics Laboratory in the University of Strathclyde. Finally, the various chapters of the book have to be organised and formatted, notoriously difficult tasks that Sheila Vioche now seems to perform with consummate ease and serenity.

We are also pleased to welcome our new publishers, Sage, on board. The transition has gone remarkably smoothly, thanks especially to Lucy Robinson, Vanessa Harwood and Vicky Price at Sage.

As always, however, our most heartfelt tribute is reserved for our anonymous respondents in England, Scotland and Wales who gave their time to participate in our 1999 survey. Like their 40,000 or so predecessors, they are the stars of this enterprise. We hope that some of them will one day come across this volume and read about themselves with interest.

The Editors

1 The generation game

*Alison Park**

British society is ageing. The government estimates that by 2026 there will be over 17 million people aged 60 or over – an increase of nearly 50 per cent in three decades (Evandrou and Falkingham, 2000). This means that while 20 to 30 year olds currently outnumber the 60-plus age group, in two decades their numbers will be roughly equal, and in three decades the older group will comfortably outnumber the younger (Foresight Ageing Population Panel, 2000). These changes not only reflect increasing life expectancy but also lower fertility rates. They also relate to fluctuations in the birth rate over time, which affect the size of particular generations. For instance, the ageing of the two large 'baby boom' generations – one born just after the Second World War and the second in the early 1960s – has a continuing dominant effect on Britain's age structure (Evandrou, 1997).

A great deal of attention has been paid to the social and economic implications of an ageing population, particularly in terms of the pressures it places on social security and health budgets. These pressures reflect both the increasing demands on health care and pensions made by an older population, and the decreasing size and proportion of younger people to contribute towards the state (and private) funds that meet such demands (Walker, 1999; Johnson and Falkingham, 1992; OECD, 1996). But little is known about the likely impact of an ageing population on Britain's social attitudes and values.

This chapter seeks partly to remedy this omission, first by exploring what age differences in attitudes there are, then by trying to uncover their origins and finally assessing their likely impact. It examines three broad categories of attitude, the first of which refers to moral values and covers such issues as sexuality, abortion and religion. Is an ageing society likely to become a more socially conservative one? The second category refers to interest and engagement in politics. Is an ageing society likely to be more or less politically apathetic? And the final category refers to attitudes to welfare. What sorts of demands might an ageing society make on state resources?

---

* Alison Park is Director of the *National Centre for Social Research* Scotland and Co-director of the *British Social Attitudes* survey series.

The fact that the young and the old have different views about certain issues is hardly surprising. But to shed light on the future, we need to know how and why these attitudes differ. If, say, older people turn out to be more religious than younger ones, is it because people become more religious as they age? If so, this would be a *life-cycle* phenomenon: changes in attitudes would accompany or follow changes in the objective circumstances of people's lives, of which chronological age is only one. Others are major life events such as getting married, having children, entering or leaving the labour market, and so on, all of which may have a profound impact on how people view themselves and their world.

But this is by no means the only explanation for age-related differences. If older people are more religious, it may instead simply be a direct consequence of having lived in a more religious world when they were young and then carrying these values with them into later life. This would be a *generational* explanation of differences, suggesting that each generation's religious attitudes and values are likely to remain relatively constant over their lifetime (Jowell and Park, 1998; Alwin and Scott, 1996; Mannheim, 1928).

Disentangling life-cycle and generational explanations of differences can provide useful clues about the implications of an ageing population for a society's future attitudes and values. If, for instance, we found that life-cycle effects best explained age differences in religiosity, then we would conclude that society would become more religious as older people become more numerically dominant. But if instead we found that generational changes best accounted for age differences in religiosity, then we would conclude that society would become less religious over time as cohort replacement took its toll. In these circumstances, we could also judge the likely speed of change according to the numerical strength of different generations and how marked the differences between them were.

In order to examine whether age differences in attitudes reflect life-cycle or generational factors we need to examine change over time both within society as a whole and among particular *age cohorts*. (Details about the cohorts we have used here can be found in the appendix to this chapter.) Only then can we begin to tell whether certain attitudes change as a particular cohort ages (a life-cycle effect), or whether they remain stable over time (a generational effect). But this analysis is always complicated by the fact that on some issues a whole society's attitudes tend to change over time (a *period effect*), permeating all age groups alike. In practice, therefore, it is impossible to be certain that we have ever definitively disentangled life-cycle, generational and period effects.[1] Nonetheless, by tracking the attitudes of particular cohorts over time, we gather valuable clues about the likely influences at work and thus of how things are likely to change.

The moral maze

Age differences in attitudes

Before trying to explain the relationship between age and moral attitudes, the following paragraphs merely attempt to document and measure it.

Nowhere is the gulf between old and young so dramatic as in their religious attachments. As the next table shows, the proportion of people who do **not** belong to a particular religion diminishes steadily as age increases – to the extent that 18-24 year olds are more than twice as likely as the 55-plus age group to have no religious attachment.

Table 1.1 Per cent not belonging to any particular religion by age, 1999

	18-24	25-34	35-44	45-54	55-64	65+	All
	%	%	%	%	%	%	%
No religion	66	59	49	44	30	24	44
Base	*240*	*588*	*588*	*492*	*450*	*783*	*3141*

In line with a long-standing cliché, clear differences exist between young and old in their sexual permissiveness. For instance, as the next table shows, 25-34 year olds (the most permissive group of all on these matters) are nearly three times more likely than people over 65 to see nothing wrong in premarital sex, and nearly five times more likely to see nothing wrong in homosexuality. However, age differences are less apparent in relation to **extra**-marital sex, of which all age groups are much more disapproving.

Table 1.2 Attitudes towards sexual relationships by age, 1999

	18-24	25-34	35-44	45-54	55-64	65+	All
% saying "not wrong at all" if:							
A man and woman have sexual relations before marriage	63	72	65	54	32	26	52
Two adults of the same sex have sexual relations	36	43	35	20	24	9	27
% saying "always wrong" if:							
A married person has sexual relations with someone other than their spouse	54	59	56	49	63	75	60
Base	*75*	*202*	*215*	*163*	*141*	*255*	*1051*

Distinct but less dramatic age differences are also evident in people's attitudes to abortion. As the next table shows, we asked respondents whether they thought abortion should be permitted by law in various circumstances, but irrespective of circumstance 25-34 year olds are again the most permissive and older age groups the least.

Table 1.3 Attitudes to abortion by age, 1998

	18-24	25-34	35-44	45-54	55-64	65+	All
% saying abortions should be allowed by law:							
The couple agree they do not wish to have the child	67	72	60	57	53	52	60
The woman decides on her own she does not wish to have the child	53	62	58	51	47	52	55
The woman is not married and does not wish to marry the man	44	58	48	56	48	49	51
Base	*72*	*184*	*171*	*136*	*123*	*188*	*874*

Explaining age differences

Are these substantial age-related differences in attitudes to such moral issues and religion just a natural life-cycle effect (with attitudes changing alongside life events, such as having children or getting closer to 'meeting one's maker')? If this were so, we would expect an ageing society to become more morally conservative. But if older people's moral views are simply a long-standing product of their formative years being spent within a more rigid moral and religious climate (a generational effect), then we would expect society to become less religious and more permissive over time. This tendency might also have been given impetus by the considerable expansion since the 1960s of higher education, which is strongly associated with a more liberal and permissive outlook (Tarling and Dowds, 1997).

On the other hand, a *period effect* might well also have been at work, with the whole of society having changed since the 1960s – among other things in response to the introduction of the contraceptive pill, the liberalisation of censorship laws and the decriminalisation of homosexuality – all of which may have dented widely held societal prejudices and values via a process of 'contagion' (Jagodzinski and Dobbelaere, 1994). If these period influences do

exist, then it is not likely that aggregate social attitudes will become more conservative as the proportion of older people rises.

We begin with religion. To assess whether the stark age differences shown earlier in Table 1.1 reflect generational or life-cycle factors, we look at change over time, both within society as a whole and within particular 'age-cohorts'.

The results are shown in the next table. The left-hand column shows when each of these cohorts were born, and the next two columns show how old they were respectively in 1983 (when the *British Social Attitudes* series started) and, 16 years later, in 1999. The upper rows in the table contain the views of younger cohorts, although the youngest two, both now aged under 33, were of course too young to have been interviewed in the first round of the survey in 1983, when they were under 18. And the lower rows contain the views of older cohorts, the oldest aged 74-plus in 1983, who can be compared with the same *age group* in 1999 (those who are now 74-plus) two rows up, but not with precisely the same cohort because of a shortage those aged 90-plus in our sample.

As the table shows, the overall proportion of people who are not attached to a religion has risen substantially since 1983, from 31 per cent then to 44 per cent in 1999 – an increase of 13 points. But there has not been nearly as much change in the religiosity of each cohort. Some, such as those born between 1950 and 1957, now in their 40s, have barely changed their religiosity at all in the last 16 years. Most other cohorts are almost equally stable – some going up a few points, some down a few points, but nothing dramatic. This adds up to a generational change in values. Religious attachments seem to assert themselves (or not) at an early age and then tend to persist. People certainly do not appear to become more religious as they age. Moreover, although attitudes within each cohort are relatively stable, younger cohorts are consistently less religious than are older ones. For instance, a striking 65 per cent of 18-25 year olds in 1999 did not belong to a religion, compared to 55 per cent of the same age group (two rows down the table) in 1983. There is thus apparently a cascade at work, with each cohort's attitudes displacing the previous one's attitudes as they replace them in the age hierarchy. As the older, more religious generations die out, they will probably give way to less religious generations, leading to an overall diminution of religious attachment in Britain. It will not, of course, be a sudden process, but nor will it be that slow: as noted, overall religious attachment has already gone down by 13 points in the last 16 years (see also Greeley, 1992, and De Graaf and Need in this volume).

Table 1.4 Per cent with no religious affiliation by age cohort

			1983	Base	1999	Base	Differ-ence
All			31	1755	44	3142	+13
Cohort	**Age '83**	**Age '99**					
1974-81	2-9	18-25	-		65	280	n.a.
1966-73	10-17	26-33	-		62	474	n.a.
1958-65	18-25	34-41	55	239	48	518	-7
1950-57	26-33	42-49	45	255	47	411	+2
1942-49	34-41	50-57	34	280	40	351	+6
1934-41	42-49	58-65	27	221	28	369	+1
1926-33	50-57	66-73	24	235	23	348	-1
1918-25	58-65	74+	21	213	24	391	+3
1910-17	66-73		13	188	-		n.a.
Pre 1910	74+		12	124	-		n.a.

n.a. = not applicable

A similar pattern is found in attitudes towards premarital sex and homosexuality. As the next two tables show (1.5 and 1.6), permissiveness in relation both to premarital and homosexual sex has increased between 1983 and 1999, in each case by ten percentage points. And once again, no similar growth in permissiveness is apparent within particular cohorts. If anything, the opposite has occurred, with each cohort becoming a little **less** permissive in these respects as they grow older (suggesting a small life-cycle effect).[2] But this small effect is outweighed considerably by generational differences. Younger cohorts are consistently less restrictive than older ones, leading to a cascade effect with relatively permissive younger generations gradually displacing relatively restrictive older generations.

Table 1.5 Per cent thinking premarital sex "not wrong at all" by age cohort

			1983	Base	1999	Base	Differ- ence
All			42	1755	52	1052	+10
Cohort	**Age '83**	**Age '99**					
1974-81	2-9	18-25	-		66	89	n.a.
1966-73	10-17	26-33	-		74	156	n.a.
1958-65	18-25	34-41	64	239	63	195	-1
1950-57	26-33	42-49	64	255	60	148	-4
1942-49	34-41	50-57	55	280	44	107	-11
1934-41	42-49	58-65	37	221	29	112	-8
1926-33	50-57	66-73	37	235	29	110	-8
1918-25	58-65	74+	21	213	22	135	+1
1910-17	66-73		13	188	-		n.a.
Pre 1910	74+		17	124	-		n.a.

n.a. = not applicable

Table 1.6 Per cent thinking homosexual sex "not wrong at all" by age cohort

			1983	Base	1999	Base	Differ- ence
All			17	1755	27	1052	+10
Cohort	**Age '83**	**Age '99**					
1974-81	2-9	18-25	-		40	89	n.a.
1966-73	10-17	26-33	-		42	156	n.a.
1958-65	18-25	34-41	19	239	32	195	+13
1950-57	26-33	42-49	28	255	32	148	+4
1942-49	34-41	50-57	26	280	21	107	-5
1934-41	42-49	58-65	20	221	16	112	-4
1926-33	50-57	66-73	18	235	11	110	-7
1918-25	58-65	74+	11	213	7	135	-4
1910-17	66-73		2	188	-		n.a.
Pre 1910	74+		0	124	-		n.a.

n.a. = not applicable

On religion and attitudes to sex, generational differences appear to dominate with the result that society is likely to continue becoming less religious and more permissive over time. But as far as attitudes to abortion are concerned, a different picture emerges.[3] Once again, attitudes have indeed become more

permissive, but this is largely because *each* of our cohorts' views have changed, in some cases to an astonishing degree. This represents a classic period effect at work: what used to be unacceptable has simply become more normative among all generations as the practice of abortion has become more widespread and, perhaps, as it has increasingly been seen as more of a feminist issue (see Scott, 1990, Heath and Martin, 1996, and Jarvis and Hinds in this volume). Moreover, views on abortion do not get less permissive with age, making it unlikely that an ageing population in Britain will reverse present trends.

This combination of generational and period effects[4] has affected the age gradient, reducing age differences in attitudes towards abortion. This suggests that generational differences will in time play a smaller and smaller role in explaining further shifts in attitudes on this issue.

Table 1.7 Per cent thinking abortion should be allowed if the woman decides she does "not wish to have the child" by age cohort

			1983	Base	1998	Base	Differ-ence
All			38	1645	55	874	+17
Cohort	**Age '83**	**Age '98**					
1974-81	2-9	18-24			53	72	n.a.
1966-73	10-17	25-32	-		66	143	n.a.
1958-65	18-25	33-40	42	227	54	147	+12
1950-57	26-33	41-48	50	248	61	117	+11
1942-49	34-41	49-56	41	268	45	109	+4
1934-41	42-49	57-64	37	206	48	98	+11
1926-33	50-57	65-72	32	218	47	100	+15
1918-25	58-65	73+	30	201	58	88	+28
1910-17	66-73		34	171	-		n.a.
Pre 1910	74+		24	106	-		n.a.

n.a. = not applicable

A more permissive future?

There is quite a bit of evidence to suggest that an ageing Britain will not, after all, become more restrictive or censorious on the sorts of moral issues we have considered here. On the contrary, not only is a smaller and smaller proportion of people likely to be attached to a religion, but attitudes towards premarital sex, homosexuality and abortion will all continue to become more permissive (although in the case of abortion this will not be so much because of generational changes but more because society as a whole has changed).

The political world

Age differences in attitudes and behaviour

Woefully low turnout at recent elections has raised concerns about levels of political participation among the young and the messages this holds for future levels of political engagement in Britain. That young people are less engaged than older ones is incontrovertible: as the next table shows, the 45-plus age group were some 15 percentage points more likely than 18-24 year olds to have voted in the 1997 general election.[5] There is a similar age gradient in political interest: while one in three of the 45-plus age group have a 'great deal' or 'quite a lot' of interest in politics, only one in ten 18-24 year olds do. Not surprisingly, then, younger groups are also less likely to be attached to any party: only one in eight 35-54 year olds have no party attachment compared to around one in four 18-24 year olds (see Table 1.9). And, among those who *have* formed an attachment to a particular party, older groups are the most likely to identify strongly with it.

Table 1.8 Political engagement by age, 1997 and 1999

	18-24	25-34	35-44	45-54	55-64	65+	All
	%	%	%	%	%	%	%
Per cent who voted in 1997 general election*	69	75	79	84	85	83	80
Base	*188*	*497*	*551*	*499*	*414*	*695*	*2857*
Per cent with 'a great deal' or 'quite a lot' of interest in politics	10	22	26	34	35	33	38
Base	*240*	*588*	*588*	*492*	*450*	*783*	*3141*
Per cent with 'very strong' or 'fairly strong' party identification	31	29	34	42	45	48	39
Base	*179*	*480*	*508*	*430*	*410*	*718*	*2725*

* Source: British Election Study 1997, based on validated turnout only

As interesting for the political parties, perhaps, is the fact that there is a clear relationship between age and party. The next table shows that those with a party attachment to the Conservatives tend to be older and those to Labour younger. Neither the Liberal Democrats nor the smaller parties appear to have a similar

age gradient in attachment (though the sample numbers are too small to be sure).

Table 1.9 Party identification by age, 1999

	18-24	25-34	35-44	45-54	55-64	65+	All
	%	%	%	%	%	%	%
Conservative	12	19	23	26	29	35	25
Labour	42	42	44	46	42	39	43
Liberal Democrat	7	11	12	9	9	12	10
Green Party	2	2	2	1	1	1	1
Other	3	2	2	3	4	2	3
None	24	18	12	12	9	8	13
Base	*240*	*588*	*588*	*492*	*450*	*783*	*3141*

Political disengagement

As before, we now need to find out why it is that young adults are so politically disengaged compared to their older counterparts and whether this is a poor omen for British democracy. Are they less engaged and involved in politics than previous generations were at their age – in which case a process of gradual disengagement would be in train, its pace ebbing and flowing with the numerical strength of different generations? On the other hand, a life-cycle explanation may fit better: perhaps young adults have always been comparatively less interested and engaged in politics, becoming more engaged only as they enter the labour market, start paying taxes, get married, have children, acquire mortgages, and so on. If so, no new threat to democracy is looming.

Looking first at political interest, the next table shows a remarkable stability in aggregate levels of interest over time, with barely any change between 1986 and 1999. But among individual cohorts, most notably those born in the 1950s, there has been a noticeable rise in political interest as they age and pass through different stages of the life-cycle. These rises do not of course influence the aggregate picture because they are counterbalanced by the entry of younger, less interested, generations.

This may seem reassuring for those who fear an impending crisis for democracy. It suggests even that the very term 'disengagement' is misleading, implying that the electorate used to be more interested in politics than it is now. On the other hand, there are some worrying signs that things may be getting worse – notably the very low levels of political interest shown by the youngest cohort in our latest survey (the 18-25 year olds). Only around ten per cent of them report being 'quite' or 'very' interested in politics, compared to over 20 per cent of the comparable age group some 13 years earlier, in the 1986 survey.

This change has drastically steepened the age gradient in the population. While in 1986, we found a 10-point gap between the most and least interested age groups, it has now become a 25-point gap. Park (1999) had earlier found a similarly worryingly low level of political interest among the cohort born in the late 1970s and early 1980s. But it is by no means certain that the size of the democratic deficit from which this cohort currently suffers will remain this large as they age. Instead they may revert to type as they move into their 30s later this decade and become comparable to today's 30 year olds. But, for this to be the case, they have a great deal of catching up to do.

Table 1.10 Per cent with "a great deal" or "quite a lot of" interest in politics by age cohort

			1986	Base	1999	Base	Differ-ence
All			29	1545	28	3142	-1
Cohort	**Age '86**	**Age '99**					
1974-81	5-12	18-25	-		11	280	n.a.
1966-73	13-20	26-33	-		24	474	n.a.
1958-65	21-28	34-41	22	241	24	518	+2
1950-57	29-36	42-49	28	241	34	411	+6
1942-49	37-44	50-57	32	237	32	351	0
1934-41	45-52	58-65	34	215	36	369	+2
1926-33	53-60	66-73	32	182	34	348	+2
1918-25	61-68	74+	32	138	31	391	-1
1910-17	69-76		31	107	-		n.a.
Pre 1910	77+		30	82	-		n.a.

n.a. = not applicable

There are thus hints of both life-cycle and generational influences on political interest. And the picture is more complicated still in relation to changes over time in party identification. As the next table shows, there has been a small, but significant, aggregate increase from eight per cent in 1983 to 13 per cent in 1999 in those who steadfastly claim *no* party identification. However, within-cohort change has only occurred among older cohorts (those born before 1941) and is notably absent among younger groups. This may reflect the fact that party identification tends to crystallise during early adulthood (Butler and Stokes, 1969), with this 'protecting' these younger groups from the process of disengagement occurring among their elders. There is also a hint that generational replacement may have a role in explaining overall societal change because the average change within each of our cohorts is smaller than the overall societal change. People now in their 20s and early 30s are especially

unlikely to identify with a political party (around one in five do not), perhaps because such identification is taking even longer these days to crystallise. In any event, the age gradient is more pronounced now than it was in 1983 and unless the youngest cohorts rapidly develop party attachments as they age, it may well signal a further drop in party loyalties in Britain over the next decade or more (see Särlvik and Crewe, 1983).

Table 1.11 Per cent with no party identification by age cohort

			1983	Base	1999	Base	Differ-ence
All			8	1755	13	3142	+5
Cohort	**Age '83**	**Age '99**					
1974-81	2-9	18-25	-		23	280	n.a.
1966-73	10-17	26-33	-		19	474	n.a.
1958-65	18-25	34-41	15	239	14	518	-1
1950-57	26-33	42-49	11	255	12	411	+1
1942-49	34-41	50-57	8	280	8	351	0
1934-41	42-49	58-65	4	221	10	369	+6
1926-33	50-57	66-73	5	235	6	348	+1
1918-25	58-65	74+	4	213	9	391	+5
1910-17	66-73		7	188	-		n.a.
Pre 1910	74+		11	124	-		n.a.

n.a. = not applicable

What then of actual turnout at elections? The next table shows that although aggregate reported turnout did not drop between 1983 and 1997 (two election years in which *actual* turnout was identical and historically low), there is considerable change in reported turnout within individual cohorts.[6] So, life-cycle does seem to play a part here as turnout increases with age, particularly among the relatively young. And although overall there is nothing to suggest that major generational changes are afoot, the youngest age group (who were almost all first-time voters in 1997) appears to be less engaged than were first-time voters in 1983.

Table 1.12 Per cent who report having voted in the most recent general election by age cohort*

			1983	Base	1997	Base	Differ-ence
All			83	3935	82	2746	-1
Cohort	**Age '83**	**Age '97**					
1974-81	2-9	18-23			68	206	n.a.
1966-73	10-17	24-31	-		75	455	n.a.
1958-65	18-25	32-39	73	636	76	538	+3
1950-57	26-33	40-47	77	587	86	505	+9
1942-49	34-41	48-55	88	612	84	419	-4
1934-41	42-49	56-63	88	508	90	389	+2
1926-33	50-57	64-71	88	481	88	392	0
1918-25	58-65	72+	89	460	87	448	-2
1910-17	66-73		83	365	-		n.a.
Pre 1910	74+		84	286	-		n.a.

n.a. = not applicable
* Source: British Election Study 1983 and 1997

So it is by no means clear that Britain is inexorably sliding into a state of mass electoral apathy. The fact that life-cycle, generational and period effects are all responsible to some degree for influencing political engagement makes future trends even more difficult to predict than usual. It is certainly likely that the young will become more interested and involved in politics as they get older. In more doubt is whether the change will be as large as it needs to be to maintain past aggregate levels of engagement.

Party politics

Another intriguing question is whether or not any one party is likely to benefit disproportionately from these trends. To answer this we must once again analyse whether age differences in party support tend to reflect life-cycle or generational differences. If on the one hand people become more sympathetic to the Conservatives as they get older, then an ageing population will tend to shift the electoral advantage toward the Conservative Party. If, however, the current pro-Labour political sympathies of younger people turn out to be adhesive, they will in time replace more Conservative generations to the long-term electoral advantage of Labour.

There is some solace for the Conservatives in the next table which examines Conservative support among those who *do* support a party. Although it confirms (in case confirmation were needed!) that support was indeed lower in

1997 than it was in 1983, it also shows that slumps of similar magnitude occurred in most cohorts. This implies that the change over time is effectively a period effect, reflecting different political circumstances at the two elections rather than a more structural generational shift. And although there is also a hint of generational change, it is a minor element in the story.[7] Nevertheless, if the current age gradient in Conservative support is maintained (it is much steeper than it was in 1983, at 19 per cent among 18-24 year olds and 42 per cent among 66-73 year olds), then even marginal generational influences could add up to a noticeable impact over the next few decades.

Table 1.13 Per cent who identify with the Conservative Party by age cohort

			1983	Base	1999	Base	Differ-ence
All			44	1535	30	2563	-14
Cohort	**Age '83**	**Age '99**					
1974-81	2-9	18-25	-		19	193	n.a.
1966-73	10-17	26-33	-		25	356	n.a.
1958-65	18-25	34-41	39	189	27	417	-12
1950-57	26-33	42-49	42	222	25	337	-17
1942-49	34-41	50-57	48	248	38	303	-10
1934-41	42-49	58-65	48	200	32	311	-16
1926-33	50-57	66-73	42	209	42	308	0
1918-25	58-65	74+	41	197	38	338	-3
1910-17	66-73		49	164	-		n.a.
Pre 1910	74+		49	106	-		n.a.

n.a. = not applicable

Naturally, the reverse is true for the Labour Party. Their growth in support was recorded in most cohorts alike, and there is a similar hint that generational replacement played a small role, to their relative advantage.

Mostly, however, what we have seen at work is the age-old pendulum of politics swinging at its usual unpredictable speed.

Government spending and welfare

Age differences in attitudes

One likely consequence of a growing ratio of older people to younger people in Britain is that the extra demand for social security and health expenditure will have to be met in large part from tax revenues generated by a shrinking working

population. Some have suggested that this is a recipe for inter-generational conflicts over the allocation of scarce resources (Turner, 1998). It may be too early to test this thesis definitively, but we can certainly discover from our data whether and in what ways young and old differ in their attitudes towards taxation and public spending.

As the next table shows, as far as taxation is concerned, there is a minor age gradient in enthusiasm for increased taxation and social spending, but the pattern is far from convincing. Least enthusiasm comes from the youngest age groups (18-34 year olds) and most from those aged 45-64. Much more important, perhaps, is the bottom row of the table, which reveals virtual unanimity in all age groups against *cutting* taxes and social spending.

Table 1.14 Attitudes towards taxation and government spending by age, 1999

	18-24	25-34	35-44	45-54	55-64	65+	All
	%	%	%	%	%	%	%
Increased taxes and more spending on health, education and social benefits	49	51	59	65	64	58	58
Keeping taxes and spending on these services the same as now	43	40	34	29	28	35	34
Reducing taxes and less spending on these services	5	4	3	3	4	4	4
Base	240	588	588	492	450	783	3141

A better acid test is whether different age groups tend to prioritise different spending areas. We asked:

> *Listed below are various areas of government spending. Please show whether you would like to see more or less government spending in each area. Remember that if you say 'much more', it might require a tax increase to pay for it*

The only spending targets to attract any serious support as priorities were health and education. No other field of spending attracted more than a four per cent vote. Even so, as the next table shows, there were clear age differences in the relative priorities given to health and education between younger and older people. While health spending as a priority broadly increases with age, reaching

its peak among the 55-plus age group, education spending as a priority broadly declines with age, reaching its trough among the 65-plus group.

Table 1.15 Priorities for extra government spending by age, 1999

	18-24	25-34	35-44	45-54	55-64	65+	All
First priority for extra spending	%	%	%	%	%	%	%
Health	41	34	48	48	57	54	47
Education	40	47	37	33	25	21	33
Base	*240*	*588*	*588*	*492*	*450*	*783*	*3141*

But the clearest age gradient of all is to be found in respect of priorities for social security benefits. We asked the sample to allocate 'extra spending' priorities between the five benefits shown in the next table. Pensions attract by far the highest support – chosen by half the sample as a top priority. But the age gradient is very steep, with those aged 65-plus over three times more likely (at 71 per cent) to choose them as a priority than are those aged 18-24 (20 per cent). Large differences also characterise support for child benefit, unemployment benefit and benefits for single parents – this time with older groups proving much less supportive than younger ones.[8]

Table 1.16 First priority for extra spending on social security benefits by age, 1996

	18-24	25-34	35-44	45-54	55-64	65+	All
	%	%	%	%	%	%	%
Retirement spending	20	37	48	54	62	71	50
Disabled benefits	24	17	18	21	21	17	19
Child benefit	21	25	15	6	4	2	12
Unemployment benefit	15	11	12	13	9	8	11
Single parent benefits	19	9	5	3	1	1	6
Base	*285*	*750*	*659*	*602*	*451*	*858*	*3620*

Conflict in store?

Do these apparently self-interested age differences presage a battle between people at different stages of the life-cycle for a bigger share of available resources? If so, an ageing society will tilt the balance somewhat in favour of

older people's preferences and priorities – notably health spending and pension rises.

To be sure, as the next table shows, these are life-cycle changes rather than generational differences, although there is also evidence of a period effect. For instance, support for prioritising extra spending on health has risen across the board from 37 to 47 per cent between 1983 and 1999, a view shared by each of our cohorts. But the increased vote within every cohort for extra spending (16 points on average) was greater than the aggregate vote for extra spending (ten points). So, in addition to the period effect, individuals naturally tend to become more favourable towards a thriving health service and a well-endowed social security system as they age.

Table 1.17 Per cent who choose health as first priority for extra government spending by age cohort

			1983	Base	1999	Base	Difference
All			37	1755	47	3142	+10
Cohort	**Age '83**	**Age '99**					
1974-81	2-9	18-25	-		40	280	n.a.
1966-73	10-17	26-33	-		34	474	n.a.
1958-65	18-25	34-41	28	239	47	518	+19
1950-57	26-33	42-49	35	255	45	411	+10
1942-49	34-41	50-57	33	280	53	351	+20
1934-41	42-49	58-65	39	221	58	369	+19
1926-33	50-57	66-73	44	235	58	348	+14
1918-25	58-65	74+	40	213	51	391	+11
1910-17	66-73		44	188	-		n.a.
Pre 1910	74+		33	124	-		n.a.

n.a. = not applicable

The importance of self-interest is also evident in the priorities attached to extra spending on education. Again, there has been an increase over time in the proportion who would make education their first priority. But although attitudes change with age, the effect does not persist in the same way through the age gradient cycle as it does for health spending. Notably, the enthusiasm of the youngest cohort has increased most markedly – from 21 per cent favouring more spending on education in 1983 (when they were 18-25) to 39 per cent in 1999 (at age 34-41). The most obvious explanation for this is that they have acquired children of their own in the interim, and this is borne out when we compare the greater enthusiasm of parents with non-parents of the same age. In

contrast, support for extra education spending *fell* between 1983 and 1999 among older cohorts.

  However, the strongest link between age and attitudes is in priorities for increased spending on pensions. As the next table shows, overall support for more spending has once again gone up – by nine points. But among each of our cohorts, support has increased by a great deal more – by an average of 20 points. Notably, the age gradient in 1996 is a great deal steeper than it was in 1983 because demand has increased more among older age groups.

Table 1.18 Per cent who choose retirement pensions as first priority for spending on social benefits by age cohort

			1983	Base	1996	Base	Differ-ence
All			41	1755	50	3605	+9
Cohort	**Age '83**	**Age '96**					
1974-81	2-9	18-22	-		16	188	n.a.
1966-73	10-17	23-30	-		31	522	n.a.
1958-65	18-25	31-38	18	239	45	638	+27
1950-57	26-33	39-46	39	255	50	488	+11
1942-49	34-41	47-54	39	280	55	460	+16
1934-41	42-49	55-62	39	221	61	361	+22
1926-33	50-57	63-70	41	235	70	376	+29
1918-25	58-65	71+	55	213	70	572	+15
1910-17	66-73		57	188	-		n.a.
Pre 1910	74+		53	124	-		n.a.

n.a. = not applicable

All these findings make it likely that an ageing population will have an impact on attitudes towards welfare spending. As people get older they increasingly favour more spending on areas such as health and pensions, and less on areas such as education, the unemployed and single parents. True, such age differences have always existed. But in a society in which older groups predominate as never before, their preferences are likely to become more and more politically relevant.

Conclusions

On moral matters, such as religion, sexual mores and abortion, we have found little evidence to suggest that an ageing society will be either more pious or less permissive. On the contrary, attitudes are likely to shift away from those

currently held by older groups because the age differences that exist tend to be more generational in origin. Thus, the attitudes currently held by younger generations will largely be carried with them into older age, replacing the more conservative values currently held by older generations.

On political matters, we found not only generational effects, but also life-cycle and period influences on attitudes which, in combination, make it more difficult to predict how attitudes might develop in the future. In the short term, it seems that an ageing society will, in aggregate, become *more* engaged than now. But in the longer term, the growing democratic deficit among the young might well remain in place as they age, causing society as a whole to become more apathetic about politics and less likely than now to participate in elections.

The clearest life-cycle effects are to be found in the priorities that different age groups attach to government spending priorities. So, as older people form a larger and larger proportion of the population, their priorities for more spending on pensions and the NHS are increasingly likely to be in conflict with younger people's preferences for more spending on education.

Reassuringly, perhaps, the battle of the generations is far from over.

Notes

1. This is known as the 'identification problem', and is explored in detail in Heath and Martin, 1996.
2. The youngest cohort in 1983 (18-25 years old then, now aged 34-41) is distinctive in its attitudes towards homosexuality. In 1983 they were among the most disapproving, and now they are among the most permissive. See Hill and Thomson in this volume for a possible explanation of a similar phenomenon.
3. These questions were last asked in 1998, so our cohorts' ages for this second reading are a year younger than they were in previous tables.
4. To obtain a rough estimate of how much overall change can be explained by generational replacement we can compare the average within-cohort change (13.5 points – the sum of each cohort's change divided by the total number of cohorts) with the overall change (17 points). This suggests that around a sixth of the overall change (3.5 out of 17 points) can be explained by generational replacement (similar findings were reported by Heath and Martin, 1996). This calculation assumes that the overall change is due to period factors or changes in the relative sizes of particular age groups (for example, the entry into the population of a particularly large generation) and that life-cycle factors have not also influenced each cohort's attitudes. It also assumes that the overall change is not due to changes in the relative size of age groups over time.
5. Surveys tend to report higher levels of turnout than do official figures (Heath and Taylor, 1999). For example, the 1997 British Election Study (BES) recorded a turnout of 82 per cent (against an official turnout of 72 per cent). One reason for this is that respondents have a tendency to over-report their turnout, perhaps because of guilt. To address this, a validation exercise was carried out on the 1997 BES which involved checking official records to see whether or not a respondent was on the Electoral Register and had *actually* voted. When the results of this validation

exercise are taken into account, the BES turnout rate falls slightly to 80 per cent. Consequently, the figures presented here are based upon the results of the turnout validation and show the proportion of respondents known to be on the Electoral Register who voted in the 1997 election. Cases where it was not possible to determine whether or not the respondent had voted (16 per cent of those on the Register) are excluded.

6. To ensure comparability over time, we concentrate here on turnout *reported* by respondents (and not on validated turnout). As noted, the lack of overall change partly reflects our choice of elections – 1983 and 1997 – both of which experienced a turnout of 72.3 per cent. Were we to look at elections which attracted higher turnout (1987, say, or 1992) we would probably find a considerable period effect with a fall in turnout among all age groups. But comparing 1983 and 1999 still allows us to examine whether an individual's propensity to vote increases as they get older or whether generational replacement promises a future characterised by lower and lower levels of democratic participation.

7. The average within-cohort change is a fall of ten percentage points, compared with an overall fall of 14 points. So if we assume that the within-cohort change is due to period factors, and that life-cycle factors have not also been at work, the remainder (just over a quarter of the total change) would be due to generational replacement.

8. This is backed up by the finding that older age groups tend to be the least supportive of the welfare state and – in particular – benefit recipients (Bryson, 1997).

References

Alwin, D. and Scott, J. (1996), 'Attitude change: its measurement and interpretation using longitudinal surveys' in Taylor, B. and Thomson, K. (eds.), *Understanding Change in Social Attitudes*, Aldershot: Dartmouth.

Bryson, C. (1997), 'Benefit claimants: villains or victims' in Jowell, R., Curtice, J., Park, A., Brook, L., Thomson, K. and Bryson, C. (eds.), *British Social Attitudes: the 14th Report - The end of Conservative values?*, Aldershot: Dartmouth.

Butler, D. and Stokes, D. (1969), *Political Change in Britain*, London: Macmillan.

Evandrou, M. (1997), *Baby Boomers: Ageing in the 21st Century*, London: Age Concern.

Evandrou, M. and Falkingham, J. (2000), 'Looking back to look forward: lessons from four birth cohorts for ageing in the 21st Century', *Population Trends 1999*, Spring, London: Office for National Statistics.

Foresight Ageing Population Panel (2000), *The Age Shift – A Consultation Document*, London: Department of Trade and Industry. See also www.foresight.gov.uk

Greeley, A. (1992), 'Religion in Britain, Ireland and the USA' in Jowell, R., Brook, L., Prior, G. and Taylor, B. (eds.), *British Social Attitudes: the 9th Report*, Aldershot: Dartmouth.

Heath, A. and Martin, J. (1996), 'Changing attitudes towards abortion: life-cycle, period and cohort effects' in Taylor, B. and Thomson, K. (eds.), *Understanding Change in Social Attitudes*, Aldershot: Dartmouth.

Heath, A. and Taylor, B. (1999), 'New sources of abstention?' in Evans, G. and Norris, P. (eds.), *Critical Elections*, London: Sage.

Jagodzinski, W. and Dobbelaere, K. (1994), 'Secularisation and church religosity' in van Deth, J. and Scarbrough, E. (eds.), *Beliefs in Government Volume Four: The Impact of Values*, Oxford: Oxford University Press.

Johnson, P. and Falkingham, J. (1992), *Ageing and Economic Welfare*, London: Sage.

Jowell, R. and Park, A. (1998), 'Young people, politics and citizenship: a disengaged generation?', London: The Citizenship Foundation.

Mannheim, K. (1928), *Essays in the Sociology of Knowledge*, London: RKP.

OECD (1996), *Ageing in OECD Countries: A Critical Policy Challenge*, Paris: OECD.

Park, A. (1999), 'Young people and political apathy' in Jowell, R., Curtice, J., Park, A. and Thomson, T. (eds.), *British Social Attitudes: the 16th Report – Who shares New Labour values?*, Aldershot: Ashgate.

Särlvik, B. and Crewe, I. (1983), *Decade of Dealignment: The Conservative Victory of 1979 and Electoral Trends in the 1970s*, London: Cambridge University Press.

Scott, J. (1990), 'Women and the family', in Jowell, R., Witherspoon, S. and Brook, L. (eds.), *British Social Attitudes: the 7th Report*, Aldershot: Gower.

Tarling, R. and Dowds, L. (1997), 'Crime and punishment' in Jowell, R., Curtice, J., Park, A., Brook, L., Thomson, K. and Bryson, C. (eds.), *British Social Attitudes: the 14th Report - The end of Conservative values?*, Aldershot: Dartmouth.

Turner, B. (1998), 'Ageing and generational conflicts', *British Journal of Sociology*, **49**: 299-303.

Walker, A. (1999), 'Ageing in Europe – challenges and consequences', *Zeitschrift fur Gerontologie unt Geriatrie*, **32**: 390-397.

Appendix

Cohorts

In order to untangle the role of generational, life-cycle and period factors in explaining age differences in attitudes we have divided our sample into a number of 'cohorts', defined by when they were born. These cohorts, and some of their key characteristics, are shown below:

- Born between 1974 and 1981, and teenagers during the 1990s. In 1999 in their teens and early 20s, and in education or entering the labour market.
- Born between 1966 and 1973, and teenagers during the 1980s. Came of age during the Thatcher era and entered the labour market during recession. In 1999 in their mid-20s and early 30s, and settling down and having children.
- Born between 1958 and 1965, and teenagers during the 1970s and early 1980s. Born at a time of prosperity, but entered the labour market as unemployment topped three million (1982). In 1999 in their mid-30s to early 40s. The second 'baby boom' generation.
- Born between 1950 and 1957, and teenagers during the late 1960s and early 1970s. Entered the labour market during a time of considerable prosperity, but shortly experienced the economic crises of the late 1970s. Also affected by the 1970 Equal Pay Act and Sex Discrimination Act, and the expansion of higher education during the 1960s. In 1999 in their 40s.
- Born between 1942 and 1949, and teenagers during the late 1950s and 1960s. Born during post-war austerity, but entered the labour market during a time of considerable prosperity. In 1999 in their 50s, and planning for retirement. The post-war 'baby boom' generation.
- Born between 1934 and 1941, and teenagers during the 1950s. The first generation to benefit directly from the 1944 Education Act. Born just before or during the Second World War during a period of austerity, but entered the labour market during a time of prosperity. In 1999 in their late 50s to mid-60s, and retired from paid work (or about to).
- Born between 1926 and 1933, and teenagers during the 1940s. The first generation to benefit from the launch of the National Health Service in 1947. In 1999 in their late 60s to early 70s, and retired.
- Born before 1925, and teenagers between the 1920s and early 1940s. Clear experiences of living through the Second World War. In 1999 in their late 70s and above, and retired.

2 Health care rationing: a cut too far?

Caroline Bryson and Bill New[*]

At its creation over 50 years ago, the NHS was charged with the duty of treating all on the basis of medical need alone. So it is understandable why debates about the rationing of health care have been steadfastly rejected by senior politicians while in government. The word 'rationing' is particularly avoided, with preference being for terms such as 'priority-setting' or 'resource allocation'. However, such distaste for the word is not shared by commentators, journalists and opposition politicians who frequently refer to rationing in discussions about the NHS.

'Health care rationing' does not just describe those highly publicised cases which involve individuals being denied treatment, or whole services being threatened. More often it is far more mundane and pervasive, an inevitable consequence of wants and needs within the NHS exceeding the resources available. Indeed, the waiting list, that perennial thorn in the NHS's side, is itself an example of rationing, with numbers having consistently risen to peak at 1.3 million on inpatient lists in April 1998 (Harrison and New, 2000).

Public attitudes towards rationing are likely to be coloured by its association with unwelcome cuts in resources and the fact that it conjures up images of people being denied life-saving treatments. Even worse, perhaps, the term may also engender fears of a different sort of NHS, one in which people would effectively be categorised into 'deserving' and 'undeserving' groups on the basis of certain characteristics or the nature of their condition, rather than on their need for treatment. Attitudes may also be influenced by a tendency to think of health care simply in terms of saving lives and curing serious illness. Of course, in reality, health care commonly involves only small probabilities of extending life (often at high cost), or only marginal improvements in symptoms with no prospect of cure (Wordsworth *et al.*, 1996). Rationing describes the limits placed on these sorts of interventions just as much as it does more colourful examples such as the removal from the NHS remit of *in vitro* fertilisation treatment.

---

[*] Caroline Bryson is a Research Director at the *National Centre for Social Research*. Bill New is an independent health policy analyst.

Rationing, whatever its form, raises a number of important questions. The first is fundamental – is it inevitable? Do people think that if funding is increased sufficiently rationing can be avoided altogether? Or is there an awareness that it may be impossible to exhaust the often marginal benefits of health care without bankrupting public finances or raising taxes to unprecedented levels? The majority of independent commentators take the latter view (see Ham and Coulter, 2000); this chapter will explore what the public thinks.

A second set of issues relates to the principles which should govern decisions about rationing if it takes place – the factors that should be taken into account and those which should not. Clinical need, the effectiveness of a treatment, personal lifestyle, the cost of treatment, the age of the recipient – all could be considered relevant to making rationing decisions (New, 1996).

Our third set of issues concerns who should make the decisions, if such decisions have to be made. Clinicians have been the traditional arbiters of rationing in the past, making decisions at an individual level and seemingly enjoying public trust (Kneeshaw, 1997). But as the issues have become more explicit, other bodies have been suggested as having a potential role – including a central, politically appointed, health care commission (Lenaghan, 1996). This raises the question of whether there should be explicit and publicly available guidelines about how decisions should be made (both to enable greater accountability and to ensure consistency across the NHS). Developments along these lines are now being implemented by NICE, the National Institute for Clinical Excellence (Coulter, 1999). However, such guidelines may be seen as disadvantageous because they restrict the ability of doctors to make judgements based purely upon their assessment of the particular circumstances of each case.

Recently, media attention to health rationing has increased, prompted initially by the introduction of Viagra, the anti-impotence drug, to Britain and the widespread discussions that ensued about the terms under which it should be available. Indeed, Ann Widdecombe, Shadow Health Secretary, credited Viagra with placing health rationing prominently on the public agenda (House of Commons Hansard, 1998). And since then the setting up of NICE has kept decisions about rationing firmly in the public eye. Examples of NICE's recommendations include the decision not to prescribe the anti-flu drug Relenza (NICE, 1999), and that routine removal of healthy wisdom teeth should no longer be performed (NICE, 2000). Health care rationing is now firmly on the public agenda, and no government can afford to ignore public concerns if confidence in its management of, and long-term plans for, the NHS are to be maintained.

The state of the NHS

We begin by setting attitudes to rationing and the potential forms this might take in the wider context of attitudes to the NHS in general. In particular, we ask whether people feel that the NHS currently provides a good level of service, and how much support exists for increased spending on the health service.

We asked how well the NHS currently 'caters for everyone's medical needs', and found there to be a general belief that there is room for improvement. Only seven per cent of people think the NHS currently caters 'very well' for everyone's medical needs. And, although half (49 per cent) think the NHS copes 'adequately', four in ten (40 per cent) feel that it falls short of that. Not surprisingly then, there is considerable support for increased government spending on the NHS. When asked whether or not the government should 'spend more on the NHS, even if this means an increase in taxes', two-thirds (67 per cent) opt for higher spending and only one per cent for lower spending (and reduced taxes). Even among those who believe that the NHS currently caters 'adequately' for everyone's medical needs around two-thirds would nevertheless like increased funding.

Support for more spending on health holds fast even when pitted against other government spending areas. Nearly eight in ten (79 per cent) opt for health as their first or second priority for extra spending (closely followed by education, chosen by 69 per cent).

The desirability and inevitability of rationing

These general attitudes towards the NHS raise interesting questions about attitudes to health care rationing. Does the existence of a significant minority who consider the NHS to be falling short suggest that resistance to further limitations on treatment via rationing will be weak or strong? And does support for extra spending suggest that this is seen as the answer to the NHS's woes – or is rationing seen as an inevitable part of a modern NHS?

We begin by looking at responses to two questions concerned with general attitudes towards health care rationing. The first is concerned with the fundamental principle of rationing. We asked people which of two statements came closest to their own view:

> *With people living longer, the NHS will always have too many demands on it and should cut down or cut out certain types of treatment*

> *Everybody has a right to health care, so the NHS should never cut down or cut out any types of treatment*

A very clear majority, eight in ten, feel the NHS should never cut down or cut out any types of treatment. But when rationing is presented as being an outcome of limited resources and increasing demand, there is clear acceptance of its inevitability. We asked people to choose between two statements:

> *The NHS will have enough money and resources to provide everyone with the treatment they need when they need it*

The NHS will not have enough money and resources for everyone and will have to cut down or cut out certain types of treatment

Nearly three-quarters (72 per cent) agreed with the second statement, namely that due to lack of funds the NHS will have cut down or cut out certain types of treatments. Thus whilst a large proportion of people are opposed to rationing in principle they are resigned to its inevitability. As the next table shows, only one in five of those who think the NHS should 'never cut down or cut out any types of treatment' also think that the NHS will have enough money to avoid doing this in the future.

Table 2.1 Whether rationing is seen as inevitable by beliefs about the principle of health rationing

	NHS should cut down on treatments	NHS should never cut down on treatments
	%	%
NHS will have enough money to treat all	6	20
NHS will not have enough money to treat all	94	70
Can't choose	-	10
Base	*95*	*650*

Belief in the inevitability of health rationing is not clear-cut. When asked to agree or disagree with the statement 'as demand on the NHS grows, it will have to ration some treatments', a far lower level (41 per cent) agreed.[1] This degree of sensitivity to question wording indicates an absence of any very fixed public view about the certainty or otherwise of health rationing, and suggests a need for more information about the role and consequences of rationing before a wider and more meaningful debate can take place.

Rationing in practice

So far we have seen that, though there is little support for cutting down or cutting out services, this is accompanied by an acceptance in practice of some kind of rationing in the future. But if rationing of health care is to take place, it is essential to establish levels of support for the various ways in which decisions might be made. When it comes to *who* should get priority for treatment there are a number of different criteria that might be used, including: the non-clinical characteristics of the patient (for example, their age or lifestyle); the severity of the illness; the cost of the treatment; and whether or not the treatment could be provided by alternatives to the NHS (for example, by

private individuals, insurance companies, or charities). We now address each of these in turn, asking whether people think decisions *should* be made on these bases at all and then whether they think this currently takes place.

We start with the age or lifestyle of the patient. The extent to which these characteristics should influence a patient's chances of getting treatment has provoked considerable debate (Williams, 1997, regarding age; Underwood *et al.*, 1993, regarding smoking). In essence, the question is whether those with a greater life expectancy or greater chances of a good quality of life after treatment should be given priority over others, even if these characteristics reflect decisions people take about their lifestyle (such as smoking) or factors beyond their control (such as age).

To assess this, we asked people to consider two scenarios, each concerning 'two equally sick people in the same area who go on a waiting list at the same time for the same heart operation'. In each scenario, the people differed on only one point:

Scenario 1   *One person was a non-smoker, the other a heavy smoker*
Scenario 2   *One person was aged 30, the other aged 70*

Around half think that whether a person smokes, or their age, should make no difference in deciding who to treat first. But a substantial minority *do* think this should be taken into account – a third think the younger person should get priority, and four in ten that the non-smoker should do so.

We also asked which person *would* currently be likely to get the operation first. As the next table shows, in both scenarios a significant proportion – well over half – believe that such rationing already happens in the NHS and that those who follow a 'healthy lifestyle' or who are younger are given priority. Less than three in ten people think that such criteria are currently irrelevant when doctors are deciding about whom to operate upon first. Clearly then, more people think rationing on these grounds already occurs within the NHS than think it should.

Table 2.2 Who *should* get priority for an NHS heart operation, and who *would* get priority?

	Who <u>should</u> get priority	Who <u>would</u> get priority
Smoking	%	%
Non-smoker	41	59
Heavy smoker	2	3
Smoking habits would/should make no difference	48	27
Can't choose	8	9
Age	%	%
Younger person	34	56
Older person	5	5
Age would/should make no difference	51	29
Can't choose	8	8
Base: 804		

Another option would be to base judgements simply on the severity of the illness or condition. This would mean that those who were most in need would be treated first. To assess support for this form of rationing we asked respondents whether they agreed or disagreed with the statement:

> *If the NHS <u>had</u> to choose, the seriousness of their condition should be the <u>only</u> basis for choosing between patients*

As the next table shows, seven in ten (69 per cent) think the severity of a person's illness should be the *only* basis for prioritising between patients. But only one in six (17 per cent) think this currently happens most of the time with a further 55 per cent thinking it happens some of the time. Many are not clear what current practice is, with one in five (19 per cent) unable to give an answer either way.

There is far less support for prioritising cheaper treatments over more expensive ones. Only a quarter (24 per cent) of people agree with the statement:

> *If the NHS <u>had</u> to choose, it should give <u>lower</u> priority to expensive treatments so that more money is available to treat a larger number of sick people whose treatment costs less*

This does not mean that the majority view is against this form of rationing as the third of people who disagree with the idea are matched by a similar proportion (29 per cent) who neither agree nor disagree with it. However, people do think that the NHS currently makes decisions on these bases. Although only six per cent of people think that this happens 'always or most of

the time', a further 59 per cent think that it happens 'some of the time'. Again, a high proportion (24 per cent) could not choose.

Table 2.3 Should priority vary according to the severity of the condition or the cost of treatment? Does priority currently vary?

	Most serious conditions	Cheaper treatments
Should get priority	%	%
Agree	69	24
Neither agree nor disagree	11	29
Disagree	11	33
Can't choose	8	11
Currently gets priority	%	%
Always or most of the time	17	6
Some of the time	55	59
Hardly ever or never	7	9
Can't choose	19	24
Base 804		

We have found there to be little support for expensive treatments being given a lower priority than cheaper ones. And that support falls away still further when we consider specific examples of expensive treatments or services. We asked:

> *Some people say the NHS should cut down on very expensive treatments or services and use the savings to provide less expensive treatments or services for more people. With this aim, how much would you be in favour of, or against, the NHS cutting down on: heart transplants; long-term nursing care of the elderly; intensive care for very premature babies whose survival is in doubt?*

In each case around two-thirds are against the NHS cutting down on the particular treatment or service. Heart transplants are the treatment that *fewest* favour cutting (only seven per cent doing so), with double this proportion thinking that intensive care for premature babies should be cut to provide savings.

Table 2.4 The NHS cutting down on expensive treatments and services

	Heart transplants	Long-term nursing care of elderly	Intensive care for premature babies
	%	%	%
In favour	7	10	13
Neither in favour nor against	16	15	13
Against	68	66	64
Can't choose	6	6	7

Base: 804

Eight in ten people do not favour cutting *any* of the three treatments. Of those who do, the majority favour cutting just one, suggesting that different people prioritise different treatments. This means that that views about cutting down on, say, the care of premature babies can not be gleaned from a person's views about cutting down on heart transplants.

   Another approach to limiting NHS spending would be to remove certain types of treatment or services from its remit altogether, leaving more money to treat other conditions. We asked:

> *Other people say the NHS should cut down on certain treatments or services that should be provided instead by private medicine or charities. With this aim, how much would you be in favour of, or against, the NHS cutting down on: fertility treatment; hospice care for the terminally ill; cosmetic surgery?*

Here we find considerable support for cutting down on NHS fertility treatment and – particularly – cosmetic surgery. Four in ten would like to see fertility treatment excluded from the NHS budget, and six in ten feel the same about cosmetic surgery. But hospice care for the terminally ill is still seen as ideally falling within the NHS's embrace, with only one in ten wanting to remove it.

Table 2.5 The NHS cutting down on treatments and services and giving responsibility for them to private medicine and charities

	Hospice care	Fertility treatment	Cosmetic surgery
	%	%	%
In favour	10	38	60
Neither in favour nor against	12	26	18
Against	72	28	15
Can't choose	3	5	7

Base: 804

Other ways of raising and saving money within the NHS have been suggested – including the introduction of charges for certain NHS services that are currently free. We asked:

One way of getting more money into the NHS is to charge people for certain things. How much would you be in favour of or against introducing charges for: visiting your GP; your GP visiting you at home; the cost of your hospital meals when you are an inpatient?

There is very little public support for charging for GP consultations, particularly in the surgery (although recent evidence suggests that around half of GPs in England do in fact favour this for "some patients" (Francombe, 2000)). However, twice as many people support charging for home visits (17 per cent). There was also limited support by a quarter of people for charging for the cost of hospital meals during a stay in hospital (perhaps a surprisingly low figure given the poor reputation of hospital food).

Table 2.6 Introducing charges for NHS services

	Visits to GP	Home visits from GP	Hospital meals
	%	%	%
In favour	8	17	25
Neither in favour nor against	8	12	18
Against	79	67	53
Can't choose	1	1	1

Base: 804

Our findings show that a clear majority opposes cutting down or cutting out NHS treatments and services in principle, and support for basing rationing decisions on the particular criteria considered here is muted. In particular, there is very little agreement with rationing on the grounds of cost, or the type, of treatment. Only rationing according to the severity of the condition attracts clear support, with seven in ten thinking this should be the only way of deciding who gets priority for treatment. Beyond this, the greatest acceptance of rationing relates to reducing non-essential treatments and withholding treatments according to patients' non-medical attributes, such as smoking and age.

Who supports and who opposes health care rationing?

Various groups might be expected to hold different views about the desirability and inevitability of rationing, as well as about the criteria that rationing might be based upon. Acceptance or opposition may well vary according to knowledge, experience and self-interest. Maybe, for example, the elderly favour priority being given to older age groups and the young take the opposite view? And are those on low incomes – who are thus less able to turn to the private sector in times of need – more opposed than average to rationing?

We need to monitor the influence of age particularly closely: if it is linked to attitudes this might be important in predicting future challenges for the NHS. We know that British society is ageing (see the chapter by Park in this Report for a more detailed discussion) and our findings could provide clues about the possible direction that attitudes might take.

We start by examining how groups differ in their responses to questions about the desirability and inevitability of rationing, and about the various criteria by which rationing decisions might be made. We focus on: age; gender; qualification level; income bracket; recent experience of NHS care; whether or not a person has private medical insurance; party political identification; and attitudes to (and experience of) the NHS. We then report on a summary 'scale' based upon some of these questions which provides an overall measure of acceptance or opposition to health care rationing within the NHS.

Age and gender

Young and old alike are united in their view that the NHS should never cut down or cut out any types of treatment, this applying to around eight in ten irrespective of age. However, older people are slightly more likely to have faith that the NHS will have enough money and resources in the future to provide treatment for everyone who needs it (and thus that rationing is not inevitable). As the next table shows, just under a quarter of the 50-plus age group take this view, double the rate among younger people who are more pessimistic. Among all age groups, however, the dominant view is that health care rationing is inevitable.

Table 2.7 Whether the NHS will have "enough money and resources to provide everyone with the treatment they need when they need it" by age

	Age				
	18-34	35-49	50-64	65 or over	Total
	%	%	%	%	%
NHS will have to ration treatments	16	11	22	23	18
NHS will not have to ration treatments	66	81	68	65	70
Can't choose	17	7	8	9	10
Base	*186*	*215*	*192*	*211*	*804*

Although age is not related to attitudes towards the *principle* of health rationing, older people are more likely than others to accept rationing on some of the specific grounds we considered earlier. For example, those aged 65-plus were more supportive than others of discriminating against smokers, with around half (49 per cent) saying they would give priority to non-smokers, compared with four in ten of younger people. As the next table shows, this group is also more accepting of cutting down on expensive treatments in favour of cheaper ones and reducing the remit of the NHS so as to exclude fertility treatment and the cost of hospital meals. Nearly half of those over 65 favour the NHS cutting down fertility treatment, compared with just over a quarter of the 18-34 age group.

Table 2.8 Specific examples of NHS health care rationing by age

	Age				
	18-34	35-49	50-64	65 or over	Total
% agree with NHS giving lower priority to expensive treatments	16	19	26	38	24
% in favour of NHS cutting down on fertility treatment	28	33	46	47	38
% in favour of charges for hospital meals	17	20	31	32	25
Base	*186*	*215*	*192*	*211*	*804*

There is some evidence of self-interest in people's responses. When asked whether a 30 year old or a 70 year old should be given priority for a heart operation, those aged 65-plus were the most likely to think the older person should go first, and those under 49 most likely to favour the young person. However, unlike other groups, the elderly have a three to one majority in favour of priority being given to the person *not* in their own age group (31 against 11 per cent). In contrast, the 18-35 year olds had a nine to one majority *in favour* of the individual in their own age group (35 against 4 per cent).

Table 2.9 Whether a 30 year old or a 70 year old should get priority for a heart operation, or whether age should make no difference by age

	Age				
	18-34	35-49	50-64	65 or over	Total
Younger person	35	39	31	31	34
Older person	4	3	2	11	5
No difference	48	49	60	49	51
Can't choose	10	9	6	7	8
Base	*186*	*215*	*192*	*211*	*804*

Men and women do not differ in their views about the general concept of health care rationing, but certain examples of rationing in practice do prove more appealing to one sex than another. In particular, women are more reluctant than men about cutting back on NHS spending on fertility treatment. One may have expected this, with fertility treatments often viewed as more of a 'women's issue'. But other forms of rationing with no clear relationship to gender also attract different responses from men and women. For example, women are more likely to favour charging for hospital meals and more likely to favour a 30 year old person being prioritised for treatment over a 70 year old person.

Table 2.10 Specific examples of NHS health care rationing by sex

	Women	Men
% in favour of NHS cutting down on fertility treatment	34	43
% in favour of charges for hospital meals	31	18
% think 30 year old should get priority over 70 year old for heart operation	39	28
Base	*442*	*362*

Education, income and private medical insurance

Graduates are substantially more likely than others to support the *principle* of health care rationing, this applying to three in ten, three times as many as among the less well qualified.

Table 2.11 Whether the NHS "should cut down or cut out certain types of treatment" by highest educational qualification

	Degree	A level	O level	None	Total
Highest educational qualification					
NHS should ration treatments	31	11	7	8	12
NHS should not ration treatments	64	81	89	84	82
Can't choose	2	7	1	6	5
Base	*86*	*92*	*163*	*248*	*804*

Graduates are also much more likely to see health rationing as inevitable. Nine in ten take this view, compared with six in ten of those with no qualifications.

Table 2.12 Whether the NHS will have "enough money and resources to provide everyone with the treatment they need when they need it" by highest educational qualification

	Degree	A level	O level	None	Total
Highest educational qualification					
NHS will not have to ration treatments	2	15	19	27	18
NHS will have to ration treatments	92	82	66	59	70
Can't choose	3	9	12	11	10
Base	*86*	*92*	*163*	*248*	*804*

Not surprisingly, given their greater acceptance of the principle of rationing, graduates are also more accepting of particular examples of rationing in practice. However, they tend to favour rationing on the grounds of severity of condition, or cutting non-essential treatments and services, rather than cutting

treatments and services purely on cost grounds. Indeed, those with no qualifications at all are the most likely to think that expensive treatments should be given lower priority than cheaper ones. A third (32 per cent) take this view, compared with 20 per cent of graduates. This results in less qualified people being less supportive than average of rationing in principle, yet more supportive of one of the least popular methods of undertaking it.

To assess the relationship between income and attitudes we divided respondents into four roughly equal groups according to their household income. While there are no significant differences between groups in their views about the principle of health care rationing, lower income groups are the most optimistic that rationing will not be an inevitable part of the NHS's future. Just over a quarter (28 per cent) of those in the lowest income quartile take this view, three times as many as in the highest quartile (ten per cent). The highest income group is much more likely than the lowest to think that rationing should be based purely on the severity of a patient's condition (74 and 47 per cent respectively). But there are no similar differences in opinion with regard to the rationing of expensive treatments in favour of a greater number of less expensive treatments.

Those with private medical insurance (19 per cent of respondents) are no more or less likely to support the concept of health rationing within the NHS. However, they are half as likely to think that the NHS will have enough money in future than those without insurance (ten per cent and 20 per cent respectively). These groups do not differ in their views about the different ways in which rationing might take place in practice.

Party identification

We turn now to consider how attitudes towards health rationing relate to a person's party identification – the party they feel closest to or support (or would vote for in a general election). As the next table shows, Conservatives and Liberal Democrats are more sympathetic about the principle of rationing (over twice as much in the case of the Conservative identifiers) than Labour identifiers.

Table 2.13 Whether the NHS "should cut down or cut out certain types of treatment" by party identification

	Party identification			
	Labour	Liberal Democrat	Conservative	Total
NHS should ration treatments	8	16	19	12
NHS should not ration treatments	86	78	76	82
Can't choose	4	5	4	5
Base	*320*	*106*	*217*	*804*

When it comes to views about the necessity – or otherwise – of future rationing, Liberal Democrat identifiers are again closer to Conservatives than to Labour identifiers. One in five Labour identifiers think rationing is *not* inevitable, compared with around one in seven Liberal Democrats and Conservatives.

Table 2.14 Whether the NHS will have "enough money and resources to provide everyone with the treatment they need when they need it" by party identification

	Party identification			
	Labour	Liberal Democrat	Conservative	Total
NHS will not have to ration treatments	21	15	14	18
NHS will have to ration treatments	67	75	75	70
Can't choose	9	8	9	10
Base	*320*	*106*	*217*	*804*

When we consider the various ways in which rationing might work in practice, Labour identifiers are consistently the most opposed. The differences are most marked in relation to devolving particular treatments to the private or charitable sector or charging for certain services. For instance, a half of Conservative identifiers (49 per cent) opt for the NHS reducing its responsibility for fertility treatment, compared with a third of Labour and Liberal Democrat identifiers (34 and 36 per cent respectively). And there is a ten percentage point gap

between the proportion of Conservative and Labour identifiers who favour charging for GP visits, either at the surgery or at people's homes.

Table 2.15 Specific examples of NHS health care rationing by party identification

		Party identification		
	Labour	Liberal Democrat	Conservative	Total
% in favour of NHS cutting down:				
Fertility treatment	34	36	49	38
Cosmetic surgery	58	54	67	60
% in favour of charges for:				
Visiting a GP	5	8	15	8
GP home visits	14	19	24	17
Hospital meals	21	29	32	25
Base	*320*	*106*	*217*	*804*

Attitudes to (and experience of) the NHS

Views about rationing did not vary between those with, and without, recent experience of NHS care (defined according to whether a person has visited their GP or hospital – as an inpatient or outpatient – over the past 12 months). Four in five (80 per cent) are recent 'users' but, although they are generally more positive than others about the current state of the NHS and keener to see extra spending and raised taxes, they do not have significantly different views about the desirability or inevitability of health care rationing.

However, differences do emerge between the views of people who currently feel that the NHS caters reasonably well for people's needs versus those who feel that the current service provided by the NHS falls below adequacy. As we reported earlier, just over half of people feel that the NHS currently copes 'very well' or 'adequately'. These people are no more or less likely than others to think that the NHS *should* cut down or cut out certain types of treatment. However, they are more likely than others to believe that the NHS *will not need* to take such measures, believing that the NHS will have enough money in the future to provide for everyone's needs.

Table 2.16 Attitudes to rationing by how well the NHS caters for everyone's needs

	NHS caters well	NHS does not cater well	Total
NHS will not have to ration treatments	21	13	18
NHS will have to ration treatments	65	77	70
Can't choose	12	7	10
Base	*464*	*340*	*804*

A rationing acceptance scale

So far we have seen that some groups are more favourable towards rationing than others, although in most cases the variation that exists is rather muted. But to compare the views of particular groups more thoroughly we have *combined* people's responses to different questions about the ways in which rationing decisions might be made. This assumes that the answers given to specific questions about the rationing of NHS care also reflect more general underlying attitudes towards the concept of rationing. If this assumption is correct, the scores on the scale are likely to be a more reliable indicator of this underlying attitude than the answer to any individual question (DeVellis, 1991). The scale gives people a score of between one and five. The higher the person's score, the more in favour – or accepting – of rationing they are, and the lower the score, the less in favour (more details of our scale are in the appendix to this chapter).

Of course, any scale is only as reliable as the questions within it. There is a chance that a person might have a low score simply because we have not included any of the forms of rationing that they would agree to. Reassuringly though, when we check the rationing scale against responses to our general question about the overall principle of rationing we find that they correlate well. So people who are the most accepting of the different ways in which rationing decisions might be made are also more accepting of the general principle behind rationing, when defined as cutting down or cutting out services.[2]

Our scale suggests that the characteristics most linked to attitudes towards health rationing are age (with those aged 65-plus being much more accepting than younger groups) and party identification (with Conservative identifiers being more accepting than other groups). There is also a high correlation between people's rating of how well the NHS currently 'caters for everyone's medical needs' and attitudes to rationing. Those who feel the NHS is currently doing at least 'adequately' are more accepting of rationing than those who think the NHS is not doing well.

The *British Social Attitudes* survey series includes three attitude scales, which aim to measure where respondents stand on certain underlying value dimensions – left-right, libertarian-authoritarian and welfarist-individualist (see Appendix I of this Report for more details). We begin by considering the welfare scale. At one end of this scale are those most in favour of welfare provision and its role in redistributing income from rich to poor. At the other are those who take a more 'individualist' approach and would rather minimise the government's involvement. Those with a pro-welfare stance are *less* likely than those with a more individualistic approach to accept the notion of health care rationing. (Those in the most pro-welfare quartile score 2.31 on our scale, compared with a score of 2.72 for those in the most anti-welfare quartile.)

We saw earlier that Labour identifiers were less accepting of rationing than Conservative or Liberal Democrats. Not surprisingly, then, we find that a person's position on the left-right scale is also linked to their views about rationing. Those with the most left-wing views (and thus the most in favour of redistribution) are less accepting of the idea of health care rationing, and those with right-wing views the most accepting. (Those in the most left-wing quartile score 2.42 on our scale, compared with a score of 2.66 for those in the most right-wing quartile.)

Attitudes to rationing do not prove to be related to whether a person takes a libertarian or authoritarian stance on issues to do with tradition, authority and punishment.

Disentangling relationships using regression analysis

It is clear that attitudes to health rationing vary according to a variety of characteristics – including age, party identification, and a person's views about the welfare state. However, because many of these characteristics are themselves related to one another, it is difficult to untangle the effect of one characteristic *independently* from the effect of another. For example, is it being aged 65-plus which gives a person a particular view about health rationing, or being a Conservative identifier (as the Conservatives happen to have an older age profile than identifiers with other parties)? To this end, we use multivariate analysis in order to establish the relationship between a range of different characteristics and attitudes towards health rationing. (Regression analysis is described in more detail in Appendix I of this Report.)

If we include in our model all the characteristics we considered earlier (including the left-right, welfare, and libertarian-authoritarian scales) we find confirmation of the strong relationship between attitudes to rationing and age, with older groups being the most accepting. (Details of the model are in the appendix to this chapter.) Education also matters, with those who have qualifications at A-level standard or above being more accepting than less well-educated groups. So too does how 'welfarist' a person is, with those taking a more 'individualist' and anti-welfare approach also being the most accepting of health rationing. In fact, this relationship is so strong that it overshadows some other relationships, suggesting that both attitudes to welfare and to health

rationing tap very similar underlying values – the 'rolling back' of the state's responsibility. If we *exclude* the welfare scale from our model, we find that two other characteristics also emerge as significantly linked to a person's views about health rationing. Those who think the NHS is currently doing an adequate job are more accepting of rationing, as are those with the most right-wing views on our left-right scale.

It is not clear why age is so strongly linked to attitudes to health rationing. On the one hand, it may indicate a 'generational' difference between older and younger groups (see the chapter by Park in this Report for a more detailed discussion of this). The distinctiveness of current older generations might reflect their being brought up during post-war austerity (perhaps making them less demanding) or, conversely, the fact that they witnessed the birth of the NHS (perhaps making them more valuing of its services). This would imply that people's views on these matters are shaped considerably by experiences during youth and do not alter markedly as they get older. But of course age differences could also reflect 'life-cycle' differences – differences to do with the ageing process itself. Perhaps people's attitudes towards public services and medicine mellow with age, becoming more realistic as a result of experience and changing expectations.

The relationship between beliefs about welfare and those about rationing raises rather different issues. Those who are anti-welfare are also more accepting of rationing – making their 'acceptance' of health rationing less to do with improving the NHS than with a basic scepticism about public services. Meanwhile, those who are pro-welfare (and less accepting of health rationing) may well object because they perceive rationing to be a betrayal of the egalitarian principles of the NHS.

Potentially these findings do not bode well for the NHS. If attitudes to rationing do reflect generational differences then the dying out of older generations, who are more accepting of rationing, and their replacement by younger ones, who are less accepting, implies that support for rationing may fall further still. Moreover, the very people who support the NHS from a political and ideological perspective (the pro-welfarists) are also the *least* likely to support the rationing of health care. If commentators are right – and future rationing is inevitable – this may result in the NHS's 'natural' supporters becoming increasingly disillusioned.

However, all is not lost for those who would argue that rationing is both necessary and desirable. It may be that the age differences we have found reflect nothing more than a tendency for people to become more accepting of rationing as they get older. So, as the population ages, attitudes towards rationing should become more positive.[3] Similarly, the fact that better qualified people are more accepting suggests that opposition may mellow as the educational qualifications of the population continue to increase.

Who decides?

If rationing is to take place, there are a variety of different groups who might have an interest in participating in making decisions about how priority should be assessed. We turn now to examine people's views about who should be involved in making these decisions – and who they believe currently is.

To assess attitudes towards who should make decisions, we asked:

> *Suppose that the NHS did have to make these sorts of choices about who to treat, or the order in which they should be treated ... How much say do you think each of these groups should have: the government; GPs; hospital or health service managers; hospital doctors; the general public; independent health experts?*

Hospital doctors were by far the most popular group to have 'all or most of the say' in these sorts of decisions, with over half of people opting for them (and the remainder thinking they should have 'some' say). GPs are also popular choices, though far fewer consider they should have the most say in decision making. In contrast, the idea of leaving most decisions to politicians or hospital bureaucrats attracts very little support. Only four per cent of people would like rationing decisions to be centralised at government level, and only one in ten think that hospital or health service managers – rather than doctors – should have 'all or most of the say'. Over half think that government should have *no* say whatsoever in these sorts of issues. Attitudes towards the public participating in decision making is more mixed, with similar proportions thinking they should, and should not, play a part.

A third (32 per cent) of people think no single one group should have all or most of the say. Rather, they support the idea of the responsibility being spread across two or more groups.

Table 2.17 How much say should different groups have in health rationing decisions?

	Hospital doctors	GPs	Experts	Man-agers	Public	Govern-ment
	%	%	%	%	%	%
All or most of the say	56	29	11	10	7	4
Some of the say	35	62	55	43	35	29
None of the say	1	2	18	34	44	55
Can't choose	4	4	11	7	9	7

Base: 804

These findings suggest that people favour flexible decision-making which can take into account individual circumstances (as opposed to decisions being made at a central and more impersonal level and then implemented by way of a prescribed set of rules). This interpretation is backed up by responses to a further question which required respondents to choose between two statements:

There should be publicly available guidelines about who should get priority for health care

Medical experts should be allowed to make these sorts of decisions as they see best

Only a quarter (25 per cent) would rather have publicly available guidelines, with the majority (60 per cent) preferring a more opaque system allowing medical experts to make their own decisions. One in eight (13 per cent) could not choose between either option.

There is a gulf between who people would rather have make decisions about rationing, and who they think currently does. Two of the *least* popular sources of decision making (hospital managers and government) are the most likely to be seen as having all or most of the say at the moment. Only one in five consider hospital doctors to have this same level of influence (although around three times this amount think they should). However, only six per cent think that hospital doctors currently play no role in the decision-making process.

Table 2.18 How much say *do* groups currently have in health rationing decisions?

	Hospital doctors	GPs	Experts	Man-agers	Public	Govern-ment
% saying ...						
All or most	19	7	6	35	1	30
Some	63	68	47	47	12	45
None	6	13	25	5	73	11
Can't choose	6	7	17	8	9	9

Unweighted base: 804

People's views about decision making also relate to their attitudes towards health rationing. In particular, as the next table shows, those who think doctors should have "all or most of the say" (whether GPs or hospital doctors) are more opposed to rationing. In contrast, those who think government should have at least some of the say[4] in decision making score 2.78 (which indicates a more sympathetic stance to rationing), compared with a score of 2.5 among those who think government should not be involved at all.

Table 2.19 How much say should doctors have in health rationing decisions and attitudes to rationing?

	GPs should have ...	Base	Hospital doctors should have ...	Base
Mean scale score				
All or most of the say	2.46	221	2.46	431
Some or none of the say	2.7	490	2.82	280

These findings show that those who are opposed to rationing in principle are – if pushed to nominate a group to make decisions about rationing – more trusting of doctors' ability to make the right decisions than they are of any other group, particularly government. There is certainly little evidence here of a desire for public guidelines to help prioritise people needing treatment or care. However, those who are more ready to accept rationing do see a role for government, perhaps because they believe the fairest way to implement decisions is by way of politically accountable mechanisms. Certainly decision making at a central level is the most likely to avoid 'post-code' rationing, whereby place of residence affects the services one receives. It may of course be that those most accepting of rationing are also the most aware of these sorts of issues, and thus keen to address them.

Conclusions

One of the most difficult tasks in researching people's attitudes to rationing is to ask the appropriate question. Rationing is an emotive issue. For some it conjures up images of treatment denial and system failure; for others it is a neutral 'fact of life', the necessary consequence of natural scarcity making it impossible to do all things for all people. Within both these conceptions, beneficial things will be denied to people. But the understanding of what that implies in practice is quite different. On the one hand, the denial may be seen as immoral and unnecessary, involving cutbacks and the withdrawal of public welfare. On the other, the denial may be viewed as inevitable and thus uncontroversial. In this latter case, the only relevant questions relate to what extent rationing should take place in any given circumstance, and how, and by whom, decisions about rationing should be taken.

Researching attitudes to rationing health care – in particular the question of whether it is inevitable in the NHS – is thus complicated by the possibility that people are responding to one particular conception of what rationing might mean. In the survey reported here this problem is addressed by specifically focusing on the more 'controversial' perception of rationing, namely that "the NHS will always have too many demands on it and should *cut down and cut out*

certain types of treatment" (emphasis added). It needs to be borne in mind that one can be opposed to this point of view and yet still accept the broader notion of rationing as an inevitable, natural consequence of limited resources. 'Cutting down and cutting out' is not the only way in which rationing manifests itself. Often the issues relate to technological advances and how much we are able to make use of the opportunities these potentially offer. So rationing is not necessarily about providing fewer or poorer services than in the past but about not being able to exhaust every last drop of new benefit offered by medical science over time. The most obvious manifestation of this is the fact that very significant real resource increases in expenditure on the NHS over the past 20 years, resulting in substantially increased service provision (Harrison *et al.*, 1997), have not nearly exhausted all the demands made on the NHS. Choices still have to be made, even when we provide more and provide it better.

Notwithstanding these difficulties, valuable evidence emerges about how people think rationing decisions should be made (and by whom) and the kinds of people who are most likely to support rationing in principle and practice. The results are unequivocal: over 80 per cent of people believe that the NHS should never cut down and cut out any types of treatment. If pushed, they would rather doctors took the lead in making rationing decisions, and most are opposed to the prospect of non-clinical characteristics guiding which patients should have priority. People with 'pro-welfare' attitudes are more likely to be opposed to rationing, whereas the elderly are more likely to be accepting – as well as acknowledging that if age is to be a relevant factor then it should be in favour of the young. Many of these findings mirror other work in the same area (Judge *et al.*, 1997; Kneeshaw, 1997).

These results offer mixed messages for the NHS. Clearly much has to be done if the natural supporters of the NHS are to be convinced that rationing does not signify an abandonment of its egalitarian principles. But the more accepting attitude of the elderly and the better educated – both growing proportions of the population – might point to a bolstering of support for a 'rationing' NHS. That said, the views of the elderly might simply reflect a particular generation of elderly people who, by living through post-war austerity and witnessing the birth of the NHS, have a unique view about these sorts of health matters that may well not be passed on to subsequent generations.

Notes

1. This is backed up by other survey work on the same subject which used different questions to assess attitudes to rationing (Kneeshaw, 1997). In these surveys, the proportion of people taking an 'anti-rationing' line was either 77 per cent, 51 per cent or 16 per cent, depending on the question asked. The three questions/statements were, respectively, 'Everyone should have all the health care they need no matter how much it costs' (1991), 'Do you think that the NHS should have unlimited funding?' (1993), 'The NHS will always be able to provide everyone with every treatment they need' (1994).

2. Those who agree with the general principle of rationing score 2.88 on the scale, and those who do not score 2.45. The relatively small difference between these scores substantiates our general finding that people are more likely to disagree with the general principle of rationing than with some of the specific ways in which rationing decisions might be made.
3. If is not yet possible to identify whether the age differences we have found reflect generational or life-cycle differences as to do this would require the same questions to have been asked over a long period of time. This would allow us to track the views of different 'cohorts' of people and examine how their views have changed (or remained the same) as they have aged.
4. For the questions relating to GPs and hospital doctors it was necessary to combine the "some of the say" and the "none of the say" responses due to the small bases involved, whereas for the question about the government "some of the say" was instead combined with "all or most of the say".

References

Coulter, A. (1999), 'NICE and CHI: reducing variations and raising standards' in Appleby and Harrison (eds.), *Health Care UK 1999/2000*, London: King's Fund.

DeVellis, R. (1991), 'Scale Development: Theory and Applications', *Applied Social Research Methods*, **26**: Newbury Park, Ca: Sage.

Francombe, C. (2000), personal communication.

Ham, C. and Coulter, A. (eds.) (2000), *The Global Challenge of Health Care Rationing*, Buckingham: Open University Press.

Harrison, A., Dixon, J., Judge, K., and New, B. (1997), 'Can the NHS cope in future?', *British Medical Journal*, **314**: 139-42.

Harrison, A. and New, B. (2000), *Access to Elective Care: What should really be done about waiting lists*, London: King's Fund.

House of Commons Hansard (1998), Volume 321, 26 November, col 339.

Judge, K., Mulligan, J. and New, B. (1997), 'The NHS: New Prescriptions needed?' in Jowell, R., Curtice, J., Park, A., Brook, L., Thomson, K. and Bryson, C. (eds.), *British Social Attitudes: the 14th Report - The end of Conservative values?*, Aldershot: Ashgate.

Kneeshaw, J. (1997), 'What does the public think about rationing? A review of the evidence' in New, B. (ed.), *Rationing: Talk and Action in Health Care*, London: King's Fund/British Medical Journal.

Lenaghan, J. (1996), *Rationing and rights in health care*, London: IPPR.

National Institute for Clinical Excellence (1999), 'NICE Guidance – zanamivir (Relenza) in the Treatment of Influenza', NICE Press Release 1999/08, 8 October 1999.

National Institute for Clinical Excellence (2000), 'NICE issues Guidance to the NHS on the removal of Wisdom Teeth', NICE Press Release 03-27, 27 March 2000.

New, B. (1996), 'The Rationing Agenda in the NHS', *British Medical Journal*, **312**: 1593-1601.

Underwood, M.J. and Bailey, J.S. (1993), 'Coronary bypass surgery should not be offered to smokers', *British Medical Journal*, **306**, 1047-49.

Williams, A. (1997), 'Intergenerational equity: an exploration of the "fair innings" argument', *Health Economics*, **6**: 117-132.

Wordsworth, S., Donaldson, C. and Scott, A. (1996), *Can we afford the NHS?*, London: IPPR.

Acknowledgements

The authors would like to thank the King's Fund for funding this module of questions on health care rationing in 1999.

Appendix

Construction of the rationing acceptance scale

The scale consisted of the following items:

Should priority be given to people on the basis of:
1. whether or not they smoke?
2. their age?

Should the NHS cut down on the expensive treatments and services:
3. heart transplants?
4. long-term nursing care for the elderly?
5. intensive care for very premature babies whose survival is in doubt?

Should the NHS reduce its remit – by passing to private insurance and charities:
6. fertility treatment?
7. hospice care for the terminally ill?
8. cosmetic surgery?

Should the NHS charge for:
9. visits to GP surgeries?
10. GP visits to people's homes?
11. the cost of inpatient meals?

Responses to the statements were recoded so that five equals the most accepting view and one equals opposition to rationing for all the items. Answers of 'can't choose' were recoded as 'neither agree nor disagree'. The scale score was calculated by averaging the scores for each respondent on each of the 11 items, giving a maximum value of five (accepting) and a minimum value of one (opposed). The 11 statements have a Cronbach's alpha of 0.86, a measure of reliability (internal consistency) of the scale which can be regarded as very good for an attitude scale of this sort (DeVellis, 1991).

Regression models

Each model is based upon all respondents who answered all the relevant questions. The models report the coefficients (or parameter estimates) for each of the characteristics specified on the left side of the table. Each coefficient shows whether that particular characteristic differs significantly from its comparison group in its association with the dependent variable – in this case the acceptance of rationing scale. Details of the comparison group are supplied in brackets. Two asterisks indicate that the coefficient is statistically significant at a 99 per cent level and one asterisk that it is significant at a 95 per cent level.

In each model, a positive coefficient indicates that those with the characteristic are more likely than the comparison group to score as more accepting of health care rationing; a negative coefficient means that they are less likely to accept rationing.

Linear regression model on the acceptance of rationing scale

Characteristic (comparison group in brackets)	Coefficient
Age (65+)	
18-34	-0.111*
35-49	-0.148**
50-64	-0.099*
Gender (female)	
Male	0.006
Income quartile (lowest)	
High	-0.029
Second	-0.014
Third	-0.069
Recent experience of NHS (None)	
Experience in past year	-0.021
Private health insurance (None)	
Has insurance	0.009
Party identification (Conservative)	
Labour	-0.009
Liberal Democrat	-0.016
Other	-0.033
Highest qualification (Less than A level)	
A level or above	0.079*
How well NHS doing (not well)	
NHS doing very well/adequately	0.068
Welfare scale	
Low score = pro-welfare	0.303**[1]

---

[1] In the welfare scale, a score of 1 indicates a pro-welfare stance and a score of 5 indicates an anti-welfare or individualist stance. In the rationing scale, a score of 1 indicates a rejection of rationing and a score of 5 indicates an acceptance of rationing. Thus, as the coefficient 0.303 is positive (rather than negative), this shows that there is relationship between scoring highly on the welfare scale (anti-welfare/individualist) and highly on the rationing scale (pro-rationing). Similarly, there is a relationship between having a low score on the welfare scale (pro-welfare) and having a low score on the rationing scale (anti-rationing).

Libertarian scale
Low score = libertarian -0.080^2

Left-right scale
Low score = left 0.029^3

---

[2] In the libertarian scale, a score of 1 indicates a libertarian stance and a score of 5 indicates an authoritarian stance. In the rationing scale, a score of 1 indicates a rejection of rationing and a score of 5 indicates an acceptance of rationing. Thus, as the coefficient -0.080 is negative (rather than positive), this shows that there is a (non-significant) relationship between scoring highly on the libertarian scale (authoritarian) and having a low score on the rationing scale (anti-rationing). Similarly, there is a relationship between having a low score on the libertarian scale (libertarian) and having a high score on the rationing scale (pro-rationing).

[3] In the left-right scale, a score of 1 indicates a left-wing stance and a score of 5 indicates a right-wing stance. In the rationing scale, a score of 1 indicates a rejection of rationing and a score of 5 indicates an acceptance of rationing. Thus, as the coefficient 0.029 is positive (rather than negative), this shows that there is a (non-significant) relationship between scoring highly on the left-right scale (right-wing) and highly on the rationing scale (pro-rationing). Similarly, there is a relationship between having a low score on the left-right scale (left-wing) and having a low score on the rationing scale (anti-rationing).

3 The working class and New Labour: a parting of the ways?

Geoffrey Evans[*]

Much recent public debate about social class has focused on whether, in its apparently successful move to capture the support of middle England, New Labour is likely to lose its working-class heartland.[1] At the heart of this debate is the assumption that class divisions are at their strongest in attitudes towards the economy, spending and redistribution – the core of the traditional left-right division in British politics. The argument goes that as the government has moved to the centre on these questions, it has moved closer to the position of the Conservatives, effectively leaving its traditional working-class supporters without effective parliamentary representation. For some commentators, although the 2000 budget was a gesture in the opposite direction, as was the Chancellor's comprehensive spending review later in the year, the damage had already been done.

This chapter examines the latest *British Social Attitudes* data to discover how far the New Labour government has actually moved away from the attitudes and preferences of Old Labour's traditional working-class base. As we shall see, economic policy and redistribution turn out not, after all, to be the main areas of divergence between Labour and the working classes. There are in fact two types of class-related issues, and thus two potential sources of divergence between the working class and New Labour: traditional economic issues to do with redistribution, on which the working class are on 'the left', and social issues to do with tolerance, morality, traditionalism, prejudice and nationalism, on which the working class are on 'the right'.[2] This picture of class differences in attitudes is rather different from the commonly held one that places the government in the centre, the Conservatives on the right and the working-class on the left. It opens up the possibility that the Conservatives can gain support on social issues from working-class voters who roundly reject New Labour's image of a 'progressive', multicultural, pro-European, pro-minority Britain. On these issues, many working class voters appear to embody the very 'forces of conservatism' that the Prime Minister and his party have disparaged.

[*] Geoffrey Evans is Official Fellow in Politics, Nuffield College Oxford and University Reader in the Sociology of Politics.

Rather than try to cover the complexities of the modern class structure here, the focus will be confined to divisions between, on the one hand, a broadly defined 'middle class' of higher and lower level professionals and managers (also referred to as the 'salariat'), and on the other, a 'working class' of employees who work in manual occupations. The views of the smaller but politically interesting category of the 'petty bourgeoisie'[3] – mainly the self-employed, but also owners of small businesses and farmers – will also be referred to. This latter group are sometimes lumped into what market researchers call the 'C2s' alongside skilled manual workers, but their views are generally as distinct from skilled manual workers as they are from professionals and managers, so it is preferable to treat them as a distinct category.

Traditional class divisions

The principal 'class' issues in British politics are usually thought to revolve around economic policy and social spending, referring in particular to the perennial subject of *redistribution*. This is regarded as the classic class divide because the working classes with their lower incomes, poorer health and education, and their lower likelihood of climbing up the income ladder, are bound to be more left wing than the middle classes with all their relative advantages.

As the next table shows, they are, but there is rather less difference between the salariat and the working class on this issue than might be expected. While the middle classes (and the self-employed), are quite a bit more *opposed* to redistribution than are the working classes, the proportions of the middle and working classes who actually endorse redistribution by the government are strikingly similar.

Table 3.1 "Government should redistribute income from the better-off to those who are less well-off" by class

	Salariat	Self-employed	Working class
	%	%	%
Agree	37	29	40
Disagree	42	45	26
Base	*737*	*189*	*749*

So, the working classes seem to be somewhat more fainthearted, and the middle classes somewhat more enthusiastic, supporters of redistribution than we might have anticipated. This is also the case when we look at various means of achieving redistribution. One way of doing this is via public spending to reduce

social inequalities. Respondents were asked for their priorities with respect to public spending in ten different areas. Omitted from the next table are those spending areas – defence, social security, police and prisons, overseas aid – that were ranked as first priority by fewer than five per cent of respondents. The rest are shown in the table.

Table 3.2 Priorities for public spending by class

	Salariat	Self-employed	Working class
First priority for extra government spending	%	%	%
Health	46	43	48
Education	37	33	30
Public Transport	6	4	3
Roads	2	6	4
Housing	1	2	5
Base	*907*	*258*	*984*

Again, there is little evidence of any major differences in emphasis between the social classes. Health is the clear priority for all classes, and education is the only other area of spending that attracts any substantial vote. Despite shades of difference among the other less popular priorities, the overall picture on spending preferences is one of broad correspondence rather than conflict.

Table 3.3 Support for more spending on benefits by class

	Salariat	Self-employed	Working class
Per cent in favour of more government spending on benefits for:			
Carers for those who are sick or disabled	83	79	83
Disabled people who cannot work	68	72	77
Working parents on low income	67	59	71
Retired people	66	67	74
Single parents	29	25	35
Unemployed people	19	17	29
Base	*907*	*258*	*984*

Only when we come to some unambiguously *redistributive* areas of public spending as seen in Table 3.3 – in particular, on the unemployed, pensioners and the disabled – do we at last find larger differences in the expected direction between the salariat and the working class. Even so, these differences hardly amount to a chasm.

So on the measures presented so far, it appears that the working class are slightly more in favour of higher public spending than are the middle class. But these are not the only measures available in the series nor perhaps the best ones, based as they are on questions that make no explicit link between greater public spending on the one hand and the likelihood of higher taxes on the other.[4] Some people's support for higher public spending tends to disappear in the face of this trade-off. The next table shows the answers in response to two questions that do explicitly make this link between taxes and spending. And the differences between the classes all but disappear: all classes are solidly in favour of higher taxes and spending rather than the reverse, and all (less enthusiastically by far, but to much the same degree as one another) endorse more spending on welfare benefits *per se*, "even if it leads to higher taxes".

Table 3.4 Attitudes to taxation and public spending by class

	Salariat	Self- employed	Working class
Government should:	%	%	%
Reduce taxes and spend less on health, education and social benefits	3	4	4
Increase taxes and spend more on health, education and social benefits	60	58	57
Base	*907*	*258*	*984*
Spend more on welfare benefits for the poor even if it leads to higher taxes	%	%	%
Agree	43	39	40
Disagree	31	33	29
Base	*737*	*189*	*749*

Thus the picture is by no means a simple division between a solidaristic working class supporting redistribution to help the poor and a unified middle class opposing such measures to guard their own position. In fact, on some issues, such as concern for the homeless and beggars, as discussed in more detail in the chapter by Adler, Bromley and Rosie, it is the middle class (73 per cent) rather than the working class (50 per cent) who express sympathy for the view that it is 'everyone's responsibility' to help them.

Why are class differences so blurred?

There are, of course, many ways of examining and explaining similarities and differences in class attitudes. This chapter focuses on what the different classes believe about opportunity, responsibility and fairness, all important words in the New Labour dictionary.

As the next table shows, a large majority of respondents in *all classes* regard inequalities in British pay as too great. Similarly, only around one in five people within each class believes that large income inequalities are good for the economy. Meanwhile, working-class respondents are by far the *most* sceptical about the legitimacy of begging and are almost as likely as the middle classes to believe that unemployment benefits are too high.

Table 3.5 Attitudes towards economic inequality by class

	Salariat	Self-employed	Working class
Per cent who agree that:			
The gap between high and low incomes is too large	79	80	83
Base	*583*	*183*	*645*
Large differences in income are necessary for Britain's prosperity	20	21	19
Benefits for the unemployed are too high and discourage them from finding jobs	43	49	41
Base	*233*	*56*	*239*
Begging is just an easy way of making a living	35	48	56
Base	*300*	*84*	*318*

It is hardly surprising that working-class people are more inclined than their middle-class counterparts to believe that they are personally underpaid (57 per cent, as opposed to 47 per cent of the middle class, believe they get paid less than a 'fair wage'). More interestingly, however, while those *middle-class* people who regard themselves as underpaid are rather more likely to be in favour of more redistribution generally, the relationship goes the other way in the case of working-class people. In their case, a sense of injustice about their own pay is associated with scepticism about helping the poor, as the next table shows.

Table 3.6 Evaluation of own pay by support for redistribution

	Own pay is less than fair	Own pay is fair or more than fair
Salariat		
Per cent who agree:		
Government should redistribute income from the better-off to those who are less well-off	39	31
Government should spend more on welfare benefits even if it leads to higher taxes	41	36
Base	*126*	*105*
Working class,		
Per cent who agree:		
Government should redistribute income from the better-off to those who are less well-off	46	41
The government should spend more on welfare benefits even if it leads to higher taxes	32	37
Base	*117*	*133*

Thus it appears that redistributive efforts on the part of the New Labour government towards people on benefits will not particularly appeal to its working-class heartland. While working-class people tend to support redistribution *in principle* to a greater degree than their middle-class counterparts, they are rather less sympathetic to the claims of the very poor as potential beneficiaries.

Wider social issues, and Europe

So far we have seen that class attitudes to economic and redistributive policies are not very polarised. But when we broaden the investigation to issues such as law and order, European integration, transport policy, sexual morality and minorities, far larger divisions begin to emerge. On these sorts of issues, the working class appears consistently to be more 'conservative' or 'right-wing' than their middle-class counterparts and more out of tune with many of New Labour's policies and programmes.

Looking first at attitudes to crime and punishment we find noticeably higher levels of punitiveness among the working class, particularly in respect of the death penalty – a relatively dead issue in politics that none of the three major parties has seriously attempted to resuscitate.

Table 3.7 Punitiveness by class

	Salariat	Self-employed	Working class
Per cent who agree:			
People who break the law should be given stiffer sentences	70	76	85
For some crimes, the death penalty is the most appropriate sentence	46	62	66
Base	*737*	*189*	*749*

Similarly, as the next table shows, working-class views on libertarian issues such as censorship and tolerance of homosexuality are considerably to the right of middle-class views. Although middle- and working-class support for censorship in principle, in order to "uphold moral standards", is almost identical, views diverge most sharply in relation both to the portrayal of, and the moral acceptability of, homosexuality (see also the chapter by Hill and Thomson). Some 60 per cent of working-class people, and a clear majority of the self-employed (56 per cent) believe that homosexuality is 'wrong', as opposed to 37 per cent of middle-class people who still hold this view. The New Labour government's intention to repeal 'Section 28' might thus well alienate Labour's traditional heartland more than it does its newer middle-class recruits.

Table 3.8 Attitudes towards censorship and homosexuality by class

	Salariat	Self-employed	Working class
Per cent who agree:			
Censorship is necessary to uphold moral standards	67	71	66
Base	*737*	*189*	*749*
Films showing a man and a woman having sex should be banned from cinemas	12	16	17
Films showing two men having sex should be banned from cinemas	29	37	44
Sexual relations between two adults of the same sex are wrong	37	56	60
Base	*321*	*84*	*316*

The fact that showing a heterosexual scene in a film is so much less controversial than showing a homosexual one confirms that this issue probably has less to do with prudishness *per se* than with disapproval of homosexuality. But sexual minorities are no exception. The working class and the self-employed are also more anti-immigration and racist in their attitudes than are the middle class. As the next table shows, they are much more inclined to believe that "immigrants take jobs away from people born in Britain", and to support the view that "to be truly English you have to be white".

Table 3.9 Attitudes towards minorities by class

	Salariat	Self-employed	Working class
Per cent who agree:			
Immigrants take jobs away from people born in Britain	34	45	57
Attempts to give equal opportunities to black people and Asians have gone too far	30	47	39
To be truly English you have to be white	17	32	31
Base	*744*	*208*	*808*

Note: These frequencies do not include ethnic minority respondents and cover England only

These negative attitudes towards minorities appear to be fuelled in part by ethnic competition. We asked respondents which groups in society they thought had been "getting ahead" in recent years and which were "losing out". Follow-up questions in each case established whether such trends were "a good thing", "a bad thing", or neither. The proportion of the sample who perceived minorities to have been improving their position *and* considered this to be a "bad thing" is highest among the self-employed (at 31 per cent), but the working-class figure (20 per cent) is nonetheless a full seven points greater than the middle-class proportion. In fact, given the rather high hurdle required to be included in the first row of the next table (both the perception that ethnic minorities are getting ahead fastest *and* the belief that this is a bad thing), these figures might be considered rather high.

The fact that ethnic competition has played a part in these judgements is underlined by the fact that the comparable answers about whether "ordinary working people" have been getting on or losing out produce much more sympathetic responses. New Labour's aspiration to pursue appropriate numerical representation of minorities in public institutions such as the police and fire brigade may thus be likely to increase the prevalence of these responses.[5]

Table 3.10 Attitudes towards ethnic minorities "getting ahead" by class

	Salariat	Self-employed	Working class
In the past few years, ethnic minorities have been getting ahead and ...	%	%	%
... this is a bad thing	13	31	20
... this is a good thing	28	17	17
Base	*713*	*195*	*738*

Note: These frequencies do not include ethnic minority respondents and cover England only

But, as the next table shows, by far the most pronounced divisions between the salariat and the working class are over the question of European Monetary Union. In short, people who want to keep the pound outnumber those who favour the euro by more than nine to one among the working class, four to one among the self-employed and less than two to one among the salariat. Class differences on this issue are higher than for any other political issue, including the death penalty.[6] The euro thus seems to have become *the* 'hot potato' for a government that wishes to promote it to the electorate in a referendum. And it could now promote strong opposition within the very heart of what used to be Labour territory (see Evans, 1999).

Table 3.11 Attitudes towards the euro by class

	Salariat	Self-employed	Working class
	%	%	%
Adopt euro	23	14	8
Keep pound	43	58	75
Base	*297*	*81*	*328*

Other programmes of change that are being pursued by New Labour, notably in relation to constitutional issues, also appeal more to the middle class than the working class. Surprisingly, perhaps, the radicals on House of Lords reform are the middle classes (70 per cent of whom want changes) rather than the working classes 60 per cent). Similarly, while 45 per cent of the middle class supports electoral reform, only 31 per cent of the working class does. Though not enormous, these differences do underline the fact that liberal-progressive

agendas tend to be more in keeping with middle-class than with working-class tastes.

Some of these differences in social liberalism between the views of Labour's middle-class and working-class constituency are by no means new (see Heath and Evans, 1988, in the *5th Report*). They were almost certainly present during the era of the 1960s when Harold Wilson's Labour government managed to introduce major social changes, including the abolition of the death penalty, the decriminalisation of homosexuality and abortion, and the lifting of some forms of censorship.

But have things changed since then? Certainly, the parties have radically changed their policy positions more than once – the Conservatives, most notably under Margaret Thatcher, and Labour, first under Neil Kinnock with the major Policy Review of the late 1980s (see Heath and Jowell, 1994) and then again under Tony Blair leading to the adoption of his 'Third Way' agenda in the late 1990s (see Bromley and Curtice, 1999, in the *16th Report*).

Has the electorate changed in tandem? For our purposes here, the key question is whether New Labour's blend of social and constitutional reform (modernisation) and economic stability (rather than change) continues to appeal sufficiently to its traditional working-class base to sustain their long-term support. We do have some evidence from the *British Social Attitudes* series itself to suggest that class differences in attitudes towards certain issues have changed. If we compare our present findings with those from 1987 (see Heath and Evans, 1988, in the *5th Report*), we find there has indeed been class convergence on several of the questions about redistribution and state intervention, accompanied by further class polarisation on most of the social issues.

The next table shows the 1987 distributions of answers by class during the height of Thatcherism. Then, in the last two columns it shows the extent of class polarisation on each of the issues then and now. The first five issues in the table refer to economic management and related issues of taxation and public spending. On all of these class polarisation has decreased or, in one case, stayed the same. The next four issues are to do with social or moral policies. And in three out of four of these cases, the years between 1987 and 1999 have seen a greater shift towards liberalism in the salariat than in the working class, so widening the class gap over time.

Table 3.12 Changes in attitudes by class, 1987

	Sal-ariat	Self-empl.	Work. Class	Salariat Working-class gap	
				1987	1999
Government should redistribute					
income	%	%	%		
Agree	40	36	54	+14	+3
Disagree	43	46	23	-20	-16
Base	*596*	*174*	*851*		
First priority for extra government					
spending:	%	%	%		
Health	45	45	54	+9	+2
Education	31	26	18	-14	-7
Government should:	%	%	%		
Reduce taxes and spend less on					
health, education and social benefits	3	3	4	+1	+1
Increase taxes and spend more on					
health, education and social benefits	53	41	51	-3	-2
Base	*652*	*206*	*1003*		
Per cent who agree:					
Spend more on welfare benefits for the					
poor even if it leads to higher taxes	55	45	61	+6	-3
People who break the law should get					
stiffer sentences	71	84	83	+12	+15
For some crimes, the death penalty					
is the most appropriate sentence	66	80	79	+13	+20
Censorship is necessary to uphold					
moral standards	68	76	68	0	-1
Bases	*305*	*91*	*433*		
Sexual relations between two					
adults of the same sex are wrong	65	79	81	+16	+23
Bases	*329*	*102*	*498*		

Class, attitudes and politics

Two processes seem therefore to be at work. The less marked one is that New Labour is seen as somewhat 'too centrist' on the economy and redistribution by its slightly more left-wing working-class voters. The more pronounced one is

that it is increasingly seen as 'too soft' on social issues (such as the death penalty, immigration, homosexuality, and ethnic competition) for its own traditional supporters. In particular, they are a long distance from New Labour's likely resting place on the euro.

The key issue then is whether these sorts of social issues count for votes. Do they, for instance, divide working-class Tories from working-class Labour supporters, and has this become more clearly the case as the Labour Party has modernised? If we examine the attitudes of Labour, Liberal Democrat and Conservative supporters within the middle and working classes we can obtain some evidence of whether differences of opinion on these issues might provide a basis for supporting one party or the other.

From the next table, we can see that there is substantial polarisation within the middle class between pro-redistributive Labour supporters and anti-redistributive Conservatives on all three traditional left-right issues. The Liberal Democrats are meanwhile much closer to Labour than to the Conservatives on these issues. In the working class, the polarising issues are redistribution and public spending on welfare benefits, while taxation *versus* social spending does not divide either party's working-class supporters. Working-class Liberal Democrats tend to fluctuate considerably on different questions, mainly as a result of a large presence of 'don't knows' and similarly non-committal answers, and in any case their numbers in our sample are too small to be sure. The numbers of self-employed within each party are also small, but it looks as if redistribution is the main polarising issue among them.

As the last column in the next table shows, redistributive issues do nonetheless seem to be a source of strong *partisan* division, despite the fact that they are no longer a cornerstone of *class* division.

Table 3.13 Traditionally left-right issues by class and vote

	Conserva-tive	Liberal Democrat	Labour	Con-Labour gap
Salariat				
Per cent left-wing views:				
Redistribution	26	40	48	+22
Tax and spend	50	67	72	+22
Welfare benefits	33	48	47	+14
Bases	*252-301*	*109-122*	*257-321*	
Self-employed				
Per cent left-wing views:				
Redistribution	16	24	41	+25
Tax and spend	59	73	58	-1
Welfare benefits	34	43	44	+10
Bases	*70-97*	*21-28*	*63-81*	
Working class				
Per cent left-wing views:				
Redistribution	23	45	46	+23
Tax and spend	57	42	60	+3
Welfare benefits	25	39	46	+19
Bases	*123-150*	*62-69*	*388-520*	

Table 3.14 Social and moral issues by class and vote

	Conserva-tive	Liberal Democrat	Labour	Con-Labour gap
Salariat				
Per cent right-wing views:				
Death penalty	60	33	41	+19
Stiffer sentences	77	59	70	+7
Censorship	74	64	67	+7
Homosexuality	45	20	36	+9
Immigration	39	23	27	+12
Equal opportunities for				
Blacks and Asians	39	15	25	+14
The euro	59	25	30	+29
Bases	*96-272*	*41-104*	*96-281*	
Self-employed				
Per cent right-wing views:				
Death penalty	73	57	56	+17
Stiffer sentences	79	81	77	+2
Censorship	77	81	67	+10
Homosexuality	63	57	46	+17
Immigration	47	42	48	+1
Equal opportunities for				
Blacks and Asians	53	46	39	+14
The euro	78	40	29	+4
Bases	*26-90*	*9-24*	*22-69*	
Working class				
Per cent right-wing views:				
Death penalty	64	76	66	-2
Stiffer sentences	90	90	85	+5
Censorship	61	76	67	-6
Homosexuality	59	74	62	-3
Immigration	49	66	52	-3
Equal opportunities for				
Blacks and Asians	81	36	34	+6
The euro	83	67	75	+8
Bases	*47-144*	*21-61*	*170-443*	

As the previous table shows, the divides on social and moral issues tell a different story. These issues divide the middle class most, with Liberal Democrats rather than Labour occupying the most liberal positions. By a substantial margin, the euro is the most powerful issue differentiating partisanship. In contrast, the working-class divisions are weak and inconsistent and, somewhat surprisingly, the working-class Liberal Democrats turn out to be the most illiberal on the death penalty, censorship and immigration. In contrast to the redistributive issues, however, the source of division on social and moral issues is mainly class rather than partisanship.

In 1987, the only non-redistributive issue that divided middle-class and working-class voters alike was the debate over nuclear weapons (Heath and Evans, 1988, in the *5th Report*) – an issue that has so disappeared from the political agenda that it is no longer covered in the *British Social Attitudes* surveys. So, partisan issues do change fairly dramatically from time to time. As Heath and Evans did in 1988, however, it is helpful to map where the classes and the party supporters currently lie on the main axes of political division in Britain. To do this, respondents' answers to various questions in the latest survey have been boiled down into a set of underlying dimensions via a technique known as principal components analysis.[7] The plotting of this analysis appears in Figure 3.1 and confirms the existence of three distinct issue types: those to do with redistributive policies those to do with social and moral issues; and those to do with the euro and the European Union.[8] And we find that that the Labour Party has an even more pronounced politically divided class basis than we found in 1987, with its socially liberal middle-class support quite distinct from other groups. What has also changed since 1987 is the extent to which the Liberal Democrats have become divided on class lines – now showing a similar pattern of division to the one afflicting Labour, but an even more pronounced one.

As can be seen from a detailed look at Figure 3.1, middle-class Liberal Democrat and Labour voters are isolated from all other groups of classes and partisans principally on social issues and the euro; but they are left-wing on redistributive issues as well, which was not the case in 1987. Figure 3.1 also confirms the relatively limited extent of division between most groups along the redistributive axis. Most intriguingly, however, the diagram reveals the euro as a basis for a class split in the otherwise impressively consensual Conservative cross-class alliance. The fact is that working-class Conservatives (and self-employed Conservatives) are significantly more euro-sceptical than are their middle-class Conservative counterparts. In 1987, this was not the case. At that stage, Conservative supporters from both the working and the middle classes spoke with more or less one voice. Now, on the ever more dominant issue of European integration, all three major parties seem to be riddled with class division.[9]

Figure 3.1   Party supporters by class and scores on the pro/anti-European, socially Liberal/socially Conservative and pro/anti-redistribution dimensions

9. If we model the potential influences on partisanship simultaneously, including measures of redistributive, social and moral, and European attitudes, we find that attitudes towards the euro have the strongest impact on voting Conservative rather than Labour in both the middle class and the petty bourgeoisie, but not in the working class, where its effects are statistically non-significant.

10. Though this is most likely to be effective if they present a unified view on this issue: Evans (1998b) shows that in the 1990s divisions within the Conservative Party over European integration probably cost them support among Eurosceptic voters.

References

Bromley, C. and Curtice, J. (1999), 'Is there a third way?' in Jowell, R., Curtice, J., Park, A., Thomson, K. (eds.), *British Social Attitudes: the 16th Report - Who shares New Labour values?*, Aldershot: Ashgate.

Budge, I. (1999), 'Party policy and ideology: Reversing the 1950s?' in Evans, G. and Norris, P. (eds.), *Critical Elections: British Parties and Voters in Long-term Perspective*, London: Sage.

Evans, G. (1998a), 'How Britain views the EU' in Jowell. R., Curtice, J., Park, A., Brook, L., Thomson, K. and Bryson, C. (eds.), *British − and European − Social Attitudes: the 15th Report - How Britain differs*, Aldershot: Ashgate.

Evans, G. (1998b), 'Euroscepticism and Conservative electoral support: how an asset became a liability', *British Journal of Political Science*, **28**: 573-90.

Evans, G. (1999), 'Europe: a new electoral cleavage?' in Evans, G. and Norris, P. (eds.), *Critical Elections: British Parties and Voters in Long-term Perspective*, London: Sage.

Evans, G., Heath, A. and Lalljee, M. (1996), 'Measuring left-right and libertarian-authoritarian values in the British electorate', *British Journal of Sociology*, **47**: 93-112.

Evans, G., Heath, A. and Payne, C. (1999), 'Class: Labour as a Catch-All Party?' in Evans, G. and Norris, P. (eds.), *Critical Elections: British Parties and Voters in Long-term Perspective,* London: Sage.

Heath, A. and Evans, G. (1988), 'Working class conservatives and middle class socialists' in Jowell, R., Witherspoon, S. and Brook, L. (eds.), *British Social Attitudes: the 5th Report*, Aldershot: Gower.

Heath, A., Jowell, R. and Curtice, J. (1985), *How Britain Votes*, Oxford: Pergamon Press.

Heath, A. and Jowell, R. (1994), 'Labour's policy review' in Heath, A., Jowell, R. and Curtice, J. (eds.), *Labour's Last Chance?*, Aldershot: Dartmouth.

Heath, A., Taylor, B., Brook, L. and Park, A. (1999), 'British national sentiment', *British Journal of Political Science*, **29**: 155-175.

Lipset, Seymour M. (1981), *Political Man*, 2nd edition, Garden City, NY: Doubleday.

Sanders, D. (1999), 'The impact of left-right ideology', in Evans, G. and Norris, P. (eds.), *Critical Elections: British Parties and Voters in Long-term Perspective*, London: Sage.

4 Sex and the media: a shifting landscape

Annette Hill and Katarina Thomson[*]

If 'sex sells', as the media cliché has it, then in recent years sales have burgeoned. High profile cases such as the Clinton/Lewinsky affair have helped make the detailed reporting of sexual relations more explicit than ever, as has the rise of day-time talk shows such as *Jerry Springer*, which deal openly and *ad infinitum* with topics such as prostitution, love triangles, fetishes and trans-sexuality.

Moreover, modern consumers who wish to see the portrayal of sex in the media now have a variety of converging technologies to choose from. In Britain, for instance, nudity and 'soft porn' are frequently available on some terrestrial television channels as well as on satellite and cable channels, digital television, pay per view subscription channels, at the cinema, on video, in print media, on DVD, on CD-ROM, in computer games, and on the world wide web. Connoisseurs of *Playboy* can now not only buy the magazine, as they always have, but they can also subscribe to the adult *Playboy* satellite/cable/digital channel, visit the *Playboy* website, and chat online (cybersex optional). And access to all these new technologies is becoming more and more widespread.

Yet it is the rise of television's portrayal of sex that seems to dominate popular press discussion, with synthetically outraged headlines such as "Everybody's doing it", or "Gay sex at prime time".[1] Whereas subscription channels used to be the main site for more explicit sex programmes, nowadays several other channels – both satellite and free to air – are getting in on the act with sexually explicit dramas and documentaries, all having the effect of making sex on television more mainstream. As Paul Dunthorne, the channel controller for TVX: the Fantasy Channel, said of Channel 4 and Channel 5: "A lot of their late-night stuff is unadulterated porn. It's not often put into context and it's not erotica – it's actually porn and it's free-to-air, simple as that".[2]

[*] Annette Hill is Reader in Communication at the Centre for Communication and Information Studies, University of Westminster. Katarina Thomson is a Research Director at the *National Centre for Social Research* and Co-Director of the *British Social Attitudes* survey series.

The press regularly complains about the fact that sex on television is no longer confined to 'adult' drama, but is becoming commonplace in prime time and even family programming too.[3] Thus, the *Times* reports that "Sex scenes in television soap operas treble in three years", while the *Daily Mail* indignantly asks "Has *The Bill* degenerated into television porn?" Other programmes complained about regularly are Channel 4's *Queer as Folk*, a popular drama series about gay life in Manchester, and Channel 5's *Sex and Shopping*, both of which epitomise the changing landscape where neither homosexuality nor pornography are any longer forbidden topics for primetime television.

As far as free-to-air channels are concerned, Channel 4 and Channel 5 have been the most controversial in their programming. Indeed, Michael Grade, former head of Channel 4, was dubbed "pornographer in chief" by the *Daily Mail* when the channel set the tone in the mid-1990s with 'themed' weekend schedules such as *The Red Light Zone*. But it was Michael Jackson, his successor, who introduced the gay drama, *Queer as Folk*, which attracted a 17 per cent audience share (2,374,000 viewers) and 321 telephone calls after its first transmission, nearly half of which were from outraged viewers. Other controversial offerings from Channel 4 include *Sex in the City*, *Ibiza Uncovered*, *Sex Bomb*, *Sex Lives*, *Fetishes*, and as part of their *Censored Weekend*, *Caligula*, a film featuring Roman orgies. More recently *Film Four*, a subscription channel, showed an edited version of Lars Von Trier's film *The Idiots*, the original of which contains explicit penetrative sex scenes, but it later showed the uncensored version on the Internet.[4] In fact, while British broadcasters are still forbidden from showing erect penises or explicit penetrative sex on television, even on subscription channels, no such bans are imposed on their Internet sites, a subject we shall return to.

As for Channel 5's late night programming, which has included shows such as *Sex and Shopping*, *Compromising Situations*, *Hotline*, and a game show where the contestants were naked, Dawn Airey, director of programming, explained: "We are simply meeting an audience need."[5] As far as free-to-air channels are concerned, while BBC1's drama series *The Lakes* and *The Tribe*, and ITV's documentary and chat shows *Vice*, *The Sex Trade* and *Jerry Springer*, all also include some explicit sexual material, Channel 4 and Channel 5 have been the most controversial in their programming. *Sex and Shopping* attracted one and a half million viewers, and a regular audience share of 14 per cent in its late night slot.

In short, as satellite/cable and now digital television channels open up the television market and court the British public with a variety of specialist adult programming, mainstream terrestrial channels are under increasing commercial pressure to compete for television audiences. And the fact remains that sexual content – whether in chat shows, factual programmes or erotica – is not only a 'ratings-grabber', but usually a cheap form of programming. Indeed, Dawn Airey of Channel 5 claims that erotica consumes only 1 per cent of the Channel's £115m programme budget.[6]

Regulating sex in the media

As discussed in the *13th Report* (Barnett and Thomson, 1996), the debate about freedom to publish *versus* freedom to consume is an age-old concern and as difficult to resolve as ever. We shall present findings here which suggest that while the precise balance between regulation on the one hand, and freedom to watch sexual content on the other is shifting, there is still a strong public recognition that balance is called for.

We have no wish to go over the ground covered in the *13th Report* on the patterns of institutional regulation of traditional media. But we shall refer briefly to some changes in UK media regulation since 1995 to do with cinema, satellite/cable and digital services and the Internet.

The British Board of Film Classification (BBFC) continues to age-classify films, such that 15-rated films are able to show 'impressionistic sex', and 18-rated films are able to show more detail. Its classifications are rarely challenged, though sometimes criticised. The BBFC also has a statutory role under the Video Recordings Act 1984, which requires videos, DVDs and some games to carry a BBFC classification. This role includes the classification of R18 videos which are only available in licensed sex shops. When classifying videos, the BBFC, under the direction of the 1984 Act, and its 1994 amendment, must take into account the context of the home viewing environment, where children may be exposed to videos not intended for their age group.

In the 1996 BBFC *Annual Report*, James Ferman, then director of the BBFC, expressed concern about the two tier system of adult classification (BBFC, 1996). He argued that the extra cuts in R18 movies would drive adult movies of a more explicit nature underground. In the 1997 *Annual Report*, Ferman reiterated his concerns about this issue after the Home Office had urged it to be more severe than it had been in its treatment of non-violent erotica. Ferman wrote: "Pornography will once again be swept under the carpet where, in the name of the law, it will be mixed up with violence and degradation." (BBFC, 1997: 38). In the same year, the BBFC came under attack for allowing *Crash*, a controversial film about sex and car crashes, to be released uncut with an 18 rating. The *Daily Mail* labelled the film 'pornographic' and started a campaign to overhaul the BBFC. And although Ferman retired in 1998, the issue of 'acceptable' standards has continued to be contentious. In 1998 13 hours of sex material were cut from R18 and 18 videos. Under the new director, Robin Duval, the Board's guidelines on sexual explicitness were tested once again with three European art house films, *The Idiots*, *Romance*, and *Seul Contre Tous*, all portraying explicit non-violent sex of a kind that is more commonplace in mainland Europe than in Britain.[7] In the same year, two companies challenged the Board's strict policy for R18 films and lodged appeals with the Video Appeals Committee concerning seven pornographic films which the Board had rejected (BBFC, 1999). The appeals were upheld and the BBFC sought a Judicial Review, which it lost. As a result of this, the BBFC published new R18 guidelines which are more relaxed and reflect the content of the seven appeal titles. The new classification guidelines draw upon the results of BBFC research in public opinion. In the report Sense and Sensibilities 46 per cent of

the national sample thought 'people over 18 have a right to see graphic portrayals of real sex in films and videos' (Hanley, 2000: 4). The public also supported a relaxation in sex guidelines at '15' and '18'. The new R18, 18 and 15 categories are more liberal towards consenting sex between adults and also make no distinction between heterosexual and homosexual activity.

The disagreements between the BBFC and the Home Office, the porn industry, the Video Appeals Committee and the High Court illustrate how difficult it is to have a common agreement in relation to acceptable sex in the media. The BBFC *Annual Report* for 1999 openly acknowledges this difficulty: "The question of whether the Board's Guidelines for the level of acceptable sex at different categories match the expectations of the British public is one of the major considerations in the extensive public consultation exercise set underway during the course of the year" (BBFC, 1999: 32) – partly via the *British Social Attitudes* survey itself.

As for terrestrial television, there has also been controversy over how the Broadcasting Standards Commission (BSC) and the Independent Television Commission (ITC) determine acceptable standards and levels of sex on television. The ITC regulates all non-BBC television, under the conditions of the 1990 Broadcasting Act, and the BSC is the statutory body which monitors issues of taste and decency, sex, violence, bad language and fairness. The Broadcasting Act also has specific guidelines, which are included in the updated BBC *Producers' Guidelines*. All terrestrial television follows a 'family viewing policy', which designates 9pm as a watershed, allowing a gradual increase in more adult material later in the evenings. Programmes before the 9pm watershed must be suitable for a general audience including children. Other agreed policies are that clear sign-posting should be available to viewers, context should be taken into account in decisions about the legitimacy of certain scenes, and that programme-makers and schedulers should be sensitive to the expectations of their audiences.

According to a survey in 1998 (ITC, 1998b), the regulation of television channels is widely understood and accepted by the majority of the British public. Nearly 60 per cent of terrestrial, satellite and cable viewers thought not only that there was 'quite a lot' of regulation in the UK, but also that the amount of regulation was 'about right'. Inevitably, however, mainstream broadcasters try to push back the boundaries, while the ITC and BSC try in turn to protect them. In their annual review of broadcasters' performance (ITC, 1998a), the ITC noted a growing emphasis on sex, and expressed concern about the amount of adult material that was being screened immediately after the 9pm watershed. It singled out Channel 5 in particular for its "tacky erotica". Similarly, the latest BSC annual report reprimands broadcasters for taking liberties with sex on television and urges them to become more responsible. Otherwise, they warn, they might have to abandon their 'light touch' regulation.[8] In response, however, broadcasters do not appear to have taken heed and re-drawn any boundaries.[9]

In maintaining their current role, the various television regulators appear to sense that public attitudes are relatively liberal towards extending boundaries so

long as the situation does not get out of hand. As the BBC *Producers'* *Guidelines* acknowledge, "audiences in the United Kingdom have become more liberal in their acceptance of sexually explicit material" (BBC, 2000: 86), while the most recent ITC annual review is at pains to point out blandly that: "We are not against or opposed to erotic material on television in any shape or form."[10]

In respect of digital services, for which the ITC, BSC and BBC are all responsible, they are at present treated similarly to terrestrial, satellite and cable channels. However, all regulators agree that viewers must be able to determine clearly, while watching, whether they are in a free-to-air or a 'buying' environment.[11]

The Internet is, of course, governed largely by self-regulation. But two independent organisations active in the UK (the Internet Watch Foundation – IWF and the Internet Content Ratings Association – ICRA) are involved in regulation of sorts. The IWF (http://www.iwf.org.uk) was launched in 1996 to address the issue of illegal pornography on the Internet, particularly child pornography, and to encourage the classification of legal material on the Net. ICRA (http://www.icra.org) was set up in 1999 and works with Internet industries on self-regulation and rating of sexually explicit and other potentially offensive material.

What other research says

There has been little research to date on what people think about sexually explicit material on the Internet, though a 1998 survey found that one-half of their sample of Internet users wanted ratings of, and the ability to filter out, sexually-explicit, violent or other offensive or insulting material.[12] Rather more research evidence has been compiled on attitudes to television sex. For instance, according to an ITV survey, almost two-thirds of people are relaxed about the amount of sex scenes shown on television, *as long as the scenes continue to be relevant to the story*.[13] The BSC have also found that over three-quarters of people (78 per cent) would not want sex to be removed from television when it is relevant to the storyline (BSC, 1999b). Even so, television analyst, William Phillips, doubts that programmes with sexual content are all that popular, citing ratings to show that "cosy, nostalgic dramas" attract the biggest audiences.[14]

The British Film Institute's Audience Tracking Study reveals women are less happy than are men about the levels and types of sex on television, especially on satellite and cable services. Even so, most people thought that sexual content was acceptable after the 9pm watershed, yet often embarrassing when seen in front of other people, especially parents or children. Elderly viewers were, on the whole, more restrictive, and preferred 'gentle' programmes from which 'gratuitous' sex was absent (Gauntlett and Hill, 1999).

More importantly, perhaps, an ITC survey in 1998 found that two-thirds of the sample could not recall anything they had seen or heard on television that they had found offensive. Of the one-third who had been offended by something, women outnumbered men by almost two to one, and older viewers (over 55) were more likely to take offence than were their younger counterparts. But

among those who had taken offence at something, only around half cited sex and nudity as the culprits. Larger proportions were offended by violence and bad language. The survey also showed that people were more likely to object to sexually-explicit material if it was on terrestrial television than if it was on satellite or cable channels (see later sections of this chapter).

  Not surprisingly, the latest BSC findings suggest that public attitudes towards sex on television have become more permissive over the years (BSC, 1999b). Only 36 per cent felt there was "too much" sex on television nowadays, and the proportion who felt that the portrayal of homosexual relations on television was acceptable had grown from 46 per cent to 58 per cent in the last seven years. This growth in tolerance was attributed partly to the growth in television shows about homosexuality, as well as the growth in talk shows, and partly to the fact that more homosexuals had 'come out' in the intervening period. For instance, 54 per cent of their sample knew someone who was homosexual (BSC, 1999b). In common with the ITC research findings, women and older viewers were more likely to feel there was too much sex on television.

Increasing permissiveness

The 1995 *British Social Attitudes* survey included a set of questions on attitudes to the portrayal of sex in the media, the results of which appeared in the *13th Report* (Barnett and Thomson, 1996). We then asked an analogous set of questions a year later about the portrayal of violence in the media (see Barnett and Thomson, 1997). In this chapter we report on the 1999 survey in which we repeated many of the earlier questions four years on, as well as asking some new questions tapping attitudes to digital television and the Internet. Thus, our analysis here is of change – in public attitudes, in technology, in media regulation and in social and cultural responses to the portrayal of sex in the mass media.

  We asked respondents both in 1995 and 1999 whether the following two scenes should be allowed to be shown:

> *A frank scene in a film showing **a man and a woman character having sex**.*

And:

> *Instead of a male and a female character, … a frank scene with **two adult male characters** having sex.*

For each scenario, we asked respondents for their opinions about whether the scene should be allowed to appear in six different media outlets. For the moment, we refer only to those three outlets which we asked about in both years so as to measure change. They were:

- the regular television channels
- the cinema
- a video for sale or hire

For television, respondents were allowed to choose between an outright ban, watersheds at midnight, 10pm, 9pm or 8pm, and no restrictions. For the cinema and video, respondents were allowed to choose between an outright ban, age limits of 18, 15 and 12, and no restrictions – supplemented in the case of the cinema by special adult cinemas, and in the case of video by special adult shops. As in our previous analyses, our working assumption is that a 10pm watershed is roughly equivalent to an 18 age limit, 9pm to a 15 age limit and 8pm to a 12 age limit. These are the rough equivalences applied by the ITC to terrestrial television (ITC, 1998a: 4-6). The watersheds are slightly more lenient in the case of premium subscription channels, on which the main watershed is 8pm rather than 9pm, in accordance with the ITC's policy that parents who subscribe to these channels should share responsibility for who watches them. Some adult subscription channels are also available only from 10pm until 5.30am.

As seen in the next table, the broad pattern of public attitudes to the portrayal of heterosexual sex remains similar to what it was in 1995, but less restrictive for all outlets. The dominant choice is still for such a scene not to be shown before 10pm on the regular television channels, and not to be accessible to people under 18 in cinemas or on video. We suggested in the *13ᵗʰ Report* that public attitudes might well become more permissive over time as new cohorts with more permissive attitudes replaced older, more restrictive-minded cohorts. And, as can be seen in the table, this is precisely what appears to have happened. A clear decline has taken place in the proportions who would want to see the scene prohibited or access severely restricted – whether from peak time television, cinemas or videos. Meanwhile, the proportion who would allow completely unrestricted viewing is still almost non-existent.

Table 4.1 Heterosexual sex scene, 1995 and 1999

	1995	1999
	%	%
(i) Regular TV channels		
Should not be allowed to be shown at all	27	23
Only after midnight	18	18
Only after 10pm	40	35
Only after 9pm	13	18
Only after 8pm	1	2
Allowed to be shown at any time	1	2
(ii) Cinema		
Should not be allowed to be shown at all	19	14
Only at special adult cinemas	19	17
At ordinary cinemas but only to aged 18+	47	45
At ordinary cinemas but only to aged 15+	12	17
At ordinary cinemas but only to aged 12+	2	3
Allowed to be shown to anyone at all	1	1
(iii) Video for sale or rent		
Should be banned altogether	20	13
Only in special adult shops	22	24
In any shop but only to aged 18+	45	46
In any shop but only to aged 15+	10	11
In any shop but only to aged 12+	1	2
In any shop available to anyone	1	1
Base	*1172*	*1052*

The next table shows a similar picture for the male homosexual sex scene. As in 1995, the most popular choice is still an outright ban, but that view is now held by a significantly smaller proportion of the population than it was in 1995. For instance, the proportion of people who would ban the scene from regular television channels has fallen from 54 to 48 per cent, and the overall change in attitudes has been greater for the male homosexual scene than for the heterosexual one. So, while views on the portrayal of homosexual sex are still much more restrictive than those on heterosexual sex, the gap has narrowed in the last four years.

Table 4.2 Male homosexual sex scene, 1995 and 1999

	1995	1999
	%	%
(i) Regular TV channels		
Should not be allowed to be shown at all	54	48
Only after midnight	19	18
Only after 10pm	19	20
Only after 9pm	6	10
Only after 8pm	1	1
Allowed to be shown at any time	*	1
(ii) Cinema		
Should not be allowed to be shown at all	45	36
Only at special adult cinemas	25	24
At ordinary cinemas but only to aged 18+	25	29
At ordinary cinemas but only to aged 15+	4	7
At ordinary cinemas but only to aged 12+	1	1
Allowed to be shown to anyone at all	*	1
(iii) Video for sale or rent		
Should be banned altogether	42	32
Only in special adult shops	27	28
In any shop but only to aged 18+	26	29
In any shop but only to aged 15+	3	5
In any shop but only to aged 12+	*	1
In any shop available to anyone	*	1
Base	*1172*	*1052*

To decipher the broad picture more easily, we have constructed two 'permissiveness indices' that combine information from several responses – one for the heterosexual sex scene and one for the homosexual sex scene. Again for reasons of comparability, we use only those questions that were asked in both 1995 and 1999. The score on these indices varies from 1 (most restrictive) to 6 (most permissive). (See the appendix to this chapter for more details about the construction of the indices). The table below confirms the impression of the earlier tables that there has been a shift towards more permissive attitudes and that this shift has been larger in respect of the portrayal of homosexual sex than of heterosexual sex.

Table 4.3 Permissiveness indices, 1995 and 1999
(Low score = restrictive attitudes; high score = permissive attitudes)

	1995		1999		Change 1995-99
		Base		*Base*	
Heterosexual sex scene	2.53	*1150*	2.69	*1009*	+0.17
Homosexual sex scene	1.87	*1152*	2.07	*1012*	+0.20

The link between age and attitudes

In the *13th* and *14th Reports* we looked at the various characteristics that may affect people's attitudes towards the portrayal of sex and violence in the media – such as a person's age, gender, religiosity, socio-economic position and education, whether or not they have young children, their levels of exposure to different media, and how libertarian they are on other issues. In order to take all these factors into account simultaneously, we employed multivariate modelling, thus allowing the independent effect of each factor to be measured while holding all other factors constant. We can now repeat this analysis, four years on, to look at changes. (See the appendix to this chapter for more details of this analysis.)

The next table shows – in order of importance – those characteristics that turn out to be significant in influencing people's degree of permissiveness or restrictiveness in relation to the portrayal of sex.[15] It is clear that the broad picture has barely changed in the last four years. Indeed, allowing for sampling variation, it has in all probability not changed at all.

A person's age is by far the most important factor in predicting his or her opinions on these issues: the older one is on average, so the more restrictive are one's views on the portrayal of sex. Other characteristics that are also significantly associated with one's views are one's position on the wider libertarian-authoritarian scale and one's religiosity: people who are generally more authoritarian and religious also tend to be more restrictive in their attitudes to the portrayal of sex. Education tends to go with permissiveness of the homosexual sex scene, but not of the heterosexual one. In contrast, women are more restrictive than men of the heterosexual scene, but not of the homosexual one. The effects of one's socio-economic group, and the regularity of cinema-going and video-watching on one's response are patchy or non-existent. Meanwhile, it appears that the presence of very young children in one's household makes little difference to one's views, while being responsible for older children does make one a little more restrictive, independent of one's own age.

Table 4.4 Factors significantly related to attitudes to the heterosexual and male homosexual sex scene, 1995 and 1999

Heterosexual sex scene		Male homosexual sex scene	
1995	**1999**	**1995**	**1999**
Age	Age	Age	Age
Libertarian-authoritarian values	Libertarian-authoritarian values	Libertarian-authoritarian values	Libertarian-authoritarian values
Religiosity	Religiosity	Education	Education
Cinema attendance	Socio-economic group	Religiosity	Religiosity
Video film viewing		Socio-economic group	Cinema attendance
Gender		Video film watching	
		Parental responsibility	

As noted, age is the overwhelming factor in predicting attitudes. To illustrate just how dominant it is, we show in the next table that the proportion of the sample who wish to ban the heterosexual scene from regular television channels altogether ranges from a tiny five per cent of 18-25 year olds to over 50 per cent of people over 65. Similarly stark age gradients are apparent for cinema and video.

Table 4.5 Heterosexual sex on regular television by age of respondent

	18-25	26-33	34-41	42-49	50-57	58-65	66-73	74+
	%	%	%	%	%	%	%	%
Not allowed at all	5	8	12	12	22	45	52	55
Only after midnight	18	14	18	23	28	16	12	9
Only after 10pm	51	36	42	34	42	26	25	19
Only after 9pm	19	33	23	26	8	8	4	8
Only after 8pm	3	4	2	-	-	1	1	2
Allowed any time	2	1	2	2	-	2	4	1
Base	*88*	*156*	*195*	*148*	*107*	*112*	*110*	*135*

Table 4.6 Male homosexual sex on regular television by age of respondent

	18-25	26-33	34-41	42-49	50-57	58-65	66-73	74+
	%	%	%	%	%	%	%	%
Not allowed at all	32	27	41	34	56	67	77	79
Only after midnight	22	22	20	26	20	15	11	3
Only after 10pm	34	24	24	20	23	11	6	9
Only after 9pm	9	21	13	17	-	2	3	1
Only after 8pm	-	1	1	-	-	2	-	-
Allowed any time	1	-	1	1	1	1	1	-
Base	88	156	195	148	107	112	110	135

While for the homosexual sex scene, attitudes are more restrictive in all age groups, the age gradient is still very much in evidence – from one-third of 18-25 year olds (32 per cent) who opt for an outright ban on regular television, to nearly four in five people over 65. Interestingly, however, the 26-33 age group appears to be more permissive than the very youngest age group – a point we shall return to. Again, similar age gradients are apparent for cinema and video, including the non-linear pattern among 26-33 year olds.

In the next table we summarise these findings in terms of the indices we used earlier. As can be seen, every age group is more permissive than the one that precedes it about both scenes, with the notable exception of the 26-33 year olds (in 1999).

As noted in the 13th and 14th Reports, links between age and attitudes can be caused either by *cohort replacement* (where younger age cohorts with more permissive attitudes tend to carry these attitudes with them as they age), or by *life-cycle effects* (where people tend to grow more restrictive as they age in response, say, to parental responsibilities). We hypothesised that cohort replacement was the more likely explanation of what was happening in this case, particularly because we had found only a weak link between attitudes and parenthood.

Now, with data from two surveys four years apart, we can begin to test that hypothesis by examining the views of particular birth cohorts (say, 1954-1961) in 1995 and then again in 1999. This *same cohort* would of course have been aged between 34 and 41 in 1995 and between 38 and 45 in 1995, and we can see whether their views have remained much the same (a cohort effect) or become more restrictive (a life-cycle effect). So, if attitudes *within* cohorts stay fairly constant over time, and younger cohorts are consistently more permissive than older ones, this is a classic cohort effect. If on the other hand the cohorts themselves change their attitudes as they age, say becoming more restrictive, then we have a classic life-cycle effect. The problem is that these analyses are complicated by the possible presence of *period effects* (where external events change the views of society at large, regardless of age).

Table 4.7 Permissiveness indices by age groups, 1995 and 1999
(Low score = restrictive attitudes; high score = permissive attitudes)

Age	1995		1999	
(i) Heterosexual sex	**Mean**		**Mean**	
scene	**scores**	*Base*	**scores**	*Base*
18-25	3.14	*111*	3.12	*85*
26-33	3.05	*193*	3.22	*150*
34-41	2.78	*179*	3.00	*192*
42-49	2.59	*156*	2.96	*143*
50-57	2.33	*136*	2.47	*106*
58-65	2.18	*126*	2.09	*107*
66-73	1.89	*125*	2.10	*104*
74+	1.50	*121*	1.86	*121*
(ii) Male homosexual				
scene				
18-25	2.39	*111*	2.43	*85*
26-33	2.33	*193*	2.63	*151*
34-41	2.15	*178*	2.34	*192*
42-49	1.96	*156*	2.36	*142*
50-57	1.60	*136*	1.83	*106*
58-65	1.50	*127*	1.59	*109*
66-73	1.31	*125*	1.47	*107*
74+	1.15	*123*	1.27	*119*

The grid below summarises the expected findings if only one of these effects was in operation at a time.

Type of effect	Observation of cohorts	Observation of age groups
Period effect	Change over time in same direction in all cohorts	Change over time in same direction in all age groups
Cohort effect	No change within cohorts over time, but cohorts different from each other	Change over time within age groups
Life-cycle effect	Change over time within cohorts	No change over time within age groups, but age groups different from each other

Often, several of these effects coexist, e.g. a period effect and a cohort effect. Although it is impossible to determine with certainty the relative importance of the effects,[16] we can nonetheless go some way by carefully examining cohort and age group change. In effect, we need to find out whether the within-cohort

change is larger than the within-age group change. (If it is, it is likely to be a life-cycle effect. If the opposite, it is likely to be a cohort effect.)

Starting with the heterosexual sex scene, the table below presents a complex picture. Looking at *within-cohort* change first, people born in the first fifteen years after the war, from 1946-61 (now aged between 39 and 54, have become more permissive, as have those born before 1930 (now aged 70 and over). In contrast, the views of those born since 1962 (aged under 39) have been relatively static, and those of people born between these two periods (between 1930 and 1945, now aged 55-69) have become more restrictive. So there is a hint of a life-cycle effect, which does not kick in at the time of becoming a parent, but later (perhaps as their children leave home (see also Gauntlett and Hill, 1999).

In contrast, almost all *age groups* have become more permissive. The exceptions are those aged 58-65, who have become slightly more restrictive, and 18-25, whose views have not changed. Since the within-cohort changes are smaller than the within-age group changes, the cohort effect appears to be stronger overall than the life-cycle effect.[17]

Table 4.8 Change in permissiveness index 1995-1999 by age cohort and age group: heterosexual scene
(Low scores = restrictive attitudes; high scores = permissive attitudes)

Approximate birth years	Change within cohort	Age groups	Change within age group	Base in 1995	Base in 1999 cohort, age group
1970-1977	+0.04	18 – 25	-0.02	111	111, 85
1962-1969	+0.08	26 – 33	+0.17	193	195, 150
1954-1961	+0.20	34 – 41	+0.22	179	152, 192
1946-1953	+0.11	42 – 49	+0.37	156	128, 143
1938-1945	-0.06	50 – 57	+0.14	136	104, 106
1930-1937	-0.04	58 – 65	-0.09	126	103, 107
1922-1929	+0.16	66 – 73	+0.21	125	94, 104
1921 or earlier	+0.28	74+	+0.35	121	81, 121

But when we consider the male homosexual sex scene (see the next table), the dominant trend here is a movement in a more permissive direction within *all* cohorts and *all* age groups. This not only adds up to a much larger overall change in views than for the heterosexual sex scene, but also suggests the major additional impact of a *period effect*, or in other words a culture change.

Even so, since the most substantial change occurs within the group born after 1970 who are now aged under 30, there is also a hint of a life-cycle effect, but this time in the direction of greater permissiveness. It seems then that people grow more permissive about the portrayal of male homosexual sex as they get

into their late twenties, perhaps as they gain more friends and acquaintances with different sexual orientations. However, since the within-age group change is still larger than the within-cohort change, the predominant pattern is one of cohort replacement.

Table 4.9 Change in permissiveness index 1995-1999 by age cohort and age group: homosexual scene
(Low scores = restrictive attitudes; high scores = permissive attitudes)

Approximate birth years	Change within cohort	Age groups	Change within age group	Base in 1995	Base in 1999 cohort, age group
1970-1977	+0.32	18 – 25	+0.05	111	111, 85
1962-1969	+0.16	26 – 33	+0.30	193	197, 151
1954-1961	+0.19	34 – 41	+0.19	178	150, 192
1946-1953	+0.12	42 – 49	+0.40	156	128, 142
1938-1945	+0.13	50 – 57	+0.23	136	105, 106
1930-1937	+0.13	58 – 65	+0.09	127	105, 109
1922-1929	+0.02	66 – 73	+0.16	125	97, 107
1921 or earlier	+0.10	74+	+0.12	123	78, 119

The fact that a cohort effect seems to be the dominant explanation of attitude change in relation to the portrayal of sex means that average attitudes are likely to become still more permissive as cohort replacement continues. If a life-cycle effect had been the dominant explanation of differences, there would have been no reason to expect any further movement towards permissiveness. On the contrary, with an ageing population in Britain, we might have anticipated the opposite effect (see also the chapter by Park for a more detailed discussion of these effects).

Portraying lesbian sex

The 1995 module asked only about heterosexual and male homosexual sex scenes. The 1999 module added the following question:

> *What if the film showed a frank scene of two adult **female** characters having sex. ... what would your opinion be of a film at the **cinema** including a scene like that?*

Like the other scenes, the question was then repeated for each of the media.

The next table shows the answers for regular television, but the picture is very similar for the other media too. It shows that views about showing lesbian sex are similar to those about gay male sex (the differences are not statistically

significant), and are once again less permissive than they are of heterosexual sex scenes. Thus the index score for the lesbian sex scene is 2.13 (close to the male homosexual scene score of 2.07) while that for the heterosexual scene is 2.69 (see Table 4.3).

Table 4.10 Heterosexual, male homosexual and lesbian scene: regular television

	Heterosexual scene	Lesbian scene	Male homosexual scene
	%	%	%
Should not be allowed to be shown at all	23	43	48
Only after midnight	18	21	18
Only after 10pm	35	22	20
Only after 9pm	18	10	10
Only after 8pm	2	1	1
Allowed to be shown at any time	2	1	1

Base: 1052

In general, men are more permissive than women, but does that apply to the portrayal of lesbian sex? In fact it does: the table below shows that while nearly one half of women (46 per cent) would ban the lesbian sex scene from regular television, only two-fifths of men (39 per cent) would do so. And while gender did not quite make the cut in the multivariate analysis of factors behind attitudes to the portrayal of male homosexual sex, it does become a significant factor in relation to lesbian sex. The other factors are much the same. (See the appendix to this chapter for more details about the multivariate analysis).

Table 4.11 Lesbian sex scene by gender: regular TV channels

	Male	Female
	%	%
Should not be allowed to be shown at all	39	46
Only after midnight	22	20
Only after 10pm	25	19
Only after 9pm	10	9
Only after 8pm	1	1
Allowed to be shown at any time	1	1
Base	*483*	*569*

Relevance to the plot

The *13th* and *14th Report*s pointed to the importance that people attached to the context in which the sex or violent scene was shown. As in 1995, we asked in 1999:

> *We have been talking about films and videos in general, but there are, of course, different types of film. Some contain sex scenes which are part of a developing relationship between the main characters. Others show sex scenes which don't seem to be essential to the plot.*
> *Think first of films in which a frank sex scene between a man and a woman character does **not** seem to be essential to the plot.*
> *Should they **ever**, in your view, be allowed to be seen . . .*
>
> *. . . by **12** year olds?*
> *. . . by **15** year olds?*
> *. . . by **18** year olds?*
> *. . . by **anyone at all**?*

And then:

> *And how about films in which a frank sex scene between a man and a woman character **is** part of a developing relationship between the main characters.*
>
> *Now how about **educational videos** containing a frank scene of a man and a woman character having sex.*

But in 1999 we added two further questions to tap attitudes to erotica and pornography more directly:

> *Now think of films made for entertainment rather than education in which showing frank sex scenes between a man and a woman character is the **main purpose** of the film.*

and

> *Of course, most films shown on television and at the cinema do **not** show the **actual sex act in detail**. How about films that do show that?*

The results are shown in the next table. The answers about context have barely changed in the last four years. As we noted in the *13th Report*, the results suggest that respondents must have had a 'gratuitous' sex scene in mind in answering the earlier questions, because they are considerably more permissive when they believe such a scene is essential to the plot.

Turning to the new questions, we find that views on erotica (defined here as a film whose "main purpose" is to show sex scenes) are rather similar to views

about the gratuitous sex scene (defined as a sex scene "not essential to the plot"). Views about pornographic (films showing "the actual sex act in detail") are more restrictive, but not perhaps as much as might have been anticipated. While one in five (19 per cent) would ban such films outright, a not dissimilar proportion (17 per cent) would allow them to become available at 15. And the majority (54 per cent) would allow such films to become available at 18. So, overall, the British public is perhaps not quite so censorious about the portrayal of sex in films as the earlier 'context free' questions had suggested.

Table 4.12 The impact of context

	Gra-tuitous sex scene	Plot based sex scene	Edu-cational video	Erotica	Porno-graphy
	%	%	%	%	%
Not allowed to anyone	15	10	8	14	19
Not allowed to 18+ except in certain circumstances	2	1	1	3	3
Allowed for age 18+	52	38	18	50	54
Allowed for age 15+	22	34	32	23	17
Allowed for age 12+	6	14	38	7	5

Base: 1052

New media, new technologies

The *13th Report* found differences in attitudes between the portrayal of sex in different media. In particular, the more unrestricted the access to the medium (such as regular television channels and radio), so the more restrictive were attitudes. In contrast, the most permissive views were held about cinema and video, with satellite and cable television falling somewhere between the two. These findings were confirmed in the *14th Report* in respect of attitudes to the portrayal of violence. In both cases, however, the differences between the media were not large.

  Since then there has been an explosion in access to cable and satellite channels, as well as the arrival of digital television and a massive expansion of the Internet. A recent survey concluded that the proportion of viewers with satellite access rose from 15 to 20 per cent, with cable access from six to 13 per cent, and with Internet access from zero to eight per cent between 1995 and 1998 (ITC, 1999). One-third of households now have access to general subscription television (BSC, 2000). Meanwhile, Sky Digital alone is used by 3.4 million households, with numbers increasing by approximately 50,000 every

week.[18] And in the UK, the ratio between the number of people registered with Internet Service Providers and members of the public is up to one in 12 (around eight per cent).[19]

Our 1999 questions made a distinction between different types of subscription channels and asked also about digital television. In addition to the questions already outlined about the heterosexual and male homosexual sex scenes, respondents were asked:

> *Thinking now of a **subscription channel** for which people pay a regular amount, and which regularly shows **adult films**. How would you feel about a film with this same scene ... being shown on this channel?*

> *And how would you feel about this same scene being shown on a different subscription channel which does **not** normally show this sort of film?*

> *Thinking now of the new **digital channels** some people have, which need a special piece of equipment but no regular subscription. How do you feel about this same scene in a film being shown on one of these channels?*

As we see in the table below, the public do still distinguish between what is acceptable on different channels. Regular television channels still attract more restrictive attitudes, now joined by *general* subscription channels and by digital channels. But subscription channels which regularly show adult material are given more leeway. So, while around a third (35 per cent) would ban the heterosexual scene altogether from the general subscription channel, only half that proportion (17 per cent) would ban it from an adult subscription channel. And similar large differences apply to the homosexual scene. There is some evidence of a polarisation of attitudes on the adult subscription channel: almost one in five (18 per cent) would allow the heterosexual sex scene to be any time and one in eight (12 per cent) the homosexual scene. There is no similar polarisation for any other media. There is a suggestion here of minority support for dividing the television market by type of channel rather than by watersheds. But there is still strong majority support for watersheds on *all* channels. Indeed, a majority would impose a 10pm or earlier barrier on the heterosexual scene, even on *adult* subscription channels, and a midnight barrier on the homosexual scene. As can be seen, the most restrictive attitudes of all apply to *general* subscription channels, perhaps because they are associated in people's minds most closely with family entertainment.

Table 4.13 Acceptability across different media

	General sub-scrip.	Reg-ular TV	Digital	Adult sub-scrip.	Video	Cin-ema
(i) heterosexual scene	%	%	%	%	%	%
Should not be allowed						
to be shown at all	35	23	22	17	13	14
After midnight/special						
adult cinema/shop	15	18	19	20	24	17
After 10pm/Aged 18+	26	35	32	28	46	45
After 9pm/Aged 15+	12	18	13	10	11	17
After 8pm/Aged 12+	2	2	1	2	2	3
Allowed to be shown at						
any time/ to anyone	5	2	5	18	1	1
(ii) homosexual scene	%	%	%	%	%	%
Should not be allowed to						
be shown at all	52	48	42	35	32	36
After midnight/special						
adult cinema/shop	15	18	19	22	28	24
After 10pm/Aged 18+	17	20	20	20	29	29
After 9pm/Aged 15+	8	10	9	8	5	7
After 8pm/Aged 12+	1	1	1	1	1	1
Allowed to be shown at						
any time/ to anyone	3	1	3	12	1	1

Base: 1052

We also asked about material of this sort on the Internet:

> *And what if this same scene was in a film available through the* **Internet** *or* **World Wide Web**. *... please say how you would feel about that.*

Since it is not very clear how watersheds or age limits could be implemented on the Internet, we were forced to use different answer categories which are therefore not directly comparable with the other media. But it is clear from the next table that there is barely any support for free access. A majority would support an 18 age limit for the heterosexual scene.

Table 4.14 Heterosexual and homosexual sex scenes on the Internet

	Heterosexual scene	Homosexual scene
	%	%
Should not be available at all	38	52
Access should be available only to authorised subscribers aged 18+	51	40
Should be available to anyone with Internet access	5	4

Base: 1052

To what extent does one's access and exposure to the new media affect one's attitudes? If indeed increased permissiveness goes with increased exposure, then we should expect a great growth in permissiveness over the next few years. We have already seen that increased exposure to cinema and videos goes with more permissive attitudes, although the relationship was not very strong.

Respondents who reported having cable or satellite access in 1999 was 36 per cent – up 14 points from our 1995 reading. Digital television was still somewhat in its infancy in 1999, though it has grown since, and was available to 8 per cent of our respondents. And some 22 per cent of our respondents had home Internet access at the time of our survey in 1999.

It is important to note that even if we do find a link between access and permissiveness, we cannot be sure which causes which. Nonetheless, as a first step, it is important to know whether such a link exists. According to the table below, there is no significant difference in attitudes to the *general* subscription channel between those who have access to cable and satellite and those who do not. There is, however, a slight tendency for those with cable or satellite access to be more permissive about *adult* subscription channels (it is statistically significant only for the heterosexual scene). This tendency seems to be stronger among younger than older respondents, suggesting the possibility of greater permissiveness via cohort replacement in the future.

There was also no difference in attitudes to sex on digital channels according to whether or not respondents had access to digital television (though the numbers are still too small to be certain).

Table 4.15 Attitudes to general and adult subscription channel by access to cable/satellite

	General subscription channel		Adult subscription channel	
	Has cable/ satellite	Does not have cable/ satellite	Has cable/ satellite	Does not have cable/ satellite
(i) heterosexual sex scene	%	%	%	%
Should not be allowed to be shown at all	35	35	13	20
Only after midnight	16	15	24	17
Only after 10pm	29	25	30	27
Only after 9pm	12	12	10	11
Only after 8pm	1	2	2	3
Allowed to be shown at any time	4	6	19	18
(ii) homosexual sex scene	%	%	%	%
Should not be allowed to be shown at all	51	53	33	35
Only after midnight	16	14	24	20
Only after 10pm	18	17	21	19
Only after 9pm	10	7	9	7
Only after 8pm	-	1	1	1
Allowed to be shown at any time	2	4	10	13
Base	*332*	*720*	*332*	*720*

In the case of the Internet, however, we do see a substantial difference in attitudes between those with and without Internet access at home (see the next table). Those with access are much less likely to want an outright ban and much more likely to opt for the 18+ restriction. Only 29 per cent of those with Internet access would ban the heterosexual scene compared with 41 per cent of those without such access. Although these differences are largely a function of age, they continue to exist at a lower level even after age differences are discounted.

Table 4.16 Attitudes to Internet by access to Internet

	Has Internet	Does not have Internet at home
(i) heterosexual sex scene	%	%
Should not be available at all	29	41
Access should be available only to authorised subscribers aged 18+	64	47
Should be available to anyone with Internet access	6	6
(ii) homosexual sex scene	%	%
Should not be available at all	37	56
Access should be available only to authorised subscribers aged 18+	57	35
Should be available to anyone with Internet access	6	4
Base	*201*	*850*

Conclusions

As predicted in the *13th Report* four years ago, the British public is becoming more permissive towards the portrayal of sex in the media as a result of cohort replacement. This trend is thus likely to continue. People are more restrictive about terrestrial television and *general* subscription television, and less so about adult subscription channels, video films and cinema, suggesting that the social context of viewing and in particular access by (older) children affect attitudes. They are also less restrictive when the scene is relevant to the plot than when it is not, which suggests that the *narrative* context is also influential.

Our findings not only reinforce other research in this area, such as ITC (1998b), BSC (1999) and Gauntlett and Hill (1999b), but also support current regulatory practice in relation to heterosexual sex and television 'watersheds'. In any event, there seems to be no reason for introducing stricter policies on television than at present, and some suggestion that present restrictions should before long be relaxed by degree.

In relation to gay sex, whether lesbian or gay male sex, while broadcasters are perhaps increasingly willing to deal with such themes in more mainstream programmes, the public are on the whole still rather cautious, though less so than four years ago.

Our findings reveal no great perceived public distinction in these matters between free-to-air television, digital television and *general* subscription channels. Since the ITC at present adopts a slightly different approach to subscription television, with the watershed at 8pm rather than 9pm, public attitudes will need to be monitored closely over the next few years.

There is some public support for a more relaxed regime in respect of *adult* subscription channels, with nearly one in five respondents believing that they should be allowed to show frank heterosexual sex scenes at any time. This may well become a more widely held view as a multi-channel environment becomes more common in Britain. Since at present, adult subscription channels are available only from 10pm to 5.30am on satellite, cable and digital services, this may before long seem to be too restrictive and in need of review.

It must be said, however, that popular press anxiety about the portrayal of sex and nudity on mainstream television does to some extent mirror public concerns. While broadcasters are pushing back the boundaries in early and late evening programmes, their claim that they are simply giving the public what they want is somewhat exaggerated. Equally, although people may be concerned about the spread of sex on television, only a very small proportion wish to ban it outright. They see it as acceptable at the right time and in the right context. When it comes to media other than mainstream television – especially cinema – public attitudes to the portrayal of sex are much more permissive, reflecting their confidence in the effective imposition of age barriers. This must be good news for the BBFC with their new relaxed guidelines for the portrayal of sexual activity in '15', '18' and 'R18' categories.

As for the Internet, there is anxiety about unregulated sex on the web and about the difficulty of imposing regulation – in particular of illegal sex acts. Such anxiety is, however, less common among those with access to the Internet, possibly because they are more familiar with the various rating and filtering systems available.

Attitudes towards erotica and outright pornography are similarly critical, but do not extend to a widespread wish to ban them. Most people believe they should be available to adults.

Notes

1. *Guardian Media* 14/9/98, pp2-3; *Daily Express* 4/11/98, p15.
2. Quoted in *Broadcast* 7/5/99, p18.
3. For example *Blackeyes*, the Dennis Potter study of male sexuality in 1989, or Beth Jordache's lesbian kiss in *Brookside* in 1995.
4. See the *Guardian* 24/4/2000, p8.
5. *Broadcast* 7/5/99, p19.
6. Quoted in *Broadcast* 7/5/99, p19.
7. The Board passed all three films at 18, but not before a cut was made to *Romance* (on video), and modifications made to *Seul Contre Tous* (cinema and video). As was already noted, when Channel 4 attempted to show the BBFC uncut version of *The Idiots* on subscription television, they were unable to do so, and screened the uncut version on the Internet.
8. See BSC (2000) and the *Guardian* 27/6/2000, p5.
9. See *Broadcast* 9/1/1999, p1.
10. See *Daily Express* 29/5/2000, p15.
11. See the *Guardian* 2/8/99, p17.

12. See the website http://www.iwf.org.uk/consultation-report.docUK Consultation Summary.
13. See *Broadcast* 3/9/1999, p5.
14. See *Broadcast* 5/3/1999, p16
15. In order to make this table comparable over time, the indices used here are based only on those questions asked in both 1995 and 1999 and are therefore slightly different to those presented in the *13th* and *14th Report*s which used all available questions. The broad picture remains the same when using the full indices, although there are some differences in the detail. For example, cinema attendance and video film watching carry more weight with the short index, which is not surprising since the media covered are cinema, videos and the regular television channels. In the full index, where the score is 'diluted' by attitudes to various types of television channels etc, cinema attendance and video watching lose their statistical significance.
16. See Heath and Martin (1996) for a discussion of life-cycle, period and cohort effects.
17. The cohorts and age groups cover a longer time span than the period between the two survey measures. Thus cohort and age group change are not fully separated. For example, the 18-25 year age group in 1999 includes some people who were 18-25 in 1995. However, each cohort covers exactly the same group of people in each year. This means that it is more difficult to pick up within-age group changes than within-cohort changes. We may therefore be under-estimating within-age group change. Since our argument is that within-age group change is *greater* than within-cohort change, this strengthens our argument rather than weakens it.
18. Of course this includes the number of satellite subscribers who have switched to digital at no extra cost (figures accurate in July 2000). OnDigital on the other hand, who do not have existing satellite subscribers, have only 670,00 subscribers in July 2000.
19. Figures compiled by Professor Colin Sparks, University of Westminster.

References

Andrews, F., Morgan, J. and Sonquist, J. (1967), *Multiple Classification Analysis: a report on a computer program for multiple regression using categorical predictors*, Ann Arbor, Michigan: Survey Research Centre, Institute for Social Research.

Barnett, S. and Thomson, K. (1996), 'Portraying sex: the limits of tolerance' in Jowell, R., Curtice, J., Park, A., Brook, L. and Thomson, K. (eds.), *British Social Attitudes: the 13th Report*, Aldershot: Dartmouth.

Barnett, S. and Thomson, K. (1997), 'How we view violence' in Jowell, R., Curtice, J., Park, A., Brook, L., Thomson, K. and Bryson, C. (eds.), *British Social Attitudes: the 14th Report - The end of Conservative values?*, Aldershot: Ashgate.

British Broadcasting Corporation (2000), *Producers' Guidelines*, London: BBC.

British Board of Film Classification (1996), *Annual Report*, London: BBFC.

British Board of Film Classification (1997), *Annual Report*, London: BBFC.

British Board of Film Classification (1999), *Annual Report*, London: BBFC.

Broadcasting Standards Commission (1999a), *Annual Review*, London: BSC.

Broadcasting Standards Commission (1999b), *Sex and Sensibility*, London: BSC.

Broadcasting Standards Commission (2000), *Annual Review*, London: BSC.

Gauntlett, D. and Hill, A. (1999), *TV Living: Television, Culture and Everyday Life*, London: Routledge.

Hanley, P. (2000), *Sense and Sensibilities: Public Opinion and the BBFC Guidelines*, London: BBFC.

Heath, A. and Martin, J. (1996), 'Changing attitudes towards abortion: life-cycle, period and cohort effects' in Taylor, B. and Thomson, K. (eds.), *Understanding Change in Social Attitudes*, Aldershot: Dartmouth.

Independent Television Commission (1998a), *The ITC Programme Code*, London: ITC.

Independent Television Commission (1998b), *Television: the Public's View*, London: ITC.

Independent Television Commission (1999), *Annual Report*, London: ITC.

Acknowledgements

The *National Centre for Social Research* is grateful to the British Board of Film Classification, the Broadcasting Standards Commission, the British Broadcasting Corporation, Flextech Television, and the Independent Television Commission for their financial support which enabled us to ask the questions reported in this chapter.

Appendix

Permissiveness indices

In this chapter, the permissiveness indices are used primarily to compare attitudes in 1995 to those in 1999. The indices have therefore been restricted to the three questions which were asked in both years (cinema, regular television, and video for sale or rent) and are not directly comparable to the indices used in the *13th* and *14th Reports*. The choice of independent variables was guided by those found to be important in the analyses in the *13th* and *14th Reports*. All analyses were repeated also on the full indices which use all possible questions (not just those common to 1995 and 1999) and, although some of the detail differs, the broad picture was the same in each case.

The indices were constructed by averaging the (ordinal) answer codes for the three questions and index scores were then treated as interval variables. Cases with missing data were excluded. Since code 1 is 'ban' and code 6 is 'allowed at any time/to anyone at all', low scores on the indices indicate restrictive attitudes and high scores indicate permissive attitudes.

Cronbach's alpha for the indices are:

Heterosexual sex index	0.88
Homosexual sex index	0.92
Lesbian sex index	0.93

Multivariate modelling

The multivariate modelling was done using Multiple Classification Analysis (MCA). MCA is a technique for examining interrelationships between several independent (explanatory) variables and an interval (or above) dependent variable (here the indices scores). The independent variables need be no more than nominal level measures. MCA shows the effect of each independent variable after taking into account the effects of all other independent variables that are entered in the model (Andrews *et al.*, 1967).

MCA produces a partial beta for each independent variable roughly equivalent to a standardised partial regression coefficient. This is a measure of the ability of the variable to explain variation in the dependent variable after adjusting for the effects of all other independent variables. For the model as a whole, MCA produces a multiple correlation coefficient, which when squared (R^2) indicates the proportion of the variance in the dependent variable explained by all the independent variables together (after adjusting for degrees of freedom).

A major limitation of this technique, however, is that it requires large amounts of computer power. The number of independent variables, and the number of levels within each variable, entered into the model therefore needs to be kept strictly limited. Some summarising of variables was therefore necessary before carrying out the modelling.

The models presented here are main effects models as there were difficulties with computing interaction effects due to empty cells. Cases with missing data on any of the variables were excluded from the analysis affected.

Independent variables:

RAGECAT2 – respondent's age
1   18-24
2   25-44
3   45-64
4   65+

RSEX – respondent's gender
1   Male
2   Female

CHATTEN2 – religious attendance ('religiosity')
1   Once a week or more
2   Less often but at least once a month
3   Less often than that
4   No religion

RSEGGRP3 – socio-economic group
1   Professional/employer
2   Intermediate non-manual
3   Junior non-manual
4   Supervisor/skilled manual
5   Semi-skilled manual/Personal services
6   Unskilled manual/armed forces

HEDQUAL2 – highest educational qualification
1   Degree
2   Higher education below degree
3   A-level or equivalent
4   O-level or equivalent
5   CSE or equivalent
6   None/foreign qualification

CHILDRE2 – children of the respondent in the household
0   No children
1   Child(ren) under 11, no child 11-19
2   Child(ren) under 11 and child(ren) 11-19
3   Child(ren) 11-19, no child under 11

VIDFILM2 – how often watches video films
1   once a week or more
2   less often than once a week, but at least once a month
3   less often than once a month, but at least once a year
4   less often than that
5   doesn't have a video

5 The gender gap

*Kerstin Hinds and Lindsey Jarvis**

For much of the twentieth century, most British women were expected to follow the well-established tradition of marrying, bearing children and working in the home, leaving men to go out to work and earn the family income. Even as late as 1942, the Beveridge Report simply takes it for granted that "during marriage most women will not be gainfully employed" (cited in Timmins, 1996: 55). Not until 1970 was legislation in place to establish a woman's right to the same pay as a man for equivalent work. So until very recently, women's participation in the labour market has always been regarded as somewhat marginal.

But long-standing prejudices and practice have both been changing very rapidly in recent times. In particular, both employment and educational opportunities are much more open to women than in the past. For instance, while only one half of women were in (or seeking) any sort of work in 1971, this proportion had grown to two-thirds by 1983 and to almost three-quarters by 1999[1] (ONS, 2000). There are also now four times as many women enrolled in higher education than there were in the early 1970s (ONS, 2000). Moreover, since women now tend to marry at a later age than in the past and have fewer children, they generally possess greater choice than ever over how (and if) to combine work with their family responsibilities (Scott *et al.*, 1998).

Nonetheless, as the following table shows, the experiences of women and men still differ substantially in many respects. Though relatively better-off economically than they used to be, women still lag behind men in terms of income (Rake, 2000). One reason is that they are four times as likely as men to work part-time (ONS, 2000). Another is that the jobs they do are concentrated disproportionately in the low pay service sector (Thair and Risden, 1999). So, for instance, a man is still twice as likely as a woman to be in a professional occupation.

Another contributory factor in gender inequality is that women's greater labour market participation has not been accompanied by a more equal sharing of

* Kerstin Hinds is a Senior Researcher at the *National Centre for Social Research* Scotland. Lindsey Jarvis is a Senior Researcher at the *National Centre for Social Research* and Co-director of the *British Social Attitudes* survey series.

childcare responsibilities (La Valle *et al.*, 2000; Witherspoon and Prior, 1991). In addition, the proportion of lone parent households headed by women has doubled since 1981, now amounting to around 20 per cent of households with children (ONS, 2000).

We shall investigate in this chapter how much these differences between women and men, coupled with their different patterns of socialisation and unequal exposure to discrimination, are reflected in different values and attitudes.

Table 5.1 Differences between women and men, 1983-1999[+]

	1983	1991	1999
% in lowest household income quartile			
Women	28	23	29
Men	20	14	19
% in full-time work (of working age)			
Women	34	35	39
Men	78	75	74
% in part-time work (of working age)			
Women	20	22	25
Men	*	1	4
% with A-level or equivalent or higher qualifications[++]			
Women	21	29	33
Men	34	40	44
% in professional socio-economic group			
Women	5	13	14
Men	22	30	29
% in household with children aged 16 or under			
Women	31	31	29
Men	32	27	22
Base			
Women	*954*	*1626*	*1748*
Men	*807*	*1292*	*1395*
Women of working age	*672*	*1114*	*1157*
Men of working age	*668*	*1012*	*1074*

[+] For each of the characteristics shown there *are* significant differences between women and men in each year (the single exception is that the same proportion of women and men were living in a household with a child aged 16 years or under in 1983)

[++] Figures in first column for 1985, as the question was not asked in 1983

Recognising the existence of gender differences, the recently established Women's Unit[2] was set up "to ensure that Government policies knit together properly to take account of the interests of women" (The Women's Unit, 1998).

Advances within recent decades in women's educational and employment opportunities are, of course, likely to have had a greater impact on younger rather than older generations. For instance, among the under-35s, women and men have similar educational qualifications (48 per cent of women and 53 per cent of men in this age group have at least A-level or equivalent qualifications). So we shall investigate, using age cohort analysis (see the chapter by Park in this volume), whether any gender gaps in attitudes that we discover turn out to be getting smaller than they used to be among the under-35s.

We start our exploration of women's and men's attitudes by turning first to look at economic issues, in particular employment.

Employment

Women have been increasingly joining the labour market to the extent that there is now only a 12-point difference between the proportion of economically active women and men (ONS, 2000). Are these changes having any impact on the gender gap in attitudes?

Should women work?

The traditional view that men should go out to work while women stay at home was still held by substantial proportions of women (41 per cent) and men (45 per cent) in 1984. In our latest reading in 1998, that view has diminished substantially among both women and men and is now held by around one in six women and one in five men – not a statistically significant gender gap. Moreover, looking at findings from 1994, we see again that only a fifth of women and a quarter of men are in principle against a reversal of gender roles where "the man stays at home and cares for the children and the woman goes out to work". So, although men are more resistant to such an idea, in general the traditional notion of women as housewives seems to be all but extinct.

We turn now to attitudes towards single mothers with young children working which, as shown in the next table, are much more ambivalent. In 1994 and 1998 we asked respondents whether they thought that a single mother (first with a pre-school child, and next with a school-aged child) ought to go out to work, stay at home or do as she chooses.

Here we find that women are much more likely than men to consider that the mother should decide for herself whether to work or not, while men are more likely to prescribe that the mother should work or should stay at home.

Our logistic regression analysis included a range of possible factors other than gender which might better explain differences in work orientation, but to no avail. Being male turns out to be the best predictor of claiming to work only as hard as necessary, just as being female is the best predictor of not letting work interfere with other aspects of life. However, the last and marginally most popular of our three statements about work above – doing the best one can at work even if it does interfere with other aspects of life – is better predicted by job and family type than by gender *per se*. In particular, middle-aged managers with children, whether male or female, are most likely to take this view.

Commitment to work is, however, only part of the picture. What of job satisfaction?

Job satisfaction

Since women earn less than men and, on average, perform more menial roles at work, it seems strange that they have always been found to enjoy at least as much job satisfaction (Berch, 1982; Hodson, 1989; Curtice, 1993). As the next table shows, figures from our latest readings confirm that this is still the case.

Table 5.5 Job satisfaction by sex, 1989 and 1998

	1989	1998
	%	%
Very satisfied		
Women	37	35
Men	38	29
Fairly satisfied		
Women	47	45
Men	42	49
Not very satisfied/not at all satisfied[+]		
Women	13	19
Men	17	22
Base		
Women	*337*	*767*
Men	*401*	*661*

[+] For 1989 this includes "neither satisfied nor dissatisfied" as the answer categories were different

Overall levels of job satisfaction for both women and men have remained remarkably stable since 1989. However, the proportion of men who are "*very* satisfied" with their job seems to have diminished in the last ten years or so, meaning that women are now more likely to say this.

Recognising the existence of gender differences, the recently established Women's Unit[2] was set up "to ensure that Government policies knit together properly to take account of the interests of women" (The Women's Unit, 1998).

Advances within recent decades in women's educational and employment opportunities are, of course, likely to have had a greater impact on younger rather than older generations. For instance, among the under-35s, women and men have similar educational qualifications (48 per cent of women and 53 per cent of men in this age group have at least A-level or equivalent qualifications). So we shall investigate, using age cohort analysis (see the chapter by Park in this volume), whether any gender gaps in attitudes that we discover turn out to be getting smaller than they used to be among the under-35s.

We start our exploration of women's and men's attitudes by turning first to look at economic issues, in particular employment.

Employment

Women have been increasingly joining the labour market to the extent that there is now only a 12-point difference between the proportion of economically active women and men (ONS, 2000). Are these changes having any impact on the gender gap in attitudes?

Should women work?

The traditional view that men should go out to work while women stay at home was still held by substantial proportions of women (41 per cent) and men (45 per cent) in 1984. In our latest reading in 1998, that view has diminished substantially among both women and men and is now held by around one in six women and one in five men – not a statistically significant gender gap. Moreover, looking at findings from 1994, we see again that only a fifth of women and a quarter of men are in principle against a reversal of gender roles where "the man stays at home and cares for the children and the woman goes out to work". So, although men are more resistant to such an idea, in general the traditional notion of women as housewives seems to be all but extinct.

We turn now to attitudes towards single mothers with young children working which, as shown in the next table, are much more ambivalent. In 1994 and 1998 we asked respondents whether they thought that a single mother (first with a pre-school child, and next with a school-aged child) ought to go out to work, stay at home or do as she chooses.

Here we find that women are much more likely than men to consider that the mother should decide for herself whether to work or not, while men are more likely to prescribe that the mother should work or should stay at home.

Table 5.2 Attitudes towards whether single mothers should work by sex, 1994 and 1998

% who agree that:	1994		1998	
	Women	Men	Women	Men
A single mother with a **pre-school child:**				
Has a special duty to go out to work to support her child	8	9	14	20
Has a special duty to stay at home to look after her child	17	26	20	29
Should do as she chooses, like everyone else	67	52	58	42
Can't choose	7	12	7	9
A single mother with a **school-aged child:**				
Has a special duty to go out to work to support her child	25	31	39	51
Has a special duty to stay at home to look after her child	4	8	4	5
Should do as she chooses, like everyone else	67	53	51	38
Can't choose	4	8	6	5
Base	*536*	*448*	*1500*	*1031*

There has been an important change between the earlier and later readings, with a drop in the proportions of both sexes who opt for the woman to "do as she chooses" to the extent that now only a minority of men take this view. In line with government thinking in its New Deal for Lone Parents, both sexes are now much more inclined than they were to believe that single mothers of school-going children *should* go out to work, with half of men holding this opinion. Although there has also been a rise in those who say the same of mothers of pre-school children, this view is still held by a small minority overall. Our cohort analysis suggests that the changes have occurred among people of *all* ages.

Reasons for working

We asked all respondents in paid work in 1999 to tell us *why* they worked – from a list of eight reasons. Not surprisingly, the most common reason selected by both women and men was "money for basic essentials". But, as the next table shows, men were more likely to say this than were women, while women were more likely than men to say "money to buy extras", or "to earn money of my own".

Table 5.3 Main reason for working by sex, 1999

	Women	Men
	%	%
Need money for basic essentials such as food, rent or mortgage	44	67
I enjoy working	13	10
To earn money to buy extras	15	3
To earn money of my own	10	5
Working is the normal thing to do	5	8
To follow my career	7	6
For the company of other people	3	0
For a change from my children or housework	2	0
Base	*750*	*848*

Logistic regression analyses[3] we subsequently undertook confirmed the gender gap in why people work, particularly in relation to essentials versus 'extras' or independence. Some of this increase in women's participation in the labour market therefore seems to be driven less by financial necessity than by the desire for a greater sense of financial freedom. As we shall see, this might well be reflected in different attitudes toward work among women and men.

Work orientation

Perceptions of the extent to which work impinges on other aspects of life certainly seem to differ among women and men. As the next table shows, women are more likely than men to say that they do not let work interfere with the rest of their lives (49 per cent against 39 per cent), while men are more likely to claim that they work only as hard as they have to.

Table 5.4 Attitudes to own job by sex, 1999

% stating:	Women	Men
I only work as hard as I have to	6	11
I work hard, but not so that it interferes with the rest of my life	49	39
I make a point of doing the best I can even if it sometimes does interfere with the rest of my life	45	50
Base	*750*	*848*

Our logistic regression analysis included a range of possible factors other than gender which might better explain differences in work orientation, but to no avail. Being male turns out to be the best predictor of claiming to work only as hard as necessary, just as being female is the best predictor of not letting work interfere with other aspects of life. However, the last and marginally most popular of our three statements about work above – doing the best one can at work even if it does interfere with other aspects of life – is better predicted by job and family type than by gender *per se*. In particular, middle-aged managers with children, whether male or female, are most likely to take this view.

Commitment to work is, however, only part of the picture. What of job satisfaction?

Job satisfaction

Since women earn less than men and, on average, perform more menial roles at work, it seems strange that they have always been found to enjoy at least as much job satisfaction (Berch, 1982; Hodson, 1989; Curtice, 1993). As the next table shows, figures from our latest readings confirm that this is still the case.

Table 5.5 Job satisfaction by sex, 1989 and 1998

	1989	1998
	%	%
Very satisfied		
Women	37	35
Men	38	29
Fairly satisfied		
Women	47	45
Men	42	49
Not very satisfied/not at all satisfied[+]		
Women	13	19
Men	17	22
Base		
Women	*337*	*767*
Men	*401*	*661*

[+] For 1989 this includes "neither satisfied nor dissatisfied" as the answer categories were different

Overall levels of job satisfaction for both women and men have remained remarkably stable since 1989. However, the proportion of men who are "*very satisfied*" with their job seems to have diminished in the last ten years or so, meaning that women are now more likely to say this.

But our logistic regression analysis found (just as the analysis by Curtice in1993 had done), that the best predictor of being "*very* satisfied" with one's job is working part-time rather than full-time (which is, of course, dominantly a woman's preserve). This may explain why women with seemingly unrewarding jobs nonetheless derive great satisfaction from them. It is the very fact that they are part-time that enables them to combine work with the rest of their lives, which is itself a source of considerable satisfaction.

In summary then, women and men have both largely abandoned traditional notions that a woman's place is in the home. But by no means have all gender differences in relation to work disappeared. The fact is that many women still work under less financial pressure than men do, in that their incomes are less likely to be required for basics. While they work hard, they nonetheless try to keep work and other aspects of their lives in balance. By virtue of the fact that they are more likely to work part-time, women's levels of job satisfaction are higher than their job content would suggest.

Overall, our evidence does not suggest that the gender gap between young women and men in particular has begun to be eroded.

Politics

We know from this series and other sources (see Curtice and Jowell, 1997) that public trust and confidence in Britain's political system has been declining in recent years and that turnout in elections seems to be declining in tandem. But the same sources suggest that individual political 'efficacy' – the perceived ability to influence the political system – has been rising.

We investigated whether these trends were equally evident among women and men. While in the late 1980s men were more likely than women to be disillusioned with the political system, this gap has all but disappeared almost entirely as a result of an increase in disillusionment among women, particularly younger women. Similarly, women in the late 1980s had significantly lower levels of personal efficacy than men and, while still true, this gap has also diminished substantially, again largely due to changes in younger women. The one exception to this general picture is that women are still much more likely than men to say that politics and government these days are too complicated to understand. As we shall see, this difference may not only be a function of different propensities between the sexes to *admit* ignorance, but also to quite different levels of political interest.

Women have long expressed less interest in politics than have men (Greenstein, 1973; Butler and Stokes, 1974; Francis and Peele, 1978; Verba *et al.*, 1997). More recent research based on this series (Park, 1999) suggests that even among teenagers, girls are less knowledgeable about and interested in politics than are boys of the same age. Since 1997, however, when the number of women MPs doubled, a raft of measures have been introduced that might spark the interest of young women in particular, so we wondered whether things might have changed.

In fact they have not. Women in 1999 still report lower levels of interest in politics than men do, with only one in four of them (24 per cent) claiming at least "quite a lot" of interest in politics, compared to one in three men (33 per cent). Moreover, despite fluctuations, the gender gap in political interest has not changed appreciably within the last 13 years. But, since we know that political interest tends to increase with age (Heath and Park, 1997), we decided to check whether this is equally true for both women and men.

To some extent it is. Each age cohort of women has shown a small rise in political interest (of two to seven percentage points) from 1986 to 1999. This has not led to a rise in overall levels of interest because new generations of uninterested young women undermine this trend. But within each cohort women were less interested in politics than were their male counterparts both in 1986 and 1999, and there is no evidence that this gap is closing.

Again, in order to test the impact of gender on political interest independently of other factors, we carried out a regression analysis. It confirmed that gender is indeed a significant and key determinant of political interest.

The question then arises whether, with their lower expressed interest in and understanding of politics, women are less likely than their male counterparts to turn out to vote in elections. To answer that question, we turned to data from the 1997 *British Election Study*, which suggests that if anything the opposite is true (Norris, 1999) – at least as far as 'claimed' vote is concerned, which is always higher than actual vote. The proportion of eligible women who said they had voted in the 1997 election narrowly outnumbered that of their male counterparts (by some three percentage points). Indeed, women have been as likely as men to vote in general elections since 1979. So, despite their lower levels of interest and knowledge, perhaps women simply take their 'duties' of citizenship more seriously than men do?

Public spending

We know that women earn less than their male counterparts and are more likely to work in modest public sector jobs (Thair and Risden, 1999). These differences could well combine to create a gender gap in policy preferences, particularly those to do with tax and spending.

The *British Social Attitudes* series has shown growing support over the years for higher social spending and, if necessary, higher income tax to pay for it (Hills and Lelkes, 1999). As the next table shows, by 1999 almost 60 per cent supported increases in taxes to provide more public spending and only four per cent opted for reductions in taxes if they led to lower social spending. Throughout the last 16 years women's and men's views have been largely consistent.

Table 5.6 Opinions about taxation and public spending by sex,1983-1999

% in favour of:	1983	1990	1999
Increased taxes and more spending on health, education and social benefits	%	%	%
Women	34	53	57
Men	31	55	59
Keeping taxes and spending on these services the same as now			
Women	54	38	34
Men	55	37	35
Reducing taxes and less spending on these services			
Women	6	3	4
Men	11	4	4
Base			
Women	*954*	*1541*	*1748*
Men	*807*	*1256*	*1395*

However united as they may be in their support for extra public spending, are women and men in agreement about how that extra spending should be allocated? We asked the sample to select priorities from a list of ten areas of public spending. As always, the top priorities are health (overwhelmingly) and education, though as Judge *et al.* (1997) showed priorities do vary according to fluctuations in actual levels of public spending in particular time periods.

In the next table we show the gender distributions over the years in support for health and education spending (no other areas of spending attracted remotely such high priorities). Here we find a substantial gender difference in 1999 in relation to health spending, but not in relation to education spending. Women (as the more likely carers in society and greater users of NHS services (Bryson and Jarvis, 2000)) have been keener supporters of health spending ever since 1983, and while this support has tailed off somewhat during the 1990s, men's support has tailed off considerably more. But we find that these differences between women and men cannot be accounted for by the fact that women tend to use the NHS more than men do.

Table 5.7 Trends in spending priorities by sex, 1983-1999

% support for extra spending on:	1983	1990	1999
Health			
Women	39	57	52
Men	34	54	43
Education			
Women	24	24	33
Men	24	24	34
Base			
Women	*807*	*1541*	*1748*
Men	*954*	*1256*	*1395*

Our logistic regression analysis confirms the gender gap in relation to prioritising health spending. Even when other possible contributory factors are discounted, the odds of women choosing health spending as their top priority are one and a half times greater than for men.

While neither women nor men tend to give top priority to social security benefits as a target for extra spending (only two per cent do so), we do find gender differences when we look at particular areas of social spending. As the next table shows, we asked whether respondents wanted to see more or less public spending on benefits for a range of specific target groups.

Interestingly, women are more likely than men to favour extra spending on benefits for low income families and single parents, while men are more likely than women to opt for extra spending on the unemployed. These contrasting preferences possibly derive from self-interest rather than different forms of altruism. After all, women's low household incomes arise in the main from low pay (women are twice as likely as men to be in households claiming top-up benefits for working parents) whereas far more men than women are unemployed.

Table 5.8 Level of spending on benefits by sex, 1999

% saying spend more on benefits for:	Women	Men
People who care for those who are sick or disabled	83	81
Disabled people who cannot work	72	72
Parents who work on very low incomes	72	66
Retired people	71	69
Single parents	35	31
Unemployed people	22	26
Base	*1748*	*1395*

Moral issues

It is on a range of moral issues – such as religion, and attitudes towards marriage, cohabitation, sex and abortion – that we find some of the largest and most persistent gender differences (see also Scott, 1990 and Scott *et al.,* 1998).

Religion

As the next table shows, women have throughout the series been far more likely than men to have religious attachment, although this is no longer the case for those under 35. True, this greater religiosity is partly a function of the fact that there are more older women in the population, and religion is highly related to age (see the chapter by Park in this Report). Moreover, our logistic regression confirms that, although age is the best predictor of religiosity, gender is not that far behind (when other factors are controlled for).

Table 5.9 Religious beliefs of women and men, and those aged 18-34, 1983-1999

% with some religion	1983	1999
All women	75	60
All men	61	49
Women aged 18-34	57	39
Men aged 18-34	44	35
Base		
Women	*954*	*1748*
Men	*807*	*1395*
Women aged 18-34	*269*	*442*
Men aged 18-34	*256*	*387*

This series has formerly thrown up the fact that religion is highly associated with morally prescriptive views about family roles, abortion and sex (Heath *et al.*, 1993). Does it follow therefore that women who are more religious than men are also more morally prescriptive?

Marriage, cohabitation and sex

Surprisingly, perhaps, men are more likely than women to subscribe to the notion that "married people are generally happier than unmarried people", but the proportion of both sexes who believe this has been in decline (down to 27 per cent of men and as few as 21 per cent of women at the last reading in 1994). On the other hand, men are more permissive than women about couples living

together without any intention of marrying, (67 per cent of men now say it is "all right" compared to 59 per cent of women).

As the next table shows, women were more opposed to premarital and extramarital sex than men were in the early years of this series. Since then, women's opposition to premarital sex has halved while men's opposition has changed in the same direction but to a lesser extent. The result is a convergence in attitudes. The loss of the gender gap in relation to extramarital sex results from men taking an increasingly moral stance. So the outcome is more convergence. In examining age cohort differences, it is clear that a period effect is at work here.

We also ask in the questionnaire about attitudes towards sex between two adults of the same sex and here we find men to be persistently less tolerant than women are. In the latest reading in 1999, there was a 12 percentage point gap (44 to 32 per cent) between the proportion of men and women believing homosexual sex to be "always wrong". Attitudes to gay sex have fluctuated over the years. Hostility increased among both women and men in the mid-1980s when AIDS first became prominent and was at the time associated almost exclusively with gay sex. Then it abated during the 1990s and is now at its lowest level since the series began, but with women still leading this trend of increasing tolerance.

Table 5.10 Attitudes towards premarital, extramarital and gay sex by sex, 1983-1999

% choosing "always wrong"	1983	1989	1993	1999
A man and woman having sexual relations before marriage				
Women	19	13	12	8
Men	13	10	7	9
A married person having sexual relations with someone other than his or her partner				
Women	-	58	60	60
Men	-	52	52	60
Two adults of the same sex having sexual relations				
Women	44	52	48	32
Men	56	60	54	44
Base				
Women	*954*	*831*	*873*	*569*
Men	*807*	*682*	*611*	*483*

Replicating analyses carried out by Hayes (1997), our logistic regression confirmed that gender continued to be a significant predictor of attitudes to gay sex even after other factors were controlled for.

Abortion

Abortion has, arguably, a more immediate significance to women than it does for men suggesting that views on this issue would be quite clearly demarcated by gender. Previous analyses of attitudes to abortion (Scott, 1998) found that women's attitudes had liberalised more swiftly than men's had done between 1984 and 1994. Looking at our most recent data from 1998, there appears to have been some convergence in the interim, primarily because women's previously high levels of support have waned. Overall, there is now less social disapproval of abortion than there was in the early 1980s, but slightly more than there was in the early 1990s.

At each survey round when this subject is tackled, we present the respondents with seven circumstances in which a woman may contemplate an abortion and ask in each case whether it should be allowed by law. As the next table shows, not until 1994 was a clear majority of the sample willing to allow abortions in *all* the circumstances we presented. As always, permissiveness is greater when an abortion is needed on medical grounds and lower when it is sought for social reasons. So, as many as 90 per cent of both women and men in Britain nowadays sympathise with an abortion if the woman's health is endangered, and over 80 per cent do so where there is a strong chance of a defect in the baby. Women have consistently been more supportive of abortion in the latter circumstance than men throughout the past two decades (although the difference in 1998 was not statistically significant). A high proportion (among both women and men) is also sympathetic when the woman has become pregnant as a result of rape. Not surprisingly, men are rather more prepared to sanction abortions when *both partners* agree they do not want the child.

Table 5.11 Attitudes towards abortion by sex, 1983-1998

% saying an abortion should be allowed by law if:	1983	1989	1994	1998
The woman's health is seriously endangered by the pregnancy				
Women	87	92	93	91
Men	88	91	90	92
The woman became pregnant as a result of rape				
Women	87	91	94	92
Men	84	90	91	91
There is a strong chance of a defect in the baby				
Women	84	89	88	86
Men	79	85	82	81
The couple agree they do not wish to have the child				
Women	42	57	65	57
Men	51	63	63	65
The couple cannot afford any more children				
Women	45	56	62	55
Men	49	57	60	58
The woman decides on her own she does not wish to have the child				
Women	34	48	58	54
Men	41	50	51	55
The woman is not married and does not wish to marry the man				
Women	42	56	58	51
Men	47	59	49	51
Base				
Women	*893*	*720*	*536*	*503*
Men	*757*	*587*	*448*	*374*

As expected also, the logistic regression analyses we conducted showed that religion rather than gender was the key predictor of attitudes to abortion. For instance, Catholics had six times the odds of those with no religion of opposing abortion on the grounds of a predicted defect in the baby.

In one example, where the couple decide they do not want the child, there has been a large shift over time. Although the numbers in 1998 were too small to sustain a full cohort analysis, the evidence available seems to suggest a period effect on this issue such that people in every age group have become more accepting of abortion over time.

Conclusions

Our aim was to investigate whether changes in women's education and employment opportunities over the last two decades of the twentieth century have led to a narrowing of the gender gap. It turns out, however, that the question was too simplistic.

What we have seen here shows that opinions cannot, and perhaps never could be, divided neatly according to gender. True, certain enduring differences in the circumstances and life experiences of women and men lead to certain enduring differences in attitudes (say to issues such as the availability of abortion). But on many issues, since women and men inhabit the same social world, they share similar views and where attitudes have been changing over time, the trend has been towards convergence.

Rather more common than starkly different stances on certain issues, women and men tend to differ in the *strength* of their views. So, while both claim to work primarily to make money for essentials, men are significantly more likely than women to do so. Similarly, while the majority of women and men express satisfaction with their jobs, women now do so with greater enthusiasm than their male counterparts. And although women and men give health the highest priority for extra public spending, women are again more emphatic in this view.

On the other hand, divergence is also apparent on certain subjects. For instance, men are increasingly more likely than women to believe that single mothers should get jobs – doubtless reflecting the fact that only two per cent of single-parent households are headed by a man (ONS, 2000). Here, then, is an example of an issue on which women and men have somewhat different *interests*, and thus where the 'battle' of the sexes seems to be uninterrupted by period changes in attitudes.

In other cases, differences seem to persist because of abiding socio-demographic differences rather than any underlying gender fault line. Thus the greater job satisfaction among women is attributable in part to the fact that part-time workers are particularly satisfied with their lot at work.

Some differences are not accounted for by the reasons outlined above but rather they seem to arise instead from early socialisation and society's different expectations of girls and boys. This could explain why women are more tolerant of homosexuality than men. And also why it is that young women, in particular, admit to less knowledge of, and interest in, politics than young men do – a gender divide that narrows but does not disappear with age.

Nonetheless, the overall picture is much more one of convergence rather than divergence, sometimes because women's attitudes have shifted more (they have become relatively less disapproving of premarital sex than they were) and sometimes because men's attitudes have shifted more (they have become relatively more disapproving of extramarital sex). And on a host of other issues, women's and men's attitudes have changed in tandem across all age groups.

It seems therefore that the Women's Unit within the Cabinet Office still has a large role to play not only in pointing to and trying to eradicate objective disadvantages for women, such as in the labour market, but in the longer term to

influence much more insidious and adhesive cultural norms which continue to inhibit women from engaging in the political system as effectively as men do.

Notes

1. The difference in the labour market participation rates shown in Table 5.1 and those reported in ONS (2000) are accounted for by the fact that the Labour Force Survey (on which the ONS data is based) includes people aged 16 and 17 and that it includes all people economically active, that is in work and seeking work. The *British Social Attitudes* figures include only those in work.
2. The Women's Unit was established in 1997 and is situated within the Cabinet Office with a cross-departmental remit
3. Due to the large number of regression analyses in this chapter, it is not possible to present the results in an appendix. The following independent variables were entered into each regression model (some models contained additional items): age, sex, highest educational qualification, household income, economic activity, socio-economic group, religion, and presence of children in household. When sex remains significant within the regressions, other significant factors are not discussed in the text. However, full details of these analyses can be obtained from the authors.

References

Berch, B. (1982), *The Endless Day: The Political Economy of Women and Work*, New York: Harcourt Brace Jovanovich.

Bryson, C. and Jarvis, L. (2000), *Trends in Attitudes to Health Care 1983-1998: Report based on results from the British Social Attitudes surveys*, London: *National Centre for Social Research*.

Butler, D.E. and Stokes, D. (1974), *Political Change in Britain*, 2nd edition, London: Macmillan.

Curtice, J. (1993), 'Satisfying work – if you can get it' in Jowell, R., Brook, L. and Dowds, L. (eds.), *British Social Attitudes: the 10th Report*, Aldershot: Dartmouth.

Curtice, J. and Jowell, R. (1997), 'Trust in the Political System' in Jowell, R., Curtice, J., Park, A., Brook, L., Thomson, K. and Bryson, C. (eds.), *British Social Attitudes: the 14th Report - The end of Conservative values?*, Aldershot: Ashgate.

Francis, J.G. and Peele, G. (1978), 'Reflections on Generational Analysis: Is there a shared political perspective between men and women?', *Political Studies*, Vol. 26, **3**: 363-374.

Greenstein, F. (1973), 'Sex related political differences in childhood' in Dennis, J. (ed.), *Socialization to Politics*, New York: John Wiley.

Hayes, B.C. (1997), 'The influence of gender on public attitudes toward homosexual rights in Britain', *International Journal of Public Opinion Research*, **9**: 361-385.

Heath, A. and Park, A. (1997), 'Thatcher's Children?' in Jowell, R., Curtice, J., Park, A., Brook, L., Thomson, K. and Bryson, C. (eds.), *British Social Attitudes: the 14th Report - The end of Conservative values?*, Aldershot: Dartmouth.

Heath, A., Taylor, B. and Toka, G. (1993), 'Religion, morality and politics' in Jowell, R., Brook, L. and Dowds, L. (eds.), *British Social Attitudes: the 10th Report*, Aldershot: Dartmouth.

Hills, J. and Lelkes, O. (1999), 'Social security, selective universalism and patchwork redistribution' in Jowell, R., Curtice, J., Park, A., and Thomson, K. (eds.), *British Social Attitudes: the 16th Report - Who Shares New Labour Values?*, Aldershot: Ashgate.

Hodson, R. (1989), 'Gender differences in job satisfaction: Why aren't women more dissatisfied?', *The Sociological Quarterly*, **30**: 385-399.

Judge, K., Mulligan, J. and New, B. (1997), 'The NHS: new prescriptions needed?' in Jowell, R., Curtice, J., Park, A., Brook, L., Thomson, K. and Bryson, C. (eds.), *British Social Attitudes: the 14th Report - The end of Conservative values?*, Aldershot: Ashgate.

La Valle, I., Finch, S., Nove, A. and Lewin, C. (2000), *Parents' Demand for Childcare*, DfEE Research Report RR 176, London: The Stationery Office.

Norris, P. (1999), 'Gender: A Gender-Generation Gap?' in Evans, G. and Norris, P. (eds.), *Critical Elections: British Parties and Voters in Long-term Perspective*, London: Sage.

Office for National Statistics (ONS) (2000), *Social Trends 30*, London: The Stationery Office.

Park, A. (1999), 'Young People and Political Apathy' in Jowell, R., Curtice, J., Park, A. and Thomson, K. (eds.), *British Social Attitudes: the 16th Report - Who shares New Labour values?*, Aldershot: Ashgate.

Rake, K. (ed.) (2000), *Women's incomes over the lifetime*, London: The Stationery Office.

Scott, J.(1990), 'Women and the family' in Jowell, R., Witherspoon, S. and Brook, L. (eds.), *British Social Attitudes: the 7th Report*, Aldershot: Gower.

Scott, J. (1998), 'Generational Changes in Attitudes to Abortion: A Cross-national Comparison', *European Sociological Review*, **14**: 177-190.

Scott, J., Braun, M. and Alwin, D. (1998), 'Partner, parent, worker: family and gender roles' in Jowell, R., Curtice, J., Park, A. and Thomson, K. (eds.), *British and European Social Attitudes: how Britain differs - the 15th Report*, Aldershot: Ashgate.

Thair, T. and Risden, A. (1999), 'Women in the labour market', *Labour Market Trends*, **107**: 103-128.

Timmins, N. (1996), *The Five Giants – a Biography of the Welfare State*, London: Fontana Press.

Verba, S., Burns, N. and Lehman Schlozman, K. (1997), 'Knowing and Caring about Politics: Gender and Political Engagement', *The Journal of Politics*, Vol. 59, **4**: 1051-1072.

Witherspoon, S. and Prior, G. (1991), 'Working mothers: free to choose?' in Jowell, R.. Brook, L. and Taylor, B. (eds.), *British Social Attitudes: the 8th Report*, Aldershot: Darmouth.

The Women's Unit (1998), *Delivering for women: Progress so far*, London: The Cabinet Office.

6 Losing faith: is Britain alone?

*Nan Dirk De Graaf and Ariana Need**

Britain and the secularisation debate

Religious life in Britain has largely been characterised by falling levels of involvement with the main Christian churches, accompanied by a decline in religious belief more generally (Bruce, 1995b). This process, often referred to as secularisation, has been seen as having numerous negative societal consequences (such as a decline in social cohesion), but our concern in this chapter is not the *consequences* of secularisation but whether what is happening in Britain is mirrored in other industrialised nations. This question is of particular interest because the Church of England differs in certain key respects from churches in other countries. Perhaps Britain,[1] because of the unique organisational structure of the Church of England, has been better able to resist the 'threat' of secularisation than other countries?

Until a decade ago most scholars argued that there was a process of secularisation at work in most European countries, irrespective of the organisation of their churches (Dobbelaere, 1985; Lechner, 1991; Tschannen, 1991; Wilson, 1982). Secularisation theory (largely derived from modernisation theory) has been interpreted in various ways (Hadden, 1987), but most agree that secularisation implies religious institutions, actions, and consciousness losing their social significance (Wilson, 1982). This should manifest itself in lower church membership, fewer people attending church services, and a gradual fading in the power and presence of religion in public life.

According to secularisation theory, increasing social modernisation should lead to higher levels of secularisation. Often advances in a society's levels of technology are taken to illustrate a higher degree of modernity, but we would also add to this the acceptance of democratic, and more generally activist, ideologies (Lenski, 1970; Ultee *et al.*, 1992). Recent research examining the importance of ideologies has also shown that the development of the welfare

* Nan Dirk De Graaf is a Reader at the Department of Sociology, Nijmegen University, the Netherlands. Ariana Need is a Reader at the Department of Sociology, Amsterdam University, the Netherlands.

state is a particularly important predictor of differences between countries in religiosity (Te Grotenhuis *et al.*, 1997; Verweij *et al.*, 1997).

Today there is less agreement as to whether secularisation is actually taking place. A rival approach has developed in the United States which, though one of the most modern countries in the world, is nevertheless a country in which religion still seems to prosper (Verweij *et al.*, 1997). These rival theories are inspired by rational choice literature (Stark and Bainbridge, 1985; Stark and Bainbridge, 1987), with many being based upon the assumption that *demand* for religion is stable over time and place. So the need for religion is the same everywhere, and for everyone, meaning that variations in religiosity and church membership cannot be explained by different religious preferences – the explanatory factor at work has to be differences in *supply*. In this chapter, we refer to theorists who use this version of rational choice theory as 'supply-side theorists'.[2]

There are two major areas of controversy between secularisation theorists and rational choice theorists. The first concerns the effect of *religious pluralism* on secularisation. According to secularisation theorists, more religious competition leads to lower levels of religious participation (Berger, 1967), while rational choice theorists claim that more religious competition increases levels of religious participation (Finke and Stark, 1988). However, while rational choice theorists continue to find evidence in favour of the claim that competition increases religious participation (Chaves and Cann, 1992; Finke *et al.*, 1996; Finke and Stark, 1988; Finke and Stark, 1998; Hamberg and Pettersson, 1994; Stark *et al.*, 1995; Stark and Iannaccone, 1994) others – often using the same data! – find no evidence that this is the case (Breault, 1989a; Breault, 1989b; Lechner, 1996a; Lechner, 1996b; Olson, 1998; Olson, 1999). Supply-side rational choice theories have also been criticised for failing to describe adequately the kind of society which is the opposite to one in which different religions compete peacefully. Is it, for instance, a society where church and state are separated but a natural monopoly has nevertheless emerged – or is it one where the state has forcefully imposed some particular religion on its inhabitants and discriminates against those who do not belong to it?

The second area of controversy is a difference of opinion as to whether it is the United States or Europe that is the exception to the rule. Secularisation theorists argue that the United States is the exception to the secularising rule – though they also try to show that religiosity in the United States is not actually so different from that in Europe (Bruce, 1996; Demerath, 1998; Wilson, 1982). Conversely, rational choice theorists argue that Europe is the exception to the religious rule and that the focus of research should be not so much on religious decline but rather on religious *change* (Stark and Iannaccone, 1994).

This chapter explores the issues raised by secularisation and supply-side theories of religion. It examines the evidence of a long-term decline in religosity (either in terms of religious membership or belief) and considers whether people in countries where one religion enjoys a monopoly position are any more or less religious than those in countries with a multiplicity of religious groups. It also assesses whether there is any relationship between levels of welfare and religious belief. We address these issues by comparing Britain with typical

Catholic, Protestant and religiously mixed countries, and examining their levels of church membership, church attendance and religious faith.

Although debates about religosity often deal with time periods spanning centuries (Bruce, 1995a; Bruce, 1996), our ambitions here are more modest. We base our work on data from the 1991 and 1998 *International Social Survey Programme* of which the *British Social Attitudes* survey is the British member (see Appendix I in this Report for more details about this programme). Although the time-span is rather short, the data have the advantage of being highly comparable across countries.

Classifying countries according to religion

There are a number of ways in which we can divide up countries in terms of their religious characteristics, the most obvious being to distinguish between Catholic and Protestant nations. Another would be to differentiate between countries with a majority religious denomination and those where no one religious denomination dominates, and a third (partly overlapping) method is to distinguish between countries with high and low levels of religious competition. Throughout this chapter we use a classification based on these first two divisions: Catholic *versus* Protestant and majority denomination *versus* no majority denomination. We shall return to the question of religious competition later.

We classify a country as Protestant if the difference between the proportion of Protestants and the proportion belonging to any other denomination is larger than 25 percentage points.[3] We label a country as Catholic if this difference is to the advantage of Catholics, and classify a country as mixed if the difference is smaller. But this leaves us with a problem as to how to classify Britain. Because of the history of the Reformation in Britain, the Church of England – or, more widely defined, the Anglican Church – is neither typically Catholic nor typically Protestant, in either a doctrinal or a practical sense. In fact, Bruce describes the Church of England as an "uneasy coalition between Protestants and Catholics" (Bruce, 1995b). For this reason, we treat Britain as unique and compare it with the other more straightforwardly Protestant and Catholic countries. In addition, the denominational structures of England, Scotland and Wales are, of course, very different from each other, but the focus of this chapter is on the Church of England.

The next table shows our classification of the countries which participated in the 1991 and 1998 *International Social Survey Programme*, together with membership rates of various churches in each country.

Of course, every classification is arbitrary and vulnerable to criticism. In particular, our classification differs from common practice in its treatment of the United States. Using our rules, we have classified it as a majority Protestant country. But, in contrast to most other countries in the 'majority' categories, it has a large number of *different* churches and so can also be seen as a country with a competitive religious 'market'. We shall return to this issue later in the chapter.

Table 6.1 Church membership in the different countries in 1998

Country		Roman Catholic	Pro-testant	Ang-lican	Other	None	Base
Great Britain	%	9	5	28	11	47	804
Mixed – no majority denomination							
Australia	%	25	16	25	3	31	1310
Eastern Germany	%	5	26	0	1	69	1006
Netherlands	%	19	17	0	5	58	2020
New Zealand	%	14	7	22	28	29	998
Northern Ireland	%	39	6	16	30	9	812
Western Germany	%	38	44	0	3	15	1000
Large Protestant majority							
Norway	%	0	85	0	4	10	1532
United States	%	26	51	0	9	14	1284
Large Catholic majority							
Austria	%	80	5	0	3	13	1002
Hungary	%	51	17	0	1	31	1000
Ireland	%	88	0	4	1	7	1010
Italy	%	90	0	0	2	8	1008
Poland	%	92	0	0	1	7	1147
Slovenia	%	72	1	0	3	24	1006
Orthodox							
Russia	%	0	0	0	65	35	1703

Note: Bases exclude 'don't know' and 'not answered' cases

Religion in Britain

In his classical study of the elementary forms of religious life first published in 1912, Durkheim defined religion as "a unified system of beliefs and practices relative to sacred things, that is to say, things set apart and forbidden – beliefs and practices which unite into one single moral community called a Church, all those who adhere to them" (Durkheim, 1969: 46). This identifies three elements as central ingredients in all religions – religious belief, religious practices and church membership. We begin by looking at where Britain stands.

Church membership[4]

Questions on church membership have been asked regularly on the *British Social Attitudes* survey since 1983. As the next table shows, there is considerable variation over time in denominational membership, with the most striking finding being the 13 point fall (to 27 per cent) in the proportion identifying with the Church of England (although the percentage of people identifying with the other denominations hardly declined at all – and the percentage in the category 'other religion' actually increased). Meanwhile, the proportion without a denomination increased from 31 in 1983 to 44 per cent in 1999. This substantial increase in the number of people without a denomination supports secularisation theory.

Table 6.2 Church membership in Britain, 1983-1999

	1983	1987	1991	1995	1999
	%	%	%	%	%
Church of England	40	37	36	32	27
Roman Catholic	10	10	10	9	9
Church of Scotland	5	5	5	3	4
Other Protestant	7	7	6	6	6
Other religion	7	7	8	9	10
No religion	31	34	35	40	44
Base	*1761*	*2847*	*2918*	*3633*	*3143*

Church attendance

By comparison, there has been no real decline in church attendance. True, church attendance rates may not have been very high in 1999 – but they were at about the same level as in 1991, when the question was first asked in its present format.

Table 6.3 Church attendance (apart from such special occasions as weddings, funerals and baptisms) of those with current religion or brought up in a religion, 1991-1999

	1991	1995	1999
	%	%	%
Once a week	12	13	13
At least every two weeks	3	3	2
At least once a month	7	6	6
At least twice a year	13	12	10
At least once a year	7	7	8
Less often	4	5	6
Never or practically never	51	55	54
Base	*2687*	*3333*	*2834*

Belief in God

Perhaps the most straightforward measurement of belief in God are responses to the following question which was asked on *British Social Attitudes* as part of the 1991 and 1998 *International Social Survey Programme* modules on religion:

> *Which best describes your beliefs about God?*
>
> *I don't believe in God now and I never have*
> *I don't believe in God now but I used to*
> *I believe in God now, but I didn't used to*
> *I believe in God now and I always have*

As the next table shows, there has hardly been any change in belief about God over the last decade. In both years, just over half the British population claimed to believe in God and just under a quarter not to know how to answer the question.

Table 6.4 Belief in God in Britain, 1991 and 1998 (i)

	1991	1998
	%	%
Don't believe in God now and never have	12	13
Don't believe in God now but used to	12	12
Believe in God now but didn't used to	6	4
Believe in God now and always have	46	48
Don't know	23	22
Base	*1257*	*807*

Two further questions, which tap the same type of issues, are shown in the next two tables. Again there is hardly any change over time.

Table 6.5 Belief in God in Britain, 1991 and 1998 (ii)

	1991	1998
Which statement comes closest to expressing what you believe about God	%	%
I don't believe in God	10	10
I don't know whether there is a God and I don't believe there is any way to find out	14	15
I don't believe in a personal God, but I do believe in a Higher Power of some kind	13	14
I find myself believing in God some of the time, but not at others	13	14
While I have doubts, I feel I do believe in God	26	23
I know God really exists and I have no doubts about it	23	21
Base	*1257*	*807*

Table 6.6 Belief in God in Britain, 1991 and 1998 (iii)

	1991	1998
There is a God who concerns Himself with every human being personally	%	%
Agree strongly	11	10
Agree	22	19
Neither agree nor disagree	25	25
Disagree	17	20
Disagree strongly	13	12
Don't know	8	9
Base	*1257*	*807*

We can use these three questions together to conceptualise religious belief or devoutness (see also Felling *et al.*, 1991; Kelley and De Graaf, 1997). Not surprisingly, answers to one question correlate highly with answers to the others, suggesting that they all measure the same underlying factor. Combining them, we get an index of religious belief, to which we shall return later on.[5]

Cross-national comparisons

Church membership

We turn now to the various countries we considered earlier, beginning with church membership. The first three columns in Table 6.7 show the levels of church membership found in each country in 1991 and 1998, and then the change between these years. The highest levels of church membership are generally found in the countries with a majority denomination, with Catholic and Protestant countries showing broadly similar figures. Many of these countries have church membership of around 90 per cent and more, with somewhat lower levels in Hungary and Slovenia. The mixed countries show far wider variation, ranging from 36 per cent in eastern Germany and 42 per cent in the Netherlands to 85 per cent in western Germany and 91 per cent in Northern Ireland.[6] Britain, with 53 per cent church membership, would seem to fit most neatly into this group.

These findings do not support the prediction by supply-side rational choice theorists that countries with monopoly religions should have *lower* levels of church membership than countries with a more mixed religious profile. Some would contest this conclusion on the grounds that a country like the United States, though having a large Protestant majority, can hardly be seen as having a monopoly religion because of the diverse nature of the different Protestant denominations that coexist within it. But even if we accept this argument it remains true that it is the Catholic countries, all typical monopolistic societies,

which have the highest levels of church membership of all. And it turns out that church membership rates in the United States are not so different from those in western European countries (such as western Germany). Moreover, between 1991 and 1998 church membership declined from 93 to 86 per cent in the United States, the largest decline of any of the countries in the table with the exception of Britain and the eastern European countries Hungary and Slovenia.

To examine the validity of the secularisation thesis, we need to look at *trends* in church membership for all countries. With the exception of Australia, Russia, and New Zealand there has been a general fall in the proportion of the population who identify themselves with a denomination, with Britain having one of the sharpest declines. These findings confirm secularisation theory's prediction that church membership will continue to decline in modern society. However, Russia shows a clear religious revival. Apparently, Greeley (1994) was right in expecting a resilience of religion in Russia.

Table 6.7 Per cent church membership and attendance across countries, 1991 and 1998[7]

Country	% church membership			% who attend church at least once a month		
	1991	1998	Change	1991	1998	Change
Britain	66	53	-13	22	20	-2
Mixed – no majority denomination						
Australia	73	73	0	24	25	+1
Eastern Germany	36	31	-5	7	8	+1
Netherlands	45	42	-3	29	24	-5
New Zealand	70	71	+1	23	24	+1
Northern Ireland	92	91	-1	67	60	-7
Western Germany	89	85	-4	24	22	-2
Large Protestant majority						
Norway	94	90	-4	12	10	-2
United States	93	86	-7	52	48	-4
Large Catholic majority						
Austria	90	87	-3	n.a.	25	
Hungary	95	70	-25	25	20	-5
Ireland	98	93	-5	80	71	-9
Italy	94	92	-2	56	48	-8
Poland	97	93	-4	97	96	-1
Slovenia	89	76	-13	n.a.	27	
Orthodox						
Russia	35	65	+30	2	10	+8

Notes: Bases for percentages exclude 'don't know' and 'not answered' cases

n.a. = not available

Church attendance

The second set of columns in Table 6.7 shows the proportion who attend church at least once a month. This proportion is generally *much* lower than the proportion who consider themselves members of a church. Attendance has declined slightly between 1991 and 1998, with the British fall very much in line with the other countries.

If supply-side theorists are right to assume that demand for religion is stable and only competition affects church membership, then attendance should be highest in countries with no majority denomination. This is clearly not the case – it is the monopolistic, Catholic countries like Italy, Ireland and Poland that have the levels of highest church attendance.

Belief in God

The next table shows the proportion of the population who believe in God and the index we constructed from the questions considered in Tables 6.4, 6.5 and 6.6. Britain, with seven in ten believing in God in 1991, is close to the average.

Here we find considerable variation *within* each of our categories of countries, implying that our classification does not give much information about the religious faith of the population. The highest proportion of people who believe in God is found in Poland, Ireland and the United States (this applying to over nine in ten in each country), closely followed by Northern Ireland and Italy. The lowest proportion believing in God is found in eastern Germany (around one in four). Apparently the former communist regime has been very effective in suppressing religious feelings (this is also indicated by very low levels of church membership and attendance). A number of other former communist countries (such as Slovenia and Hungary) also show relatively low percentages believing in God. The exceptions, as we have seen, are Poland (here religious belief has remained strong throughout the 1990s) and Russia (which has witnessed a religious revival). The index of religious belief shows a similar picture, with a strong increase in religiosity only in Russia.

Although the proportion of people believing in God fell slightly between 1991 and 1998, this fall was muted in comparison with the decline in church membership over the same period. This pattern is not very supportive of theories of secularisation and better suits the supply-side argument that demand for religion is stable over time (Stark and Bainbridge, 1987). However, supply-side theory is dealt a blow by the considerable variation that exists between countries in levels of belief about God (levels which, it predicts, should be largely stable).

Table 6.8 Indicators of religious beliefs across countries, 1991 and 1998

Country	% who believe in God			Index of religious belief		
	1991	1998	Change	1991	1998	Change
Britain	70	68	-2	59	58	-1
Mixed – no majority denomination						
Australia	69	65	-1	61	59	-2
Eastern Germany	25	26	+1	28	25	-3
Netherlands	59	55	-4	51	53	+2
New Zealand	70	69	-1	62	61	-1
Northern Ireland	95	89	-6	85	78	-7
Western Germany	67	63	-4	59	55	-4
Large Protestant majority						
Norway	59	58	-1	55	53	-2
United States	94	92	-2	83	81	-2
Large Catholic majority						
Austria	79	78	-1	63	62	-1
Hungary	66	63	-3	54	54	0
Ireland	95	92	-3	83	79	-4
Italy	87	87	0	75	75	0
Poland	94	94	0	83	83	0
Slovenia	61	63	+2	51	51	0
Orthodox						
Russia	47	61	+24	43	51	+8

Note: Bases for percentages exclude 'don't know' and 'not answered' cases

In summary then, most countries (Britain, western Germany, eastern Germany, United States, Hungary, Italy, Ireland, Norway, Austria, Poland, and Slovenia) show a large decline in church membership between 1991 and 1998, and a much smaller decline in church attendance and belief in God. These trends are especially visible in Britain. These latter findings are largely in line with the supply-side perspective. However, the variations that we find *between* the countries contradict the supply-side theory, as does the marked decline in church membership over time.

The steeper fall in church membership than in belief in God tallies with the view that those in modern societies are becoming increasingly individualistic. Examples of this in Britain would include the fact that people are becoming increasingly educated and more independent of authorities such as the Church of England. As a consequence, they adopt a more personal approach towards religion and no longer automatically follow the lead of organised religion (see also Inglehart, 1990).

Competition in the religious 'market place'

Next we turn to another aspect of the supply-side theory which arises from its origin in economic theory (see Stark and Iannaccone, 1994) – the importance of competition. In this context, competition describes a situation in which a number of different religious 'suppliers' vie with one another, the assumption being that offering 'consumers' a wider range of 'religious commodities' will force suppliers to be more responsive and efficient.

As we have seen, our classification of countries on the basis of their majority denomination does not adequately capture this angle of religious competition. To do this we turn to the Herfindahl index of religious concentration (Iannaccone, 1991).[8] A low score on the index indicates strong competition on the religious market, and a high score low level of competition. The next table shows the score for those countries where it is available.

Table 6.9 Herfindahl index of religious concentration by country

Country	Herfindahl index
United States	12
New Zealand	25
Australia	27
Britain	41
Netherlands	38
Western Germany	46
Norway	85
Austria	85
Ireland	95
Italy	98

According to the supply-side theory we should expect to find that those countries with the strongest religious beliefs have the highest levels of religious competition (and thus the lowest scores on the Herfindahl index). But we find no evidence to support this. On average, the population of typical monopolistic societies like Ireland and Italy (with their high scores on the index) also show a high level of religious belief. And while the low index score for the United States indicates very high levels of religious competition, we find the population there to be no more religious than the population in Italy and Ireland.

Supply-side theory also implies that levels of religious participation will be lower in countries with religious monopolies than in more religiously pluralist societies. This is because the failure of 'competition' means nations with religious monopolies have substantial unmet religious needs, while nations with religious competition do a better job of meeting diverse religious needs. More specifically, the supply-side argument implies that non-attenders in

monopolistic societies should be more religious than those in religiously competitive societies, since those in the latter societies with religious needs are more likely than those in monopolistic societies to find a church that meets them (Kelley and De Graaf, 1997).

If anything, Table 6.10 shows quite the reverse. Thus, non-attenders in the United States (with its high degree of religious competition) have a relatively high level of religiosity (62 in 1998), whereas in Britain (with its much lower degree of religious competition) the non-attenders have a much lower devoutness score of 47. And the non-attenders in monopolistic societies like Ireland and Italy *are* clearly more devout than non-attenders in Britain. These findings are exactly the opposite of what we would expect from supply-side theory's prediction of low levels of religiosity among non-attenders in highly competitive countries.

Table 6.10 Index of religious belief of those who do not attend church by country, 1991 and 1998

Country	1991	1998
Britain	47	49
Mixed – no majority denomination		
Australia	39	36
Eastern Germany	13	29
Netherlands	32	37
New Zealand	43	36
Northern Ireland	70	56
Western Germany	35	39
Large Protestant majority		
Norway	32	33
United States	64	62
Large Catholic majority		
Austria	n.a.	39
Hungary	28	29
Ireland	51	45
Italy	36	50
Poland	31	43
Slovenia	n.a.	24
Orthodox		
Russia	36	35

n.a. = not available

Religion and the welfare state

In general, secularisation theory states that religiosity and modern society are incompatible. Inglehart argues:

> The shift to Postmaterialism and the decline of traditional forms of religion tend to go together because they share a common cause: the unprecedented levels of personal security of contemporary advanced industrial society, which in turn can be traced to the postwar economic miracle and the rise of the welfare state. (Inglehart, 1990: 205)

Inglehart implies that improved levels of social security are important causes of a decline in the importance of religion. In the past, churches made a substantial contribution to the support of the poor. But within a modern welfare state their role is less clear cut. Now the government, not the church, is responsible for helping the poor and needy.

This suggests that measures of social security might be important predictors of secularisation (Te Grotenhuis *et al.*, 1997). Were this the case we would expect to find that those countries with higher levels of social security have lower levels of religious belief. We do indeed find such a negative relationship when we compare the average score on the index of religious belief for each of our countries and their OECD social security levels in 1990 and 1997 (a negative correlation of -0.27). While this correlation is not statistically significant, considering the very few cases on which it is based, it does provide some support for this interpretation of secularisation theory. However, if we carry out the same comparison of social security levels with church membership and attendance we also do not find significant support for secularisation theory.

Conclusions

The Church of England does not appear any more capable of offering resistance to the secularisation process than churches in other countries. Over the last decade, there has been no sign that the secularisation process in Britain (or most other Christian countries) has been halted. The exception is former communist Russia where religion appears to have survived seventy-five years of socialism and is now experiencing a religious revival (although it should be noted that church membership and attendance rates in Russia were very low to begin with).

In *British Social Attitudes: the 9th Report*, Greeley (1992: 68) concluded that "perhaps the worst thing for religion in England was the establishment of the Church of England". This conclusion was based on a comparison of Britain with three other English speaking nations: the United States, the Irish Republic, and Northern Ireland. However, our more extensive international comparison suggests the Church of England is doing no worse than churches in countries such as the Netherlands.

If we take into account the fact that older cohorts are generally substantially more religious than younger cohorts (De Graaf, 1999; Need and De Graaf, 1996; Te Grotenhuis *et al.*, 1997), we cannot expect that this trend towards secularisation will stop.[9] Nor does it seem likely that religious competition will increase church membership or religious belief. In contrast to the predictions of supply-side theorists, it is typical monopolistic Catholic countries such as Italy and Ireland which are marked by high levels of religious belief and belonging, rather than countries in which diverse religious groups compete for the hearts and minds of the populace.

Notes

1. The focus of this chapter is the Anglican Church, which of course predominates only in England and (to a lesser extent) in Wales. However, since English data make up the majority of cases in the *British Social Attitudes* survey, the discussion throughout this chapter refers to Britain.
2. Since most work in the field of religion by rational choice theorists is done by supply-side theorists, most authors fail to distinguish between different versions of rational choice theory (cf. Bruce, 1999). However, it is possible to use a rational choice approach without making any assumptions about a stable demand for religion. In a forthcoming article, De Graaf *et al.* (2000) use a different version of rational choice theory to explain differences in disaffiliation in the Netherlands. They specifically distance their approach from that of supply-side theorists.
3. The proportion of Catholics and Protestants is based on proportion of the total population belonging to religious denominations falling into these categories.
4. The discussion in this chapter focuses on Christian religions and so we use the term 'church' to refer to all religious institutions. Of course, many of the countries considered have sizeable non-Christian minorities and the survey questions take such variation into account (by referring, for example, to "meetings connected with your religion").
5. In order to combine them, we score the answers in equal intervals, from 0 to 100, and take the average. The index thus runs from 0 to 100 where a low score indicated low religious belief and a high score high religious belief.
6. By western Germany we mean the geographical area known until unification as the Federal Republic of Germany. By eastern Germany we mean the area formerly known as the German Democratic Republic.
7. The bases for Tables 6.7 and 6.8 (including 'don't know' and 'not answered' cases) are as follows:

Table 6.11 Bases for Tables 6.7 and 6.8

	1991	1998
Britain	1,257	804
Australia	1,310	1,310
Eastern Germany	1,486	1,006
Netherlands	1,635	2,020
Western Germany	1,346	1,000
New Zealand	1,070	998
Northern Ireland	838	812
Norway	1,506	1,532
United States	1,359	1,284
Austria	984	1,002
Hungary	1,000	1,000
Ireland	1,005	1,010
Italy	983	1,008
Poland	1,063	1,147
Slovenia	2,080	1,006
Russia	2,964	1,703

8. To calculate the Herfindahl index, we first take the market share of denominations S_{ij}. This is the number of people in country j affiliated with denomination i, divided by the total number of people in country j affiliated with any religious denomination. The Herfindahl index H_j is the summation of all squared S_{ij}s. The disadvantage of the Herfindahl index is that it does not distinguish between religions. Some religions do a better job in attracting potential members than other religions. Furthermore, in this measure there is no difference between a country with one per cent Catholics, one per cent Protestants, and 98 per cent without a denomination and a country with 50 per cent Catholics, 50 per cent Protestants, and 0 per cent without a denomination. These are rather strong assumptions (cf. Bruce 1999).

9. Note, however, that this does not take into account differences in fertility rates between denominations and between religious and non-religious people (cf. De Graaf *et al.*, 2000). For example, if religious people are more fertile than the non-religious we will tend to overestimate the secularisation process.

References

Berger, P.L. (1967), *The Sacred Canopy*, New York: Anchor.

Breault, K.D. (1989a), 'A re-examination of the relationship between religious diversity and religious adherents', *American Sociological Review*, **54**: 1056-1059.

Breault, K.D. (1989b), 'New evidence on religious pluralism, urbanism, and religious participation', *American Sociological Review*, **54**: 1048-1053.

Bruce, S. (1995a), 'A novel reading of nineteenth-century Wales: A reply to Stark, Finke, and Iannaccone', *Journal for the Scientific Study of Religion*, **34**: 520-522.

Bruce, S. (1995b), *Religion in Modern Britain*, Oxford: Oxford University Press.

Bruce, S. (1996), *From Cathedrals to Cults. Religion in the Modern World*, Oxford: Oxford University Press.

Bruce, S. (1999), *Choice and Religion. A Critique of Rational Choice*, Oxford: Oxford University Press.

Chaves, M. and Cann, D.E. (1992), 'Regulation, pluralism, and religious market structure. Explaining religion's vitality', *Rationality and Society*, **4:** 272-290.

De Graaf, N.D. (1999), 'Event History Data and Making a History Out of Cross-Sectional Data', *Quality & Quantity*, **33:** 261-276.

De Graaf, N.D., Need, A. and Ultee, W.C. (2000 forthcoming), Levensloop en kerkverlating. Een nieuwe en overkoepelende verklaring voor enkele empirische regelmatigheden' , *Mens en Maatschappij*, **74**.

Demerath, N.J. (1998), 'Excepting exceptionalism: American religion in comparative relief', *Annals of the American Academy of Political and Social Science*, **558:** 28-40.

Dobbelaere, K. (1985), 'Secularization theories and sociological paradigms: a reformulation of the private-public dichotomy and the problem of social integration', *Sociological Analysis*, **46:** 377-387.

Durkheim, E. (1969), 'The social foundations of religion' in Robertson, R. (ed.), *Sociology of Religion*, Middlesex: Penguin Books.

Felling, A., Peters, J. and Schreuder, O. (1991), *Dutch Religion*, Nijmegen: Instituut voor Toegepaste Sociale Wetenschappen.

Finke, R., Guest, A.M. and Stark, R. (1996), 'Mobilizing local religious markets: Religious pluralism in the empire state, 1855 to 1865', *American Sociological Review*, **61:** 203-218.

Finke, R. and Stark, R. (1988), 'Religious economies and sacred canopies: religious mobilization in American cities, 1906', *American Sociological Review*, **53:** 41-49.

Finke, R. and Stark, R. (1998), 'Religious choice and competition', *American Sociological Review*, **63:** 761-762.

Greeley, A. (1992) 'Religion in Britain, Ireland and the USA' in Jowell, R., Brook, L., Prior, G. and Taylor, B. (eds.), *British Social Attitudes: the 9th Report*, Aldershot: Dartmouth.

Greeley, A. (1994), 'A religious revival in Russia?', *Journal for the Scientific Study of Religion*, **33:** 253-272.

Goldthorpe, J.H. (1998), 'Rational action theory for sociology', *British Journal of Sociology*, **49:** 167-192.

Goldthorpe, J.H. (2000), *On Sociology. Numbers, narratives, and the integration of research and theory*, Oxford: Oxford University Press.

Hadden, J.K. (1987), 'Toward desacralizing secularization theory', *Social Forces*, **65:** 587-611.

Hamberg, E.M. and Pettersson, T. (1994), 'The religious market: Denominational competition and religious participarion in contemporary Sweden', *Journal for the Scientific Study of Religion*, **33:** 205-215.

Iannaccone, L.R. (1991), 'The consequences of religious market structure: Adam Smith and the economics of religion', *Rationality and Society*, **3:** 156-177.

Inglehart, R. (1990), *Culture shift in advanced industrial society*, Princeton: Princeton University Press.

Kelley, J. and De Graaf, N.D. (1997), 'National context, parental socialisation, and religious belief: Results from 15 nations', *American Sociological Review*, **62:** 639-659.

Lechner, F.J. (1991), 'The case against secularization: A rebuttal', *Social Forces*, **69:** 1103-1119.

Lechner, F.J. (1996a), 'Rejoinder to Stark and Iannaccone: "Heads, I win ...": On immunizing a theory', *Journal for the Scientific Study of Religion*, **35:** 272-274.

Lechner, F.J. (1996b), 'Secularization in the Netherlands?', *Journal for the Scientific Study of Religion*, **35:** 252-264.

Lenski, G. (1970), *Human Societies*, New York: McGraw-Hill.

Need, A. and Graaf, N.D. de (1996), '"Losing my Religion": a dynamic analysis of leaving the church in the Netherlands', *European Sociological Review*, **12:** 87-99.

Olson, D.V.A. (1998), 'Religious pluralism in contemporary US counties', *American Sociological Review*, **63:** 759.

Olson, D.V.A. (1999), 'Religious pluralism and US church membership: A reassessment', *Sociology of Religion*, **60:** 149-173.

Stark, R. and Bainbridge, W.S. (1985), *The Future of Religion: Secularization, Revival, and Cult Formation*, Berkeley: Berkeley University Press.

Stark, R. and Bainbridge, W.S. (1987), *A Theory of Religion*, New Brunswick, NJ: Rutgers University Press.

Stark, R. and Iannaccone, L.R. (1994), 'A supply-side reinterpretation of the "secularization" of Europe', *Journal for the Scientific Study of Religion*, **33:** 230-252.

Stark, R., Finke, R. and Iannaccone, L.R. (1995), 'Pluralism and piety: England and Wales, 1851', *Journal for the Scientific Study of Religion*, **34:** 431-444.

Te Grotenhuis, M., De Graaf, N.D. and Peters, J. (1997), 'Komt religiositeit met de jaren? De invloed van leeftijd, welvaart, sociale zekerheid en religieuze opvoeding op kerkbezoek en christelijk geloof in West-Europa', *Mens en Maatschappij*, **72:** 210-226.

Tschannen, O. (1991), 'The secularization paradigm: a systematization', *Journal for the Scientific Study of Religion*, **30:** 395-415.

Ultee, W., Arts, W. and Flap, H. (1992), *Sociologie: vragen, uitspraken, bevindingen*, Groningen: Wolters-Noordhoff.

Verweij, J., Ester, P. and Nauta, R. (1997), 'Secularization as an economic and cultural phenomenon: a cross-national analysis', *Journal for the Scientific Study of Religion*, **36:** 309-324.

Wilson, B.R. (1982), *Religion in Sociological Perspective*, Oxford: Oxford University Press.

7 Images of council housing

*Peter A Kemp**

Throughout the European Union, private landlords and non-profit housing associations are the main providers of rented housing. Britain (like Ireland) is an exception in its promotion of councils as the main providers of subsidised or 'social' rented housing (Harloe, 1995). This was originally conceived as a public sector solution to the private sector problem of slum housing and the failure of the market to provide sufficient homes at rents that ordinary people could afford (Merrett, 1979).

Local councils in Britain were first given subsidies to build homes to rent after the First World War, and their role as housing providers became increasingly important up until the late 1970s. But the future of council housing is now being questioned and seems less certain than before (Burns and Timmins, 2000). The recent housing Green Papers for England and Scotland envisage that, if tenants vote in favour of it, much of the existing stock of council housing will gradually be transferred to housing associations, arms-length housing companies,[1] and other types of 'social landlord' (Scottish Office, 1999; DETR and DSS, 2000). Meanwhile, the Department of Environment, Transport and the Regions intends to "encourage local authorities to consider the benefits which [stock] transfer can bring to tenants and local communities" (DETR and DSS, 2000). Similar views have been expressed by the Scottish Executive (Scottish Executive, 2000).

Calls for reform have come from 'think-tanks' as well as government. The influential Institute for Public Policy Research (IPPR) set up a forum of housing experts charged with considering the future of social housing. The result was a call for nothing less than the 'reinvention' of social housing and the recommendation, among other things, that the management or ownership of all council housing should be transferred to arms-length, community housing organisations (IPPR, 2000).

The Deputy Prime Minister has emphasised that "there is a continuing role for council housing" (House of Commons Hansard, 2000). But it remains true that substantial amounts of council housing could be transferred to other forms of

---

* Peter A Kemp is Professor of Housing and Social Policy at the University of Glasgow.

social landlord over the next decade. If this transfer process gathers pace, some experts are predicting the virtual end of council housing as a major tenure in Britain (Burns and Timmins, 2000). That is an outcome that few would have predicted when Labour published their previous housing policy Green Paper in 1977 (DoE, 1977). While that document and its Scottish equivalent (Scottish Office, 1977) presented home ownership as the most attractive housing tenure, they nevertheless argued that local authorities had an important and continuing role to play in the provision of rented housing. At the time, councils accounted for over six million homes – 70 per cent of all rented housing, and 30 per cent of the entire housing stock. Although there were growing problems with council housing, its future appeared not to be in question.

Things changed rapidly after the election of the Conservative government of Mrs Thatcher, which came to power in 1979 with a manifesto commitment to give council tenants the 'right to buy' their home at a very substantial discount from its market value. The policy was a popular one, not just among council tenants, but also among other households as well (Curtice, 1991). Indeed, in no other area of social policy has privatisation extended so far or with such popular public support. The new government also aimed to promote home ownership more generally, to reduce public spending on housing and to minimise the role of local authorities as landlords.

Although the promotion of home ownership remained an important and popular goal of Conservative housing policy, from 1986 there was an important shift in emphasis as attention increasingly focused on 'demunicipalising' the provision of rented housing (Kemp, 1989). As well as persuading council tenants to take up the right to buy, the government now aimed to encourage the remaining tenants to consider voting to transfer the ownership of their homes to alternative owners, such as private landlords and housing associations (DoE, 1987).

In support of this policy, the Conservatives argued that council housing was inefficient and paternalistic, and that it was unhealthy to have one landlord dominating the local rental market. As Housing Minister John Patten put it, we should "get rid of these monoliths" and transfer council estates to landlords "who will be closer in touch with the needs and aspirations of individual tenants" (quoted in Kemp, 1989: 52). With this aim in mind, the Conservatives followed their 1987 general election victory with a housing White Paper which set out a radical agenda for rented housing (DoE, 1987). The aim was to shift local councils from being providers of homes to being 'enablers' who would help others provide accommodation. Where possible, *existing* council housing estates were to be hived off to other types of social housing landlord. Meanwhile, *new* social housing was to be constructed by housing associations using private finance, rather than by local councils. The Housing Act of 1988 deregulated housing associations and private rents and measures were taken to expand the provision of homes by private landlords. Subsequently, an increasing number of local councils opted to transfer their entire stock, rather than individual estates, to newly established housing associations (Mullins, 1998).

By the time New Labour came to power in 1997, the nature and image of council housing had significantly changed (Kemp, 1999). Capital spending by local authorities on new housing and renovation had been substantially reduced and the number of new council houses constructed each year had fallen from 86,000 in 1980 to only 2,000 in 1995 (Hills, 1998). Between 1979 and 1999, around two million council homes were sold, mainly under the right to buy scheme. The net result was that the number of council homes in Britain fell by a third, from 6.4 million homes in 1981 to 4.2 million in 1997. Local councils now accounted for about 53 per cent of all rented homes, while housing associations had trebled their share, from 5 per cent to 15 per cent. Meanwhile, the share of rented housing owned by private landlords had increased from 25 to 32 per cent over the same period (Wilcox, 1999).

The consequences of these changes have been profound, particularly in terms of the characteristics of council housing tenants. Compared with the late 1970s, these now include proportionately far more unemployed, retired and economically inactive households. The proportion who are middle aged has fallen, and far more tenants are now either young or elderly. The turnover of tenants within the sector has increased and far fewer see council housing as a tenure for life (Burrows, 1999; DETR and DSS, 2000).

Table 7.1 Respondent's economic activity by current tenure

	Owner-occupiers	Council tenants	Housing association tenants	Private tenants
	%	%	%	%
In paid work	61	32	30	61
Unemployed	2	11	10	5
Full-time education	2	3	3	10
Permanently sick or disabled	3	10	10	7
Wholly retired from work	21	26	25	6
Looking after the home	10	17	22	10
Base	*2183*	*500*	*204*	*222*

Housing associations have also re-positioned themselves within the housing market over the past twenty years. They have essentially moved 'down market' and become increasingly important as providers of accommodation to households in need. As a result, there has been a convergence in the types of household who rent from councils and housing associations, such that they now house pretty much the same kinds of people. There are now no significant differences between the two tenures in terms of the age, gender, ethnic background, social class, marital status, economic activity, or income of their

tenants. This makes it possible, at least so far as the socio-economic composition of tenants is concerned, to talk in terms of a 'social housing' sector that comprises both local councils and housing associations. But, as the next table shows, the characteristics of these tenants are very different from those of private tenants or owner-occupiers, who are much more likely to be in paid work or education and less likely to be retired.

This chapter examines public attitudes to council housing by addressing three key questions. Firstly, does the public have faith in council housing? Second, are councils seen as better or worse than private landlords at providing rented housing? And third, what role should council housing have nowadays: should it be targeted at the very poor or aimed at a variety of income groups?

Public faith in council housing

Choice of landlord

We begin by considering whether people would rather rent from a council than from some other types of landlord, such as a housing association or private landlord. If the public has little faith in council housing, we would expect to see a high proportion of respondents, including many council tenants, preferring other types of landlord.

In fact, if they had a free choice, the great majority of people (including most tenants) would rather not rent at all and would choose to buy their home. We asked:

> If you had a free choice would you choose to rent accommodation, or would you choose to buy?

A near unanimous nine in ten (87 per cent) would choose to buy, with 13 per cent saying they would choose to rent. This is backed up by previous *British Social Attitudes* surveys which have shown that, while the preference for owner-occupation may have weakened a little following the housing market recession of the late 1980s and early 1990s, the great majority of people would still rather be owner-occupiers than tenants (Ford and Burrows, 1999).

In reality, some households have little option but to rent their accommodation, either in the short term or permanently. Many will rent accommodation before becoming homeowners. Some former owner-occupiers will rent, at least for a short period, following events such as relationship breakdown or divorce. And each year, 50,000 to 70,000 owner-occupiers rent accommodation in the private sector in between buying and selling their home (Green and Deacon, 1998). Some, of course, will never be able to afford to buy their own home and so will always be reliant upon rented accommodation.

We turn now to consider the types of landlord that existing tenants favour, focusing particularly on those in social housing. Would existing council tenants rather rent from housing associations, as the government implicitly hopes? Are

housing association tenants renting from their preferred type of landlord or would they really rather rent from a council – or even a private landlord?

Our findings show that preferences about landlords vary considerably according to people's current tenure and that the majority of tenants would rather continue with their current type of landlord. The most 'loyal' are those currently renting from a local authority, among whom a clear majority (about eight in ten) would rather rent from this landlord if given a choice. Of the remainder, two-thirds (14 per cent) would rather rent from a housing association and a third from a private landlord. If we look at housing association tenants we find that, as with council tenants, the majority are currently renting from their preferred type of landlord. But over a quarter say they would rather rent from a council instead. Thus, in proportionate terms, more housing association tenants would rather rent from a council, than council tenants would rather rent from an association.

Table 7.2 Preferred landlord by current tenure

	Owner-occupiers	Council tenants	Housing association tenants	Private tenants	All
	%	%	%	%	%
Housing association	33	14	63	22	31
Council	31	78	27	16	36
Private landlord	28	7	9	56	26
Base	*2183*	*500*	*204*	*222*	*3137*

Of course, people may not always be able to rent accommodation from their preferred type of landlord. So, irrespective of who they would most prefer as a landlord, would people take up a council tenancy if they were offered one? To assess this, we asked those who are not currently council tenants how strongly they agreed or disagreed with the statement "I would like to live in council housing if I could get it". A clear majority (75 per cent) would *not* like to live in council housing and disagree with the statement. Only 13 per cent agree. Those who disagree feel far more strongly about the issue, with 35 per cent saying they "strongly disagree" (compared with the two per cent who "strongly agree").

On the face of it, the fact that three-quarters of people would not like to live in council housing suggests a public with very little liking for this tenure. But, once again, our results are strongly influenced by tenure, with owner-occupiers – who account for the majority of households – showing by far the highest level of disagreement with the statement. This is hardly surprising because 95 per cent of owner-occupiers would rather own than rent their home. They therefore have no wish to take a council house, even if one were to be offered to them.

And, as Table 7.2 shows, if this group *had* to rent, only 31 per cent would choose to rent from a council; roughly similar proportions would prefer to rent from a housing association or a private landlord.

If we focus only on current housing association tenants we find far greater enthusiasm for council housing. Nearly half agree that they would like to live in council housing if they could get it, while only a third disagree (and one in five feel unable to say one way or the other). Again, this does not suggest a lack of faith in council housing. Among private tenants a different pattern emerges, with over half saying they would *not* like to live in council housing even if they could get it. The latent desire for council housing is thus much lower among tenants renting from private landlords than it is among housing association tenants. (In fact, compared with housing association tenants, we shall see that private tenants have a consistently less favourable view of councils across the range of issues examined in this chapter.)

Table 7.3 "I would like to live in council housing if I could get it" by current tenure

	Owner-occupiers	Housing association tenants	Private tenants	All
	%	%	%	%
Agree	10	46	27	13
Neither	10	20	18	12
Disagree	80	34	55	75
Base	*2180*	*204*	*221*	*2633*

Perceptions of council property

We now examine whether attitudes to council property have changed over time, focusing on views about council estates, council rents, and the standard of repairs and maintenance that councils offer. This allows us to examine whether the apparent loss of confidence in council housing among policy makers over the past decade and a half has been shared by council tenants and the public more generally.

Satisfaction with one's housing relates not only to the dwelling itself but also to its location – the neighbourhood within which it is situated (Murie, 1997). Indeed, many of the problems that beset council housing relate to the concentration of dwellings in relatively large housing estates. Consequently, one of the first priorities of the Social Exclusion Unit, set up by the government following the 1997 general election, was to undertake an investigation into the 'worst estates' in Britain and to propose a strategy for tackling the problems they face (Social Exclusion Unit, 1998).

Of course, attitudes to council estates may well be affected by whether or not respondents live on estates themselves, and we will need to take this into account. The 1999 survey shows that while most people do not live on housing estates, eight out of ten council tenants do (along with nearly two-thirds of housing association tenants).

We asked respondents whether they agreed or disagreed with the statement "council estates are generally pleasant places to live". As the next table shows, only about a third of respondents agree with this view, a slightly lower proportion than in 1985. However, council tenants themselves have not become more pessimistic about estates as being pleasant places to live. Indeed, the proportion who take this view has increased slightly, from 47 per cent in 1985 to 52 per cent today. Whether or not a person themselves lives on a council estate makes no difference to their answer. Nevertheless, it remains the fact that almost half of all council tenants do *not* think council estates are generally pleasant places in which to live.

Table 7.4 "Council estates are generally pleasant places to live" by tenure, 1985 and 1999

	1985		1999	
	Council tenants	All	Council tenants	All
	%	%	%	%
True	47	36	52	32
False	46	57	47	61
Base	*434*	*1530*	*364*	*2450*

One of the defining characteristics of social housing is that the rents charged are lower than market rents. However, over the last two decades (and especially since the late 1980s), the rents charged by local councils – and by housing associations and private landlords – have increased in real terms. Council rents increased over this period at a faster rate than the Retail Price Index, average earnings and house prices. As a percentage of average male earnings, they have increased from 9.5 per cent in 1985 to 12.8 per cent in 1998 (Wilcox, 1999). It would be no surprise, therefore, to find that public perceptions of council rents have also changed.

To assess this, we asked people whether they agreed or disagreed with the statement "council tenants pay low rents". Despite real increases in council rents, around a half of people think council rents are low, nearly double the proportion who thought this when we first asked the question in 1985. Even among council tenants (who are less likely to take this view), the proportion who agree that their rents are low has tripled over this period. A possible reason

for this is that private rents have increased more rapidly than council rents over the last decade

Table 7.5 "Council tenants pay low rents" by tenure, 1985 and 1999

	1985		1999	
	Council tenants	All	Council tenants	All
	%	%	%	%
True	11	26	29	47
False	82	66	62	46
Base	434	1530	364	2450

We have already seen that council tenants are less likely than average to think they pay low rents. These perceptions may reflect both the substantial increases that council tenants have experienced over this period, and the fact that many more of them are now drawn from very low income groups.

Table 7.6 "Council tenants pay low rents" by tenure, 1999

	Owner-occupiers	Council tenants	Housing association tenants	Private tenants	All
	%	%	%	%	%
True	49	29	33	68	47
False	44	62	62	28	46
Base	1763	364	136	158	2450

As the table above shows, the perceptions of council rent levels held by housing association tenants are similar to those held by council tenants. In contrast, over twice as many private tenants think that council rents are low – perhaps not surprisingly given that, on average, they pay significantly higher rents. Owner-occupiers are less likely than private tenants to think council rents are low, although a half agree that they are (perhaps reflecting the fact that average mortgage repayments tend to be higher than council and housing association rents).

In the 1985 survey we asked whether people agreed or disagreed with the view "councils give a **poor** standard of repairs and maintenance". At that time, responses to this question were relatively negative. This was especially true

among council tenants, 68 per cent of whom agreed that councils gave a poor standard of repairs and maintenance, compared with 58 per cent of those in other forms of accommodation (Bosanquet, 1986). However, in the 1999 survey, the responses to a similar statement ("councils give a **low** standard of repairs and maintenance") are more evenly balanced. While council tenants remain more pessimistic than other people, the proportion who agree that councils give a low standard of repairs and maintenance is – at 56 per cent – rather less than in 1985. There has been a similar decline among non-council tenants. It is not clear whether this apparent change in attitudes over time represents a real improvement in how councils' repair and maintenance performance is perceived or merely reflects the change in wording (from 'poor' to 'low').

Is there enough council housing?

The number of council houses in Britain has been substantially reduced because of a combination of sales to sitting tenants and the virtual cessation of council house building. Some commentators have argued that councils should be encouraged and helped to build substantial numbers of new homes once again. But recent governments, including New Labour, have instead relied on housing associations and, to a lesser extent, private landlords to add to the rented housing stock. However, the government has noted that, in some cases, "new social housing has been developed in areas where it was not needed in the longer term, while insufficient amounts of new affordable housing have been developed in areas of acute pressure" (DETR and DSS, 2000).

To assess public perceptions of these issues, we asked respondents:

> *Thinking now about the amount of **affordable council** accommodation available to rent in your area, do you think there is enough, more than enough or too little?*

A similar question, this time about 'affordable private accommodation' was also asked. Our purpose here is to ascertain whether responses to these questions shed light on the notion that the public has little faith in council housing. If we find a belief that there is insufficient affordable private accommodation but sufficient (or even too much) council accommodation, that might be one indication that councils should not provide more new homes to rent and that this should be left to the private sector.

In fact, around two-fifths of respondents believe there is *not* enough council housing in their area and a similar proportion feel the same about affordable private accommodation. Council tenants are the most likely to say there is too little affordable private housing to rent (52 per cent compared with 44 per cent of private tenants and 45 per cent of housing association tenants). Meanwhile, housing association tenants are the most likely to say there is insufficient affordable *council* housing (56 per cent, compared with 46 per cent of council tenants and 40 per cent of private tenants). Perhaps not surprisingly, 61 per cent

of people who say they would take a council house if they could get it, also say that there is too little affordable council housing.

Table 7.7 Views on the availability of rented accommodation

	Affordable council accommodation to rent	Affordable private accommodation to rent
	%	%
Enough	27	28
More than enough	6	7
Too little	42	44

Base: 3143

There is a significant correlation between whether people think there is enough affordable private housing to rent and whether they think there is enough council housing. Seven out of ten people who think there is too little affordable *private* housing think the same about affordable council housing. This certainly does not suggest that the public favour confining the supply of rented homes to non-council landlords.

Previous experience of council housing

If there is a lack of faith about council housing among the public, we might expect this to manifest itself most strongly among those most affected by it – that is, those either living in council accommodation or who have done so in the past. We have seen already that attitudes do vary according to people's current experience – we turn now to see whether past experience also makes a difference. We find that, far from past experience generating a dislike for councils, those who have previously lived in council housing (either as tenants or as children) and no longer do so have a more favourable view than those with no such experience. For example, this group are much more likely than those without past experience to say they would prefer to rent from the council than from any other landlord, and would actually like living in this form of housing if they could get it. They view council estates more positively too, with a higher proportion agreeing they are generally pleasant places to live.

So, when it comes to council housing, familiarity apparently does not breed contempt. People who have actually lived in council housing, either as tenants before buying a home or as the children of council tenants, are much more positive about the tenure than those who have no such experience.

Private *versus* public landlords

The past two decades have seen a significant shift from public to private provision in the public utilities and, to a lesser extent, in the welfare state. Housing has witnessed the most extensive privatisation of all by way of the sale of council houses to sitting tenants under 'right to buy' legislation. However, for the most part, privatisation in housing has involved the transfer of public (that is, council and new town) homes to owner-occupation rather than to the private rented sector. In so far as council housing has been shifted to another landlord, this transfer has been to housing associations ('registered social landlords' as the government now calls them in England) – in other words, from one part of the social housing sector to another.

Although the Conservative governments of Thatcher and Major took steps to encourage the transfer of council housing to the private rented sector, they largely failed. Private investors have been reluctant to take over council housing estates and, at the same time, council tenants have proved unwilling to have their homes transferred to the private rented sector (Kemp, 1989). Interestingly, opponents of the transfer of council housing in Glasgow to community housing associations have, in an attempt to discredit the proposal, described the transfer as being one of 'privatisation' to private landlords. This perhaps reflects long-standing folk memories of 'Rachmanism' in which 'unscrupulous' private landlords are said to have exploited tenants by charging 'exorbitant' rents for slum property.

Advocates of a market based approach to the provision of goods and services argue that the private sector is generally more efficient and more responsive to consumer wishes than the public sector. Certainly, this argument has been used to justify privatisation over the last two decades. But does the public agree with that view when it is applied to the rented housing market? To assess this we now examine people's responses to a series of questions that asked them whether "from what you know or have heard" councils or private landlords are generally better at a number of different aspects of housing provision.

First of all, we asked which type of landlord – councils or private landlords – is generally better at providing "a good quality of housing" As Table 7.8 shows, in this respect councils are generally seen as being better than private landlords, with just under half thinking this, and only a quarter believing it to be the other way around.

One of the potential attractions of renting rather than owning accommodation is that someone else – the landlord – is responsible for repairs and maintenance. We have already seen that many people think councils give a low standard of repairs and maintenance – but do they think private landlords would do any better? It appears not. About half believe that councils are generally better than private landlords at providing a "good standard of repairs and maintenance". And only one in six believe that private landlords are better than local councils.

Since council rents are on average about 40 per cent lower than private market rents, it comes as little surprise to learn that councils come out much better than private landlords when it comes to charging 'reasonable' rents. In total, two-

thirds of all respondents believe that councils are generally better at this and hardly any think private landlords are better than councils in this respect.

Security of tenure is one of the most critical issues for people who rent their home. Having the freedom to stay there for as long as they like is especially important for tenants who want long-term accommodation. The security of tenure arrangements in the council and private rented sector are very different, with council tenants having 'secure tenancies' which provide strong security of tenure. In essence, provided the tenant pays the rent and complies with the other requirements of their tenancy, they can stay in council housing for as long as they like. By contrast, in the non-regulated part of the privately rented sector – which accounts for about eight out of ten tenancies – most tenants have 'assured shorthold' tenancies, which are fixed term tenancies for periods of six months or more (known as 'short tenancies' in Scotland). Hence, private tenants have much weaker security of tenure than council tenants. It is not surprising then that security is the aspect of renting accommodation on which councils do best of all in the public's view. Three-quarters of all respondents believe that councils are generally better than private landlords at giving their tenants long-term security.

So far councils have been seen in a consistently more positive light than private landlords. But, while their image is better in terms of rent, maintenance, security and quality, they are not seen to do so well when it comes to providing homes in good neighbourhoods. Three times as many think that private landlords are generally better than councils at providing housing in good areas as hold the opposite view. However, a substantial minority – almost two-fifths of all respondents – feel either that private landlords and councils are equally able to provide housing in good neighbourhoods or were not able to choose between them on this scale.

Finally, we asked respondents which type of landlord – councils or private landlords – they thought was generally better at giving "good value for money". In total, just over a half think councils are generally better than private landlords at giving value for money. A further one in five considers private landlords and councils to be about the same, and only one in twelve thinks private landlords offer better value.

So, in most respects, councils are generally seen as better landlords than those in the private sector. The exception is their ability to provide housing in good neighbourhoods, something which private landlords are seen as better able to do. However, it is notable that a significant minority – between a fifth and two-fifths, depending on the feature in question – either believe that the performance of councils and private landlords is the same or are unable to choose between them. This signifies a relatively high degree of uncertainty as to whether councils or the private sector are the better landlords.

Table 7.8 "From what you know or have heard, which type of landlord do you think is generally better at ..."

		Council better	Same	Private landlords better	Can't choose	Base
Giving tenants long-term security	%	74	11	4	9	2392
Charging reasonable rents	%	67	15	4	12	2390
Giving good value for money	%	54	19	8	16	2386
Providing a good standard of repairs and maintenance	%	51	19	16	13	2390
Providing a good quality of housing	%	46	16	24	13	2411
Providing housing in good neighbourhoods	%	16	24	45	13	2380

Attitudes towards the relative merits of councils and private landlords vary significantly by tenure. In particular, council tenants are especially likely to say that councils are better at providing all the aspects of housing provision asked about. So too are those with previous experience of council accommodation (either as a tenant or during childhood). By contrast, private tenants do not show the same loyalty towards their landlords, rating them above councils only in respect of providing good quality housing and housing in good neighbourhoods. In the four remaining areas – repairs and maintenance, long-term security, charging reasonable rents, and value for money – they too believe that councils do better than private landlords (though by smaller proportions than was the case with council tenants).

Housing association tenants are *more* likely than private tenants to see councils as better than private landlords at providing a good quality of housing and housing in good neighbourhoods. They are *equally* as likely as private tenants to say that councils are better at giving tenants long-term security and value for money. And they are *less* likely than private tenants to say that councils are better at charging reasonable rents. Nevertheless, with the exception of providing housing in good neighbourhoods, they consistently rate councils more highly than private landlords.

Table 7.9 Per cent saying that councils are better at ...

	Owner-occupiers	Council tenants	Housing association tenants	Private tenants
	%	%	%	%
Giving tenants long-term security	76	82	67	67
Charging reasonable rents	67	79	57	66
Providing a good standard of repairs and maintenance	51	65	46	44
Giving good value for money	55	63	50	49
Providing a good quality of housing	45	62	49	30
Providing housing in good neighbourhoods	14	33	21	6
Smallest base	*1718*	*346*	*133*	*155*
Largest base	*1738*	*353*	*134*	*157*

Council housing for the poor?

One of the long-running debates in post-war social policy in Britain has concerned whether the welfare state should be universal and available to all *or* more selective and targeted at the poorest households. 'Universalists' argue that means-testing stigmatises beneficiaries and requires costly and complicated administrative procedures. Meanwhile, 'selectivists' claim that universal services waste resources on people who do not really need help, whereas means-testing allows assistance to be targeted towards those who are most in need (Deacon and Bradshaw, 1983; Pratt, 1996).

The recent controversy over the allocation of additional resources for pensioners is a case in point. The government has argued that it would be wasteful to increase the basic state pension since that would benefit all pensioners, rich and poor alike, whether they need extra help or not. Rather, it has preferred instead to raise the level of benefits paid to pensioners in receipt of the Minimum Income Guarantee, thereby ensuring that additional help is targeted only on the poorest pensioners. This issue was examined in the *16th Report* (Hills, 1999).

In housing, as we have seen, council housing has focused increasingly over time on the poorest households. On the one hand, this is partly because it has been better-off households, especially those in work, who have tended to take up their option to buy their home at a discount under the 'right to buy' scheme.

On the other hand, it is also because new entrants to the sector are much more likely than in the past to be among the poorest households or to be homeless (Burrows, 1999). This has led to concerns that council housing may become, like public housing in the USA, a highly stigmatised 'ambulance service' for those very poor who cannot fend for themselves in the housing market. Unlike public housing in the USA, however, council housing in Britain has never yet explicitly targeted this group to the exclusion of all others (Harloe, 1995).

In contrast, in much of the rest of the EU (especially the Scandinavian countries and the Netherlands), social housing is more of a universal service than in Britain, and is open to people in all income categories. Although there are 'problem estates' in these countries, these are not on a par with the difficulties that beset council housing in Britain and, to an even greater degree, public housing in the USA.

What stance do the British public take on these matters? Do they feel that council housing should be *only* for people on very low incomes who cannot find other suitable forms of housing? Or should it instead be for a mixture of people with different incomes? In fact, as the next table shows, most people would opt for a universal rather than a targeted approach. Three out of five believe that council housing should be for a mixture of people on different incomes, and two out of five that it should be only for those on very low incomes who cannot find any other suitable accommodation. Thus only a minority, albeit a substantial one, support pushing council housing further in the direction of a residual housing tenure, focused only on those who cannot fend for themselves in the housing market.

Council tenants are particularly supportive of the view that council housing should contain a social mix, three-quarters doing so. People with previous experience of council housing are also more likely than others to sympathise with this view. The strongest support for a highly residual council sector can be found among those renting or buying in the private market – but nonetheless the majority of these groups still believe council housing should be socially mixed. Housing association tenants fall mid-way between these two extremes: two-thirds would prefer council housing to be socially mixed while the remaining third favour a residual sector.

Attitudes to the role of council housing also vary according to income. If we divide respondents into four groups according to their household income we find that those in the bottom three-quarters are more likely – by a ratio of about two to one – to say that council housing should have a wider, rather than a purely residual, role. Among respondents in the highest income quartile (the 'well-off'), opinion is evenly divided between those who think council housing should encompass a mix of income groups and those who believe it should be targeted only at the poor who cannot obtain other suitable accommodation. So, even among the well-off, there is no majority support for confining council housing to the very poor.

Table 7.10 Views on whether council housing should be universal or selective by tenure

	Owner-occupiers	Council tenants	Housing association tenants	Private tenants	All
	%	%	%	%	%
Should only be for people with very low incomes who cannot find other suitable forms of housing	44	21	34	43	40
Should be for a mixture of people with different incomes	55	77	65	56	59
Base	*2183*	*500*	*204*	*222*	*3137*

Conclusions

Our findings reveal relatively little support among the public for the view held by many experts and policy makers that council housing has passed its 'sell by' date and should be transferred to other landlords such as housing associations. As might be expected, opinions differ, with people living in private housing (rented or owned) having a less favourable view of council housing than social housing tenants. But overall the public generally has not lost faith in council housing and, more significantly, nor have council tenants, or those with past experience of living in council housing. There is only muted support for confining council housing to those very poor households who are unable to find suitable accommodation elsewhere.

In most respects councils are seen, and not just by council tenants, as being better than private landlords. Moreover, the great majority of council tenants say they prefer councils to private landlords or housing associations. And, despite a tendency for people to favour their current landlord when asked about their preferred landlord, a significantly greater proportion of housing association tenants would rather rent from a council than *vice versa*.

Where councils do seem to fall down in the public's mind is in relation to council housing *estates* (rather than the accommodation itself) and, to some extent, the standard of their repair service. This provides support for the government's emphasis on improving the quality and efficiency of council housing and on putting resources into the improvement of the worst estates. However, because of the limits placed on public spending, the additional resources required to improve council estates will have to come from the private

sector. Consequently, the use of private finance and the transfer of stock to other types of social landlord may be the price that council tenants have to pay to improve their estates, even though most would currently rather rent from the council.

Note

1. Arms-length housing companies are organisations set up by local authorities to manage or take over the ownership of council housing.

References

Bosanquet, N. (1986), 'Interim report: housing' in Jowell, R., Witherspoon, S. and Brook, L. (eds.) *British Social Attitudes: the 1986 Report*, Aldershot: Gower.

Burns, J. and Timmins, N. (2000), 'Council housing "set to disappear within a decade"', *Financial Times*, 22 February.

Burrows, R. (1999), 'Residential mobility and residualisation in social housing in England', *Journal of Social Policy*, **28**: 27-52.

Curtice, J. (1991), 'House and home' in Jowell, R., Brook, L. and Taylor, B. (eds.), *British Social Attitudes: the 8th Report*, Aldershot: Dartmouth.

Deacon, A. and Bradshaw, J. (1983), *Reserved for the Poor. The Means Test in British Social Policy*, Oxford: Basil Blackwell and Martin Robertson.

Department of the Environment [DoE] (1977), *Housing Policy: A Consultative Document*, London: HMSO.

Department of the Environment (1987), *Housing: the Government's Proposals*, London: HMSO.

Department of the Environment, Transport and the Regions [DETR] and Department of Social Security [DSS] (2000), *Quality and Choice: A Decent Home for All*, London: Department of the Environment, Transport and the Regions.

Ford, J. and Burrows, R. (1999), 'To buy or not to buy? A home of one's own' in Jowell, R., Curtice, J., Park, A. and Thomson, K. (eds.), *British Social Attitudes: the 16th Report – Who shares New Labour values?*, Aldershot: Ashgate.

Green, H. and Deacon, K. (1998), *Housing in England 1996/97*, London: The Stationery Office.

Harloe, M. (1995), *The People's Home: Social Rented Housing in Europe and America*, Oxford: Basil Blackwell.

Hills, J. (1998), 'Housing: a decent home within the reach of every family?' in Glennerster, H. and Hills, J. (eds.), *The State of Welfare*, 2nd edition, Oxford: Oxford University Press.

Hill, J. and Lelkes, O. (1999), 'Social security, selective universalism and patchwork redistribution' in Jowell, R., Curtice, J., Park, A. and Thomson, K. (eds), *British Social Attitudes: the 16th Report- Who shares New Labour values?*, Aldershot: Ashgate.

House of Commons Hansard (2000), *Parliamentary Debates*, Vol. 347, 4 April 2000, Col. 814.

Institute for Public Policy Research (2000), *Housing United*, London: Institute for Public Policy Research.

Kemp, P. A. (1989), 'The demunicipalisation of rented housing' in Brenton, M. and Ungerson, C. (eds.), *Social Policy Review 1*, London: Longman.

Kemp, P. A. (1999), 'Making the market work? New Labour and the housing question' in Dean, H. and Woods, R. (eds.), *Social Policy Review 11*, Luton: Social Policy Association.

Merrett, S. (1979), *State Housing in Britain*, London: Routledge & Kegan Paul.

Mullins, D. (1998), 'More choice in rented housing?' in Marsh, A. and Mullins, D. (eds.), *Housing and Public Policy*, Buckingham: Open University Press.

Murie, A (1997), 'The housing divide' in Jowell, R., Curtice, J., Park, A., Brook, L., Thomson, K. and Bryson, A. (eds.), *British Social Attitudes: the 14th Report – The end of Conservative values?*, Aldershot: Dartmouth.

Pratt, A (1996), 'Universalism or selectivism? The provision of services in the modern welfare state' in Lavalette, M. and Pratt, A. (eds.), *Social Policy. A Conceptual and Theoretical Introduction*, London: Sage.

Scottish Executive (2000), *Better Homes for Scotland's Communities*, Edinburgh: Stationery Office.

Scottish Office (1977), *Scottish Housing. A Consultative Document*, Edinburgh: Stationery Office.

Scottish Office (1999), *Investing in Modernisation – An Agenda for Scotland's Housing*, Edinburgh: Stationery Office.

Social Exclusion Unit (1998), *Bringing Britain Together: A National Strategy for Neighbourhood Renewal – Report by the Social Exclusion Unit*, London: Stationery Office.

Wilcox, S. (1999), *Housing Finance Review 1999/2000*, Coventry: Chartered Institute of Housing, and London: Council of Mortgage Lenders.

Acknowledgements

We are grateful to the Department of the Environment, Transport and the Regions whose financial support for the *British Social Attitudes* survey since 1996 has enabled us to ask a module of questions about housing. The author is grateful to the Department and to Joanne Neale for helpful comments.

8 Is the English lion about to roar? National identity after devolution

John Curtice and Anthony Heath[*]

'There'll always be an England', says the old song. Yet, politically at least, there has not been an England since Wales was subsumed under the English crown by Edward I in 1284. Subsequently both Scotland and Ireland also joined what was to become the United Kingdom. While most of Ireland left the Union to form the Irish Republic in 1922, England continues to share its statehood with Scotland, Wales and Northern Ireland.

The English have never seemed to be unhappy with this state of affairs. After all, their nation is by far the largest partner in a Union that once enjoyed the fruits of a great and prosperous empire. And although part of a multinational state, the English have always tended to think of themselves as English and British interchangeably. Meanwhile, the advantage to the Union of the existence of a British identity was that it was something to which many people in Scotland, Wales and Northern Ireland could feel an affinity too (Smith, 1981; Kellas, 1991).

But is this apparently benign state of affairs for the English now under threat? Certainly the ties that hitherto have bound the peripheral nations of the United Kingdom to the Union appear to have loosened. Not only have Scotland and Wales been granted forms of devolution – with Scotland acquiring its first legislature since the Act of Union in 1707, and Wales its first assembly since its incorporation under the English crown. But in addition, after nearly three decades, devolution has now been restored (if somewhat shakily) to Northern Ireland, and joint governmental institutions have been established with the Irish Republic.

The only part of the United Kingdom for which little has changed is England. Perversely, therefore, while the rest of the United Kingdom has secured greater autonomy within the Union, England's affairs are still run exclusively by a

[*] John Curtice is Deputy Director of the ESRC Centre for Research into Elections and Social Trends, and Professor of Politics and Director of the Social Statistics Laboratory at Strathclyde University. Anthony Heath is Professor of Sociology at the University of Oxford, and Co-director of the ESRC Centre for Research into Elections and Social Trends.

United Kingdom Parliament in which there is a full contingent of Scottish, Welsh and Northern Irish MPs. (In fact, both Scotland and Wales are over-represented in the House of Commons relative to their populations.) Meanwhile, Scotland, Wales and Northern Ireland also enjoy significantly higher levels of public expenditure per capita than England does. So, while England effectively helps to pay for other parts of the UK to run their own affairs, it still lacks full control over any of its own affairs.

Several commentators have speculated about the possibility of an English backlash in response to this state of affairs (Paxman, 1998; King, 2000). But such a backlash might take one of two forms. The first is a 'me too' backlash. People in England might seek – if only for the sake of symmetry – some form of devolution along the lines of, say, their Scottish counterparts. At the same time they might develop a stronger attachment to their 'Englishness' than to their 'Britishness'. Such a reaction would probably be a greater threat to the continuation of the Union than would any of the nationalisms in Scotland, Wales and Northern Ireland.

But an English backlash could take quite another form. Annoyed at the advantages granted to the rest of the UK but wishing to maintain Great Britain, people in England might seek to withdraw the 'privileges' granted to Scotland, Wales and Northern Ireland. With no interest in the establishment of equivalent institutions of their own, they would adhere to the still fairly popular view in England that Britain is one country and should be ruled as such (Gellner, 1983; Heath *et al.*, 1999). To the extent that this view succeeds, however, it might well generate an equivalent and opposite reaction in Scotland, Wales and Northern Ireland, which would also threaten the continuation of the Union.

We use various sources to examine national identity in England in the wake of devolution, to explore whether there has been an English backlash and, if so, what form it is taking. Has devolution so far undermined or reinforced English people's commitment to the British state, or is it treated with benign indifference?

However, any change in the pattern of national identity in England may have wider effects too. For instance, as a multinational identity, Britishness might be expected to have a rather more inclusive quality than does Englishness (Heath and Kellas, 1998). Indeed, it has been widely noted that members of ethnic minorities are more willing to adopt a 'British' rather than an 'English' identity. So, we might also anticipate that those who are especially likely to feel 'British' are also more likely to be sympathetic to immigration (Heath *et al.*, 1999: but see McCrone and Surridge, 1998) and to closer European integration. We therefore also examine in this chapter whether any English backlash is likely to lead to less tolerance of anything 'foreign'.

Any rise in a distinctively English identity could also have implications for party politics in Britain. Devolution policies were, after all, implemented by a Labour government and opposed by the Conservatives. Now that devolution is in place the Conservatives have proposed that non-English MPs should lose their right to vote on exclusively English legislation, and the Labour government's plans for devolution to the regions of England are taking a very long time to mature. All this may have the effect of positioning the

Conservatives as the champions of English interests. We explore this possibility too.

To have a big political impact, however, English nationalism probably needs symbols to rally around that are quintessentially English rather than British, and which might be appropriated by a campaign for English devolution. We therefore look to discover whether such symbols exist.

Our evidence comes primarily from the 1999 round of the *British Social Attitudes* survey in England, which was undertaken just as the new institutions in Scotland and Wales were acquiring their powers. But we also had access to data from the 1997 *British Election Study* (Evans and Norris, 1999) and to separate Scottish and Welsh studies conducted at the same time as our survey in 1999 (Paterson *et al.*, forthcoming; Wyn Jones and Trystan, 2000).

We turn first to the present pattern of English national identity and discover how much, if at all, it has been changing. We then consider English attitudes to devolution both for England and the rest of the UK. Finally we assess how exclusive English national identity is and what symbols there might be which embody its expression.

Measuring national identity

As noted, people in England have long tended to think of themselves as both English and British, that is to have a 'dual identity' (Heath and Kellas, 1998). Our survey contained two key measures of national identity both of which allowed us to examine who feels English and British and who feels only one or the other. One of these measures is known as the Moreno scale, after its author (Moreno, 1988) and was also administered in our contemporaneous Scottish and Welsh surveys. So we can examine whether people in England are in fact more likely than are their counterparts in Scotland and Wales to hold a dual identity. The question runs as follows:

> *Some people think of themselves first as British. Others may think of themselves first as English. Which, if any, of the following best describes how you see yourself?*

> *English, not British*
> *More English than British*
> *Equally English and British*
> *More British than English*
> *British, not English*

In Scotland, 'Scottish' was substituted for 'English', and in Wales the question referred to 'Welsh'.

Table 8.1 Moreno national identity in England, Scotland and Wales

	England	Scotland	Wales
	%	%	%
English/Scottish/Welsh, not British	17	32	17
More English/Scottish/Welsh than British	15	35	19
Equally English/Scottish/Welsh and British	37	22	36
More British than English/Scottish/Welsh	11	3	7
British, not English/Scottish/Welsh	14	4	14
Other/None/Don't know	7	4	7
Base	2718	1482	1256

Additional sources: Scottish Parliamentary Election Study 1999; Welsh Assembly Election Study 1999

According to this measure nearly two in three people in England (63 per cent) express at least partly a dual identity. But in this respect, the English are hardly unique. Sixty-two per cent of the Welsh also feel some form of dual identity as do some 60 per cent of Scots. Even when we look just at those who feel equally British and English/Welsh/Scottish, England appears to be no different from Wales in its incidence of dual identity: in both cases just over one in three fall into this category, while in Scotland only around one in five choose this option.

This picture represents a change since 1997 when a higher proportion of the English than either the Scottish or Welsh professed a dual identity (Heath and Kellas, 1998; Curtice, 1999). But how has this change come about? Has dual identity become more common in Scotland and Wales, or has it declined in England? As the next table shows, it appears to be the English who have changed most. The proportions who feel exclusively English and exclusively British have both risen at the expense of those who express a dual identity. An equivalent trend is not apparent in either Scotland or Wales.

Table 8.2 Moreno national identity in England, 1997 and 1999

	1997	1999	Change
National identity	%	%	
English, not British	7	17	+10
More English than British	17	15	-2
Equally English and British	45	37	-8
More British than English	14	11	-3
British, not English	9	14	+5
Other/None/Don't know	7	7	0
Base	3150	2718	

Source: 1997 – British Election Study

But in 1997 and 1999 we also included a second measure of national identity. Rather than inviting people to say whether they are English, British or some variant of both, we presented people with a list of possible identities and invited them to indicate which applied to them. Someone with a dual identity was expected to choose more than one identity from the list.

*Please say which, if any, of the words on this card describes the way **you** think of **yourself**. Please choose as many or as few as apply. PROBE: Any other?*

British
English
European
Irish
Northern Irish
Scottish
Welsh
Other answer

In one respect, the answers in the next table confirm what the first measure told us – a marked rise in the proportion of people in England who think of themselves as English. While 47 per cent had claimed to be English in 1997, this figure has now risen to 57 per cent. But there has not been any rise (indeed if anything a small fall of three points) in the much higher proportion of people who say they are British. As a result, and in contrast to what we found with the first measure, the proportion of the English claiming to have a dual identity has in fact risen. Even so, it still constitutes well under half of the English.[1]

Table 8.3 National identity in England: an alternative measure, 1997 and 1999

	1997	1999	Change
% who think of themselves as			
British	73	70	-3
English	47	57	+10
% answering			
English only	18	21	+3
English and British	36	44	+8
British only	40	27	-13
Base	*3150*	*2718*	

Source: 1997– British Election Study

In any event, both these measures of national identity provide grounds for believing that a (still modest) English backlash may be taking place. Though

dual identities may still be common, more people express an adherence to Englishness now than two years ago. So we clearly need to investigate the possible implications of English nationalism further.

Before doing so, however, it is worth combining our two measures of national identity to develop a more sensitive scale of the degree to which someone feels English or British. After all, if someone feels truly English and not British, then we might reasonably expect them not only to say they are "English, not British" in response to the Moreno question, but also to identify themselves as English alone on our second measure. Any other combination can be relegated to the category of being 'ambiguously' rather than 'unambiguously' English and not British. A similar logic can be applied to distinguish between those who are unambiguously or ambiguously British and not English.[2] This enables us to extend the Moreno scale from a five-point measure to a seven-point one, and it is this device that we use as our principal indicator of national identity in the rest of this chapter.

The success of this extended scale is confirmed in the next table by reference to answers to another question that asked all respondents in England how much pride they had in being British and how much in being English. Those in the first three rows of the next table (all of whom prioritise feeling English over British) are all more likely to be "very proud" of being English than British. Equally, the opposite is true amongst those in the last three groups who prioritise their Britishness over their Englishness.[3] Moreover, those in the "equally English and British" category are, as expected, equally likely to be proud of being English as they are British. Thanks to the countervailing pattern between the first and last three groups in the table, we find that English people as a whole are also equally divided.

Table 8.4 Pride in being British or English by national identity

	% very proud of being		
National identity	British	English	Base
Unambiguously English	39	69	253
Ambiguously English	51	64	238
More English than British	41	56	389
Equally English and British	45	46	999
More British than English	47	33	298
Ambiguously British	42	26	119
Unambiguously British	52	20	253
All	43	44	2718

What is also apparent from this table is that pride in being English is massively higher (by 49 points) among those who we classify as unambiguously English than among those we classify as unambiguously British. On the other hand,

pride in being British is only 13 points higher among those who are unambiguously British than among those who are unambiguously English. This is despite the fact nearly three in four people in England gave the same answer to the two questions, a testament to the degree to which a distinction is still not drawn between the two. But among the minority who do draw a distinction what clearly polarises them is their attitude towards being English. For some it seems to be a label of particular pride and for others something to be avoided. In contrast, being British evokes less strong feelings, which explains perhaps why so many people feel able to hold a dual identity. Indeed, even among the unambiguously English, nearly two in five are still proud of being British.

The continuing strength of British-wide loyalties is evident in the results of two questions we asked about sporting loyalties. To those outside the UK and to some within it, a continuing peculiarity of British sport is that at many international sporting events each of the four territories fields its own separate team. On occasions, therefore, a Scottish, Welsh or Northern Irish competitor or team appears in an event in which no English competitor or team is present. In this situation, people with highly exclusive loyalties might not be expected to lend their support to a British team other than their own. And, as the next table shows, only 42 per cent of the English *would* always support a Scottish team or athlete when one from England was not involved, compared to 63 per cent who always back an English team or athlete when they can. As expected, this difference is greatest amongst those who prioritise an English over a British identity, and almost disappears amongst those who are unambiguously British rather than English. But even among our unambiguously English group, over one in three would always back a Scottish team or athlete against a competitor from outside the United Kingdom (and only around one in five would never do so). So, even to the unambiguously English, Scotland is still apparently close enough to home to evoke quite a bit of loyalty.

Table 8.5 National identity and sport

National identity	% who support the following against competition from abroad		
	English team/athlete	Scottish team/athlete	Base
Unambiguously English	66	36	253
Ambiguously English	73	44	238
More English than British	74	43	389
Equally English and British	65	42	999
More British than English	64	46	298
Ambiguously British	63	51	119
Unambiguously British	53	46	235
All	63	42	2718

Attitudes towards devolution

As we have seen, there has – in the wake of devolution – been an increase in the proportion of people in England who feel 'English'. We will, of course, have to await future readings to establish whether this is the beginning of a trend or just a fluctuation. This evidence on national identity is consistent with the beginnings of an English backlash of a 'me too' variety. To the extent that English nationalism is really rising, however, we should also find a growing demand for some form of devolution for England, and therefore growing support for devolution within the UK more generally. And those who feel English rather than British should be the most likely to adopt these views.

As far as support for devolution more generally is concerned, we shall see that the vast majority of people in England have not only come to accept devolution for both Scotland and Wales, but there are even signs of growing support amongst a minority for independence for Scotland and Wales. A majority also back the idea that Northern Ireland should unify with the rest of Ireland rather than remain within the United Kingdom. And all these opinions are indeed more common amongst those who feel English rather than British.

First, we look at attitudes towards Scotland. We asked respondents to choose one from a list of five options for governing Scotland – from independence outside both the UK and the EU at one extreme, to no Scottish parliament at all at the other extreme. As the next table shows, people in England are increasingly likely to reject the notion that Scotland should be without its own parliament: only 13 per cent (down from 23 per cent only two years earlier) now take this view. So, as far as the vast majority of the English are concerned, devolution of some sort for Scotland is now a done deed, and their growing preference is for *at least* as much devolution as now exists.

Table 8.6 English preferences for governing Scotland, 1997 and 1999

	1997	1999
Scotland should ...	%	%
... be independent, separate from UK and EU	6	8
... be independent, separate from UK, but part of EU	8	16
... remain part of UK with its own elected parliament which has **some** taxation powers	38	44
... remain part of UK with its own elected parliament which has **no** taxation powers	17	10
... remain part of UK **without** an elected parliament	23	13
Base	*3150*	*2718*

Source: 1997 – British Election Study

Moreover, as the next table shows, support for outright independence for Scotland is comfortably higher among those who are unambiguously English than among any other group. Even so little more than one in eight people in England now oppose the idea of Scotland having her own parliament. A Scottish parliament appears not only to be the settled will of Scots but also of the English. As in Scotland, the only dispute appears to be about how powerful that parliament should be.

Table 8.7 Preference for governing Scotland by national identity

National identity		Preference for governing Scotland			
		Independ-ence	Devolution	No parliament	Base
Unambiguously English	%	37	42	12	253
Ambiguously English	%	26	51	12	238
More English than British	%	25	57	13	389
Equally English and British	%	23	56	14	999
More British than English	%	22	56	14	298
Ambiguously British	%	19	56	15	119
Unambiguously British	%	17	60	16	235
All	%	24	54	13	2718

Notes:
Per cent favouring "Independence" comprises both those who think that Scotland should be independent outside the EU and those who think it should be independent inside the EU
Per cent favouring "Devolution" comprises both those who think there should be a Scottish Parliament within the UK that has some taxation powers and those who think there should be such a body without taxation powers

This picture is confirmed by the results of a second question in which we asked respondents whether they would be sorry or pleased "if in the future Scotland were to become independent and leave the UK". Given the majority preference for devolution rather than independence, we would expect more people to be sorry than pleased, and that is how it turns out. As many as 40 per cent of the English would be sorry if Scotland were to leave the United Kingdom, and as few as seven per cent would be pleased. But again the views of the unambiguously English are distinctive. Just 24 per cent of them would be sorry if Scotland were to become independent and 17 per cent would be pleased. In contrast nearly half of the unambiguously British would be sorry. But perhaps the most important message to emerge from this question is that while the clear balance of opinion among the English is for Scotland to remain in the Union, the most common feeling is one of indifference: over half the English say they would be "neither pleased nor sorry" if Scotland were to become independent.

Similar results are obtained in respect of Wales. The form of devolution currently in place in Wales is, of course, more limited than in Scotland and we

adapted question wordings accordingly. But support from the English for the broad principle of Welsh devolution (or independence) is almost as high as for Scotland. As the next table shows, as many as 56 per cent believe that Wales should enjoy at least some measure of devolution, almost identical to the 54 per cent who back it for Scotland. Meanwhile one in five back independence for Wales either within or outside the European Union, compared with one in four who do so for Scotland

Moreover, as the next table shows, support for independence has risen and opposition to any form of devolved assembly has fallen, just as for Scotland.

Table 8.8 English preferences for governing Wales, 1997 and 1999

	1997	1999
Wales should ...	%	%
... be independent, separate from UK and EU	5	6
... be independent, separate from UK but part of EU	8	14
... remain part of UK, with its own elected parliament which has law-making **and** taxation powers	37	34
... remain part of UK, with its own elected assembly which has limited law-making powers **only**	18	22
... remain part of UK **without** an elected assembly	25	15
Base	*3150*	*2718*

Source: 1997 – British Election Study

Once again, support for Welsh independence is comfortably higher among the unambiguously English (32 per cent) than for any other group. Otherwise, the only difference between English attitudes towards Scotland and those towards Wales is that there is slightly greater support for a more limited form of devolution for Wales than there is in the case of Scotland, doubtless reflecting the disparity in the actual powers of the two bodies.

So, despite growing support in England for Scottish and Welsh independence, the clear preference is for them both to remain part of the Union. Indeed, in answer to another question, no less than 65 per cent of the sample agreed that "the government should do everything it can to keep all parts of Britain together in a single state". This proportion has barely changed since 1997 (when it was 63 per cent) and, even among the ambiguously English, 59 per cent take that view. So despite increases in English sympathy for devolution and even independence for Scotland and Wales, their clear preference remains that Great Britain should be kept together in one form or another.

The same cannot be said about Northern Ireland. A majority of people in England (54 per cent) believe that Northern Ireland's long-term interests lie in unifying with the rest of Ireland rather than as part of the United Kingdom.

Among the ambiguously English no less than three people in five take this view. But in contrast to views about the governance of Scotland and Wales, there is no evidence of a change in English attitudes towards Northern Ireland. The *British Social Attitudes* series has consistently found majority British backing for Irish unification ever since its first survey in 1983 (Evans, 1996; Gallagher, 1992).

 But the acid test of the existence of a 'me too' English backlash is not just a growing acceptance of Scottish and Welsh autonomy, but also some evidence that England wants something similar for itself. So far, the debate about devolution in England has been less straightforward than about Scotland and Wales and Northern Ireland. In all of these cases, the only serious option was to devolve powers to the entities as a whole. In England, however, many advocates of devolution argue that it should take the form of regional assemblies rather than just one English assembly. After all, England is a far larger entity than any of the other nations in the UK, and if the aim of devolution is to bring government closer to the people rather than just satisfy national sentiment, then regional rather than national devolution in England would seem to fit the bill rather better. So, in asking about preferences for English devolution, we employed a rather different question:

> *With all the changes going on in the way the different parts of Great Britain are run, which of the following do you think would be best for England:*
>
> *for England to be governed as it is now, with laws made by the UK parliament,*
> *for each region of England to have its own assembly that runs services like health,*
> *or,*
> *for England as a whole to have its own new parliament with law-making powers?*

As the next table shows, those who feel most English are indeed the group most likely to want some form of English devolution. As many as 43 per cent of the unambiguously English favour either the creation of an English parliament or regional assemblies. In no other group does the figure rise much above a third. Indeed, apart from the distinctive views of the unambiguously English, there are no systematic differences between the remaining groups. And overall, nearly two out of three people in England have no wish to change the way they are governed. Since this is the first time we have asked this question, we cannot rule out the possibility that, although still low, support for English devolution may have grown. Even so, well-disposed as people in England might be to the granting of devolution to the rest of the UK, they express little demand for a taste of it themselves.

Table 8.9 Attitudes towards English devolution by national identity

National identity		Devolution preference			
		None	Regional	Parliament	Base
Unambiguously English	%	54	18	25	253
Ambiguously English	%	65	10	20	238
More English than British	%	63	16	19	389
Equally English and British	%	61	17	18	999
More British than English	%	71	13	11	298
Ambiguously British	%	61	12	22	119
Unambiguously British	%	67	15	15	235
All	%	62	15	18	2718

So, despite the fact that the current devolution settlement has been portrayed as unfair to England, and despite a growing identification among people in England with their Englishness, the new arrangements for Scotland and Wales appear to be increasingly accepted by the English without hankering for similar new arrangements for themselves. In sum, there is as yet little sign of an English backlash that might threaten the stability of the Union.

The outside world

As noted, however, a rise in English national identity may have an impact on issues other than devolution. It may also promote a less inclusive attitude towards the outside world. Those who feel particularly English may, for instance, be more hostile towards further European integration and more unsympathetic to immigration and ethnic minorities.

There is considerable evidence to support this view. Consider Europe, for example. In the next table we summarise the answers to two questions, the first of which is about attitudes to the single currency and the second to Britain's relationship with Europe more generally. In each case, we show only the proportion giving the most Eurosceptic response on offer – that is "keep the pound as the **only** currency for Britain", and "Britain's long-term policy should be to leave the European Union".

Table 8.10 Attitudes towards Europe by national identity

National identity	% who prefer		
	Pound only	Leave EU	Base
Unambiguously English	73	22	253
Ambiguously English	73	17	238
More English than British	58	17	389
Equally English and British	61	13	999
More British than English	60	15	298
Ambiguously British	54	15	119
Unambiguously British	54	12	235
All	60	15	2718

In both cases, those with a strong English national identity prove to be the most Eurosceptic by a large margin. On the other hand, there seems to be no evidence that the rise in the incidence of English national identity in recent years has made England more Eurosceptic than it was. Similar proportions wanted to keep the pound (60 per cent) and to leave the European Union (17 per cent) in 1997 as do now. Even so, any further rise in a sense of Englishness is likely to make even more difficult the task faced by those who wish to persuade the British public to adopt a single currency in a referendum.

Those who adopt a particularly English national identity are also less tolerant of immigrants and ethnic minorities. As the next table shows, while around 37 per cent of the unambiguously British subscribe to the view that "immigrants take jobs away from people who were born in Britain", no less than 70 per cent of the unambiguously English do so. Similarly, the unambiguously English are considerably more likely than average to believe that "attempts to give equal opportunities to Blacks and Asians have gone too far", that ethnic minorities in England have been getting ahead more than they should, and to admit to being racially prejudiced.[4]

Table 8.11 Attitudes towards immigration and ethnic minorities by national identity

National identity	% who think:				
	Immig- rants take jobs	Bad that ethnic minorities got ahead	Equal opps. gone too far	Racially pre- judiced	Base
Unambiguously English	70	26	46	37	253
Ambiguously English	51	21	38	38	238
More English than British	48	18	39	33	389
Equally English and British	44	14	33	26	999
More British than English	36	13	32	28	298
Ambiguously British	48	14	31	26	119
Unambiguously British	37	14	26	17	235
All	44	16	34	28	2718

Notes:
Immigrants take jobs: per cent who strongly agree or agree that "immigrants take jobs away from people who were born in Britain"
Bad that ethnic minorities got ahead: per cent who think that ethnic minority groups in England have been getting ahead in the last few years and that this is a bad thing
Equal opps. gone too far: per cent who think that "attempts to give equal opportunities to blacks and Asians in Britain have gone too far or much too far"
Racially prejudiced: per cent who say they are "very or a little prejudiced against people of other races"

As if in response to these characteristics of Englishness, members of minority ethnic groups themselves are less likely to adopt an English identity as opposed to a British one. Just six per cent of those who described their ethnic origin as 'black' and seven per cent of those who said they were Asian, classify themselves either as "English, not British" or "More English than British". In contrast, as many as 36 per cent of black people and 38 per cent of Asians classify themselves as "British, not English". Of course, since less than five per cent of our sample fall into either of these two categories, these results are only indicative, but they do suggest that perhaps the apparently more exclusive character of English national identity is recognised by members of the ethnic minorities.

Some understanding of why those who feel English appear less tolerant to those whom they consider to be 'outsiders' can be gleaned from the answers to other questions that we asked – about the qualities that someone needs to have in order to be considered English. As the next table shows, those who feel English rather than British are particularly likely to believe that in order to be "truly English", a person has to satisfy certain criteria, such as being born in

England, having English parents, living in England for most of their life, and being white. This applies particularly to being born in England and having English parents, qualities which of course are inherited rather than ones that can be acquired later in life. Little wonder then that those who feel English are less tolerant of immigrants and ethnic minorities and of the European Union too.

Table 8.12 Views of being English by national identity

	% who say the following matter a great deal to being English:				
National identity	Born in England	Have English parents	Lived most of life in England	To be white	Base
Unambiguously English	51	41	32	24	253
Ambiguously English	40	36	31	18	238
More English than British	35	29	26	12	389
Equally English and British	24	21	22	8	999
More British than English	27	22	24	12	298
Ambiguously British	26	22	19	10	119
Unambiguously British	22	21	18	14	235
All	29	25	23	12	2718

Symbolism

So far we have seen an increasing sense of an English national identity without any corresponding increase in the demand for English devolution. This may change if at any point 'standing up for England's interests' were to become a salient issue of contention between the parties. And there are some signs that the Conservative Party is beginning to adopt a more specifically pro-English agenda both in the wake of devolution and in the current absence from their parliamentary ranks of Scottish and Welsh MPs.

In order to examine the potential impact such a divide might ultimately have on the electorate, we asked the sample where they thought both the Labour and the Conservative parties stood on the 'Moreno' national identity scale. As the next table shows, the Conservative Party is seen to be more 'English' than is the Labour Party. Whereas over one in three people in England regard the Conservative Party as wholly or predominantly English rather than British, fewer than one in five take that view of the Labour Party.

Table 8.13 Perceptions of political parties

View party as:	Labour	Conservative
	%	%
English, not British	9	14
More English than British	10	22
Equally English and British	35	28
More British than English	16	12
British, not English	20	16
Neither	5	4

Base: 2718

Even so, the Conservatives are not especially popular among those who feel English rather than British. Just 28 per cent of the unambiguously English identify with the Conservative Party, much the same as the 27 per cent of the English electorate who do so. True, at 36 per cent, identification with Labour was also lower among this group than in England as a whole at the time of the survey (43 per cent). So while national identity may well influence how people vote in Scotland and Wales (Brand *et al.*, 1993; Brown *et al.*, 1999; Taylor and Thomson, 1999), it apparently remains insignificant in England.

Table 8.14 Party identification by national identity

National identity		Con	Lab	Lib Dem	Other	None	Base
				Party identification			
Unambiguously English	%	28	36	13	2	16	*253*
Ambiguously English	%	24	48	9	3	12	*238*
More English than British	%	29	43	8	3	13	*389*
Equally English and British	%	25	43	11	2	14	*999*
More British than English	%	29	45	12	1	10	*298*
Ambiguously British	%	28	41	8	7	10	*119*
Unambiguously British	%	29	40	8	2	11	*235*
All	%	27	43	10	2	13	*2718*

One explanation of this is that voters tend to attribute to parties their own beliefs. For instance, the unambiguously English are more likely than others to believe that *both* the Conservative and Labour parties are themselves predominantly English. Equally, the unambiguously British are more likely to

think that both parties are British, not English. Even those who feel equally English and British are more likely to think that both parties are similarly bi-polar. In other words, there seems at present to be insufficient agreement among voters about where the parties stand on national identity for it to be a serious candidate for partisan division.

Any party that wishes to awaken English nationalism will first need to overcome this hurdle. In addition, it will probably require an ability to appeal to a number of distinctively English symbols that immediately trigger an English identity as opposed to a British one (Edelman, 1964). In order to find out whether such phenomena actually exist, we tried out six possible symbols of England rather than Britain (not all of them by any means suitable for a rallying call) and asked the sample where each of them fell on the national identity scale. As the next table shows, distinctively English symbols may well prove difficult to come by.

Table 8.15 British and English symbols

Viewed as	Royal Navy	Union Jack	Houses of Parliament	Pubs	Guy Fawkes night	Fox hunting
	%	%	%	%	%	%
English, not British	7	8	11	14	29	31
More English	8	11	19	16	24	26
Equal	32	32	27	34	21	16
More British	22	25	18	12	8	8
British, not English	27	22	22	15	11	10
Neither	2	2	2	6	4	5

Base: 2718

As far as the Union Jack and the Royal Navy are concerned, they fare reasonably as symbols of national pride, but the nation in question is Britain rather than England. Less than one in five see either of them as wholly or predominantly English. Intriguingly, the Houses of Parliament fare a little better as a mainly or wholly English symbol, being regarded as such by a rather larger minority of around one in three. Perhaps this helps to explain why so few people in England perceive a need for English devolution? Meanwhile, pubs are just as likely to be seen as a British institution as they are to be seen as an English institution, possibly because they are correctly seen to be part of the landscape of the British Isles rather than England alone.

Which leaves only Guy Fawkes night and fox hunting that are regarded by around one in three as exclusively English institutions and by absolute majorities as at least predominantly English. But fox hunting may soon be a thing of the past.

Moreover, as in the case of the political parties, those of differing identities do not share the same perceptions about how English or British these symbols are. For example, the unambiguously English are as likely to think the Union Jack is wholly English as they are to say it is wholly British. In contrast the unambiguously British are nine times more likely to regard it as wholly British than wholly English. The fact is that these symbols seem to be as capable of uniting English people with different national identities as they are of dividing them.

Conclusions

There are signs that people in England may have become more aware of being English rather than British in response to the introduction of devolution in the rest of the UK. But, even if this proves to be a permanent shift, it does not yet appear to pose any threat to the stability of the Union. Rather, it appears as if opinion in England has simply adjusted to the new *status quo*. The English seem to be comfortable with the existence of separate institutions in Scotland and Wales without wishing to set up similar arrangements in England, whether at a national or regional level. This is probably why the somewhat muted attempts by the Conservative Party to identify itself as the party of English interests have met with an even more muted response. Meanwhile the historic intertwining of English and British identities appears to have left any English nationalist campaign bereft of obvious symbols it could call its own.

Even so, we have found that those who feel English are indeed different from those who feel British, being consistently more inclined to want to shut out the outside world. Indeed, 'Little Englanders' appear to be alive and well, if not yet very thick on the ground. And though they pose little immediate threat to the success of the devolution project within the UK, they may well be more influential in thwarting plans for closer European integration.

Notes

1. Note that it might be argued that this second measure is a less reliable indicator of the extent of dual identity than the Moreno measure. Despite interviewer probing, some of those who feel both English and British might choose either at random rather than taking the trouble to name both.
2. Thus, our unambiguously English group comprises those who said they were "English, not British" on the Moreno question and then in response to our second question said that they were English and did not say there were British. (No account is taken of any other descriptions they might have given themselves on the second question.) The ambiguously English comprise those who said they were "English, not British" on the Moreno question, but either said they were British or did not say they were English in answering the second question. The unambiguously British are those who said they were "British, not English" and went on to say they were British on the second question and did not say they were English

3. Note also that the more English someone is on this scale, the greater the likelihood that they strongly agree that "I would rather live in England than in any other part of Britain". Thus 32 per cent of the unambiguously English strongly agree with this statement compared with just 16 per cent of the unambiguously British.
4. However, as in the case of attitudes towards Europe there is no apparent evidence that the rise in adherence to an English national identity has been accompanied by growing hostility towards immigrants or ethnic minorities. For example, the proportion who said that equal opportunities for blacks and Asians had gone too far was very similar in 1997 (32 per cent) to our reading now.

References

Brand, J., Mitchell, J. and Surridge, P. (1993), 'Identity and the Vote: Class and Nationality in Scotland' in Broughton, D., Denver, D., Norris, P. and Rallings, C. (eds.), *British Parties and Elections Yearbook 1993*, Hemel Hempstead: Harvester Wheatsheaf.

Brown, A., McCrone, D., Paterson, L. and Surridge, P. (1999), *The Scottish Electorate: The 1997 Election and Beyond*, London: Macmillan.

Curtice, J. (1999), 'Is Scotland a Nation and Wales not?' in Taylor, B. and Thomson, K. (eds.), *Scotland and Wales: Nations Again?*, Cardiff: University of Wales Press.

Edelman, M. (1964), *The Symbolic Uses of Politics*, Urbana: University of Illinois Press.

Evans, G. (1996), 'Northern Ireland during the ceasefire' in Jowell, R., Curtice, J., Park, A., Brook, L. and Thomson, K. (eds.), *British Social Attitudes: the 13th Report*, Aldershot: Dartmouth.

Evans, G. and Norris, P. (1999), *Critical Elections: British Parties and Voters in Long-Term Perspective*, London: Sage.

Gallagher, A. (1992), 'Community relations in Northern Ireland' in Jowell, R., Brook, L., Prior, G. and Taylor, B. (eds.), *British Social Attitudes: the 9th Report*, Aldershot: Dartmouth.

Gellner, E. (1983), *Nations and Nationalism*, Oxford: Blackwell.

Heath, A. and Kellas, J. (1998), 'Nationalisms and Constitutional Questions', *Scottish Affairs*, Special Issue on Understanding Constitutional Change, 110-27.

Heath, A., Taylor, B., Brook, L. and Park, A. (1999), 'British National Sentiment', *British Journal of Political Science*, **29**: 155-75.

Kellas, J. (1991), *The Politics of Nationalism and Ethnicity*, London: Macmillan.

King, A. (2000), 'Will there always be an England?', *Daily Telegraph*, 22 April.

McCrone, D. and Surridge, P. (1998), 'National identity and national pride' in Jowell, R., Curtice, J., Park, A., Brook, L., Thomson, K. and Bryson, C. (eds.), *British and European Social Attitudes: how Britain differs - the 15th Report*, Aldershot: Ashgate.

Moreno, L. (1988), 'Scotland and Catalonia: The Path to Home Rule' in McCrone, D. and Brown, A. (eds.), *The Scottish Government Yearbook 1988*, Edinburgh: Unit for the Study of Government in Scotland.

Paterson, L., Brown, A., Curtice, J., Hinds, K., McCrone, D., Park, A. and Surridge, P. (forthcoming), *New Scotland: New Politics?*, Edinburgh: Edinburgh University Press.

Paxman, J. (1998), *The English: A Portrait of a People*, Harmondsworth: Penguin.

Smith, A. (1981), *The Ethnic Revival*, Cambridge: Cambridge University Press.
Taylor, B. and Thomson, K. (eds.) (1999), *Scotland and Wales: Nations Again?*, Cardiff: University of Wales Press.
Wyn Jones, R. and Trystan, D. (2000), '"A Quiet Earthquake": The First Elections to the National Assembly for Wales', paper presented at the Annual Meeting of the American Political Science Association, Washington, DC.

Acknowledgements

The collection of much of the data reported in this chapter was financed by a grant from the Economic and Social Research Council R000222960 for a study of English nationalism. We are grateful to Robert Andersen for helpful comments.

9 Town and country life

Nina Stratford and Ian Christie[*]

Rural issues have had a high profile during the life of the present government. Campaign groups such as the Countryside Alliance claim that rural areas are facing unprecedented economic and social pressures, and that people living there experience poor services and high levels of deprivation. Rural discontent, centred on a severe recession in farming, has been loudly voiced in public demonstrations (with another demonstration threatened if the government fulfils its pledge to ban fox hunting before the next election). Concern has also been expressed over the demise of many village services such as shops and public transport. Recently announced plans to pay benefits directly into bank accounts are seen to threaten the viability of village post offices, and come shortly after Barclays Bank announced the closure of large numbers of its rural branches. To highlight these concerns, a new Countryside Party has just been formed which aims to put up protest candidates at the next general election.

The government has challenged the case of the countryside campaigners by publishing a controversial report (Cabinet Office, 2000) claiming that quality of life is in fact much higher in the countryside. It argues that employment rates and educational performance are higher there, poverty less prevalent, lifestyles healthier, mortality rates, risks of crime and homelessness lower. Set against this, however, is a Countryside Agency report which highlights the presence of poverty and 'social exclusion' in rural areas, problems exacerbated by the lack of affordable housing, by poor public transport and by the decline in everyday services in villages and small towns (Countryside Agency, 2000). Other studies also suggest that the countryside is full of under-recognised problems of poverty and social exclusion, these being rendered 'invisible' by the dispersion of households and the absence of the concentrated clusters of deprivation that are found in cities (Alexander *et al.*, 2000).

 [*] Nina Stratford is a Senior Researcher at the *National Centre for Social Research* and Co-director of the *British Social Attitudes* survey series. Ian Christie is Associate Director of the consultancy The Local Futures Group and an associate of Forum for the Future.

The pressure on policy makers to act on the demands of countryside campaigners has mounted, and the government has made a number of moves to respond: for example, the announcement in July 2000 of increased funding for rural community transport schemes and rural bus services, and the decision to create a 'universal bank' with services available through post offices. Meanwhile, the Countryside Agency has launched a range of initiatives to strengthen rural communities, including a programme of 'health checks' for market towns in order to spot potential danger signs concerning access to services, employment, housing, transport and loss of economic vitality (Cassell, 2000).

So the countryside campaigns of the last few years have undoubtedly made an impact on politicians and public agencies. But do the campaigners have a valid case in all respects, or are their complaints about the overall state of rural life overstated? In this chapter, we explore whether rural people are really as dissatisfied as those who claim to represent them maintain. In doing so, we will make a vital comparison with people living in urban areas. How do rural and urban people perceive their own and each other's areas and quality of life? Do they experience similar problems, or are there distinct rural problems which do not occur in urban locations (or *vice versa*)?

Of course, satisfaction or otherwise with one's area can depend on the extent to which the choice to live there was a free one. As with most other aspects of life, higher income groups have more choice over where they live, both within and between different areas. They are more likely to be able to realise a desire to live in the countryside, as the associated housing and commuting costs will be more easily within their reach. And, if they choose the city, they will be able to live in the more 'desirable' areas. Wherever they live, higher income groups will be better placed to 'buy themselves out' of any real or perceived disadvantages of their location, via private health care, schooling, transport, and so on. In other words, the affluent are able to afford a lifestyle which 'sprawls' over space – larger homes, bigger gardens, longer commuting journeys and shopping trips – while the poor are increasingly 'squeezed' spatially, more restricted in their mobility and very limited in their choices of where to live. This greater element of choice for the affluent will, we hypothesise, mean that higher income groups are more content with their area, wherever they are located; by contrast, we might expect that lower incomes and poorer choices will be associated with greater discontent, whether in town or country.

Comparing the views of urban and rural people allows us to explore whether their needs and values conflict (MacFarlane, 1998), a long-standing notion often alluded to by both campaigners and the media. Certainly, there is a sense among rural campaigners of a predominantly 'urban' government imposing national policy which does not take into account the specific needs of rural areas. Some commentators have suggested, for example, that there is a degree of conflict between urban and rural residents in terms of land use and protection issues. This position can be summarised as the tendency of urban users of the countryside to see it as a vast recreational space, whereas those who live and work there have quite different needs and expectations of the land (and will thus be more concerned than urban people with issues such as housing and jobs).

This can lead to conflict, particularly in areas concerning development and environmental protection (Mormont, 1987). We will look for evidence of this conflict in relation to countryside planning and farming policy.

In addition to a possible urban-rural divide, there may also be divisions *within* those living in the countryside. Newby (1979) has suggested that the migration of a large number of people from urban areas has resulted in conflict between such rural newcomers and rural locals. He argues that the newcomers bring with them an urban middle-class lifestyle and stereotyped expectations of village life in which the quality of the rural environment is highly valued. This leads to conflict over housing and environmental issues as the newcomers seek to preserve the area and locals seek improvements in their standard of living. If such conflict exists, it may be discovered by comparing lifetime rural residents to those who previously lived in a big city. Although not a perfect indicator, this should enable some assessment of the accuracy of Newby's analysis.

Who lives in the countryside?

Before beginning our examination of urban-rural differences we need to define what we mean by these terms. This is not straightforward, as different definitions are used for different research or administrative purposes. We base our categorisation on respondents' own views about whether they live in a rural or urban area, on the assumption that attitudes about rural issues are most likely to be linked to where people situate *themselves*. Their answers tally with the fact that Britain is an overwhelmingly urban nation – a third say they live in a big city or its suburbs and half in a small city or town. The following table shows that people's subjective view of where they live is in fact closely related to the *objective* measure of population density, taken from data about the areas respondents live in. As some of the groups are quite small, we have collapsed them into three categories: a big city or its suburbs; a small city or town; and a country village or home in the country, which will be used in tables throughout this chapter.

Table 9.1 How respondents describe the area where they live and the mean population density, 1999

	%	Mean population density*	Base
A big city	8	6,484	260
The suburbs or outskirts of a big city	24	3,298	743
A small city or town	49	2,032	1554
A country village	17	469	501
A farm or home in the country	2	141	49
Base	3143		

* persons per square kilometre

In order to explore attitudes differences between town and country, we must first examine the characteristics of people living in these areas. Otherwise, if we do find urban-rural attitude differences, we will not know whether these are simply a reflection of other urban-rural differences which are themselves linked to attitudes (such as age and income).

We start by examining whether rural people differ in simple demographic terms from the urban population. As the next table shows, the rural population is older on average. The mean age of someone living in a country village or a home in the country is 50, whereas it is 42 among big city residents. This is due to fewer young people living in rural areas (only 18 per cent are aged 18-34 compared to 31 per cent elsewhere). Country residents are more likely to be married than those elsewhere, which probably reflects their greater age, but could also be due to more traditional attitudes. Rural people are not, however, any more religious than their urban counterparts, although the prevalence of the various religions differs in urban and rural areas. Roman Catholics are more likely to be found in cities, as are those who hold a non-Christian faith. There also appear to be differences in income and standards of living. Fewer country than urban dwellers rate their income as low and they are more likely to describe their area as a 'better off part of the district'. They are also more likely to be in a higher social class, with more rural people in social class II (intermediate) and fewer in III (skilled).

As well as demographic differences, there are attitudinal differences between country and town dwellers. There is evidence of greater rural support for traditional institutions such as the House of Lords and the Monarchy, and rural people are also more likely to vote Conservative or Liberal Democrat. The more traditional values of those in rural areas are further illustrated by their considerably more restrictive views about homosexuality (only 18 per cent feel that it is "not wrong at all" compared with 30 per cent elsewhere).

Table 9.2 Characteristics of urban and rural people, 1999

	Big city or suburbs	Small city or town	Country village or home in country
Age	%	%	%
18-24	10	11	7
25-34	21	20	11
35-44	19	18	20
45-54	16	17	22
55-59	7	7	9
60-64	8	7	9
65+	19	21	22
Religion			
Church of England/Anglican	22	28	34
Roman Catholic	12	8	6
Other Christian	16	16	17
Non-Christian	6	2	1
No religion	42	46	42
Economic activity			
Education	3	3	2
Work/training	58	56	53
Unemployed/sick	9	9	6
Retired	20	20	24
Home/other	10	11	16
Base	*1003*	*1554*	*548*
Social class			
I (professional)	6	4	4
II (intermediate)	26	22	34
III (skilled)	48	48	38
IV (semi-skilled)	15	19	17
V (unskilled)	5	7	7
Base	*978*	*1527*	*530*
Self-rated income			
High	3	3	5
Middle	52	51	54
Low	45	46	40
Base	*649*	*1050*	*371*

Who would rather live where?

Stemming the flow from urban to rural areas is now an important part of Government policy on planning and regeneration. Although the decline in population seems to have been checked in some areas, there has been a steady and substantial fall in the population of our big cities. Since 1961, inner London and the other conurbations of England have lost some 1.5 million residents, a decline of over 20 per cent. People have tended to move from inner city districts to the edge of metropolitan districts, and into outer suburban or rural fringe areas. Although cities have drawn in young people, ethnic minority householders and single people, they have tended to push affluent families out into the distant suburbs and rural edges of conurbations (Champion, 1997; Rudin, 1998). In some areas loss of employment and local economic vitality has propelled the exodus, leading to the abandonment of many properties and further depression of urban neighbourhoods (Power and Mumford, 1999).

The Urban Task Force chaired by Lord Rogers has called for an 'urban renaissance' in order to stem the flow of people to rural areas and the consequent pressure on countryside and on travel services, and to help revitalise cities which are losing many affluent households (Urban Task Force, 1999). The government's Urban White Paper, due to be published in autumn 2000, aims to produce a strategy to make city living more attractive.

Our findings illustrate the problems our cities have in retaining residents, despite the billions spent in recent years on urban regeneration. Most urban people, given a free choice in the matter, would rather live elsewhere. Over one in three have a yearning for the country life, whereas a mere one in seven respondents from the countryside would like to move to more populated areas. The following table shows that only 30 per cent of big city residents would stay put, and those in the suburbs are only marginally happier (42 per cent). It is rural residents who are the most content, with seven in ten being happy to remain where they are.

Table 9.3 Where respondents would choose to live given a free choice by area of residence, 1999

	Area of residence				
	Big city	Suburbs/ outskirts of big city	Small city/ town	Country village	Farm/home in the country
% who would like to live in:	%	%	%	%	%
Big city	**30**	3	3	4	3
Suburbs/outskirts of big city	16	**42**	6	3	3
Small city or town	16	13	**48**	6	8
Country village	28	32	29	**72**	13
Farm/home in the country	6	9	14	16	**74**
Base	168	510	1014	334	36

This pattern between area of residence and the desire to move seems clear-cut, but there are many other characteristics that are also linked. Younger people, the unmarried, lower income groups, Londoners, those with no political affiliation, semi-skilled and unskilled workers, and the unemployed are all more likely to want to move. As many of these characteristics are also linked to the type of area in which people live, the relationship we observe between where they live now and where they want to live could be due to these confounding factors. However, logistic regression (see model 1 in the appendix to this chapter for full details) confirms that, even when these other factors are taken into account, the type of area within which a person lives is an important factor in explaining whether or not they want to move. In fact, the odds of big city dwellers wanting to move elsewhere are nearly six times greater than those for people who live in a village or home in the country.

Quality of life and problems in the countryside

There has been much recent debate over the problems faced by rural areas. Campaign groups, such as the Countryside Alliance, accuse the government of failing to understand the depth of the problems facing rural communities (Countryside Alliance, 1999a). They have been contradicted by the Prime Minister himself, who has argued in a speech to farmers that although many parts of the farming industry are in crisis, the countryside as a whole is not (Engel, 2000). Added to this, as we have already seen, is the fact that urban dwellers find the countryside more compelling than the towns and cities in which they currently live. So we turn now to examine rural and urban dwellers' views of their surroundings. Do those in the countryside experience rural life as problematic? Importantly, do their problems differ from those experienced in urban areas, or do rural and urban people share more troubles than is commonly supposed?

The economy

The unemployment rate among our rural respondents (two per cent) is half that of those in big cities (five per cent). However, rural economic inactivity rates are higher, with both retirement and 'looking after the home' being more common in these areas. Thus, the smaller proportion unemployed might be compensated for by more hidden joblessness. The proportion with a job is similar in all areas, ranging from 53 to 57 per cent.

The same proportion everywhere (15 to 17 per cent) are finding it difficult to cope on their present income, although rural people are less likely to see themselves as belonging to a low income group (40 per cent) than those living in towns or big cities (46 per cent and 45 per cent respectively). Taken with the employment data above, this does not support the assertion that rural areas have worse economic problems in general than do urban ones.

It is striking that those country residents who have previously lived in a big city (they are either newcomers or returned migrants) are much better off than rural residents who have never done so. None of the latter place themselves in a high income group, compared to 14 per cent of city migrants to the country. In addition, 43 per cent of city migrants live "comfortably" on their income, compared with 34 per cent of country residents with no experience of urban living. Logistic regression confirms that location history is a predictor of high income, independent of occupational, class and educational differences.

Access to services

One concern of countryside campaigners that appears justified is that rural people have less easy access to a range of vital services, most notably medical and shopping facilities.[1] The next table shows the proportion who live within a 15-minute walk of various services. Without exception, those living in urban areas have greater access to these facilities, but – that said – most of the differences are only in the region of five to ten percentage points. Rural people are greatly disadvantaged in their access to a doctor, with only two-thirds living this near to one, compared to almost all urban residents. They are also much less likely to have a supermarket this close at hand (only one in three doing so, compared to eight out of ten urban residents).[2]

Table 9.4 Access to facilities by area of residence, 1999

	Big city or suburbs	Small city or town	Country village or home in country	Total
% who have the following within 15-minute walk				
Public transport stop	97	97	89	94
Small shop	96	95	84	92
Pub/bar/restaurant	93	94	88	92
Primary school	94	92	82	90
NHS doctor	92	85	66	83
Supermarket	82	81	33	72
Base	*678*	*1014*	*370*	*2083*

It should not be assumed that lack of proximity to services is always experienced as problematic by rural people. Rather, they may accept this as an inevitable part of rural life, and car ownership (which is, after all, higher in rural areas) may lessen or remove the disadvantage altogether. This interpretation is backed up by responses to questions asking people whether they thought it

important to have these sorts of services nearby. This shows that nearly two-thirds (64 per cent) of rural residents without a nearby GP did *not* rate this as important, and 72 per cent with no local supermarket felt the same about this. By contrast, people in inner cities without such services are much less happy about it: 60 per cent of those with no nearby GP do rate this as important, and 57 per cent with no supermarket feel similarly about this.

Traffic problems

We might expect urban and rural dwellers to differ in their experience of traffic problems. In fact, rural people do not see traffic as a more or less serious problem than those living in urban areas. Regardless of where they live, 73 per cent think that "the amount of traffic on the roads is one of the most serious problems for Britain", and 86 per cent think that this will be true within the next 20 years or so.

The next table considers more specific traffic problems, making reference to problems located in towns and cities, and in the countryside, and asking whether they personally pose a serious problem to respondents. Over seven in ten perceive exhaust fumes and traffic congestion in towns and cities as problematic to them. It is not surprising that we find that big city dwellers are more concerned about these urban problems than those living in rural areas (although they are the two top causes of concern for all, irrespective of area of residence). Rural people, on the other hand, see increased traffic on country roads and congestion at popular countryside sites as a bigger problem for them, presumably because they encounter it more frequently. Motorway congestion was viewed as problematic by only one in three with people from cities being more likely to take this view than those from the country.

Table 9.5 Traffic problems by area of residence, 1999

% saying the following is a serious problem for them	Big city or suburbs	Small city or town	Country village/ home in country	Total
Exhaust fumes from traffic in towns and cities	82	73	70	75
Traffic congestion in towns and cities	77	69	68	71
Increased traffic on country roads and lanes	37	41	58	43
Traffic congestion at popular places in the countryside	39	40	60	43
Congestion on motorways	45	30	37	36
Base	*324*	*510*	*191*	*1031*

Since these questions were first asked in 1997, there has been little change in attitudes except for a small increase in the feeling that rural traffic and motorway congestion are serious problems. Rural traffic has been increasing at a greater rate than in urban areas and traffic growth has been most pronounced of all on motorways (DETR, 1998; Macafee, 2000) so this change in opinion is not unexpected.

Housing

Since large numbers of people started to migrate to rural areas in the 1950s, there have been complaints of a shortage of affordable housing. Newby (1979) argues that wealthy newcomers push up prices beyond the reach of most locals and then, to add insult to injury, oppose new housing schemes on the grounds that they spoil the rural nature of the area. These ideas are now commonplace in reporting of the housing problems facing rural citizens as more in-migration by affluent people from the cities takes place. Unfortunately, we cannot address this here directly by examining urban-rural differences in perceptions of house prices, but we can examine whether there are urban-rural differences in the availability of affordable places to *rent*. We find that less than a quarter (23 per cent) of country dwellers think there is enough affordable privately-rented housing in their area, compared to 29-30 per cent of urban residents. Country dwellers are also less likely to think there is enough affordable *council* housing (23 per cent compared to 27-29 per cent of urban people). As social housing accounts for only 14 per cent of the total housing stock in rural districts, as opposed to 23 per cent in urban ones (Cabinet Office, 2000), this perception is not surprising. However, the differences in opinion are small – the poor supply of affordable rented housing is regarded as a problem *everywhere*, and only slightly more so in rural areas than in urban ones.

Quality of the local area

The government has argued that quality of life is higher in rural areas. Much of the debate sparked by the Urban Task Force report (Caplin and Falk, 2000) centred around the perception by many that cities can be risky, poorly maintained and unhealthy areas with a low quality of life. By contrast, it was argued, rural areas are regarded by many as more reassuring and healthy places for families. To assess whether these views are commonplace, we asked respondents whether they agreed or disagreed with a list of statements about living in the countryside or a country village, compared to living in a town or city. The next table shows that, in many respects, most people view the countryside very positively indeed. Substantial majorities agree that it "provides a healthier environment to live in", that it "is a better place to bring up children", that "there is more community spirit" and perhaps linked to this, "there is less crime in the countryside". Very few agree that life there is "very boring". On the other hand, most people also believe that there are some

drawbacks to rural living, namely that "if you live in the countryside, you are more likely to need a car to get around", that "it is harder to get a good job" and "it is more expensive".

For most of the statements, there is a good deal of agreement between rural and urban residents, although those who live in the countryside are more likely to defend it against the claim that it is harder to get a good job, and that it is boring. They also stress its positive features, being more likely to think that the schools and environment are better, that it is more suited to bringing up children, and that there is more of a sense of community. There is little evidence here that rural people are more dissatisfied with their overall quality of life than townspeople, except perhaps with employment opportunities and access to transport (which we return to later in this chapter).

Table 9.6 Advantages and disadvantages of living in the countryside by area of residence, 1999

	Big city or suburbs	Small city or town	Country village or home in country	Total
% who agree				
Positive statements				
Healthier environment to live in	89	91	94	91
Better place to bring up children	67	69	88	72
More community spirit	63	64	70	65
Less crime	59	60	62	60
Schools tend to be better	27	34	42	33
Negative statements				
More likely to need a car	93	92	95	93
Harder to get a good job	62	62	57	61
More expensive	43	57	52	52
Very boring	13	10	6	10
Base	*505*	*816*	*317*	*1646*

The view that the countryside is a better place to bring up children is held particularly keenly by those who themselves want to move to the country, 79 per cent of whom think it has this advantage (compared to only 58 per cent and 62 per cent of those who want to stay in a big city or small town). This is in line again with much recent debate on trends in city living: while much new housing and leisure facilities in London and other big cities are designed to attract affluent single people (converted Docklands 'lofts', for example), there is much to deter families and those planning one (high costs of family-sized homes, lack of green space, traffic congestion and fumes, crime rates, perceived lack of 'good schools'). Policy makers concerned to keep people in our cities need to

think carefully about why people do not consider them suitable places for children.

So far we have found that the countryside is clearly seen as advantageous in a number of respects, and that it contains much to attract city dwellers. But we have not yet considered the factors that might 'push' urban residents towards a more rural environment, and it is to this that we now turn.

It is clear that certain social problems are more visible in urban areas, and this is strikingly demonstrated by the proportion of people who have come across someone begging in the last four weeks. Sixty-one per cent of big city dwellers had done so, compared to 43 per cent of small town and city residents and 39 per cent of rural residents.[3] It seems plausible that the greater visibility of problems such as begging might contribute to a perception that city society is afflicted by social decay and disturbing or personally threatening problems. Of course, this might be at odds with the *facts* of city life overall, but it is the subjective impression that counts when people weigh up the pros and cons of remaining in a city, especially when family life is the issue.

Further strong evidence for this is found in the 1998 *British Social Attitudes* survey, which included a series of questions about problems people may encounter in their local area. For almost everything mentioned, those in urban areas saw it as a greater problem than did rural residents. Thus, substantial minorities of those living in big cities (and to a lesser extent small cities and towns) feel that a wide variety of low-level social disorder and crime is common in their area, the most widespread being groups of teenagers hanging around, rubbish, car theft and burglary, drug-dealing, vandalism, poor maintenance of homes, and graffiti. This points to the importance for urban policy of dealing with the perception that certain areas are not cared for, or are becoming threatening. It also demonstrates the importance of tackling the evidence of decay and poor maintenance of the 'streetscape' in order to reassure residents and foster pride and confidence in urban neighbourhoods (Worpole, 2000.)

Table 9.7 Problems in respondents' local area by area of residence, 1998

	Big city or suburbs	Small city or town	Country village or home in country	Total
% saying "very" or "fairly common" in their area				
Teenagers hanging around on the streets	48	44	35	43
Rubbish and litter lying about	46	43	24	39
Cars broken into or stolen	44	33	23	35
Homes broken into	38	26	20	29
People dealing in illegal drugs	28	24	18	24
Vandalism and deliberate damage to property	24	25	13	22
Homes and gardens in bad condition	24	17	7	17
Graffiti on walls and buildings	23	14	6	15
Noisy neighbours or loud parties	14	16	7	14
Drunks or tramps on the streets	14	13	5	12
People attacked in the streets	10	7	3	7
Insults or attacks to do with someone's race or colour	5	5	3	4
Base	*343*	*511*	*202*	*1075*

Urban people are also not as satisfied as rural ones with certain local services. Only one in five (21 per cent) of those in big cities declare themselves "very satisfied" with local doctors, compared with a third (32 per cent) of rural residents. Rural people are also more content with other aspects of medical services, including inpatient, outpatient and accident and emergency services. This might merely reflect the older age profile of the rural population, as older people in general are more satisfied with NHS services than younger ones (Bryson and Jarvis, 2000). However, when age (and other key urban-rural differences) are taken into account, location continues to matter – though age is the most important predictor of satisfaction with local doctors.

The importance of income

In our introduction, we hypothesised that *income* might be a more important determinant of people's attitudes than their location. In particular, we predicted that higher income groups would be happier with their location wherever they lived, as they could afford to take measures to overcome any problems with their area. We will now examine the evidence for this, our basic question being

whether higher income groups are more positive about their location than lower income groups – regardless of the type of area they live in. For simplicity, the following table compares the proportion in the highest and lowest income groups in the most urban and rural areas who perceive various problems with their area.

Table 9.8 Problems in respondents' local area by annual household income and area of residence, 1998

% saying the following are "very" or "fairly common" in their area	Big city/ suburbs	Base	Country village/ home in country	Base
Rubbish and litter				
Lowest income	48	132	33	66
Highest income	36	77	19	46
Cars broken into or stolen				
Lowest income	50	132	30	66
Highest income	38	77	21	46
Homes broken into				
Lowest income	44	132	18	66
Highest income	31	77	23	46
Vandalism/deliberate damage				
Lowest income	30	132	16	66
Highest income	16	77	11	46
Homes in bad condition				
Lowest income	36	132	7	66
Highest income	13	77	9	46
Graffiti				
Lowest income	26	132	12	66
Highest income	15	77	4	46
Noisy neighbours/parties				
Lowest income	19	132	11	66
Highest income	9	77	10	46
People attacked in the streets				
Lowest income	15	132	7	66
Highest income	5	77	4	46

Lowest income = less than £12,000 per year; highest income = £29,000 per year or more

In both big city areas and rural areas, there are differences in the level of problems encountered by different income groups. The prevalence of vandalism, graffiti, homes in bad condition, noisy neighbours, and attacks perceived in urban areas by the least well-off is two to three times that reported by the most affluent. In rural areas, the wealthiest also experience fewer problems than the least well-off, but the disparity is less pronounced, with fewer

items showing a large difference.[4] The table also shows that urban dwellers remain more likely to experience problems than rural ones, even when we take urban-rural differences in income into account. So, for example, among those on the lowest income, 48 per cent of those living in big cities say that rubbish and litter are common in their area compared with 33 per cent of those in the countryside. Similarly, higher earners living in cities are almost twice as likely as those in the country to perceive rubbish as a problem (39 per cent and 19 per cent respectively).

A multiple regression model (see model 2 in the appendix to this chapter) shows that location and income each bear a separate relationship to the number of problems perceived as "very" or "fairly common". Whatever their income, those who live in a big city, its suburbs or a small city or town, are all more likely to experience problems than those who live in the countryside. And wherever they live, those with the highest incomes are less likely to perceive problems than those with the lowest incomes. The model reveals that where a person lives makes a bigger contribution than income in predicting the number of problems they perceive. Age emerges as the most important predictor, with the older the respondent, the less likely they are to observe these problems.

Table 9.9 Perception of services and opportunities in local area by annual household income and area of residence, 1998

% saying the following is better than average in their area	Big city/ suburbs	Base	Country village/ home in country	Base
Public transport				
Lowest income	36	132	11	66
Highest income	24	77	4	46
Schools				
Lowest income	16	132	40	66
Highest income	42	77	57	46
Job chances				
Lowest income	11	132	19	66
Highest income	32	77	37	46
Place to bring up children				
Lowest income	37	132	58	66
Highest income	58	77	83	46

Lowest income = less than £12,000 per year; highest income = £29,000 per year or more

Location and income are also linked to people's happiness with the access their area gives them to important life chances. As the table above shows rural residents are more positive than urban dwellers about all aspects of their area, apart from the public transport system. For example, the urban-rural gap in appreciation of schools is 24 percentage points for those in the lowest income

group and 15 percentage points for those in the highest income group. And, once again, income also matters, with the less affluent being much more critical than those on higher incomes of their area, be this in terms of its schools, its suitability as a place to bring up children, or the chances of someone living there getting a job interview.

Does the greater rate of 'area' problems experienced by lower income groups lead them to think that 'the grass is greener' in other types of area? The most sensitive indicator we have of this is whether, given a free choice, people would choose to stay where they are. If our hypothesis is correct, we should find that the better off would rather stay put, whether in a rural or urban location, and that the less affluent would rather move. Looking again at the regression model 1 in the appendix to this chapter we see this is confirmed. Wherever they live, people with the lowest incomes are twice as likely to want to move to a different type of area than the highest earners.

Countryside policy

We have so far shown that there is a clear urban-rural divide, with those in urban areas perceiving their quality of life and local area in a more negative light than rural residents. Next, we consider whether there is a similar division when it comes to attitudes. There tends to be a perception among countryside campaign groups that rural policy is imposed on the countryside by urban-based politicians who do not understand its problems. According to campaigners such as Nigel Burke, "the government's view of the countryside is a view through the windows of a Jaguar in the bus lane of a motorway" (Countryside Alliance, 1999b). But do such deep urban-rural divisions over countryside policy exist, with urban people generally backing government policy in the face of rural opposition? The major issue that is exercising campaigners at present is the banning of hunting with hounds, but unfortunately the survey did not cover this. However, we are able to explore several other areas of countryside policy.

Planning and development

If there is urban-rural conflict over countryside policy then it should be particularly apparent when it comes to planning and development. Building homes and developing industry in rural areas may be seen as beneficial by residents as this provides goods which, as we have shown, are perceived to be in short supply. However, urban people may see such developments as detrimental, believing them to degrade the rural environment. Migrants from the cities to the countryside may hold this view particularly strongly, as they have made a considerable effort to take advantage of the rural environment and are unlikely to welcome a new housing estate or business park obscuring their view.

These issues were explored in the *British Social Attitudes* survey by two questions asking respondents to choose which of two statements came closer to their view:

Industry should be prevented from causing damage to the countryside, even if this sometimes leads to higher prices,
or,
Industry should keep prices down, even if this sometimes causes damage to the countryside

The countryside should be protected from development, even if this sometimes leads to fewer new jobs,
or,
New jobs should be created, even if this sometimes causes damage to the countryside

Contrary to the hypothesis outlined previously, rural and urban residents have identical views about this. Between 87 per cent and 89 per cent in all areas agree that industry should be prevented from damaging the countryside, and 74 to 75 per cent agree that the countryside should be protected from development. There are no signs here that rural and urban people perceive their interests to differ in relation to countryside development. This said, we have already seen that rural dwellers are more aware than urban residents of a shortage of rented housing – perhaps their views differ more when we ask directly about building housing in rural areas? But here too there are few differences. We asked whether "new housing should be built in cities, towns and villages rather than in the countryside": 72 to 74 per cent in all areas agree with this. A similar proportion (78 to 82 per cent) agree that "it is more important to keep green-belt areas than to build new homes there". Indeed, people living in the countryside are actually *more* opposed than city dwellers to relaxing planning laws "so that people who want to live in the countryside may do so".

The only indication that urban people are more protectionist comes from a question which specifically pits countryside protection against the ability of rural people to make a living. Rural residents are more likely to agree that "people should worry less about protecting the countryside, and more about those who have to make their living there" than those who live in a big city (26 per cent compared with 19 per cent). However, although statistically significant, this difference is small and the most common position for all groups is disagreement with this statement (42 to 43 per cent).

Given the evidence from these questions, the idea that there is much urban-rural conflict over planning and development does not seem plausible. However, despite this, we do find evidence of conflict between 'newcomers' to the countryside and rural 'locals', as predicted. The next table shows that rural residents who have previously lived in a big city are considerably more protectionist than those who have never done so. This is particularly evident with attitudes towards relaxing planning restrictions, which 37 per cent of 'locals' agree with, compared to only 19 per cent of 'newcomers'.

Table 9.10 Attitudes to development in the countryside among rural residents by residential history, 1999

	Never lived in big city	Has lived in big city
% who agree		
Industry should be prevented from causing damage to the countryside, even if this sometimes leads to higher prices	84	94
The countryside should be protected from development, even if this sometimes leads to fewer new jobs	73	76
New housing should be built in cities, towns and villages rather than in the countryside	69	81
It is more important to keep green-belt areas than to build new homes there	77	87
Planning laws should be relaxed so that people who want to live in the countryside may do so	37	19
Base	162	155

This difference between 'newcomers' and 'locals' may, however, reflect their different socio-economic characteristics. In particular, rural residents who have lived in a big city are older than those who have not, and are also more highly educated, better-off and belong to a higher social class. So it is possible that the distinctiveness of their attitudes could be linked to these other characteristics, rather than the fact that they previously lived in a city. Perhaps, we have uncovered not so much an urban-rural divide as an age and social class one? To test this, we ran logistic regression models for each of the questions shown in Table 9.9 (see models 3a, 3b, 4, 5 and 6 in the appendix to this chapter). In most cases whether a person was a local or a newcomer was *not* significant once the socio-economic differences between these groups were taken into account. The exception relates to whether or not house-building should be restricted to already built-up areas. Here migrants from big cities proved more likely than average to support restrictions, and rural 'locals' less likely (see model 4).

Farmers and farming

Britain's rural landscape is predominantly a farmed one, and so its appearance depends to a large extent on what farmers do. Rural and urban people may have different expectations of farmers and the priority they should place on looking after the countryside. Most people are content for farmers to have a central role in the countryside – only 29 per cent agree that "compared with other users of the countryside, farmers have too much say", and as many as 77 per cent feel that "farmers do a good job in looking after the countryside". However, most

feel that modern methods of farming have caused damage to the countryside, and, as the next table shows, this perception has increased since the question was first asked in 1985.

Support has increased for farming policies that treat countryside protection as a priority. In 1999, 56 per cent agree with the policy of re-allocating some farming subsidies to pay for countryside protection, even if this results in higher prices. In 1985, this was only 47 per cent. Similarly, people are now much less keen on farmers prioritising food production over looking after the countryside. In 1985, 53 per cent agreed that if farmers had to choose, they should produce more food rather than looking after the countryside. Now only 31 per cent do so.

Table 9.11 Attitudes to farmers and farming, 1985-1999

	1985	1986	1987	1989	1991	1994	1999
% who agree							
Modern methods of farming have caused damage to the countryside	63	63	68	72	71	71	69
All things considered, farmers do a good job in looking after the countryside	75	78	74	72	-	74	77
Government should withhold some subsidies from farmers and use them to protect the countryside, even if this leads to higher prices	47	49	51	60	-	54	56
If farmers have to choose between producing more food and looking after the countryside, they should produce more food	53	45	36	36	37	34	31
Base	*1530*	*1321*	*1212*	*1297*	*1224*	*975*	*1646*

There is no evidence that the views of those living in towns and cities differ from those living in the countryside when it comes to farming. So there is little evidence of an 'urban' government forcing farming policies onto rural areas and failing to take into account their different attitudes and experiences. Both urban and rural residents are equally likely to agree that modern farming methods have damaged the countryside, or to feel that government should use farm subsidies to protect it.

However, when we compare rural 'locals' and urban migrants to rural areas, we observe a similar pattern as found with views on development. Once again, rural residents who have lived in a big city are more likely to support countryside protection than those who have never done so.

Table 9.12 Attitudes to farming and countryside protection among rural residents by residential history, 1999

	Never lived in big city	Has lived in big city
% who agree		
Modern methods of farming have caused damage to the countryside	64	75
All things considered, farmers do a good job in looking after the countryside	76	70
Government should withhold some subsidies from farmers and use them to protect the countryside, even if this leads to higher prices	54	62
If farmers have to choose between producing more food and looking after the countryside, they should produce more food	33	23
Base	*162*	*155*

Transport choices

Transport policy has gained steadily in prominence over the government's lifetime. This reflects both the increase in demand for road and rail use as the economy has grown, and historic failures of maintenance of the infrastructure – as recognised by government in *Transport 2010 – The 10 Year Plan* (DETR, 2000), which envisages expenditure of some £180 billion over the next decade on rail, roads and public transport. Opinion polls suggest that public discontent with the state of transport in general has grown. We have already seen that access to public transport is regarded as less convenient in rural areas than in cities and towns, and that there is a strong perception overall that living in the countryside makes car use essential. We now investigate whether there are other major differences between the perceptions of rural and urban citizens in relation to transport.

One reason we might expect rural and urban residents to differ in this respect is that levels of car ownership and access are higher in the countryside: just 11 per cent say they do not have use of a car, compared with 20 per cent in cities, towns and suburbs. Country dwellers are more likely also to own two or three cars than are those in cities, reflecting both the affluence of many rural households and also the greater dependence of families on cars given the lower

availability of public transport services. Consequently, it is not surprising to find that 80 per cent of rural respondents say that they drive a car these days, compared to just 65 per cent of those who live in cities or suburbs. And while 38 per cent of respondents in big cities say they drive a car every day or nearly every day, for rural residents the proportion is 58 per cent.

These differences are reflected in the extent to which people use public transport services. Sixty per cent of rural respondents say they *never* travel by bus nowadays, compared to only 33 per cent of big city residents. And the great divide between urban and rural rail provision is reflected in the findings on use of train services. While 34 per cent of people in cities and suburbs say they never use the train nowadays, the proportion for country dwellers is 49 per cent. However, there are few differences between urban and rural residents in the number of journeys they make by bicycle or on foot. Urban dwellers (79 per cent) are slightly more likely to say they never cycle than rural people (72 per cent), and when it comes to taking a 15-minute walk every or nearly every day, the proportion doing so is around one-third in both cases.

Reducing car dependence

These are problematic results for a government which is concerned with reducing dependence on cars and increasing the proportion of journeys by rail, bus, bike and foot. Much of the government's long-term strategy for transport will depend on new measures to improve the attractiveness of public transport (this acting as a 'carrot' to tempt people towards the services), as well as on 'stick' measures to make driving a car more expensive. Previous editions of *British Social Attitudes* have shown respondents to agree that there is a need for radical measures of both the carrot and stick kind to tackle transport problems in general. However, we have also found that people are much less likely to favour any particular measures which would hit their purses and wallets and make car use less convenient (Christie and Jarvis, 1999). What then do rural and urban respondents feel about different policy options for reducing car dependence, particularly in light of the greater car dependence in rural areas?

Much depends on how important people feel that access to a car is for their daily lives. On the basis of our earlier results, we might expect that attachment to cars would be stronger in rural areas than in cities, towns and suburbs. To investigate this, we asked how inconvenient respondents would find it if they had to give up half their regular car trips. Surprisingly, the differences between urban and rural respondents are not significant. In every category of residential location, at most 10 per cent of respondents say it would be "not at all" or "not very inconvenient" to reduce their car use by half, and two-thirds or more say it would be "very inconvenient". Similarly, when asked about cutting a quarter of their car trips, respondents in rural and urban areas do not differ although obviously this reduction is thought to be less inconvenient. Around a half in all areas thought it would be "very inconvenient" but fewer than one in five thought it would be "not at all" or "not very inconvenient". However, the fact that those in the countryside are more likely to use a car in the first place does

mean that a higher proportion of rural residents than urban ones would be inconvenienced were they to reduce their use in this way.

Table 9.13 Impact of reducing car trips by half by area of residence, 1999

	Big city or suburbs	Small city or town	Country village or home in country	Total
	%	%	%	%
Not at all inconvenient	2	2	1	2
Not very inconvenient	5	8	6	7
Fairly inconvenient	20	20	19	20
Very inconvenient	71	68	74	70
Base	118	209	96	428

So dependence on cars is high everywhere. But are there urban-rural differences in how people feel about the various measures which have been canvassed as ways of reducing road congestion and promoting more use of alternatives to the car? Certainly, people in rural and urban areas alike agree on the importance of reducing car use and improving public transport. In all residential categories, over two-thirds agree that it is "very" or "fairly important" to cut down on car use. And an overwhelming majority in both urban and rural categories agrees that it is important to improve public transport. More than 90 per cent in all areas take this view, and the great majority see improving public transport as "very" rather than just "fairly" important.

At the same time, however, resistance to measures which would make life harder for motorists, as opposed to those making life easier for public transport users, is strong, especially among rural people. Only eight per cent of country dwellers agree that car users should pay higher taxes, whereas almost twice as many in urban areas agree with the proposition. Rural residents are also more likely to oppose increased taxes on car users (77 per cent) than big city residents (65 per cent).

Table 9.14 Attitudes to making car users pay higher taxes for the sake of the environment by area of residence, 1999

	Big city or suburbs	Small city or town	Country village or home in country	Total
	%	%	%	%
Agree strongly	4	2	2	3
Agree	11	7	6	8
Neither agree nor disagree	17	18	14	17
Disagree	39	45	44	43
Disagree strongly	27	24	32	26
Base	*234*	*413*	*162*	*813*

People living in the countryside are more likely to oppose most of the ways suggested of raising money for public transport shown in the next table (although not all of the differences are significant). This greater rural opposition is particularly pronounced with regard to cutting spending on new or existing roads, and taxing employers for car parking spaces. By contrast, fewer than half of big city dwellers oppose these two measures.

Once again, however, we must bear in mind the different characteristics of those living in urban and rural areas. In particular, we must take into account the higher rates of car ownership and use in the countryside. This is confirmed by logistic regression models which show that, once differences in car ownership and use are taken into account, the urban-rural divide in attitudes shown in the next table vanishes. The only exception relates to taxing employers for car parking – here rural dwellers remained more opposed than urban residents, even when these differences are taken into account, presumably because they are more dependent on cars for commuting to work (see model 7 in the appendix to this chapter).

Table 9.15 Ways of raising money to improve public transport by area of residence, 1999

	Big city/ suburbs	Small city/ town	Country village/home in country	Total
% who oppose	%	%	%	%
Doubling the cost of petrol	75	72	83	75
Cutting in half maintenance of existing roads	71	75	83	75
Increasing taxes like VAT	72	68	77	71
Increasing road tax for all vehicles	67	68	75	69
£2 peak-time city centre tolls	55	60	54	57
£1 motorway tolls	50	58	56	55
Cutting in half spending on new roads	47	55	61	54
Taxing employers for car parking spaces	40	54	54	50
Base	234	413	162	813

Sticks and carrots

On the basis of previous *British Social Attitudes* survey results, we expect that people will be much more likely to approve of measures which offer 'carrots' to tempt drivers out of their cars than policies which are perceived to penalise them. However, conventional political wisdom, and our previous survey experience, also suggest that while people approve of *others* cutting their car use as a result of improved access to more attractive public transport, they are less likely to say they would use public transport far more themselves. But do urban and rural people differ in this respect? To assess this, we asked about attitudes to a variety of both carrot and stick measures that could be introduced by central and local government:

> *I am going to read out some of the things that might get people to **cut down** on the number of car journeys they take. For each one, please tell me what effect, if any, this might have on how much **you yourself** use the car to get about*

The next table shows the proportions in urban and rural areas saying that they would use their car "quite a bit less" or give it up altogether in response to each measure. Perhaps surprisingly, there are no significant differences in urban and rural responses. In both cases, there is a very high level of perceived dependence on the car, and resistance to 'stick' measures to reduce this. The message for policy-makers would seem to be that either we need to rely on

long-term improvements to public transport to make marginal differences to transport patterns, or that there will need to be much more leadership of public debate on the issues and more exploration of alternatives to reducing car use which do not depend only on public transport.

Table 9.16 Impact of different transport policies on own car use by area of residence, 1999

% who say would use car "quite a bit less" or "give up using car"	Big city/ suburbs	Small city/ town	Country village/home in country	Total
'Stick measures'				
Doubling the cost of petrol	34	32	29	32
£2 peak-time city centre tolls	28	30	33	30
Severe parking penalties	21	24	23	23
£1 motorway tolls	17	21	23	20
'Carrot measures'				
Halving long distance rail and coach fares	37	33	38	35
Improving the reliability of local public transport	34	32	34	33
Halving local public transport fares	34	28	33	30
Improving long-distance rail and coach services	28	24	25	25
Special cycle lanes on roads	15	14	15	14
Base	*182*	*300*	*133*	*620*
Free school bus service*	20	32	33	28
Base	*47*	*69*	*37*	*155*

* This question was asked only of those with school-age children in the household

Conclusions

A major message coming from our sample of urban respondents is that they perceive themselves as having a much worse deal than do those living in rural areas. They report that they are less affluent, that low level disorder, acquisitive and violent crime are more common in their area, and that their locality is not such a good place to bring up children. They are also less satisfied with local services such as schools and health facilities. And both urban and rural people agree that the most serious traffic problems are to be found in urban areas.

That is not to say that people in rural areas do not have problems too. They have less easy access to a range of local services, perceive more of a shortage of

affordable rented housing and find rural traffic congestion more problematic. However, it seems that overall they do not consider these problems serious enough to want to move. The fact that rural people obviously view alternative locations as worse, whereas urban residents view them as better is telling. Consequently, the *British Social Attitudes* survey provides little evidence for the claims of countryside campaigners that there is a generalised rural crisis. Rather, there is a general crisis of attitudes towards the cities: most people regard them as offering a lower quality of life than the countryside.

This suggests that the nature of the much-debated division between town and country is more complex than suggested by the controversies sparked by the Countryside Alliance. Although its campaigners see urban interests dominating those of rural dwellers, our results indicate that there is little evidence of urban interests and preferences being imposed upon the rural minority. When it comes to attitudes towards the countryside and its management, urban and rural residents are more united than divided.

There is a substantial divide between the affluent and the poor, in city and countryside alike: wherever they live, unsurprisingly, the affluent feel they have a better quality of life and are less likely to wish to move, regardless of location. The importance of income cuts across the urban-rural divide, with the urban poor seeming to experience the most problems with their local area and the services and opportunities it offers. This does not so much indicate a division between town and country as point to the shared problems of the 'socially excluded' wherever the area, although policies for poor urban neighbourhoods may well need to be designed very differently from those for the more dispersed 'excluded' households in rural areas.

None of this should detract attention from the real problems of service provision, housing and transport experienced by the poor in the countryside. But it does put the problems of rural exclusion and quality of life in perspective. For all the campaigning efforts of the Countryside Alliance, the issues it raises seem to be less pressing for the majority of citizens, rural and urban alike, than those highlighted by the Urban Task Force. Perhaps the UK now needs an Urban Alliance to march on Whitehall and Westminster?

Notes

1. Although not covered by this survey, other evidence points to declining access to other vital services such as post offices and banks, in rural areas.
2. It is worth noting that although 89 per cent of rural people said they were within a 15-minute walk of a public transport stop, this does not necessarily mean thay have a frequent or peak-time service. Only 16 per cent of rural households have access to a bus service operating at least every half-hour (Countryside Agency, 2000).
3. It is likely that many of the encounters rural people have with beggars actually take place in urban areas – they were simply asked whether they had come across anyone in Britain begging in the last four weeks.
4. Due to the small sample size involved, none of the differences observed among rural people here are statistically significant. However, as with the urban respondents,

almost all of the differences are in the same direction, with the higher income group perceiving fewer problems than the lower income group.

References

Alexander, D., Dix, M. and Stratford, P. (2000), 'Planning policies for rural social exclusion', *Town and Country Planning*, April 2000.

Bryson, C. and Jarvis, L. (2000), *Trends in Attitudes to Health Care 1983-1998: Report based on results from the British Social Attitudes surveys*, London: National Centre for Social Research.

Cabinet Office (2000), *Sharing the Nation's Prosperity, Economic, Social and Environmental Conditions in the Countryside*, London: Cabinet Office.

Caplin, E. and Falk, N. (2000), *My Kind of Town?*, London: Building Centre Trust.

Cassell, D. (2000), 'Market forces', *New Start*, Vol. 2, **70**: 21 July 2000.

Champion, T. (1997), 'The facts about the urban exodus', *Town and Country Planning*, March 1997.

Christie, I. and Jarvis L. (1999), 'Rural spaces and urban jams' in Jowell, R., Curtice, C., Park, A. and Thomson, K. (eds.), *British Social Attitudes: the 16th Report - Who shares New Labour values?*, Aldershot: Ashgate.

Countryside Agency (2000), *State of the Countryside*, Cheltenham: Countryside Agency.

Countryside Alliance (1999a), 'Countryside says the Government does not understand', Press Release, 10 August 1999.

Countryside Alliance (1999b), 'Chairman pledges new web-driven political movement to empower rural communities', Press Release, 25 October 1999.

Department of the Environment, Transport and the Regions (DETR) (1998), *Focus on Roads*, London: The Stationery Office.

Department of the Environment, Transport and the Regions (DETR) (2000), *Transport 2010, The 10 Year Plan*, London: DETR.

Engel, M. (2000), 'Blair begins seduction of country folk', *The Guardian*, 4 February.

Macafee, K. (2000), 'Traffic trends', *Transport Trends 2000 Edition*, London: The Stationery Office.

MacFarlane, R. (1998), 'What – or who – is Rural Britain?', *Town and Country Planning*, June 1998.

Mormont, M. (1987), 'Rural nature and urban natures', *Sociologia Ruralis*, Vol. XXVII, **I**: 3-20.

Newby, H. (1979), *Green and Pleasant Land? Social change in rural England*, London: Wildwood House.

Power, A. and Mumford, K. (1999), *The Slow Death of Great Cities: urban abandonment or urban renaissance*, York: Joseph Rowntree Foundation.

Rudin, D. (1998), *Tomorrow: a peaceful path to urban reform*, London: URBED/Friends of the Earth.

Urban Task Force (1999), *Towards an Urban Renaissance*, London: Department of the Environment, Transport and the Regions.

Worpole, K. (2000), *In our Own Backyard: the social promise of environmentalism*, London: Green Alliance.

Acknowledgements

The *National Centre for Social Research* is grateful to both the Department of the Environment, Transport and the Regions and to the Countryside Agency, whose financial support enabled us to ask the modules of questions about attitudes towards the countryside and transport.

Appendix

Multivariate analysis

Models referred to in the chapter follow. Two multivariate techniques were used: logistic regression (models 1, 3a, 3b, 4, 5 and 6) and multiple regression (model 2). These are explained in more detail in Appendix I to this Report.

For the logistic regression models, the figures reported are the odds ratios. An odds ratio of less than one means that the group was less likely than average to be in the group of interest on the dependent variable (the variable we are investigating), and an odds ratio greater than one indicates a greater than average likelihood of being in this group. For the multiple regression models, it is the coefficients (or parameter estimates) that are shown. These show whether a particular characteristic differs significantly from its 'comparison group' in its association with the dependent variable. Details of the comparison group are shown in brackets. A positive coefficient indicates that those with the characteristic score more highly on the dependent variable and a negative coefficient means that they are likely to have a lower score. For both methods, those variables which were selected as significant in predicting this are shown in order of the importance of their contribution. Two asterisks indicate that the coefficient or odds ratio is statistically significant at a 99 per cent level and one asterisk that it is significant at a 95 per cent level.

Model 1: Predictors of wanting to move to a different type of area

Logistic regression was used for this model. The dependent variable was whether people wanted to stay in the same type of area or whether they wanted to move to a different type of area. Thus the table shows how much more or less likely than average the various groups are to want to move to a different type of area.

Variables also entered into the model which were shown not to have an independent relationship with the dependent variable were social class, political identification, marital status, sex, ethnic origin, and educational attainment.

Model 2: Correlates of perceiving social disorder and crime problems in the area

Multiple regression was used for this model, which is based on data from the 1998 *British Social Attitudes* survey. The dependent variable was the number of area problems people reported as being "very" or "fairly common" in their local area.

Variables also entered into the model which were shown not to have an independent relationship with the dependent variable were sex, marital status, ethnic origin, and educational attainment.

Models 3a, 3b, 4, 5 and 6: Predictors of wanting to prevent countryside development

Logistic regression was used for these models. The models are predicting a pro-protection stance in all cases, in other words showing agreement with each of the following dependent variables apart from PlanLaws.

CtryJobs – "The countryside should be protected from development, even if this sometimes leads to fewer new jobs."

Damage – "Industry should be prevented from causing damage to the countryside, even if this sometimes leads to higher prices."

HousBuil –"New housing should be built in cities, towns and villages rather than in the countryside."

KeepBelt – "It is more important to keep green-belt areas than to build new homes there."

PlanLaws – "Planning laws should be relaxed so that people who want to live in the countryside may do so." (Disagree)

The table shows how much more or less likely than average the various groups are to want the countryside protected from development/house-building. Note that the analysis was restricted to those living in rural areas in order to investigate whether being a 'newcomer' or a 'local' was linked to attitudes.

  Variables also entered into the model which were not shown to have an independent relationship with any of the dependent variables were sex, age, educational attainment and tenure.

Model 7: Predictors of opposition to taxing employers for car parking spaces

Logistic regression was used for this model, which predicts opposition to the following statement:

PTIMPR8 – "Taxing employers for each car parking space they provide for their employees."

The table shows how much more or less likely than average the various groups are to oppose this. Note that the analysis was restricted to those who filled in the self-completion questionnaire.

  Variables also entered into the model which were not shown to have an independent relationship with any of the dependent variables were sex, age, region, frequency of driving, frequency of travel as a car passenger, household income, social class, economic activity, educational attainment and marital status.

Model 1: Predictors of wanting to move to a different type of area

Higher odds ratio = more likely to want to move to different type of area

	Odds ratios (Exp(B))	
Baseline odds	0.9182	
Type of area		Sig =0.0000
Big city	2.0728	**
Suburbs or outskirts of a big city	1.2985	**
Small city or town	1.0044	
Country village/farm or home in the country	0.3699	**
Annual household income		Sig =0.0002
Less than £12,000	1.3795	**
£12,000-£28,999	1.0865	
£29,000 or more	0.7458	**
Not answered/refused	0.8946	
Age		Sig = 0.0008
18-24	1.2966	
25-34	1.3541	**
35-44	1.2326	
45-54	1.1104	
55-59	1.2427	
60-64	0.5890	**
65+	0.5684	**
Region		Sig =0.0151
Scotland	0.5988	**
North	1.0572	
Midlands	0.9502	
Wales	1.5604	*
South	1.0587	
Greater London	1.0065	
Economic activity		Sig =0.0453
Education	0.7062	
Work/training	1.1078	
Unemployed/sick	1.3625	*
Retired	1.1876	
Looking after home/other/not answered	0.7900	

Note: Number of cases included in the model: 2041

Model 2: Correlates of perceiving social disorder and crime problems in the area

Individual characteristics (comparison group in brackets)	Standardised Beta coefficient	
Age	-0.180	**
Type of area (village/home in country)		
Big city	0.151	**
Suburbs or outskirts of a big city	0.159	**
Small city or town	0.122	**
Annual household income (less than £12,000)		
£12,000-28,999	-0.029	
£29,000 or more	-0.108	**
Refused/not answered	-0.127	**
Region (London)		
Scotland	-0.004	
North	0.089	**
Midlands	0.050	
Wales	0.008	
South	-0.054	
Economic activity (work)		
Education	0.090	**
Unemployed/sick	0.021	
Retired	0.019	
Home/other	0.027	
Car ownership (no car)		
Owns car	-0.071	*
Social class (I – professional)		
II – intermediate	-0.041	
III – skilled non-manual	-0.004	
III – skilled manual	0.050	
IV – semi-skilled	0.065	*
V – unskilled	0.008	
Political identification (Conservative)		
Labour	0.058	*
Liberal Democrat	-0.011	
Other/missing	-0.013	
None	0.041	

Note: Based on the 1998 *British Social Attitudes* survey

Models 3a, 3b, 4, 5 and 6: Predictors of wanting to prevent countryside development

Higher odds ratio = more likely to want to prevent countryside development
All figures shown are odds ratios except the figures in italics which are significance levels.

	Odds ratios (Exp(B))				
	3a	3b	4	5	6
	CtryJobs	Damage	HousBuil	KeepBelt	PlanLaws
Baseline odds	4.1946	13.8738	2.6435	4.7209	0.5150
Economic activity	*0.0081*	*0.0128*		*0.0008*	*0.0388*
Work/education/ training	0.5282 **	0.4020 **	-	0.7579	1.3281
Unemployed/sick/ home/other/NA	2.0503 *	1.7032	-	0.4206 **	0.5618 *
Retired	0.9234	1.4604	-	3.1368 **	1.3404
Party identification	*0.0129*		*0.0052*		
Conservative	1.4201	-	1.2467 *	-	-
Labour	1.2445	-	1.5074	-	-
Other/None	0.5658 **	-	0.5321 **	-	-
Household income		*0.0012*	*0.0180*	*0.0411*	
< £12,000	-	0.3495 **	0.5714 *	0.5784 *	-
£12,000-£28,999	-	1.2066	1.6951 *	1.5909 *	-
£29,000 or more	-	2.3713 *	1.0325	1.0867	-
Marital status			*0.0087*		*0.0031*
Married/living as	-	-	1.5773 **	-	1.5889 **
Separated/ not married	-	-	0.6340 **	-	0.6294 **
Social class				*0.0477*	*0.0005*
I/II – prof/intermediate	-	-	-	1.8256 *	1.9359 **
III – skilled	-	-	-	0.8555	0.9504
IV/V – semi/unskilled	-	-	-	0.6403 *	0.5435 **
Residential history			*0.0482*		
Lived in city	-	-	1.3616 *	-	-
Never lived in city	-	-	0.7344 *	-	-
No. of cases in the models	269	272	274	274	274

Model 7: Predictors of opposition to taxing employers for car parking spaces

Higher odds ratio = more likely to oppose taxing employers for car parking

	Odds ratios (Exp(B))	
Baseline odds	0.6809	
Access to car		Sig =0.0002
Yes	1.4966	**
No	0.6682	**
Type of area		Sig =0.0017
Big city/suburbs or outskirts of a big city	0.6639	**
Small city or town	1.2493	*
Country village/farm or home in the country	1.2056	
Party identification		Sig =0.0122
Conservative	1.4583	*
Labour	1.1398	
Liberal Democrat	0.5477	**
Other/DK/Ref	0.9067	
None	1.2116	

Note: Number of cases included in the model: 703

10 Begging as a challenge to the welfare state

Michael Adler, Catherine Bromley and Michael Rosie[*]

Begging is neither a new nor an exclusively British phenomenon. However, the apparent growth of street begging in Britain represents a return to practices which were common in previous centuries but which the welfare state appeared, until quite recently, to have eliminated. In *The Needs of Strangers*, Ignatieff (1984, 9-10) points out that the institutions of the welfare state effectively distance those who give from those who receive. As he puts it,

> My encounters with [the poor] are a parable of moral relations between strangers in the welfare state. They have needs and, because they live in a welfare state, these needs confer entitlements – rights – to the resources of people like me. Their needs establish a silent relationship between us ... They are dependent on the state not upon me, and we are both glad of it. We are responsible for each other but we are not responsible to each other.

In the welfare state, a large number of welfare professionals are employed to make difficult moral decisions on the public's behalf and front-line staff in large charitable organisations like *Oxfam* or *Shelter* perform similar functions in distancing donors from recipients. What is peculiar about begging, and arguably what makes it problematic, is that the public are, once again, confronted with the task of making such decisions themselves. How the public have reacted to this and whether they find it problematic are explored in this chapter.

---

[*] Michael Adler is Professor of Socio-Legal Studies in the Department of Social Policy, University of Edinburgh. Catherine Bromley is a Researcher at the *National Centre for Social Research* and Co-director of the *British Social Attitudes* survey series. Michael Rosie is a Research Associate in the Governance of Scotland Forum, University of Edinburgh.

Although street begging has recently been the subject of empirical research (see, for example, Dean, 1999; Fitzpatrick and Kennedy, 2000), there are still many gaps in our knowledge. Most of the research consists of small-scale studies and there are no reliable estimates of how often the public encounter beggars on the streets, and no systematic data on where those encounters take place or whether those who encounter beggars actually give money to them. Thus there is an absence of good data on the reasons why some people are prompted to give while others are not and, more generally, on public attitudes to beggars and to begging.

We focus in this chapter on three areas. First, we explore public attitudes. How do people feel about beggars? How do their views vary – who is the most sympathetic and who is the least? We also consider whether people blame the government for the apparent increase in begging and examine attitudes towards a range of possible initiatives to reduce it. These initiatives range from measures that aim to help beggars ('carrots' such as providing more accommodation for homeless people and increased training opportunities) to those that seek to deter them ('sticks' such as arresting people for begging in public).

Secondly, we examine how often people come across people begging, and whether those who do so give any money to them. Is giving best typified as a random – perhaps unconscious – act of benevolence? Or is there a particular 'type' of person who is consistently sympathetic towards the plight of beggars and more likely than other people to give them money? We also explore the difference between people's responses to begging and their responses to busking and people selling *The Big Issue* (a newspaper sold by homeless people, with a proportion of the selling price being kept by the vendor).[1] Although *Big Issue* sellers are encouraged to see themselves as newspaper vendors, it is not clear whether the public perceive them to be any different from beggars. This comparison also allows us to throw light on what guides people in their actions – kindness, charity or the desire to get something in return (Gouldner, 1960, 1973).

Finally, we explore how people's views about begging influence their willingness to give. Does not giving to a beggar reflect a wish to avoid making difficult decisions about, say, whether his or her needs are genuine? Or does it indicate a perceived lack of reciprocity in the transaction, or a belief that an individual donation is not the most useful action to take? Or are those who do not give to beggars simply those who are most critical of them, and hostile towards what it is that they do?

Attitudes to begging

There is a widespread belief that begging has become more common in Britain. A clear majority (62 per cent) think there are more people begging now than there were five years ago. Fewer than one in ten (seven per cent) think that begging has become less common.

As the table below indicates, many people are hostile towards begging. Nearly half think it to be an easy way of making a living, and six in ten think that the welfare state gives those who beg no excuse for doing so, indicating that many people see them as responsible for their own plight, and do not regard this as an indication of society's failure to support those in need. Nearly half *disagree* with the view that no one would beg for money unless they were really desperate, and two-thirds cannot imagine that they could ever be so desperate that they would have to beg. But, despite these views, only a quarter think that no one should ever give to beggars – and even fewer that beggars should not be treated with the same respect as other people. So, although paupers were deprived of their rights as citizens under the Poor Law, there is no evidence here of any popular demand to treat beggars as second-class citizens today.

Table 10.1 Attitudes to begging

		Agree	Neither agree nor disagree	Disagree
In today's Welfare State there is no excuse for anyone to beg	%	60	12	26
Begging is just an easy way of making a living	%	44	18	37
I could never be so desperate that I needed to beg for money	%	65	13	19
People should never give to beggars	%	26	26	47
People who beg don't deserve to be treated with the same respect as the rest of us	%	19	19	60
No-one begs for money unless they are really desperate	%	35	16	47

Base: 1060

These negative views about begging make it unsurprising that less than a third (29 per cent) agree with the statement "I generally feel guilty if I do not give anything to someone who is begging". Only two in five "feel angry that more is not done to help people who beg".

To help us examine attitudes to begging further we constructed a 'scale' to act as a summary measure of people's answers to the first five questions shown in Table 10.1. Factor analysis (see Appendix I of this Report) shows that it is these questions which most accurately tap people's underlying beliefs about begging.[2] The scale is scored from one to five, with high scores indicating what we will call an 'understanding' attitude to begging, and low scores a more

'hostile' one. By looking at the average scores of various groups we can begin to identify who holds particular views.

What characteristics might be linked to attitudes to begging? Three possible candidates suggest themselves. The first relates to people's demographic and socio-economic characteristics (such as their age and sex, their income, class and education), factors that we know are often associated with considerable differences in attitudes. But views about begging might also be shaped by their underlying beliefs about, for example, politics or religion. Finally, attitudes might also be shaped by experience, in this case, by encounters with those who beg.

As the following table shows, when we examine the average scores of different social groups on our begging scale we find women to be more understanding than men, and younger people more understanding than their elders.

Table 10.2 Mean scores on the attitudes to begging scale by sex, age, income, class and education

	Mean score	Base
All	2.86	1055
Sex		
Male	2.78	472
Female	2.93	583
Age		
18-24	3.22	81
25-44	2.99	372
45-59	2.91	253
60+	2.52	349
Annual household income		
£32,000 or more	3.13	155
£20,000-£31,999	2.93	206
£12,000-£19,999	2.87	177
£6,000-£11,999	2.68	211
Less than £6,000	2.62	185
Class		
Salariat	3.01	295
Intermediate	2.91	403
Working class	2.67	327
Highest educational qualification		
Degree or other higher education	3.14	268
Intermediate	2.91	440
No qualifications	2.54	343

Sympathy also climbs steadily with household income, and education. Given this, it is not surprising that those in middle-class occupations have a more understanding view than those in working-class ones.

And as the next table shows, attitudes to begging also vary by party identification, with supporters of the Conservative Party being more critical of begging than Labour or Liberal Democrat supporters. But there is also a clear relationship with a person's wider ideological views – with their attitudes to welfare, that is how supportive they are of welfare provision and its redistributive role, as measured on the 'wefarism' scale, and towards issues relating to freedom of expression, law, discipline and 'tradition', as measured on the 'libertarian-authoritarian' scale. (These scales are discussed in more detail in Appendix I of this Report.) There is no relationship between church attendance and attitudes to begging.

Table 10.3 Mean scores on the attitudes to begging scale by party identification, attitudes to welfare and libertarian-authoritarian beliefs

	Mean score	*Base*
Party identification		
Conservative	2.68	274
Labour	2.87	427
Liberal Democrat	3.07	120
Attitudes to welfare		
Most pro-welfare	3.41	198
Second quartile	2.87	183
Third quartile	2.81	175
Most anti-welfare	2.38	216
Libertarian-authoritarian beliefs		
Most libertarian	3.23	244
Second quartile	2.82	183
Third quartile	2.76	166
Most authoritarian	2.54	185

The frequency with which beggars are encountered also influences attitudes towards begging, with those who come across beggars on a weekly basis (or more often) being more sympathetic than those who never encounter beggars.

Of course, many of the characteristics that are related to attitudes to begging in general are strongly related to one another (for example, income, class and education), and this makes it difficult to assess which are the most significant. To identify those characteristics which have the greatest influence on attitudes to begging we use regression techniques (see Appendix I of this Report for details of this analysis method). This identifies a number of characteristics as

being significantly and independently linked to having an understanding view of begging. Age, sex, income, education, attitudes to welfare, and one's position on the libertarian-authoritarian scale all matter (reported in full in the appendix of this chapter). So those who are most understanding will tend to be young, well-educated (and high-earning) women who are supportive of welfare and have liberal attitudes more generally. Our analysis also confirms that those who support the Conservative Party are less likely to be understanding, as are those living in big cities (although this is *not* because they encounter beggars more often as frequency of encounter does not prove to be significantly linked to attitudes to begging).

Perceptions of beggars

A frequent theme in discussions about begging is that of 'genuineness', a common image being that of the fake beggar who makes an easy living milking the consciences and emptying the pockets of honest citizens.[3] Numerous newspapers have reported examples of such fake beggars, commuting by car to their pitch and changing into suitable begging attire (Erskine and McIntosh, 1999). Politicians – of all parties – have often voiced such sentiments. In 1995, Labour's Jack Straw made the now infamous speech about "winos, addicts and squeegee merchants ... whose *aggressive begging* affronts and sometimes threatens decent compassionate citizens" (cited in Dean and Gale, 1999, emphasis added). More recently, when the issue of asylum seekers engaging in aggressive begging hit the headlines, politicians were quick to condemn their behaviour, prompting Conservative Ann Widdecombe, to declare "[i]t is a criminal offence to demand money with menaces and people like that should be put in prison".[4]

We turn now to examine the images people hold of those who beg, focusing particularly on whether these are sympathetic or critical. To assess this, we asked a series of questions about beggars, each of which required respondents to opt for one of two opposing views. Responses to these are shown in the next table, and reveal that public opinion about beggars is less strident than the views of some politicians and newspapers. In particular, a majority (55 per cent) think that most beggars *genuinely* need help, although a substantial minority (35 per cent) disagree. When it comes to whether people who beg are from "troubled backgrounds", are "too lazy to find a job" or "have only themselves to blame", opinion is fairly evenly divided between those who take a sympathetic and critical view. Only when it comes to whether or not beggars are in receipt of state benefits do those with more critical opinions outnumber those who are more sympathetic (although just over a fifth – 22 per cent – were unable to express an opinion on this issue).[5]

Table 10.4 Perceptions of beggars

Generally speaking ...	%
... most people who beg also get state benefits	55
... most people who beg do not also get state benefits	23
Don't know	22
... most people who beg come from no more troubled family backgrounds than the rest of us	47
... most people who beg come from very troubled family backgrounds	41
Don't know	12
... most people who beg have only themselves to blame for their situation	43
... most people who beg have been unlucky in their lives	44
Don't know	13
... most people who beg are too lazy to find a job	41
... most people who beg would work if they could find a job	45
Don't know	14
... most people who beg do not genuinely need help	35
... most people who beg genuinely need help	55
Don't know	10

Base: 1060

If we combine people's responses to these questions we find that 40 per cent never choose the 'critical' statement or do so only once. A third (33 per cent) are somewhat less sympathetic, and select the critical statement two or three times, while a quarter (26 per cent) opt for the critical statement four or five times. We return to these groups later in this section.

Although a narrow majority consider most beggars to genuinely need help, opinion is divided over the extent to which it is possible to make this assessment. Around two in five (38 per cent) agree with the statement "I can usually tell whether someone begging really needs help", while a similar proportion (36 per cent) disagrees. Nearly a quarter (23 per cent) were unable to express an opinion.

Our findings so far suggest that, while the public is not immune to negative portrayals of beggars, many people are prepared to give them the benefit of the doubt. The fact that at least one in ten could not decide between the statements provides further support for our contention that people are more guarded in their attitudes than certain politicians and newspaper editors appear to be.

We can also examine the perceptions of beggars held by different groups, using the statements in Table 10.2 to divide people into three groups: those who are most sympathetic, those who are most critical, and those whose views lie

somewhere in between.

We have already identified a number of factors that are associated with attitudes to begging. Variations are also evident when we examine people's perceptions of beggars – whether they think that those who beg are to blame for their situation, are too lazy to find work, and so on. By and large, the background variables that correlate with attitudes to begging are also correlated with perceptions of beggars.

Table 10.5 Perceptions of beggars by sex, age, income, class and education

		Sym-pathetic	Inter-mediate	Critical	Base
All	%	40	33	26	*1060*
Sex					
Male	%	35	35	30	*475*
Female	%	44	30	26	*585*
Age					
18-24	%	62	28	10	*81*
25-44	%	42	33	25	*374*
45-59	%	38	34	28	*254*
60+	%	34	31	34	*351*
Annual household income					
£32,000 or more	%	48	34	18	*155*
£20,000-£31,999	%	38	31	31	*206*
£12,000-£19,999	%	39	33	28	*177*
£6,000-£11,999	%	37	34	30	*211*
Less than £6,000	%	35	34	32	*185*
Social class					
Salariat	%	47	29	24	*297*
Intermediate (not salariat or working class)	%	46	31	24	*405*
Working class	%	28	42	31	*328*
Highest educational qualification					
Degree or other higher education	%	54	26	20	*269*
Intermediate	%	40	36	24	*440*
No qualifications	%	28	36	36	*344*

Age is important – as the above table shows, 18-24 year olds are nearly twice as likely as those aged 60 or more to have a sympathetic view of beggars – and are three times less likely to have a critical one. However, this is not really surprising, as young people tend to be more liberal than older generations on a whole range of social and moral issues (see the chapter by Park in this Report). Of course, whether this is a function of their age or of their life experiences to date is unclear, and will remain so until we can examine changes in the views of particular 'cohorts' of people over time. Sex is also related to a person's views, as are their socio-economic circumstances (whether in the form of income, class or education).

Although church attendance is not related to people's general attitudes to begging, it is related, as the next table shows, to perceptions of beggars – those who attend church on a weekly basis are more sympathetic to beggars than those who never do so (52 per cent compared to 38 per cent). This may be because religious beliefs affect people's propensity to condemn – Christian doctrine does, after all, teach that people should judge others as they would wish to be judged themselves. The influence of party identification, however, is much the same as with attitudes to begging, with those who identify with the Conservative Party the least likely to hold sympathetic views and the most likely to hold hostile views about beggars.

There is also a clear relationship with people's wider ideological views – with their attitudes towards welfare and towards issues relating to freedom of expression, law, discipline and 'tradition'. Those with the most pro-welfare views are nearly three times more likely than those with the most anti-welfare views to have a sympathetic attitude towards beggars (64 per cent compared with 22 per cent).[6] At the same time, those with the most libertarian views are over twice as likely as those with the most authoritarian to adopt a sympathetic view (56 per cent and 25 per cent respectively).

Table 10.6 Perceptions of beggars by church attendance, party identification, attitudes to welfare and libertarian-authoritarian beliefs

		Sym-pathetic	Inter-mediate	Critical	Base
Church attendance					
At least once a week	%	52	28	20	113
At least once a month	%	37	38	25	85
Less often	%	41	31	28	246
No religion	%	38	35	27	608
Party identification					
Conservative	%	31	32	37	277
Labour	%	42	35	23	428
Liberal Democrat	%	48	35	17	120
Attitudes to welfare					
Most pro-welfare	%	64	29	7	198
Second quartile	%	35	39	26	183
Third quartile	%	38	33	29	177
Most anti-welfare	%	22	32	47	216
Libertarian-authoritarian beliefs					
Most libertarian	%	56	28	16	244
Second quartile	%	38	26	36	184
Third quartile	%	31	43	26	167
Most authoritarian	%	25	40	35	185

Of course, as with attitudes to begging, many of the characteristics that are related to perceptions of beggars are strongly related to one another (for example, income, class and education), and this makes it difficult to assess which are the most significant. To identify those factors which have the greatest influence on people's perceptions of beggars, we again use regression techniques (see Appendix I of this report). As before, we find that being young, female and having pro-welfare and libertarian views are all linked to having a more sympathetic view about beggars (reported in full in the appendix of this chapter). However, the other characteristics we found to be related to attitudes to begging did not emerge as significant predictors of people's views. This time class emerges as being related to people's perceptions, with those in non-manual occupations having a more sympathetic view than those in manual ones.

Who is to blame?

Only a third (30 per cent) of those who think that begging has increased over the last five years consider this to be due to government policies, indicating, once again, that the view that beggars are 'victims of society' is not very widespread. This echoes the finding that British people are more likely to see poverty as an inevitable part of society in contrast to continental Europeans who more readily see this in terms of injustice (Golding, 1995). However, those who have the most understanding view of begging are more likely to blame government for their plight (43 per cent doing so), compared with around a quarter (22 per cent) of those who have a more hostile view.

Table 10.7 Responsibility for the increase in beggars by position on the attitudes to begging scale

	Under-standing	Inter-mediate	Hostile	All
	%	%	%	%
Result of government policies	43	25	22	30
For some other reason	48	69	73	63
Don't know	9	6	6	7
Base	*298*	*300*	*333*	*931*

What should be done?

We turn now to consider how people think begging should be tackled, and which government policies, if any, they would support. To assess this we outlined a number of possible policy responses, some of which emphasised a supportive 'carrot' approach while others best typified a more punitive 'stick' approach. Given the ambivalent attitudes towards begging and beggars we have found, it is perhaps surprising that it is the more supportive policies that garner the most enthusiasm. For example, just over half are in favour of "providing training to help people who beg get work, even if this means an increase in taxes" (52 per cent) and "providing accommodation so that people who beg can get off the street even if this means an increase in taxes" (52 per cent). Only a quarter (24 per cent) supported the far more punitive approach of "arresting people for begging in public". However, people are not entirely opposed to punitive policies. Half favour "allowing the police to move on beggars from particular areas in towns and cities" (50 per cent in favour) while just over a third (37 per cent) support "making it easier for people who beg to claim benefits".

These findings echo the current government's New Deal policies that make a virtue of work rather than continuing dependence on benefits. Thus, the public

are much more favourably disposed towards policies that aim to help people find work than they are towards measures which are intended to help people claim benefits. This reinforces previous *British Social Attitudes* surveys which have shown that public support for policies which help the unemployed find work is much greater than for increasing benefits (Hills and Lelkes, 1999). However, we should note that the support for positive measures to help people who beg also reflects the aims of the Rough Sleepers Unit,[7] which, although not aimed specifically at people who beg, will effect them (as there is a substantial degree of overlap between begging and rough sleeping – Fitzpatrick and Kennedy, 2000).

If we consider support for policy measures in terms of people's general attitudes to begging, a clear and unsurprising pattern emerges: those who are most understanding are the *least* likely to support more punitive responses to begging. However, it is not the case that the most hostile are overwhelmingly opposed to some of the more positive measures – four in ten (42 per cent) in this group support the idea of providing training to help people who beg find work, and only slightly fewer (36 per cent) support the provision of accommodation. But a clear majority of the most hostile (70 per cent) favour letting the police move beggars on from particular areas in towns and cities and getting on for half (42 per cent) are in favour of arresting them, measures which have little support among those who are more sympathetic towards beggars. Only around a quarter (28 per cent) of the most hostile group support making it easier for beggars to claim benefits (a potential policy that remains a sticking point, even for the most sympathetic – only half (49 per cent) of whom would support this strategy). Policy makers will need to be aware of this wide divergence of views about how to deal with begging when formulating policies that will command the support of the whole community.

Table 10.8 Attitudes towards policy responses to begging by position on the attitudes to begging scale

% in favour of …	Under-standing	Inter-mediate	Hostile	All
Providing accommodation so that people who beg can get off the street	70	53	36	53
Providing training to help people who beg get work	66	51	42	53
Allowing the police to move on beggars from particular areas in towns and cities	26	54	70	50
Making it easier for people who beg to claim benefits	49	35	28	37
Arresting people for begging in public	6	28	42	24
Base	*297*	*244*	*261*	*804*

Encountering beggars

A majority of people encounter begging on a fairly regular basis. Around two-thirds come across someone begging (which we defined as "asking for money for themselves without offering anything in return") at least once every few months – with nearly half this group encountering a beggar at least once a week.[8] Only one in eight say they never encounter people begging.

Table 10.9 Frequency of encounters with beggars

	%
At least once a week	30
At least once every few months	38
Less often than that	20
Never	12
Base	*3143*

In total, nearly half the sample (48 per cent) had encountered someone begging in the four weeks prior to being interviewed. There are considerable variations between different groups in this respect. Unsurprisingly, those living in big cities were much more likely to have come across someone begging in the recent past, nearly three-quarters (72 per cent) having done so, compared to 39 per cent of those living in rural areas. There are wide geographical variations – encounters with beggars are reported most often in Greater London (68 per cent) and least often in Scotland (34 per cent) and Wales (39 per cent). And the young are more likely than older groups to have encountered someone begging – with 18-24 year olds being more than twice as likely as those aged 65+ to have come across beggars in the last four weeks (66 and 31 per cent respectively). This is likely to reflect the fact that young people are more likely to visit areas such as city centres where beggars are most likely to be found. Finally, those on high incomes, those with higher education, and those in professional or managerial ('salariat') occupations are more likely to have recently encountered a beggar than those on low incomes, those with no educational qualifications and those in working-class occupations.

Responses to beggars

Although almost nine people in ten (88 per cent) encounter beggars, half of them (50 per cent) say that they *never* give them any money. Of the half who say that they do, on occasion, give money to beggars, 44 per cent report doing so "seldom" or "sometimes", leaving only a very small minority (5 per cent) saying that they do so "a lot of the time", "most of the time" or "always".

There is virtually no connection between the frequency with which people encounter someone begging and how likely they are to give money to them. Thus those who come across beggars weekly or more often are just as likely *never* to give as people whose encounters with beggars are less frequent. And, among those who do encounter beggars, there are wide geographical variations in the proportions who never give money – ranging from a high of 54 per cent in the South of England to a low of 38 per cent in Scotland.

The characteristics of those who are most likely give to beggars mirror in many ways those who are the most sympathetic to begging. Thus, it is young people, women, and those who support the provision of welfare most strongly who are the most likely to give. Nearly two-thirds (61 per cent) of those with the most anti-welfare views say that they never give to beggars, compared with 37 per cent of those with the most pro-welfare views. Similarly, the better educated, those with more liberal views, Labour party identifiers, and churchgoers are also more likely to give. Thus, over half (56 per cent) of those with no qualifications say they never give to beggars, compared with 44 per cent of graduates. And whereas just over a third (38 per cent) of those who attend church at least once a week never give to beggars, this applies to over half (56 per cent) of those who are not religious.

As is the case with attitudes towards begging and beggars, a number of different factors seem related to whether or not people give to beggars. But – once again – because many are themselves related to one another this makes it difficult to untangle those factors that have independent effects. To resolve this, we use logistic regression techniques, our aim being to pinpoint which factors best predict a person's likelihood of *ever* giving money to a beggar (see the appendix to this chapter for full details). This confirms that the young, those with pro-welfare views and those on high incomes are the most likely to give to beggars. For the first time, women do not differ notably from men (suggesting that perhaps gender is more linked to the frequency with which people give, rather than whether they give at all) but going to church does make a difference. The regression confirms that those who attend church regularly are more likely to give than those who have no religion.

How much do people give?

We now turn to look at the amounts of money people give, when they do so. As we might expect, a clear majority donate relatively small sums – over 90 per cent parted with less than £1. Only six per cent reported giving more than £1. One might speculate that those who encounter beggars, or give, most often might give the smallest amounts (reflecting the increased demand on their resources), and that people who encounter beggars, or give, less often might be able to spare slightly more. This does not seem to be the case – in fact, those who give often are twice as likely to give £1 or more than those who say they give only sometimes (11 per cent and five per cent respectively). Unsurprisingly, household income is an important factor. Two-thirds (65 per cent) of those with a household income of less than £6,000 normally gave less

than 50p compared with 38 per cent of those with a household income of more than £32,000. This high income group was also far more likely than those with lower incomes to give £1 or more.

What influences people's willingness to give?

As we have seen, the public are divided over the extent to which they are able to tell whether someone begging "really needs help" (38 per cent say they can, while 36 per cent say they can't). But what sort of factors influence the judgements people make about when, and when not, to give?

One issue that often looms large in people's minds concerns the uses to which any money will be put. Of those who claim that they do, on occasion, give to beggars, a large majority (81 per cent) say they are more likely to give if they are sure the beggar "will spend it on food or shelter". This said, nearly half (46 per cent) of them think that "most people who beg spend what they are given on drugs and alcohol" while only a small proportion (14 per cent) actually disagree. This may not be wide of the mark – a study of begging in two British cities (Fitzpatrick and Kennedy, 2000) found that many beggars cited alcohol or drug use as the main reason they begged, and concluded that helping them to reduce their dependence on these substances was the best way of getting them to give up begging.

Given that judgements about whether or not a beggar is 'in need' are hard to make, do people find that they are more likely to give to particular 'types' of beggars? In particular, to what extent do a beggar's personal characteristics, appearance or demeanour make a difference? To assess this, we asked whether respondents would be more or less likely to give in the variety of different circumstances outlined in the next table. This shows that money is much more likely to be given when the encounter is 'hassle free'. Thus, giving is more likely if the passer-by does not have to rummage in his or her pocket for change and if the beggar adopts a passive pose and does not approach the public directly. In fact, having some spare change to hand is the factor that is most strongly linked to being more likely to give. The same proportion say that seeing a young woman begging with a child would make them more likely to give, but a small minority (six per cent) say this would actually make them less likely. Young women (aged 18-34) are nearly twice as likely (62 per cent) to say they would give to a teenage girl with a baby, perhaps reflecting the fact that they are more likely than older women to have young children themselves, or to be thinking of having a baby. With the exception of the teenage girl with a baby, the personal characteristics, appearance or demeanour of a beggar only appear to make a difference to a small minority. Most people seem indifferent to such considerations.

Table 10.10 Factors which make people more or less willing to give to beggars

		More likely	Less likely	No difference
Having some spare change easily to hand	%	32	n.a.	64
Woman in late teens begging has a baby with her	%	32	6	59
Man begging is in his late fifties (as opposed to a man in his late teens)	%	11	2	85
Man in his late teens begging has a dog with him	%	10	9	77
Person in late teens begging is a woman (as opposed to a man)	%	4	1	93
Man in his late teens begging asks for money directly	%	3	26	68

Base: 804

n.a. = not applicable

Begging, busking and *The Big Issue*

To learn a little more about the competing demands placed on people's pockets by activities such as begging, busking and *Big Issue* selling we now look at how often people encounter them and whether – and how – they differentiate between them. This may also shed light upon people's thoughts about the social acceptability of begging. Does, for example, the fact that busking and *Big Issue* selling arguably provide something tangible in return for a donation affect the way that people view them?

Busking and *Big Issue* selling are both encountered more frequently than begging. 30 per cent of the sample encounter beggars at least once a week, compared with 37 per cent who come across buskers and 45 per cent who come across *Big Issue* vendors. Not surprisingly, buskers and *Big Issue* vendors are far more commonly encountered in urban areas than rural ones (this is particularly true for *Big Issue* vendors). People are most likely to give to buskers (67 per cent saying they had done so) and are least likely to buy *The Big Issue* (reported by 32 per cent).[9] As we have already seen, 44 per cent of those who encounter beggars say they give to them at times.

Patterns of giving to buskers and buying *The Big Issue* are very similar to those for giving to beggars with, for instance, younger people being more likely to give or to buy than older ones. Gender differences are even more pronounced than they are when considering giving to beggars – with women being more likely than men to buy it. However, when it comes to busking, age and gender

interact with one another – young men are considerably *more* likely than young women to contribute, while middle-aged and older men are *less* likely to do this than women of the same age. Moreover, although the proportion of women buying *The Big Issue* varies only slightly with age, among men there is a steep gradient from the 23 per cent of men under 35 who say they buy *The Big Issue* to just eight per cent among men aged over 55.

Giving to buskers or buying *The Big Issue* does not vary significantly according to social class or household income, but party identification is relevant. While Labour identifiers are the most likely to give to beggars (and Conservatives the least likely), it is Liberal Democrats who are most likely to give to buskers and to buy *The Big Issue* (with Conservatives again being least likely). Once again we also find that a person's views about welfare, and their position on our 'authoritarian-libertarian' scale, also make a difference. Those at the libertarian end of the scale are more likely to give to beggars and to buy *The Big Issue* (but not to give to buskers) and, as the next table shows, the most pro-welfare are significantly more likely to give to beggars and to buskers and to buy *The Big Issue* than those at the other end of the scale.

Finally, we find that regular churchgoers are more likely than those who do not go to church to buy *The Big Issue*, just as they are more likely to give to beggars. However, church attendance does not make a difference when it comes to giving to buskers.

Table 10.11 Giving to beggars and buskers and buying *The Big Issue* by position on the welfarism scale

% who ...	Most pro-welfare	Second quartile	Third quartile	Most anti-welfare
... give to beggars	38	28	25	21
Base	*555*	*530*	*475*	*565*
... give to buskers	50	39	32	28
Base	*192*	*177*	*164*	*196*
... buy *The Big Issue*	37	25	19	10
Base	*181*	*164*	*149*	*173*

We now examine the choices people make when confronted by beggars, buskers and *Big Issue* vendors. Here we focus only on those who encounter these groups fairly regularly (once a month or more) and at least "sometimes" give to beggars or buskers or buy *The Big Issue*. As the next table shows, among those who encounter all three groups, buying a copy of *The Big Issue* is slightly more common (applying to 30 per cent) than giving to beggars or buskers (24 per cent and 21 per cent respectively). (Those who only encounter buskers and *Big Issue* vendors are also more likely to buy *The Big Issue*, 39 per cent doing so.) The fact that, when all three groups are encountered, the

proportions giving to each are so similar suggests that the public is not necessarily more likely to part with their money when something is offered in return, and leads us to conclude – albeit tentatively – that, in this context, giving is just as likely to be motivated by kindness or charity as by a desire to get something in return.

Table 10.12 Patterns of giving to beggars, buskers and *Big Issue* sellers[10]

Encounter at least monthly		Give to beggars	Give to buskers	Buy *The Big Issue*	Base
Beggars + buskers + *Big Issue*	%	24	21	30	*345*
Big Issue + buskers	%	–	25	39	*161*

We are also in a position to judge the extent to which the efforts of *Big Issue* sellers to distinguish themselves from beggars have been successful. To assess this we asked respondents whether they agreed or disagreed with the statement that "people who sell *The Big Issue* are no different from beggars". A clear majority (59 per cent) disagreed while only one in five (20 per cent) agreed.

The characteristics of those who think that *Big Issue* vendors are *not* beggars are familiar to us from our examination of those who have the most sympathetic and understanding stance towards begging and beggars. Thus, women and young people are among the most likely to disagree with this view – this applying to almost three-quarters (71 per cent) of our youngest age group, compared with only half (48 per cent) of the oldest group. Conversely, agreement with the view that *Big Issue* vendors are no different from beggars is highest among the working class (28 per cent agreeing), those with no qualifications (25 per cent), the most authoritarian (28 per cent), and those most hostile to welfare (31 per cent).

An interesting issue here is whether those who see *The Big Issue* as little more than legitimised begging are nevertheless still prepared to buy it. The answer is a fairly resounding 'no', with a large majority (82 per cent) of those who take this view saying they never buy it. By contrast, although just over half (52 per cent) of those who *disagree* with the view that *Big Issue* vendors are the same as beggars never buy a copy, almost a third buy it often (11 per cent) or sometimes (19 per cent). Perhaps, in order to garner more support, *The Big Issue* needs to better emphasise its role as an alternative to begging?

The relationship between attitudes and behaviour

We now bring together our two earlier themes – attitudes to begging and beggars, and actual encounters with beggars – in an attempt to examine the extent to which people's views about begging affect their responses to it. We begin by looking at the views of those who give to beggars regularly (that is, those who give at least "some of the time" – 27 per cent of those who encounter beggars). Six in ten of this group report feeling guilty if they do not give (compared with three in ten overall), and they are also more likely to feel they can tell if a beggar genuinely needs help. Only two in ten of regular donors see begging as "an easy way of making a living" compared with four in ten (40 per cent) of the whole population.

Table 10.13 Attitudes to begging of those who give to beggars regularly

% of those who give to beggars regularly		Agree	Neither	Disagree
I generally feel guilty if I do not give anything to someone who is begging	%	59	15	25
I can usually tell whether someone begging **really** needs help	%	53	18	27
Begging is just an easy way of making a living	%	22	15	61

Base: 233

This apparent association between having a sympathetic and understanding view of begging and giving to beggars is confirmed when we look at our scale measuring general attitudes towards begging. We find that people who give regularly are more sympathetic than those who seldom or never do so (with mean scores of 3.3 and 2.7 respectively). But what is still not entirely clear is whether attitudes to begging and perceptions of beggars are, *per se*, important determinants of whether people give when considered in relation to all the other things we found to be significant – characteristics such as age, household income, attitudes to welfare and church attendance. Are, for instance, higher earners more likely to give to beggars because they are generally more understanding and sympathetic about begging, or is it simply that they have more money to give in the first place? Logistic regression (reported in full in the appendix of this chapter) confirms the former (that attitudes rather than income are important), as once a person's attitudes to begging are taken into account, only church attendance of all the other characteristics we examined previously remains a factor in determining giving.

Of course, we cannot solve here the recurrent problem of whether attitudes shape behaviour or behaviour determines attitudes. However, in this case it is

more likely that attitudes ultimately determine whether or not people give to beggars, rather than the other way round. It is logical to suggest that the act of giving money to a beggar will be triggered by having some sympathy with their plight in the first place, and that giving to them frequently will reinforce such views. Without such a stimulus it seems hard to think why else someone might decide to part with their money in this way.

Conclusions

Begging appears to challenge the state-mediated relationship between those with resources and those without that has been a defining characteristic of the welfare state. Once again we find ourselves having to make uncomfortable decisions about the claims of people who approach us directly for money. However, although half the people who encountered beggars seemed to be prepared to take on this responsibility and, on occasion, responded positively to requests for help, the other half were not, and did not. A widespread perception that some beggars are not 'really' desperate, a general concern about the 'undesirable' uses to which beggars might put the money they are given, and the difficulty which most people experience in telling whether a beggar really needs help, go a long way towards explaining why most people are so ambivalent about giving to beggars.

The fact that people who are sympathetic towards begging are more likely to give money to them belies the notion that giving to beggars occurs on a random, almost haphazard basis. However, the consideration which most affects people's propensity to give is having some spare change to hand, suggesting that even the behaviour of those most favourably disposed to supporting beggars is tempered by very pragmatic considerations.

Most people regard selling *The Big Issue* as something different from begging, and those who view the paper in this light are more likely to buy it. However, people who encounter buskers and *Big Issue* vendors as well as beggars are no more likely to give them money, indicating that, in this context, the norm of beneficence, which sanctions acts of kindness or altruism, may be just as influential as the norm of reciprocity, which emphasises the importance of getting something in return.

Although most people believe that begging has increased, only a third blame the government for this, indicating that people are more predisposed to individual rather than societal explanations of the causes which give rise to begging. In spite of this, people are generally supportive of positive measures which help beggars (such as providing more accommodation for homeless people and increased training opportunities) and unenthusiastic about more punitive measures (such as arresting people for begging in public). However, there is considerable support for allowing the police to move beggars on from certain parts of towns and cities, and considerable ambivalence about making it easier for beggars to claim benefits. Thus there appears to be little enthusiasm for measures which are seen as either too 'tough minded' or too 'tender hearted'.

Having sympathetic attitudes not only makes people more likely to give money themselves but also leads them to be supportive of macro level policy measures intended to help beggars. Inasmuch as more sympathetic attitudes appear to reflect a more accurate understanding of the deprived backgrounds and miserable circumstances of most beggars, it follows that the more the public understands the reasons why people beg and the circumstances in which most beggars live, the greater the likelihood that support will be forthcoming – either through more passers-by sparing some change, or through national and local strategies to provide people with routes out of begging. And perhaps, most importantly, through preventive measures designed to stop people being drawn into begging in the first place.

Notes

1. *The Big Issue* was set up in London in 1991 to give homeless people a chance to make an income. Vendors buy the magazine for 40p and sell it to the public for £1. There are now four separate Big Issue companies in the UK, each of which brings out its own magazine.
2. The scale was formed by scoring the most sympathetic sentiments towards beggars as one and the most hostile position as five for each item, and then by dividing the total score by the number of items in the scale resulting in scores ranging from one to five. Respondents who had more than two missing values (refused/not answered) out of the five questions were excluded from the scale. For all questions "neither agree nor disagree" and "don't know" were scored as three. The Cronbach's alpha for the scale was 0.79.
3. This was a recurrent theme in the focus groups that were held in early 1998 to discuss some of the issues that were subsequently included in this module of questions.
4. 'Fast-track curb on beggars', *The Guardian*, 20 March 2000.
5. Of course, believing that beggars are in receipt of benefits does not in itself indicate a critical view (they may, for example, feel that benefit levels are so low that people cannot be expected to survive on benefits alone). However, more detailed analysis of this question in relation to other more unambiguously negative statements about beggars suggests that those who believe that beggars are in receipt of benefits take a more critical stance on the other statements in Table 10.2.
6. The possibility that the two scales could in fact be picking up the same latent attitudinal dimensions was rejected after a factor analysis of all the items together revealed that they were indeed measuring different things.
7. The Rough Sleepers Unit was established in 1999 with the specific target of reducing the number of people sleeping rough in Britain by two-thirds by 2002. It replaced a programme (the Rough Sleepers Initiative) which ran from 1990-1999 and constituted a pool of money which local authorities and voluntary organisations could apply for to fund projects supporting those sleeping rough.

8. The explanatory note to interviewers for this question said: "This **includes** people using a sign to beg. It does **not** include people selling something, performing in the street, or collecting for charity."
9. These figures exclude those who never encounter any of the three groups.
10. We were not able to look at other combinations of encounters as there were too few cases.

References

Dean, H. (1999) (ed.), *Begging Questions – Street-level economic activity and social policy failure*, Bristol: The Policy Press.

Dean, H. and Gale, K. (1999), 'Begging and the contradictions of citizenship' in Dean, H. (ed.), *Begging Questions – Street-level economic activity and social policy failure*, Bristol: The Policy Press.

Erskine, A. and McIntosh, I. (1999), 'Why begging offends: historical perspectives and continuities' in Dean, H. (ed.), *Begging Questions – Street-level economic activity and social policy failure*, Bristol: The Policy Press.

Fitzpatrick, S. and Kennedy, C. (2000), *Getting by – Begging, rough sleeping and The Big Issue in Glasgow and Edinburgh*, Bristol: The Policy Press.

Golding, P. (1995), 'Public Attitudes to Social Exclusion' in Room, G. (ed.), *Beyond the Threshold: Measurement and Analysis of Social Exclusion*, Bristol: The Policy Press.

Gouldner, A. (1960), 'The Norm of Reciprocity', *American Sociological Review*, **25**: 161-178; reprinted in Gouldner, A. (1973), *For Sociology*, London: Allen Lane, pp. 226-259.

Gouldner, A. (1973), 'The Importance of Something for Nothing' in Gouldner, A., *For Sociology*, London: Allen Lane, pp. 260-299.

Hills, J. and Lelkes, O. (1999), 'Social security, selective universalism and patchwork redistribution' in Jowell, R., Curtice, J., Park, A. and Thomson, K. (eds.), *British Social Attitudes: the 16th Report - Who shares New Labour values?*, Aldershot: Ashgate.

Ignatieff, M. (1984), *The Needs of Strangers*, London: Chatto and Windus, the Hogarth Press.

Acknowledgements

We are grateful to the ESRC for funding this module of questions under grant number R000222847.

Appendix

Regression analyses

The independent variables used in the following regression analyses were:

Age
1. 18-24
2. 25-44
3. 45-59
4. 60+

Sex
1. Men
2. Women

Highest educational qualification
1. Degree or other higher education
2. Intermediate
3. No qualifications

Household income
1. Less than £6,000
2. £6,000-£11,999
3. £12,000-£19,999
4. £20,000-£31,999
5. £32,000 or more
6. DK/NA

Economic activity
1. Full-time education
2. Paid work
3. Unemployed
4. Retired
5. Looking after home

Goldthorpe social class
1. Salariat
2. Routine non-manual
3. Petty bourgeoisie
4. Manual foremen & supervisors
5. Working class

Church attendance
1. At least once a week
2. At least once a month
3. Less often
4. No religion

Party identification
1. Conservative
2. Labour
3. Liberal Democrat
4. None
5. Other party/DK/NA

Region
1. Scotland
2. North, North-West, Yorkshire & Humberside
3. Midlands (East & West)
4. Wales
5. South (East, West, & East Anglia)
6. Greater London

Urban/rural residence
1. City
2. Suburbs
3. Small town
4. Country village
5. Other

Population density
1. Less than 500
2. 500 or more

Frequency of encountering beggars
1. At least once a week
2. Less often
3. Never

Position on the welfarism scale
1. Most pro-welfare
2. Second quartile
3. Third quartile
4. Most anti-welfare

Position on the left-right scale
1.   Most left wing
2.   Second quartile
3.   Third quartile
4.   Most right wing

Position on the attitudes to begging scale
1.   Most hostile
2.   Intermediate
3.   Most understanding

Position on the libertarian-authoritarian scale
1.   Most libertarian
2.   Second quartile
3.   Third quartile
4.   Most authoritarian

Perceptions of beggars
1.   Sympathetic
2.   Intermediate
3.   Critical

Multiple regression

The multiple regression model referred to in the chapter is detailed below. The model was used to assess the relationship between the independent variables listed below and scores on the attitude to begging scale, where high scores indicate a more, and low scores indicate a less, sympathetic view about begging.

Dependent variable: Scores on the attitudes to begging scale.
Independent variables: Age, sex, highest educational qualification, household income, party identification, region, urban/rural residence, population density, frequency of encountering beggars, position on the welfarism, left-right and libertarian-authoritarian scales.

Results for multiple regression model

	Standardised Beta coefficient
Individual characteristics (comparison group in brackets)	
Welfarism scale	-.361**
Age (60+)	
18-24	.153**
25-44	.079*
45-59	.050
Income (less than £6,000)	
£6,000-11,999	-.002
£12,000-19,999	.054
£20,000-31,999	.066*
£32,000 or more	.149**
DK/NA	-.028

Education (no qualifications)
    Degree or other higher education .137**
    Intermediate   .078*

Liberal-authoritarian scale   -.136**

Sex (Women)
    Men   -.100**

Urban/rural residence[1] (country village)
    City   -.085*
    Suburbs   .028
    Small town   .011

Party identification (Conservative)
    Other party/DK/NA   .074*
    Liberal Democrat   .067*
    Labour   .011
    None   .010

Region (Greater London)
    Scotland   .016
    North   -.022
    Midlands   .008
    Wales   .001
    South-East   .008

Left-right scale   -.043

Logistic regression

The logistic regression models referred to in the chapter are detailed here. The first model was used to assess the impact of the following independent variables on whether people have sympathetic views about beggars, that is, that they agreed with at most only one negative statement about them.

---

[1] The 'other' category was set to missing as there were so few cases.

Model 1

Dependent variable: Agreeing with zero or one negative statement about beggars.
Independent variables: Age, sex, highest educational qualification, household income,
Goldthorpe social class, church attendance, party identification, region, population
density, frequency of encountering beggars.

Results for logistic regression model 1

Category	B	S.E.	R	Odds Ratio (Exp(B))	Sig
Baseline odds	-.1009	.1026		0.904	.3254
Age			.1012		.0002
18-24	.8191	.1871	.1112	2.2684	**
25-44	-.2198	.1131	-.0358	.8027	*
45-59	.1864	.1226	-.0149	.8300	
60+	-.4129	.1337	-.0737	.6617	**
Sex					
Men	-.2541	.0750	-.0827	.7756	**
Women	.2541	.0750	.0827	1.2893	**
Social class			.0782		.0024
Salariat	.0933	.1433	.0000	1.0978	
Routine non-manual	.0790	.1432	.0000	1.0822	
Petty bourgeoisie	.1549	.2027	.0000	1.1675	
Manual foremen & supervisors	.2329	.2163	.0000	1.2623	
Working class	-.5601	.1393	-.1011	.5712	**
Education			.0951		.0003
Higher education	.4746	.1198	.0994	1.6074	**
Intermediate	-.0661	.0980	.0000	.9360	
No qualifications	-.4085	.1221	-.0814	.6646	**
Party identification			.0822		.0016
Conservative	-.5517	.1359	-.1021	.5760	**
Labour	.0826	.1153	.0000	1.0861	
Liberal Democrat	.1327	.1755	.0000	1.1419	
None	.0692	.1746	.0000	1.0717	
Other/DK/NA	.2672	.1966	.0000	1.3063	

*=sig. at 0.05 level, **=sig. at 0.01 level
Number of cases in model: 1021

Model 2

Dependent variable: Agreeing with zero or one negative statement about beggars.
Independent variables: Age, sex, highest educational qualification, household income,
Goldthorpe social class, church attendance, party identification, region, population
density, frequency of encountering beggars, position on welfarism, left-right and
libertarian-authoritarian scales.

Results for logistic regression model 2

Category	B	S.E.	R	Odds Ratio (Exp(B))	Sig
Baseline odds	-.1984	.1138		1.0847	.0813
Position on the welfarism scale			.2293		.0000
Most pro-welfare	1.0978	.1481	.2269	2.9976	**
Second quartile	-.2373	.1478	-.0237	.7887	
Third quartile	-.0709	.1459	.0000	.9316	
Most anti-welfare	-.7896	.1615	-.1459	.4540	**
Age			.1374		.0000
18-24	1.1133	.2225	.1496	3.0443	**
25-44	-.2676	.1385	-.0410	.7652	*
45-59	-.4501	.1514	-.0815	.6376	**
60+	-.3956	.1542	-.0667	.6733	**
Social class			.1373		.0000
Salariat	.2276	.1545	.0128	1.2556	
Routine non-manual	-.0158	.1774	.0000	.9844	
Petty bourgeoisie	.4051	.2559	.0222	1.4994	
Manual foremen & supervisors	.2211	.2646	.0000	1.2474	
Working class	-.8380	.1667	-.1504	.4326	**
Sex					
Men	-.3066	.0927	-.0932	.7359	**
Women	.3066	.0927	.0932	1.3589	**
Position on libertarian-authoritarian scale			.0064		.0784
Most liberal	.4425	.1386	.0893	1.5567	**
Second quartile	.0588	.1461	.0000	1.0606	
Third quartile	-.3272	.1568	-.0478	.7209	*
Most authoritarian	-.1742	.1634	.0000	.8401	

*=sig. at 0.05 level, **=sig. at 0.01 level
Number of cases in model: 747

Model 3

Dependent variable: Ever gives to beggars.
Independent variables: Age, sex, highest educational qualification, household income,
economic activity, Goldthorpe social class, church attendance, party identification,
region, urban/rural residence, population density, frequency of encountering beggars,
position on welfarism, left-right and libertarian-authoritarian scales.

Results for logistic regression model 3

Category	B	S.E.	R	Odds Ratio (Exp(B))	Sig
Baseline odds	.2862	.0708		1.073	.0001
Position on the welfarism scale			.1435		.0000
Most pro-welfare	.5917	.0808	.1337	1.8070	**
Second quartile	-.0308	.0784	.0000	.9696	
Third quartile	-.1154	.0813	-.0024	.8910	
Most anti-welfare	-.4454	.0784	-.1023	.6406	**
Church attendance			.1141		.0000
At least once a week	.4886	.1178	.0726	1.6300	**
At least once a month	-.0986	.1291	.0000	.9061	
Less often	.0390	.0931	.0000	1.0397	
No religion	-.4289	.0748	-.1034	.6512	**
Age			.0995		.0000
18-24	.6605	.1291	.0915	1.9357	**
25-44	-.0263	.0774	.0000	.9740	
45-59	-.3848	.0855	-.0795	.6806	**
60+	-.2494	.0916	-.0433	.7793	**
Household income			.0314		.0000
Less than £6,000	.0903	.1316	.0000	1.0945	
£6,000-11,999	-.0639	.1038	.0000	.9381	
£12,000-19,999	-.1023	.0985	.0000	.9028	
£20,000-31,999	-.0726	.0955	.0000	.9300	
£32,000 or more	.3076	.0970	.0529	1.3602	**
DK/NA	-.1592	.1353	.0000	.8529	

*=sig. at 0.05 level, **=sig. at 0.01 level
Number of cases in model: 2072

Model 4

Dependent variable: Ever gives to beggars.
Independent variables: Age, sex, highest educational qualification, household income, economic activity[2], Goldthorpe social class, church attendance, party identification, region, urban/rural residence, population density, frequency of encountering beggars, position on welfarism, left-right and libertarian-authoritarian scales, position on the attitudes to begging scale and perception of beggars measure.

Results for logistic regression model 4

Category	B	S.E.	R	Odds Ratio (Exp(B))	Sig
Baseline odds	-.9026	.1178		0.9116	.4318
Position on the attitudes to begging scale			.1848		.0000
Hostile	-.7366	.1468	-.1600	.4787	**
Intermediate	-.0548	.1212	-.0000	.9467	
Understanding	.7914	.1408	.1808	2.2068	**
Perceptions of beggars			.1307		.0001
Sympathetic	.6082	.1389	.1377	1.8371	**
Intermediate	-.1036	.1236	.0000	.9016	
Critical	-.5046	.1549	-.0975	.6488	**
Church attendance			.0858		.0054
At least once a week	.4644	.2321	.0470	1.5910	*
At least once a month	-.2913	.2421	.0000	.7473	
Less often	.2054	.1717	.0000	1.2280	
No religion	-.3785	.1425	-.0747	.6849	**

*=sig. at 0.05 level, **=sig. at 0.01 level
Number of cases in model: 632

---

[2]   In this model the 'full-time education' category was set to missing as there were so few cases.

Appendix I
Technical details of the surveys

British Social Attitudes

In 1999, three versions of the *British Social Attitudes* questionnaire were fielded. Each 'module' of questions is asked either of the full sample (3,143 respondents) or of a random two-thirds or one-third of the sample. The structure of the questionnaire (versions A, B and C) is shown at the beginning of Appendix III.

Sample design

The *British Social Attitudes* survey is designed to yield a representative sample of adults aged 18 or over. Since 1993, the sampling frame for the survey has been the Postcode Address File (PAF), a list of addresses (or postal delivery points) compiled by the Post Office.[1]

For practical reasons, the sample is confined to those living in private households. People living in institutions (though not in private households at such institutions) are excluded, as are households whose addresses were not on the Postcode Address File.

The sampling method involved a multi-stage design, with three separate stages of selection.

Selection of sectors

At the first stage, postcode sectors were selected systematically from a list of all postal sectors in Great Britain. Before selection, any sectors with fewer than 500 addresses were identified and grouped together with an adjacent sector; in Scotland all sectors north of the Caledonian Canal were excluded (because of the prohibitive costs of interviewing there). Sectors were then stratified on the basis of:

- 37 sub-regions
- population density with variable banding used, in order to create three equal-sized strata per sub-region
- ranking by percentage of homes that were owner-occupied, from the 1991 Census figures.

Two hundred postcode sectors were selected, with probability proportional to the number of addresses in each sector.

Selection of addresses

Thirty addresses were selected in each of the 200 sectors. The sample was therefore 200 x 30 = 6,000 addresses, selected by starting from a random point on the list of addresses for each sector, and choosing each address at a fixed interval. The fixed interval was calculated for each sector in order to generate the correct number of addresses.

The Multiple-Output Indicator (MOI) available through PAF was used when selecting addresses. MOI shows the number of accommodation spaces sharing one address. Thus, if the MOI indicates more than one accommodation space at a given address, the chances of the given address being selected from the list of addresses would increase so that it matched the total number of accommodation spaces. As would be expected, the vast majority (99.5 per cent) of MOIs had a value of one. The remainder, which ranged between three and 12, were incorporated into the weighting procedures (described below).

Selection of individuals

Interviewers called at each address selected from PAF and listed all those eligible for inclusion in the sample – that is, all persons currently aged 18 or over and resident at the selected address. The interviewer then selected one respondent using a computer-generated random selection procedure. Where there were two or more households or 'dwelling units' at the selected address, interviewers first had to select one household or dwelling unit using the same random procedure. They then followed the same procedure to select a person for interview.

Weighting

Data were weighted to take account of the fact that not all the units covered in the survey had the same probability of selection. The weighting reflected the relative selection probabilities of the individual at the three main stages of selection: address, household and individual.

First, because addresses were selected using the MOI, weights had to be applied to compensate for the greater probability of an address with an MOI of

more than one being selected, compared to an address with an MOI of one. Secondly, data were weighted to compensate for the fact that dwelling units at an address which contained a large number of dwelling units were less likely to be selected for inclusion in the survey than ones which did not share an address. (We use this procedure because in most cases these two stages will cancel each other out, resulting in more efficient weights.) Thirdly, data were weighted to compensate for the lower selection probabilities of adults living in large households compared with those living in small households. This weight is called 'WtFactor' and the distribution of weights is shown in the next table:

Unscaled Weight	No.	%	Scaled weight
0.33	4	0.1	0.1856
0.40	1	0.0	0.2227
0.67	1	0.0	0.3712
0.82	1	0.0	0.4556
1.00	1141	36.3	0.5568
1.67	1	0.0	0.9280
2.00	1628	51.8	1.1136
3.00	255	8.1	1.6704
4.00	94	3.0	2.2271
5.00	9	0.3	2.7839
6.00	3	0.1	3.3407
7.00	3	0.1	3.8975
8.00	1	0.0	4.4543
10.00	1	0.0	5.5679

All weights fell within a range between 0.33 and 10.00. The average weight applied was 1.80. The weighted sample was scaled down to make the number of weighted productive cases exactly equal to the number of unweighted productive cases (n = 3,143).

All the percentages presented in this Report are based on weighted data.

Questionnaire versions

Each address in each sector (sampling point) was allocated to either the A, B or C third of the sample. The first address in the sampling point was allocated the A version, the second the B version, the third the C version, and so on. Each version was thus assigned to 2,000 addresses.

Fieldwork

Interviewing was mainly carried out between June and September 1999, with a small number of interviews taking place in October and November.

Fieldwork was conducted by interviewers drawn from the *National Centre for Social Research's* regular panel and conducted using face-to-face computer-assisted interviewing.[2] Interviewers attended a one-day briefing conference to familiarise them with the selection procedures and questionnaires.

The average interview length was 63 minutes for version A of the questionnaire, 60 minutes for version B and 68 minutes for version C.[3] Interviewers achieved an overall response rate of 58 per cent. Details are shown below:

	No.	%
Addresses issued	6,000	
Vacant, derelict and other out of scope	598	
In scope	5,402	100.0
Interview achieved	3,143	58.2
Interview not achieved	2,259	41.8
Refused [1]	1,603	29.7
Non-contacted [2]	284	5.3
Other non-response	372	6.9

1   'Refusals' comprise refusals before selection of an individual at the address, refusals to the office, refusal by the selected person, 'proxy' refusals (on behalf of the selected respondent) and broken appointments after which the selected person could not be recontacted.

2   'Non-contacts' comprise households where no one was contacted and those where the selected person could not be contacted.

As in earlier rounds of the series, the respondent was asked to fill in a self-completion questionnaire which, whenever possible, was collected by the interviewer. Otherwise, the respondent was asked to post it to the *National Centre for Social Research*. If necessary, up to three postal reminders were sent to obtain the self-completion supplement.

A total of 693 respondents (22 per cent of those interviewed) did not return their self-completion questionnaire. Version A of the self-completion questionnaire was returned by 76 per cent of respondents to the face-to-face interview, version B by 79 per cent and version C by 79 per cent. As in previous rounds, we judged that it was not necessary to apply additional weights to correct for non-response.

Advance letter

Interviewers were supplied with letters describing the purpose of the survey and the coverage of the questionnaire, which they posted to sampled addresses before making any calls.[4]

Analysis variables

A number of standard analyses have been used in the tables that appear in this report. The analysis groups requiring further definition are set out below. For further details see Bromley *et al.* (1999).

Region

The ten Standard Statistical Regions have been used, except that we generally distinguish between Greater London and the remainder of the South-East. Sometimes these have been grouped into what we have termed 'compressed region': 'Northern' includes the North, North-West, Yorkshire and Humberside. East Anglia is included in the 'South', as is the South-West.

Standard Occupational Classification

Respondents are classified according to their own occupation, not that of the 'head of household'. Their spouses or partners are similarly classified. The main Social Class variables used in the analyses in this report are Registrar General's Social Class, Socio-economic Group and the Goldthorpe schema.

Since 1991, the OPCS *Standard Occupational Classification* (SOC) has been used for the occupation coding on the BSA survey series.[5] SOC has a hierarchical structure, consisting of 371 Unit Groups which can be aggregated into 77 Minor Groups, 22 Sub-major Groups and nine Major Groups.

Registrar General's Social Class

Each respondent's Social Class is based on his or her current or last occupation. Thus, all respondents in paid work at the time of the interview, waiting to take up a paid job already offered, retired, seeking work, or looking after the home, have their occupation (present, past or future, as appropriate) classified into Occupational Unit Groups according to SOC. The combination of occupational classification with employment status generates the following six Social Classes:

I	Professional, etc. occupations	⎤
II	Managerial and technical occupations	⎬ 'Non-manual'
III (Non-manual)	Skilled occupations	⎦
III (Manual)	Skilled occupations	⎤
IV	Partly skilled occupations	⎬ 'Manual'
V	Unskilled occupations	⎦

They are usually collapsed into four groups: I & II, III Non-manual, III Manual, and IV & V.

The remaining respondents are grouped as "never had a job" or "not classifiable". For some analyses, it may be more appropriate to classify respondents according to their current social class, which takes into account only their present economic position. In this case, in addition to the six social classes listed above, the remaining respondents not currently in paid work fall into one of the following categories: "not classifiable", "retired", "looking after the home", "unemployed" or "others not in paid occupations".

Socio-economic Group

As with Social Class, each respondent's Socio-economic Group (SEG) is based on his or her current or last occupation. SEG aims to bring together people with jobs of similar social and economic status, and is derived from a combination of employment status and occupation. The full SEG classification identifies 18 categories, but these are usually condensed into six groups:

- Professionals, employers and managers
- Intermediate non-manual workers
- Junior non-manual workers
- Skilled manual workers
- Semi-skilled manual workers
- Unskilled manual workers

As with Social Class, the remaining respondents are grouped as "never had a job" or "not classifiable".

Goldthorpe schema

The Goldthorpe schema classifies occupations by their 'general comparability', considering such factors as sources and levels of income, economic security, promotion prospects, and level of job autonomy and authority. The Goldthorpe schema was derived from the SOC unit groups combined with employment status. Two versions of the schema are coded: the full schema has 11 categories; the 'compressed schema' combines these into the five classes shown below.

- Salariat (professional and managerial)

- Routine non-manual workers (office and sales)
- Petty bourgeoisie (the self-employed, including farmers, with and without employees)
- Manual foremen and supervisors
- Working class (skilled, semi-skilled and unskilled manual workers, personal service and agricultural workers)

There is a residual category comprising those who have never had a job or who gave insufficient information for classification purposes.

Industry

All respondents whose occupation could be coded were allocated a Standard Industrial Classification (SIC 1992). Two-digit class codes are used. As with Social Class, SIC may be generated on the basis of the respondent's current occupation only, or on his or her most recently classifiable occupation.

Party identification

Respondents can be classified as identifying with a particular political party on one of three counts: if they consider themselves supporters of that party, as closer to it than to others, or as more likely to support it in the event of a general election (responses are derived from Qs.119-127). The three groups are generally described respectively as *partisans, sympathisers* and *residual identifiers*. In combination, the three groups are referred to as 'identifiers'.

Attitude scales

Since 1986, the *British Social Attitudes* surveys have included two attitude scales which aim to measure where respondents stand on certain underlying value dimensions – left-right and libertarian-authoritarian. Since 1987 (except 1990), a similar scale on 'welfarism' has been asked.[6]

A useful way of summarising the information from a number of questions of this sort is to construct an additive index (DeVellis, 1991; Spector, 1992). This approach rests on the assumption that there is an underlying – 'latent' – attitudinal dimension which characterises the answers to all the questions within each scale. f so, scores on the index are likely to be a more reliable indication of the underlying attitude than the answers to any one question.

Each of these scales consists of a number of statements to which the respondent is invited to "agree strongly", "agree", "neither agree nor disagree", "disagree", or "disagree strongly".

The items are:

Left-right scale

Government should redistribute income from the better-off to those who are less well off. *[Redistrb]*

Big business benefits owners at the expense of workers. *[BigBusnN]*

Ordinary working people do not get their fair share of the nation's wealth. *[Wealth]* [7]

There is one law for the rich and one for the poor. *[RichLaw]*

Management will always try to get the better of employees if it gets the chance. *[Indust4]*

Libertarian-authoritarian scale

Young people today don't have enough respect for traditional British values. *[TradVals]*

People who break the law should be given stiffer sentences. *[StifSent]*

For some crimes, the death penalty is the most appropriate sentence. *[DeathApp]*

Schools should teach children to obey authority. *[Obey]*

The law should always be obeyed, even if a particular law is wrong. *[WrongLaw]* [8]

Censorship of films and magazines is necessary to uphold moral standards. *[Censor]*

Welfarism scale

The welfare state makes people nowadays less willing to look after themselves. *[WelfResp]*

People receiving social security are made to feel like second class citizens. *[WelfStig]*

The welfare state encourages people to stop helping each other. *[WelfHelp]*

The government should spend more money on welfare benefits for the poor, even if it leads to higher taxes. *[MoreWelf]*

Around here, most unemployed people could find a job if they really wanted one. *[UnempJob]*

Many people who get social security don't really deserve any help. *[SocHelp]*

Most people on the dole are fiddling in one way or another. *[DoleFidl]*

If welfare benefits weren't so generous, people would learn to stand on their own two feet. *[WelfFeet]*

The indices for the three scales are formed by scoring the leftmost, most libertarian or most pro-welfare position, as 1 and the rightmost, most authoritarian or most anti-welfarist position, as 5. The "neither agree nor disagree" option is scored as 3. The scores to all the questions in each scale are added and then divided by the number of items in the scale giving indices ranging from 1 (leftmost, most libertarian, most pro-welfare) to 5 (rightmost, most authoritarian, most anti-welfare). The scores on the three indices have been placed on the dataset.[9]

The scales have been tested for reliability (as measured by Cronbach's alpha). The Cronbach's alpha for the scales in 1999 are 0.82 for the left-right scale, 0.78 for the 'welfarism' scale and 0.70 for the libertarian-authoritarian scale. This level of reliability can be considered "very good" for the left-right scale and "respectable" for the other two scales (DeVellis, 1991: 85).

Other analysis variables

These are taken directly from the questionnaire and to that extent are self-explanatory. The principal ones are:

Sex (Q.34)

Age (Q.35)

Household income (Q.889)

Economic position (Q.234)

Religion (Q.657)

Highest educational qualification obtained (Q.703-765)

Marital status (Q.96)

Benefits received (Q.847-865)

Sampling errors

No sample precisely reflects the characteristics of the population it represents because of both sampling and non-sampling errors. If a sample were designed as a random sample (if every adult had an equal and independent chance of inclusion in the sample) then we could calculate the sampling error of any percentage, *p*, using the formula:

$$s.e. (p) = \sqrt{\frac{p(100-p)}{n}}$$

where *n* is the number of respondents on which the percentage is based. Once the sampling error had been calculated, it would be a straightforward exercise to calculate a confidence interval for the true population percentage. For example, a 95 per cent confidence interval would be given by the formula:

$$p \pm 1.96 \times s.e.(p)$$

Clearly, for a simple random sample (srs), the sampling error depends only on the values of p and n. However, simple random sampling is almost never used in practice because of its inefficiency in terms of time and cost.

As noted above, the *British Social Attitudes* sample, like that drawn for most large-scale surveys, was clustered according to a stratified multi-stage design into 200 postcode sectors (or combinations of sectors). With a complex design like this, the sampling error of a percentage giving a particular response is not simply a function of the number of respondents in the sample and the size of the percentage; it also depends on how that percentage response is spread within and between sample points. The complex design may be assessed relative to simple random sampling by calculating a range of design factors (DEFTs) associated with it, where

$$DEFT = \sqrt{\frac{\text{Variance of estimator with complex design, sample size n}}{\text{Variance of estimator with srs design, sample size n}}}$$

and represents the multiplying factor to be applied to the simple random sampling error to produce its complex equivalent. A design factor of one means that the complex sample has achieved the same precision as a simple random sample of the same size. A design factor greater than one means the complex sample is less precise than its simple random sample equivalent. If the DEFT for a particular characteristic is known, a 95 per cent confidence interval for a percentage may be calculated using the formula:

$$p \pm 1.96 \text{ x } complex\ sampling\ error\ (p)$$

$$= p \pm 1.96 \text{ x DEFT x } \sqrt{\frac{p(100\text{-}p)}{n}}$$

Calculations of sampling errors and design effects were made using the statistical analysis package STATA.

The following table gives examples of the confidence intervals and DEFTs calculated for a range of different questions, some fielded on all three versions of the questionnaire and some on one only; some asked on the interview questionnaire and some on the self-completion supplement. It shows that most of the questions asked of all sample members have a confidence interval of around plus or minus two to three per cent of the survey proportion. This means that we can be 95 per cent certain that the true population proportion is within two to three per cent (in either direction) of the proportion we report. The confidence intervals calculated for questions asked of only a third of the sample tend to be greater than those calculated for questions asked of the entire sample.

It should be noted that the design effects for certain variables (notably those most associated with the area a person lives in) are greater than those for other variables. This is particularly notable for the question which asks respondents to make a subjective judgement about whether they live in a city, small town or in the country. Another case in point is housing tenure, local authority tenants tend

to be concentrated in certain areas; consequently the design effects calculated for these variables in a clustered sample are greater than the design effects calculated for variables less strongly associated with area, such as attitudinal variables.

		% *(p)*	Complex standard error of *p* (%)	95 per cent confidence interval	DEFT
Classification variables (Interview)					
DV*	**Party identification**				
	Conservative	24.9	1.3	22.4-27.3	1.64
	Liberal Democrat	10.3	0.8	8.8-11.9	1.44
	Labour	42.6	1.4	39.8-45.3	1.61
DV*	**Housing tenure**				
	Owns	73.8	1.2	71.4-76.2	1.59
	Rents from local authority	12.9	1.0	10.9-14.9	1.69
	Rents privately/HA	12.1	0.9	10.4-13.9	1.57
DV*	**Religion**				
	No religion	43.8	1.2	41.3-46.2	1.40
	Church of England	27.1	1.3	24.5-29.6	1.64
	Roman Catholic	8.9	0.8	7.3-10.5	1.59
Q.1014	**Age of completing continuous full-time education**				
	16 or under	63.7	1.6	60.6-66.7	1.81
	17 or 18	17.3	0.9	15.5-19.1	1.34
	19 or over	15.8	1.1	13.6-17.9	1.66
Q.504	**Frequency of encountering beggars**				
	Most days	10.6	1.0	8.8-12.5	1.73
	At least once a week	19.0	1.1	16.8-21.1	1.58
	At least once a month	16.0	0.8	14.6-17.5	1.15
	Never	11.7	0.9	9.9-13.5	1.57
Q556	**Urban or rural residence**				
	A big city	8.0	1.6	4.9-11.1	3.28
	Small city/town	48.9	3.3	42.5-55.3	3.67
	Country village	16.6	2.2	12.3-21.0	3.35

* DV = Derived variable

	% (p)	Complex standard error of p (%)	95 per cent confidence interval	DEFT
Attitudinal variables (Interview)				
Q.425 Benefits for the unemployed are ...				
... too low	32.8	1.1	30.6-35.1	1.37
... too high	42.4	1.3	39.8-45.0	1.50
B.551 Are you personally concerned				
C.551 about things that may happen to the countryside				
Very concerned	51.3	1.6	48.1-54.4	1.47
Bit concerned	32.4	1.4	29.7-35.1	1.34
Does not concern me particularly	15.3	1.1	13.1-17.5	1.43
C.554 Should students be expected to take out loans?				
Should	29.5	1.6	26.4-32.6	1.13
Should not	58.0	1.8	54.5-61.5	1.17
C.616 Films showing two men having sex should not be allowed to be shown in cinemas at all	36.0	1.9	32.3-39.8	1.29
Attitudinal variables (Self-completion)				
B2.20c Strongly agree or agree that				
C2.22c planning laws in the country-side should be relaxed	31.1	1.3	28.5-33.7	1.16
A2.26a Strongly agree that there				
B2.10a should be a minimum wage				
C2.10a set by law	53.3	1.1	51.1-55.5	1.11
C2.19b How well state secondary schools teach basic skills				
Very well	13.2	1.5	10.3-16.1	1.25
Quite well	54.5	1.9	50.7-58.4	1.13
Not very well	23.6	1.6	20.4-26.8	1.10
Not at all well	6.6	0.8	5.0- 8.2	0.92
A2.56 Strongly agree or agree that Great Britain should introduce proportional representation	50.0	2.1	46.0-54.1	1.16

These calculations are based on the 3,143 respondents to the main questionnaire and 2,450 returning self-completion questionnaires; on the A version respondents (1,060 for the main questionnaire and 804 for the self-completion); on the B version respondents (1,031 and 813 respectively); or on the C version respondents (1,052 and 833 respectively). As the examples above show, sampling errors for proportions based only on respondents to just one of the three versions of the questionnaire, or on subgroups within the sample, are somewhat larger than they would have been had the questions been asked of everyone.

Analysis techniques

Regression

Regression analysis aims to summarise the relationship between a 'dependent' variable and one or more 'independent' variables. It shows how well we can estimate a respondent's score on the dependent variable from knowledge of their scores on the independent variables. It is often undertaken to support a claim that the phenomena measured by the independent variables cause the phenomenon measured by the dependent variable. However, the causal ordering, if any, between the variables cannot be verified or falsified by the technique. Causality can only be inferred through special experimental designs or through assumptions made by the analyst.

All regression analysis assumes that the relationship between the dependent and each of the independent variables takes a particular form. In *linear regression*, the most common form of regression analysis, it is assumed that the relationship can be adequately summarised by a straight line. This means that a one point increase in the value of an independent variable is assumed to have the same impact on the value of the dependent variable on average irrespective of the previous values of those variables.

Strictly speaking the technique assumes that both the dependent and the independent variables are measured on an interval level scale, although it may sometimes still be applied even where this is not the case. For example, one can use an ordinal variable (e.g. a Likert scale) as a *dependent* variable if one is willing to assume that there is an underlying interval level scale and the difference between the observed ordinal scale and the underlying interval scale is due to random measurement error. Categorical or nominal data can be used as *independent* variables by converting them into dummy or binary variables; these are variables where the only valid scores are 0 and 1, with 1 signifying membership of a particular category and 0 otherwise.

The assumptions of linear regression can cause particular difficulties where the *dependent* variable is binary. The assumption that the relationship between the dependent and the independent variables is a straight line means that it can produce estimated values for the dependent variable of less than 0 or greater than 1. In this case it may be more appropriate to assume that the relationship between the dependent and the independent variables takes the form of an S-

curve, where the impact on the dependent variable of a one-point increase in an independent variable becomes progressively less the closer the value of the dependent variable approaches 0 or 1. *Logistic regression* is an alternative form of regression which fits such an S-curve rather than a straight line. The technique can also be adapted to analyse multinomial non-interval level dependent variables, that is, variables which classify respondents into more than two categories.

The two statistical scores most commonly reported from the results of regression analyses are:

A *measure of variance explained*: This summarises how well all the independent variables combined can account for the variation in respondent's scores in the dependent variable. The higher the measure, the more accurately we are able in general to estimate the correct value of each respondent's score on the dependent variable from knowledge of their scores on the independent variables.

A *parameter estimate*: This shows how much the dependent variable will change on average, given a one unit change in the independent variable (while holding all other independent variables in the model constant). The parameter estimate has a positive sign if an increase in the value of the independent variable results in an increase in the value of the dependent variable. It has a negative sign if an increase in the value of the independent variable results in a decrease in the value of the dependent variable. If the parameter estimates are standardised, it is possible to compare the relative impact of different independent variables; those variables with the largest standardised estimates can be said to have the biggest impact on the value of the dependent variable.

Regression also tests for the statistical significance of parameter estimates. A parameter estimate is said to be significant at the five per cent level, if the range of the values encompassed by its 95 per cent confidence interval (see also section on sampling errors) are either all positive or all negative. This means that there is less than a five per cent chance that the association we have found between the dependent variable and the independent variable is simply the result of sampling error and does not reflect a relationship that actually exists in the general population.

Factor analysis

Factor analysis is a statistical technique which aims to identify whether there are one or more apparent sources of commonality to the answers given by respondents to a set of questions. It ascertains the smallest number of *factors* (or dimensions) which can most economically summarise all of the variation found in the set of questions being analysed. Factors are established where respondents who give a particular answer to one question in the set, tend to give the same answer as each other to one or more of the other questions in the set. The technique is most useful when a relatively small number of factors is able to account for a relatively large proportion of the variance in all of the questions in the set.

The technique produces a *factor loading* for each question (or variable) on each factor. Where questions have a high loading on the same factor then it will be the case that respondents who give a particular answer to one of these questions tend to give a similar answer to the other questions. The technique is most commonly used in attitudinal research to try to identify the underlying ideological dimensions which apparently structure attitudes towards the subject in question.

International Social Survey Programme

The *International Social Survey Programme* (*ISSP*) is run by a group of research organisations, each of which undertakes to field annually an agreed module of questions on a chosen topic area. Since 1985, an *International Social Survey Programme* module has been included in one of the *British Social Attitudes* self-completion questionnaires. Each module is chosen for repetition at intervals to allow comparisons both between countries (membership is currently standing at 37) and over time. In 1999, the chosen subject was Social Inequality, and the module was carried on the A version of the self-completion questionnaire (Qs.1-16).

Notes

1. Until 1991 all *British Social Attitudes* samples were drawn from the Electoral Register (ER). However, following concern that this sampling frame might be deficient in its coverage of certain population subgroups, a 'splicing' experiment was conducted in 1991. We are grateful to the Market Research Development Fund for contributing towards the costs of this experiment. Its purpose was to investigate whether a switch to PAF would disrupt the time-series – for instance, by lowering response rates or affecting the distribution of responses to particular questions. In the event, it was concluded that the change from ER to PAF was unlikely to affect time trends in any noticeable ways, and that no adjustment factors were necessary. Since significant differences in efficiency exist between PAF and ER, and because we considered it untenable to continue to use a frame that is known to be biased, we decided to adopt PAF as the sampling frame for future *British Social Attitudes* surveys. For details of the PAF/ER 'splicing' experiment, see Lynn and Taylor (1995).
2. In 1993 it was decided to mount a split-sample experiment designed to test the applicability of Computer-Assisted Personal Interviewing (CAPI) to the *British Social Attitudes* survey series. CAPI has been used increasingly over the past decade as an alternative to traditional interviewing techniques. As the name implies, CAPI involves the use of lap-top computers during the interview, with interviewers entering responses directly into the computer. One of the advantages of CAPI is that it significantly reduces both the amount of time spent on data processing and the number of coding and editing errors. Over a longer period, there could also be significant cost savings. There was, however, concern that a different interviewing

technique might alter the distribution of responses and so affect the year-on-year consistency of *British Social Attitudes* data.

Following the experiment, it was decided to change over to CAPI completely in 1994 (the self-completion questionnaire still being administered in the conventional way). The results of the experiment are discussed in the *11th Report* (Lynn and Purdon, 1994).

3. Interview times of less than 20 and more than 150 minutes were excluded as they were likely to be errors.

4. An experiment was conducted on the 1991 *British Social Attitudes* survey, which showed that sending advance letters to sampled addresses before fieldwork begins has very little impact on response rates. However, interviewers do find that an advance letter helps them to introduce the survey on the doorstep, and a majority of respondents have said that they preferred some advance notice. For these reasons, advance letters have been used on the *British Social Attitudes* surveys since 1991.

5. Before 1991, occupational coding was carried out according to the OPCS *Classification of Occupations 1980* (CO80). However, analysts can be confident that the change to SOC does not affect year-on-year comparability of Social Class variables in the *British Social Attitudes* survey. For further details see Appendix I in Jowell *et al.* (1992).

6. Because of methodological experiments on scale development, the exact items detailed below have not been asked on all versions of the questionnaire each year.

7. In 1994 only, this item was replaced by: Ordinary people get their fair share of the nation's wealth. *[Wealth1]*

8. *WrongLaw* was not asked in 1999 and therefore is not included in the libertarian-authoritarian scale in this year.

9. In constructing the scale, a decision had to be taken on how to treat missing values ("Don't knows" and refused/not answered). Respondents who had more than two missing values on the left-right scale and more than three missing values on the libertarian-authoritarian and welfare scale were excluded for that scale. For respondents with just a few missing values, "Don't knows" were recoded to the midpoint of the scale and not answered or 'refused' were recoded to the scale mean for that respondent on their valid items.

References

Bromley, C., Bryson, C., Park, A. and Thomson, K. (1999), *British Social Attitudes 1997 Survey: Technical Report,* London: National Centre for Social Research.

DeVellis, R.F. (1991), 'Scale development: theory and applications', *Applied Social Research Methods Series*, **26**, Newbury Park: Sage.

Jowell, R., Brook, L., Prior, G. and Taylor, B. (1992), *British Social Attitudes: the 9th Report*, Aldershot: Dartmouth.

Lynn, P. and Purdon, S. (1994), 'Time-series and lap-tops: the change to computer-assisted interviewing' in Jowell, R., Curtice, J., Brook, L. and Ahrendt, D. (eds.), *British Social Attitudes: the 11th Report*, Aldershot: Dartmouth.

Lynn, P and Taylor, B (1995), 'On the bias and variance of samples of individuals: a comparison of the Electoral Registers and Postcode Address File as sampling frames', *The Statistician*, **44:** 173-94.

Spector, P.E (1992), 'Summated rating scale construction: an introduction', *Quantitative Applications in the Social Sciences*, **82**, Newbury Park: Sage.

Appendix II
Notes on the tabulations

1. Figures in the tables are from the 1999 *British Social Attitudes* survey unless otherwise indicated.
2. Tables are percentaged as indicated.
3. In tables, '*' indicates less than 0.5 per cent but greater than zero, and '-' indicates zero.
4. When findings based on the responses of fewer than 100 respondents are reported in the text, reference is generally made to the small base size.
5. Percentages equal to or greater than 0.5 have been rounded up in all tables (e.g. 0.5 per cent = one per cent, 36.5 per cent = 37 per cent).
6. In many tables the proportions of respondents answering "Don't know" or not giving an answer are omitted. This, together with the effects of rounding and weighting, means that percentages will not always add to 100 per cent.
7. The self-completion questionnaire was not completed by all respondents to the main questionnaire (see Appendix I). Percentage responses to the self-completion questionnaire are based on all those who completed it.
8. The bases shown in the tables (the number of respondents who answered the question) are printed in small italics. The bases are unweighted, unless otherwise stated.

Appendix III
The questionnaires

As explained in Appendix I, three different versions of the questionnaire (A, B and C) were administered, each with its own self-completion supplement. The diagram that follows shows the structure of the questionnaires and the topics covered (not all of which are reported on in this volume).

The three interview questionnaires reproduced on the following pages are derived from the Blaise program in which they were written. For ease of reference, each item has been allocated a question number. Gaps in the numbering system indicate items that are essential components of the Blaise program but which are not themselves questions, and so have been omitted. In addition, we have removed the keying codes and inserted instead the percentage distribution of answers to each question. We have also included the SPSS variable name, in square brackets, beside each question. Above the questions we have included filter instructions. A filter instruction should be considered as staying in force until the next filter instruction. Percentages for the core questions are based on the total weighted sample, while those for questions in versions A, B or C are based on the appropriate weighted subsamples. We reproduce first version A of the interview questionnaire in full; then those parts of version B and version C that differ. The three versions of the self-completion questionnaire follow, with those parts fielded in more than one version reproduced in one version only.

The percentage distributions do not necessarily add up to 100 because of weighting and rounding, or for one or more of the following reasons:

(i)   Some sub-questions are filtered – that is, they are asked of only a proportion of respondents. In these cases the percentages add up (approximately) to the proportions who were asked them. Where, however, a series of questions is filtered, we have indicated the weighted base at the beginning of that series (for example, all employees), and throughout have derived percentages from that base.

(ii) If fewer than 50 respondents (unweighted) are asked a question, frequencies (the number of people giving each response) are shown, rather than percentages.

(iii)   At a few questions, respondents were invited to give more than one
         answer and so percentages may add to well over 100 per cent. These are
         clearly marked by interviewer instructions on the questionnaires.

As reported in Appendix I, the 1999 *British Social Attitudes* self-completion
questionnaire was not completed by 22 per cent of respondents who were
successfully interviewed. The answers in the supplement have been percentaged
on the base of those respondents who returned it. This means that the
distribution of responses to questions asked in earlier years are comparable with
those given in Appendix III of all earlier reports in this series except in *The
1984 Report*, where the percentages for the self-completion questionnaire need
to be recalculated if comparisons are to be made.

BRITISH SOCIAL ATTITUDES: 1999 SURVEY
Main questionnaire plan

Version A	Version B	Version C
Household grid		
Newspaper readership		
Party identification		
Housing		
Public spending and social welfare		
Health care		
Employment		
English National Identity		
Constitutional issues	Begging (short)	Begging (short)
Begging (long)	-	Education
-	Countryside	
-	Transport	Taste and decency
Classification		

Self-completion questionnaire plan

Version A	Version B	Version C
ISSP	-	-
Housing		
Public spending and social welfare		
Health care		
Health rationing	-	Education
Begging	Countryside	
Constitutional issues	Transport	GM foods
Attitude scales		

BRITISH SOCIAL ATTITUDES 1999: FACE TO FACE QUESTIONNAIRE

Contents page

VERSION A QUESTIONNAIRE

N=3143

ASK ALL

Q1 [SerialNo]
Serial Number
Range: 110001 ... 119999

Q7 [StRegion]
%   Standard Region
8.3   Scotland
6.5   Northern
9.4   North West
9.5   Yorks and Humberside
8.8   West Midlands
6.6   East Midlands
5.3   East Anglia
10.3 South West
19.9 South East (excl. Greater London)
10.3 Greater London
5.1   Wales

Q23 [ABCVer]
%   Questionnaire version
33.9   A
32.5   B
33.6   C

HOUSEHOLD GRID

N=3143

ASK ALL

Q32 [Househld]
(You have just been telling me about the adults that live in this household. Thinking now of **everyone** living in the household, **including children:**)
Including yourself, how many people live here regularly as members of this household?
CHECK INTERVIEWER MANUAL FOR DEFINITION OF HOUSEHOLD IF NECESSARY.
IF YOU DISCOVER THAT YOU WERE GIVEN THE WRONG INFORMATION FOR THE RESPONDENT SELECTION ON THE ARF:
    DO NOT REDO THE ARF SELECTION PRODECURE
    DO ENTER THE CORRECT INFORMATION HERE
    DO USE <CTRL + M> TO MAKE A NOTE OF WHAT HAPPENED.
HOUSEHOLD GRID: QUESTIONS ASKED ONCE FOR EACH HOUSEHOLD MEMBER
[Name] **(NOT ON DATAFILE)**
FOR RESPONDENT: (can I just check, what is your first name?)
PLEASE TYPE IN THE FIRST NAME (OR INITIALS) OF RESPONDENT
FOR OTHER HOUSEHOLD MEMBERS: PLEASE TYPE IN THE FIRST NAME (OR INITIALS) OF PERSON NUMBER (number)

[Rsex], [P2Sex] - [P10Sex]
PLEASE CODE SEX OF (name)(Figures refer to [RSex])
%
46.8   Male
53.2   Female

[RAge], [P2Age] - [P10Age]
FOR RESPONDENT: I would (now) like to ask you a few details about (yourself/each person in your household). (Starting with yourself,) what was your **age** last birthday?
FOR OTHER HOUSEHOLD MEMBERS: What was (Name's) **age** last birthday?
FOR 97+ YEARS, CODE 97.
%   Range: 1 ... 97
    Median: 46 years
-    (Don't know)
-    (Refusal/Not answered)

IF MORE THAN 1 PERSON IN HOUSEHOLD
[P2Rel] - [P10Rel] (figures refer to [P2Rel])
PLEASE ENTER RELATIONSHIP OF (Name) TO RESPONDENT
%
77.3   Partner/spouse/cohabitee
8.7   Son/daughter (inc step/adopted)
9.1   Parent/ parent-in-law
2.1   Other relative
2.8   Other non-relative
-      (Don't know)
-      (Refusal/Not answered)

N=3143

ASK ALL
[MarStat2]
CARD
Can I just check, which of these applies to you
at present?
CODE FIRST TO APPLY

	%
Married	56.2
Living as married	8.9
Separated (after being married)	2.7
Divorced	6.5
Widowed	8.5
Single (never married)	17.3
(Don't know)	-
(Refusal/Not answered)	-

Q96

NEWSPAPER READERSHIP

N=3143

ASK ALL
[Readpap]
Do you normally read any daily **morning** newspaper at least 3
times a week?

	%
Yes	56.2
No	43.8

Q103

IF 'Yes' AT [Readpap]
[WhPaper]
Which one do you normally read?
IF MORE THAN ONE: Which one do you read **most** frequently?

	%
(Scottish) Daily Express	4.0
(Scottish) Daily Mail	11.3
Daily Mirror	11.1
Daily Star	1.3
The Sun	14.1
Daily Telegraph	4.2
Financial Times	0.2
The Guardian	2.0
The Independent	1.2
The Times	13.1
Morning Star	0.1
Other Irish/Northern Irish/Scottish regional or local **daily morning** paper (WRITE IN)	3.4
Other (WRITE IN)	0.1
EDIT ONLY: MORE THAN ONE PAPER READ WITH EQUAL FREQUENCY	0.2
(Don't know)	-
(Refusal/Not answered)	-

Q104

VERSION C: ASK ALL
[TVHrsWk]
How many **hours** of television do you normally watch on an
ordinary **weekday or evening**?
INTERVIEWER: ROUND UP TO NEAREST HOUR
IF DOES NOT WATCH TELEVISION ON WEEKDAYS, CODE 0
IF NEVER WATCHES TELEVISION AT ALL, CODE 97
Range: 0 ... 97

Median: 3 hours

	%
(Never watches television)	0.3
(Don't know)	0.1
(Refusal/Not answered)	0.1

Q107

N=1056

N=1056

N=1056

Q108   **IF EVER WATCHES TELEVISION**
[TVHrsWke]
How many **hours** of television do you normally watch on an ordinary **weekend** day or evening?
INTERVIEWER: ROUND UP TO NEAREST HOUR
IF DOES NOT WATCH TELEVISION AT WEEKENDS, CODE 0
Range: 0 ...24
Median : 3 hours

0.3 (Never watches television)
0.1 (Don't know)
0.1 (Refusal/Not answered)

Q109   **IF 'never watches television at all' AT [TVHrsWk]**
[HaveTV]
Can I just check, is there a television set at all in your home?
%
- Yes
0.3 No
- (Don't know)
0.2 (Refusal/Not answered)

Q110   **VERSION C: IF HAS TELEVISION**
[Satellit]
Do you have a satellite dish or are you connected to a cable network in your own home?
INTERVIEWER: PROMPT FOR CORRECT PRECODE
EXCLUDE DISHES NO LONGER WORKING OR NO LONGER CONNECTED
%
19.8 Yes, satellite
15.0 Yes, cable
0.9 Yes, both
64.0 No
- (Don't know)
- (Refusal/Not answered)

Q111   [Digital]
Do you have access to any digital television channel in your own home?
IF YES: Is that through the normal aerial using a piece of equipment linked to your television, through a satellite or through a cable network?
IF SEVERAL, CODE FIRST TO APPLY
IF DON'T KNOW WHETHER HAS DIGITAL TV, USE CTRL + K
%
1.1 Yes, through aerial
4.8 Yes, through satellite
1.0 Yes, through cable network
1.1 Yes, don't know by what method
91.8 No
- (Don't know)
- (Refusal/Not answered)

Q112   [ChldTV]
CARD
How often, if at all, does anyone under 18 watch television in your home?
%
40.2 Once a week or more
4.5 Less often than once a week, but at least once a month
4.3 Less often than once a month, but at least once a year
48.6 Less often than once a year
2.0 (Don't know)
- (Refusal/Not answered)

Q113   [BlockChn]
Do you have the facility to block certain channels or certain programmes from being viewed?
%
16.6 Yes
81.4 No
- (Don't know)
1.7 (Refusal/Not answered)

Q114   **IF 'Yes' AT [BlockChn]**
[UseBlock]
Does anyone in your household use this facility to block certain channels or programmes from being viewed?
%
3.3 Yes
13.2 No
- (Don't know)
1.7 (Refusal/Not answered)

Q115   **VERSION C: IF HAS TELEVISION**
[Video]
Do you have a video recorder in your own home?
%
88.4 Yes
11.1 No
- (Don't know)
0.1 (Refusal/Not answered)

Q116   **IF 'Yes' AT [Video]**
[VidFilm]
CARD AGAIN
How often nowadays do you personally watch a rented or bought video tape?
%
13.6 Once a week or more
15.2 Less often than once a week, but at least once a month
29.6 Less often than once a month, but at least once a year
30.0 Less often than once a year
- (Don't know)
0.1 (Refusal/Not answered)

VERSION C: ASK ALL

N=1056

Q117 [CineOft]
CARD AGAIN
How often do you go to the cinema nowadays?
%
1.1   Once a week or more
10.3   Less often than once a week, but at least once a month
35.7   Less often than once a month, but at least once a year
52.9   Less often than once a year
\-   (Don't know)
\-   (Refusal/Not answered)

Q118 [Internet]
Does anyone have access to the Internet or World Wide Web from this address?
%
21.8   Yes
78.1   No
0.1   (Don't know)
\-   (Refusal/Not answered)

PARTY IDENTIFICATION

N=3143

ASK ALL

Q119 [SupParty]
Generally speaking, do you think of yourself as a supporter of any one political party?
%
38.7   Yes
61.2   No
\-   (Don't know)
\-   (Refusal/Not answered)

IF 'No/Don't know' AT [SupParty]

Q120 [ClosePty]
Do you think of yourself as a little closer to one political party than to the others?
%
26.4   Yes
34.7   No
0.1   (Don't know)
0.1   (Refusal/Not answered)

IF 'Yes' AT [SupParty] OR IF 'Yes/No/Don't know' AT [ClosePty] [PartyID1]
IF 'Yes' AT [SupParty] OR AT [ClosePty]: Which one?
IF 'No/Don't know' AT [ClosePty]: If there were a general election tomorrow, which political party do you think you would be most likely to support?

Q122 DO NOT PROMPT
%
24.9   Conservative
42.6   Labour
10.3   Liberal Democrat
1.2   Scottish National Party
0.7   Plaid Cymru
0.5   Other party
13.1   Other answer
1.4   None
1.9   Green Party
2.7   Refused to say
0.1   (Don't know)
  (Refusal/Not answered)

IF PARTY GIVEN AT [PartyID1]

Q127 [IdStrng]
Would you call yourself very strong (party given at [PartyID1]), fairly strong, or not very strong?
%
6.5   Very strong (party at [PartyID1])
27.3   Fairly strong
47.8   Not very strong
\-   (Don't know)
5.3   (Refusal/Not answered)

N=3143

Q128
ASK ALL
[Politics]
How much interest do you generally have in what is going on in politics ... READ OUT ...
%
6.5   a great deal,
21.3 quite a lot,
34.1 some,
26.4 not very much,
11.5 or, none at all?
0.1   (Don't know)
0.1   (Refusal/Not answered)

HOUSING

N=3143

Q130
ASK ALL
[AreaChng] *
Now some questions about the area in which you live.
Taking everything into account, would you say this area has got better, worse or remained about the same as a place to live during the **last two years**?
IF NECESSARY: By 'your area' I mean whatever you feel is your local area.

Q131
[AreaFut] *
And what do you think will happen during the **next two years**: will this area get better, worse or remain about the same as a place to live?

	[AreaChng]	[AreaFut]
	%	%
Better	13.4	16.6
Worse	28.6	25.6
About the same	55.0	55.1
(Don't know)	2.9	2.8
(Refusal/Not answered)	-	-

Q132
[HomeType]
CODE FROM OBSERVATION AND CHECK WITH RESPONDENT.
Would I be right in describing this accommodation as a ...
READ OUT ONE YOU THINK APPLIES ...
%
20.1 ...detached house or bungalow
37.0 ...semi-detached house or bungalow
29.2 ...terraced house or bungalow
10.6 ...self-contained, purpose-built flat/maisonette (inc. tenement block)
2.6   ...self-contained converted flat/maisonette
0.1   ...room(s), not self-contained
0.4   Other answer (WRITE IN)
-     (Don't know)
-     (Refusal/Not answered)

Q134
[HomeEst]
May I just check, is your home part of a housing estate (or scheme)?
NOTE: MAY BE PUBLIC OR PRIVATE, BUT IT IS THE RESPONDENT'S VIEW WE WANT
%
37.2 Yes, part of estate
62.4 No
0.4   (Don't know)
-     (Refusal/Not answered)

Q135 [Tenure5]   N=3143

Does your household own or rent this accommodation?

PROBE IF NECESSARY

IF OWNS: Outright or on a mortgage? IF RENTS: From whom?

	%
OWNS: Own (leasehold/freehold) outright	31.1
OWNS: Buying (leasehold/freehold) on mortgage	42.7
RENTS: Local authority/council	12.9
RENTS: Housing Association/Housing Trust	5.6
RENTS: Property company	1.7
RENTS: Employer	0.5
RENTS: Other organisation	0.3
RENTS: Relative	0.3
RENTS: Other individual	3.7
RENTS: Housing Action Trust	0.1
Rent free (other than squatting)	0.5
Squatting	-
Other answer (WRITE IN)	0.3
(Don't know)	0.2
(Refusal/Not answered)	-

Q139 [LegalRes]

IF OWNS OUTRIGHT: Are the deeds for the (house / flat) in your name or are they in someone else's.

IF IN RESPONDENT'S NAME: Are they in your name only or jointly with someone else?

IF BUYING ON A MORTGAGE: Is the mortgage in your name or is it in someone else's?

IF IN RESPONDENT'S NAME: Is it in your name or jointly with someone else?

IF RENTS: Is the rent book in your name or is it in someone else's?

IF IN RESPONDENT'S NAME: Is it in your name only or jointly with someone else?

IF RENT FREE/SQUATTING/OTHER: Are you legally responsible for the accommodation or is someone else?

IF LEGALLY RESPONSIBLE: Is that on your own or jointly with someone else?

	%
(Deeds/Mortgage/Rent book) in respondent's name only/ Yes, respondent solely responsible	31.5
Jointly with someone else	52.9
(Deeds/Mortgage/Rent book) in someone else's name/ No responsibility	15.4
(Don't know)	0.2
(Refusal/Not answered)	0.1

Q140 [RentPrf1]   N=3143

If you had a **free** choice would you choose to rent accommodation, or would you choose to buy?

	%
Would choose to rent	12.6
Would choose to buy	86.6
(Don't know)	0.7
(Refusal/Not answered)	-

Q141 IF 'Would choose to rent' AT [RentPrf1]

[RentPrf2]

CARD

Please choose an answer from this card to show from which sort of landlord you would rather rent?

	%
Housing Association, co-operative or trust	3.3
Council	6.4
Private landlord	2.6
Some other landlord (WRITE IN)	0.1
(Don't know)	0.3
(Refusal/Not answered)	-

Q143 IF 'would choose to buy'/DK/Ref/NA AT [RentPrf1]

[RentPrf3]

CARD

If you did not have the option to buy, from which sort of landlord would you rather rent? Please choose an answer from this card.

	%
Housing Association, co-operative or trust	28.1
Council	29.8
Private landlord	23.8
Some other landlord (WRITE IN)	0.9
(Don't know)	4.8
(Refusal/Not answered)	0.1

Q145 ASK ALL WHO OWN OUTRIGHT OR ARE BUYING ON A MORTGAGE   N=2329

[BuyFrm]

Did you, or the person responsible for the mortgage, buy your present home from the local authority or Housing Association as a tenant?

'LOCAL AUTHORITY' INCLUDES GLC, LONDON RESIDUARY BODY AND NEW TOWN DEVELOPMENT CORPORATION

IF 'YES', PROBE FOR WHICH

	%
Yes - from Local Authority	9.8
Yes - from Housing Association	1.4
No	87.9
(Don't know)	0.2
(Refusal/Not answered)	0.5

Q146
IF 'no' AT [BuyFrm]
[Rented]   N=2329
Have you **ever** rented your own accommodation?
That is, lived in a house or flat where the rent book was in your sole or joint name.
%
38.6   Yes
49.3   No
-       (Don't know)
1.0   (Refusal/Not answered)

ASK ALL WHO NOW OWN HAVING BOUGHT FROM LOCAL AUTHORITY/HOUSING ASSOCIATION OR HAVE EVER RENTED IN THE PAST (IF 'Yes' AT [BuyFrm] OR AT [Rented])   N=1181

Q147
[WhenRen2]
How long ago was it that you **last** lived in rented accommodation?
INCLUDES PRESENT HOUSE/FLAT
CODE 0 FOR LESS THAN A YEAR
Range: 0 ... 97
Median: 15 years
%
0.1   (Don't know)
1.9   (Refusal/Not answered)

Q148
-Q154
[TypeRent]
CARD
And which of these types of landlord have you ever rented accommodation from?
CODE ALL THAT APPLY
PROBE : Which others?
Multicoded (Maximum of 7 codes)
%
38.7   Local council (or New Town Development Corporation) [RentedLC]
5.9   Housing Association or cooperative or trust [RentedHA]
21.5   Private property company [RentedPV]
6.6   Employer [RentedEm]
2.9   Other organisation [RentedOt]
2.2   Relative [RentedRl]
35.3   Other individual [RentedIn]
1.9   (None of these) [RentedNN]
0.4   (Don't know)
1.9   (Refusal/Not answered)

ASK ALL WHO RENT   N=797
Q155
[EverOwnd]
Have you **ever** owned your own accommodation? That is, lived in a house or flat, which was in your sole or joint name?
%
24.3   Yes
74.2   No
-       (Don't know)
1.5   (Refusal/Not answered)

Q156
IF 'Yes' AT [EverOwnd]   N=797
[OwnedYrs]
How long ago was it that you last owned your own accommodation?
PROBE FOR BEST ESTIMATE
CODE 0 FOR LESS THAN A YEAR
Range: 0 ... 97
Median: 9 years
%
0.1   (Don't know)
1.5   (Refusal/Not answered)

ASK ALL   N=3143
Q157
[PTenure]
When you were a child, did your parents own their home, rent it from a local authority or rent it from someone else?
IF DIFFERENT TYPES OF TENURE, PROBE FOR ONE RESPONDENT LIVED IN LONGEST
%
48.1   Owned it
31.0   Rented from local authority
17.4   Rented from someone else
3.0   Other (TYPE IN)
0.4   (Don't know)
-       (Refusal/Not answered)

ASK ALL NOT CURRENTLY RENTING FROM LOCAL AUTHORITY   N=2737
Q159
[LikeCncl]
CARD
Please use this card to tell me how much you agree or disagree with the following statement.
I would like to live in council housing if I could get it
%
2.3   Agree strongly
11.4   Agree
11.6   Neither agree nor disagree
40.0   Disagree
34.5   Disagree strongly
0.2   (Don't know)
-       (Refusal/Not answered)

ASK ALL   N=3143
Q160
[CnclInc]
CARD
Which of these statements comes closest to your view?
%
39.9   Council housing should **only** be for people on very low incomes who cannot find other suitable forms of housing
59.0   OR, Council housing should be for a mixture of people with different incomes
1.0   (Don't know)
0.1   (Refusal/Not answered)

Q161   [PrivRent]
        Thinking now about the amount of **affordable**
        private accommodation available to rent in your
        area, do you think there is enough, more than enough
        or too little?

%
28.0   Enough
7.4   More than enough
44.2   Too little
20.4   (Don't know)
-       (Refusal/Not answered)

Q162   [CounRent]
        And what about the amount of **affordable council** accommodation
        available to rent in your area? Do you think
        there is enough, more than enough or too little?

%
27.0   Enough
6.3   More than enough
42.4   Too little
24.4   (Don't know)
-       (Refusal/Not answered)

N=3143

PUBLIC SPENDING AND SOCIAL WELFARE

N=3143

Q164   **ASK ALL**
        [Spend1] *
        CARD
        Here are some items of government spending. Which of them, if
        any, would be your highest priority for **extra** spending?
        Please read through the whole list before deciding.
        ENTER ONE CODE ONLY FOR HIGHEST PRIORITY

Q165   **IF NOT None/DK/Ref AT [Spend1]**
        [Spend2] *
        CARD AGAIN
        And which next?
        ENTER ONE CODE ONLY FOR NEXT HIGHEST

	[Spend1] %	[Spend2] %
Education	33.5	35.8
Defence	0.6	1.3
Health	47.4	31.2
Housing	3.5	7.1
Public transport	3.9	5.6
Roads	2.8	4.0
Police and prisons	2.9	5.0
Social security benefits	2.0	4.7
Help for industry	2.5	3.7
Overseas aid	0.6	0.7
(None of these)	0.3	0.3
(Don't know)	0.1	0.1
(Refusal/Not answered)	-	0.5

Q166   **ASK ALL**
        [SocSpnd1] *
        CARD
        Some people think that there should be more government spending
        on social security, while other people disagree. For each of
        the groups I read out please say whether you would like to see
        more or **less** government spending on them than now. Bear in mind
        that if you want more spending, this would probably mean that
        you would have to pay more taxes. If you want less spending,
        this would probably mean paying less taxes.
        Firstly, ...READ OUT...
        Benefits for unemployed people: would you like to see more or
        less government spending than now?

Q167 [SocSpnd2]*
CARD AGAIN
(Would you like to see more or less government spending than now)
Benefits for disabled people who cannot work

Q168 [SocSpnd3]*
CARD AGAIN
(Would you like to see more or less government spending than now)
Benefits for parents who work on very low incomes

Q169 [SocSpnd4]*
CARD AGAIN
(Would you like to see more or less government spending than now)
Benefits for single parents

Q170 [SocSpnd5]*
CARD AGAIN
(Would you like to see more or less government spending than now)
Benefits for retired people

Q171 [SocSpnd6]*
CARD AGAIN
(Would you like to see more or less government spending than now)
Benefits for people who care for those who are sick or disabled

	[SocSpnd1]	[SocSpnd2]	[SocSpnd3]
	%	%	%
Spend much more	2.2	11.6	6.7
Spend more	21.9	60.6	62.2
Spend the same as now	40.8	23.4	25.3
Spend less	28.7	1.7	2.9
Spend much less	3.7	0.1	0.2
(Don't know)	2.7	2.6	2.6
(Refusal/Not answered)	0.1	-	-

	[SocSpnd4]	[SocSpnd5]	[SocSpnd6]
	%	%	%
Spend much more	3.7	12.5	19.0
Spend more	29.2	57.9	63.2
Spend the same as now	40.8	24.9	15.2
Spend less	18.9	3.1	0.8
Spend much less	3.5	0.2	-
(Don't know)	3.8	1.3	1.8
(Refusal/Not answered)	-	-	0.1

Q172 [FalseClm] *   N=3143
I will read two statements. For each one please say whether you agree or disagree. Firstly...
Large numbers of people these days **falsely** claim benefits.
IF AGREE OR DISAGREE: Strongly or slightly?

Q173 [FailClm] *
(And do you agree or disagree that...)
Large numbers of people who are eligible for benefits these days **fail** to claim them.
IF AGREE OR DISAGREE: Strongly or slightly?

	[FalseClm]	[FailClm]
	%	%
Agree strongly	57.3	36.9
Agree slightly	26.4	43.5
Disagree slightly	7.8	10.0
Disagree strongly	4.3	3.3
(Don't know)	4.1	6.2
(Refusal/Not answered)	-	-

Q174 [Dole]
Opinions differ about the level of benefits for unemployed people.
Which of these two statements comes closest to your own view
... READ OUT ...

	%
...benefits for unemployed people are **too low** and cause hardship,	32.8
or, benefits for unemployed people are **too high** and discourage them from finding jobs?	42.4
(Neither)	17.8
EDIT ONLY: BOTH: UNEMPLOYMENT BENEFIT CAUSES HARDSHIP BUT CAN'T BE HIGHER OR THERE WOULD BE NO INCENTIVE TO WORK	0.5
EDIT ONLY: BOTH: UNEMPLOYMENT BENEFIT CAUSES HARDSHIP TO SOME, WHILE OTHERS DO WELL OUT OF IT	0.4
EDIT ONLY: ABOUT RIGHT/IN BETWEEN	2.4
Other answer (WRITE IN)	3.5
(Don't know)	0.1
(Refusal/Not answered)	-

Q176 [TaxSpend]
CARD
Suppose the government had to choose between the three options on this card. Which do you think it should choose?

	%
Reduce taxes and spend **less** on health, education and social benefits	3.8
Keep taxes and spending on these services at the **same** level as now	34.5
Increase taxes and spend **more** on health, education and social benefits	58.0
(None)	3.1
(Don't know)	0.5
(Refusal/Not answered)	-

Q177 [MstUnemp]   N=3143
Suppose two people working for a large firm each became unemployed through no fault of their own. One had a very high income, one had a very low income. Do you think the very high earner should be entitled to ...READ OUT...
... more unemployment benefit than the very low earner,
the same amount,
or, no unemployment benefit at all?
EDIT ONLY: It depends
Other answer (WRITE IN)
(Don't know)
(Refusal/Not answered)

%
9.9
74.0
11.2
2.4
1.0
0.5
1.0
-

Q179 [MstRetir]
Now suppose a very high earner and a very low earner in a large firm retired. Do you think the very high earner should be entitled to ...READ OUT...
... a bigger **state** retirement pension than the very low earner,
the same amount,
a lower **state** pension,
or, no **state** pension at all?
EDIT ONLY: It depends
Other answer (WRITE IN)
(Don't know)
(Refusal/Not answered)

%
13.6
70.4
11.4
2.8
0.9
0.1
0.7
-

Q181 [MstChild]
Now what about child benefit. Should very high earners be entitled to ...READ OUT...
... more child benefit than very low earners,
the same amount,
less,
or, no child benefit at all?
EDIT ONLY: It depends
Other answer (WRITE IN)
(Don't know)
(Refusal/Not answered)

%
1.0
46.3
25.9
25.6
0.1
0.4
0.6
0.1

Q183 [MstDisab]   N=3143
Now what about disability benefits. Should disabled people with very high incomes be entitled to ...READ OUT...
... more disability benefits than those with very low incomes,
the same amount,
less disability benefits,
or, no disability benefits at all?
EDIT ONLY: It depends
Other answer (WRITE IN)
(Don't know)
(Refusal/Not answered)

%
3.8
61.0
25.0
8.0
0.8
0.2
1.2
-

Q185 [MstWork]
Suppose two people go to claim unemployment benefit. One person has just become unemployed through no fault of their own after working for a long time and the other person has not worked for a long time.
Do you think that the person who has recently worked should be entitled to ...READ OUT...
more unemployment benefit than the person who has not worked for a long time,
the same amount,
less benefit,
or, no unemployment benefit at all?
EDIT ONLY: It depends
Other answer (WRITE IN)
(Don't know)
(Refusal/Not answered)

%
25.4
67.3
4.4
0.3
1.0
0.2
1.5
0.1

Q187   ASK ALL
[HealResp]*
CARD
Please say from this card who you think should **mainly** be responsible for paying for the cost of health care when someone is ill?

Q188 [RetResp]*
CARD AGAIN
Still looking at this card, who you think should **mainly** be responsible for ensuring that people have enough money to live on in retirement?

Q189 [SickResp]*
CARD AGAIN
And who do you think should **mainly** be responsible for ensuring that people have enough to live on if they become sick for a long time or disabled?

N=3143

Q190 [UnemResp]*
CARD AGAIN
And who do you think should **mainly** be responsible for ensuring that people have enough to live on if they become unemployed?

	[HealResp]	[UnemResp]	[SickResp]	[UnemResp]
	%	%	%	%
Mainly the government	84.7	58.0	82.6	86.6
Mainly a person's employer	8.9	9.4	7.3	3.4
Mainly the person themselves and their family	1.4	1.8	1.9	8.1
(Don't know)	1.4	1.8	1.9	1.8
(Refusal/Not answered)	0.1	-	-	-

Q191 [CareResp]
CARD
And who do you think should **mainly** be responsible for paying for the care needs of elderly people living in residential and nursing homes?

	%
Mainly the government	80.1
Mainly a person themselves and their family	15.8
(Don't know)	4.0
(Refusal/Not answered)	0.1

Q192 [MortUE]*
CARD
Please say from this card who you think should be mainly responsible for re-paying someone's mortgage if they become unemployed.

Q193 [MortIll]*
CARD AGAIN
And who do you think should be mainly responsible for re-paying someone's mortgage if they become too ill to work.

	[MortUE]	[MortIll]
	%	%
Mainly the government	31.5	55.2
Mainly a person's employer	5.8	6.8
Mainly a person themselves and their family	56.5	33.0
(Don't know)	6.2	5.0
(Refusal/Not answered)	-	-

VERSIONS A & B: ASK ALL **N=2087**

Q194 [UB1Poor]
Think of a 25 year-old **unemployed** woman living alone. Her only income comes from state benefits.
Would you say that she ... READ OUT ...

	%
... has more than enough to live on,	3.2
has enough to live on,	29.7
is hard up,	48.7
or, is really poor?	8.3
(Don't know)	10.0
(Refusal/Not answered)	0.1

Q195 [MWagPoor]
How about a 25 year-old **working** woman living alone. She is paid the minimum wage. Would you say that she ..READ OUT...

	%
... has more than enough to live on,	1.2
has enough to live on,	26.4
is hard up,	61.9
or, is really poor?	6.1
(Don't know)	4.4
(Refusal/Not answered)	0.1

Q196 [MWageAmt]
How much do you think the minimum wage per hour is for a 25 year-old?
(Many people are not exactly sure about this, but your best guess will be close enough.)
ENTER AMOUNT IN POUNDS (WITH PENCE AS DECIMALS)
Median: £3.60

Q197 **ASK ALL** **N=3143**
[MtUnmar1]
Imagine an unmarried couple who split up. They have a child at primary school who remains with the mother. Do you think that the father should always be made to make maintenance payments to support the child?

Q198 [MtUnmar2]*
If he **does** make the maintenance payments for the child, should the amount depend on his income, or not?

Q199 [MtUnmar3]*
Do you think that the amount of maintenance should depend on the **mother's** income, or not?

	[MtUnmar1]	[MtUnmar2]	[MtUnmar3]
	%	%	%
Yes	89.9	88.7	71.6
No	8.8	10.5	27.3
(Don't know)	1.2	0.8	1.0
(Refusal/Not answered)	0.1	0.0	0.0

Q200 [MtUnmar4] *
Suppose the mother now marries someone else.
Should the child's natural father go on paying
maintenance for the child, should he stop or
should it depend on the step-father's income?

N=3143

Q201 [MtUnmar5] *
Suppose instead the mother does not marry, but
the father has another child with someone else.
Should he go on paying maintenance for the first
child, should he stop or should it depend on his income?

	[MtUnmar4]	[MtUnmar5]
	%	%
Continue	49.8	71.7
Stop	11.6	1.4
Depends	37.6	26.1
(Don't know)	1.0	0.7
(Refusal/Not answered)	-	-

VERSIONS A & B: ASK ALL
Q202 [IncomGap]
Thinking of income levels generally in Britain today, would you
say that the gap between those with high incomes and those with
low incomes is
...READ OUT...

N=2087

%
81.3   ... too large,
12.7   about right,
2.8   or, too small?
3.2   (Don't know)
0.1   (Refusal/Not answered)

Q203 [SRInc]
Among which group would you place yourself ...READ OUT....
%
3.5   ... high income,
51.6   middle income,
44.3   or, low income?
0.5   (Don't know)
0.1   (Refusal/Not answered)

Q204 [HIncDiff]
CARD
Which of the phrases on this card would you say comes closest
to your feelings about your household's income these
days?
%
36.7   Living comfortably on present income
47.1   Coping on present income
11.5   Finding it difficult on present income
4.4   Finding it very difficult on present income
0.1   Other answer (WRITE IN)
0.1   (Don't know)
0.1   (Refusal/Not answered)

HEALTH

ASK ALL
Q207 [NHSSat] *
CARD
All in all, how satisfied or dissatisfied would you say you are
with the way in which the National Health Service runs
nowadays?
Choose a phrase from this card.

N=3143

Q208 [GPSat] *
CARD AGAIN
From your own experience, or from what you have heard, please
say how satisfied or dissatisfied you are with the way in which
each of these parts of the National Health Service runs
nowadays:
First, local doctors or GPs?

Q209 [DentSat] *
CARD AGAIN
(And how satisfied or dissatisfied are you with the NHS as
regards...)
... National Health Service dentists?

Q210 [InpatSat] *
CARD AGAIN
(And how satisfied or dissatisfied are you with the NHS as
regards...)
... Being in hospital as an in-patient?

Q211 [OutpaSat] *
CARD AGAIN
(And how satisfied or dissatisfied are you with the NHS as
regards...)
... Attending hospital as an out-patient?

Q212 [AESat] *
CARD AGAIN
(And how satisfied or dissatisfied are you with the NHS as
regards...)
... Accident and emergency departments?

	[NHSSat]	[GpSat]	[DentSat]
	%	%	%
Very satisfied	7.8	25.8	13.9
Quite satisfied	38.6	49.9	39.3
Neither satisfied nor dissat.	19.9	9.4	17.4
Quite dissatisfied	22.8	10.7	14.1
Very dissatisfied	10.6	3.7	9.7
(Don't know)	0.4	0.4	5.5
(Refusal/Not answered)	-	-	-

N=3143

	[InpatSat]	[OutpaSat]	[AeSat]
	%	%	%
Very satisfied	16.3	13.1	15.5
Quite satisfied	41.3	42.6	37.0
Neither satisfied nor dissat.	19.1	18.8	17.2
Quite dissatisfied	11.7	15.3	15.9
Very dissatisfied	4.9	6.1	8.3
(Don't know)	6.6	4.0	6.1
(Refusal/Not answered)	-	-	-

VERSIONS A & B: ASK ALL

Q213 [PrivMed]
Are you **yourself** covered by a private health insurance scheme, that is an insurance scheme that allows you to get private medical **treatment**?
ADD IF NECESSARY: `For example, BUPA or PPP.'
IF INSURANCE COVERS DENTISTRY **only**, CODE `No'

N=2087

	%
Yes	18.8
No	81.0
(Don't know)	0.2
(Refusal/Not answered)	0.0

IF 'Yes' AT [PrivMed]

Q214 [PrivPaid]
Does your employer (or your partner's employer) pay the majority of the cost of membership of this scheme?

	%
Yes	9.2
No	9.5
(Don't know)	0.1
(Refusal/Not answered)	0.2

ASK ALL

Q215 [OutPat1]*
CARD
Now suppose you had a back problem and your GP referred you to a hospital out-patients' department. From what you know or have heard, please say whether you think...
...you would get an appointment within three months?

N=3143

Q216 [OutPat2]*
CARD AGAIN
(And please say whether you think ...)
...when you arrived, the doctor would see you within half an hour of your appointment time?

Q217 [OutPat3]*
CARD AGAIN
(And please say whether you think ...)
...if you wanted to complain about the treatment you received, you would be able to without any fuss or bother?

N=3143

Q218 [WhchHosp]*
CARD AGAIN
Now suppose you needed to go into hospital for an operation. Do you think you would have a say about which hospital you went to?

	[OutPat1]	[OutPat2]
	%	%
Definitely would	10.6	6.7
Probably would	37.1	32.7
Probably would not	34.8	39.4
Definitely would not	14.8	19.2
(Don't know)	2.7	1.9
(Refusal/Not answered)	-	-

	[OutPat3]	[WhchHosp]
	%	%
Definitely would	12.8	5.9
Probably would	45.3	19.7
Probably would not	27.3	44.9
Definitely would not	8.2	25.5
(Don't know)	6.4	4.0
(Refusal/Not answered)	-	-

Q219 [GPChange]
Suppose you wanted to change your GP and go to a different practice, how difficult or easy do you think this would be to arrange?
Would it be ...READ OUT...

	%
...very difficult,	7.3
fairly difficult,	21.2
not very difficult,	36.9
or, not at all difficult?	27.1
(Don't know)	7.5
(Refusal/Not answered)	-

Q220 [SRHealth]
How is your health in general for someone of
your age? Would you say that is is
...READ OUT...
%
36.0 ... very good,
43.1 fairly good,
14.4 fair,
5.1 bad,
1.3 or, very bad?
- (Don't know)
- (Refusal/Not answered)

N=3143

ECONOMIC ACTIVITY AND LABOUR MARKET

N=3143

ASK ALL

Q234 [REconAct] (PERCENTAGES REFER TO THE HIGHEST ANSWER ON THE LIST)
CARD
Which of these descriptions applied to what you were doing last
week, that is the seven days ending last Sunday?

2.6 In full-time education (not paid for by employer, including on
vacation)

0.2 On government training/employment programme (eg. Youth
Training, Training for Work etc)

55.6 In paid work (or away temporarily) for at least 10 hours in
week

0.5 Waiting to take up paid work already accepted

2.7 Unemployed and registered at a benefit office

1.1 Unemployed, **not** registered, but actively looking for a job (of
at least 10 hrs a week)

0.4 Unemployed, wanting a job (of at least 10 hrs per week) but **not**
actively looking for a job

4.5 Permanently sick or disabled

20.8 Wholly retired from work

11.4 Looking after the home

0.2 (Doing something else) (WRITE IN)

- (Don't know)

- (Refusal/Not answered)

ASK ALL NOT WORKING

N=1380

Q235 [RLastJob]
How long ago did you last have a paid job of at least 10 hours
a week?
GOVERNMENT PROGRAMS/SCHEMES DO NOT COUNT AS `PAID JOBS'.
%
15.7 Within past 12 months
20.4 Over 1, up to 5 years ago
19.6 Over 5, up to 10 years ago
25.2 Over 10, up to 20 years ago
13.6 Over 20 years ago
5.3 Never had a paid job of 10+ hours a week
- (Don't know)
0.1 (Refusal/Not answered)

Q236   **ASK ALL WHO HAVE EVER WORKED**
[RTitle] **(NOT ON THE DATAFILE)**   N=3070
IF IN PAID WORK: Now I want to ask you about your
present job. What is your job? PROBE IF NECESSARY:
What is the name or title of the job?
IF WAITING TO TAKE UP PAID WORK: Now I want to ask you about
your future job. What is your job? PROBE IF NECESSARY: What is
the name or title of the job?
IF NOT WORKING BUT HAD A JOB: Now I want to ask you about your
last job. What was your job? PROBE IF NECESSARY: What was the
name or title of the job?

Q237   [RTypewk] **(NOT ON THE DATAFILE)**
What kind of work (do/will/did) you do most of
the time?
IF RELEVANT: What materials/machinery (do/will/did) you use?

Q238   [RTrain] **(NOT ON THE DATAFILE)**
What training or qualifications (are/were) needed for that job?

Q239   [RSuper2]
(Do/will/did) you directly supervise or (are you/will you
be/were you) directly responsible for the work of any other
people?
   %
36.5   Yes
63.4   No
-    (Don't know)
0.1   (Refusal/Not answered)

Q240   **IF 'Yes' AT [Super2]**
[RMany]
How many?
Median: 5 (Of those supervising any)
0.1   (Don't know)
0.1   (Refusal/Not answered)

Q242   **ASK ALL WHO HAVE EVER WORKED**
[REmplyee]   N=2704
In your (main) job (are you/will you be/were you) ...READ
OUT...
   %
88.0   an employee,
11.9   self-employed?
-    (Don't know)
0.1   (Refusal/Not answered)

Q244   **ASK ALL EMPLOYEES IN CURRENT OR LAST JOB**
[RSupman2]
Can I just check, (are you/will you be/were you) ...READ
OUT...
   %
17.3   ...a manager,
14.6   a foreman or supervisor,
67.9   or not?
-    (Don't know)
0.1   (Refusal/Not answered)

Q245   [ROcSect2]
CARD   N=2704
Which of the types of organisation on this card
(do you work/will you be working/did you work) for?
   %
70.2   PRIVATE SECTOR FIRM OR COMPANY Including, for example, limited
companies and PLCs
2.8   NATIONALISED INDUSTRY OR PUBLIC CORPORATION Including, for
example, the Post Office and the BBC
24.5   OTHER PUBLIC SECTOR EMPLOYER
Incl eg: - Central govt/ Civil Service/ Govt Agency /
Local authority/ Local Educ Auth (incl 'opted out' schools)/
Universities / Health Authority / NHS hospitals / NHS Trusts/
GP surgeries /Police / Armed forces
2.0   CHARITY/ VOLUNTARY SECTOR Including, for example, charitable
companies, churches, trade unions
0.4   Other answer (WRITE IN)
-    (Don't know)
0.1   (Refusal/Not answered)

Q247   **ASK ALL WHO HAVE EVER WORKED**
[EmpMake] **(NOT ON SPSS FILE)**   N=3070
IF EMPLOYEE: What (does/did) your employer make or do at the
place where you (work/will work/worked) (from)?
IF SELF-EMPLOYED: What (does/did) you make or do at the place
where you (work/will work/worked) (from)?

Q248   **ASK ALL CURRENTLY SELF-EMPLOYED**
[SPartnrs]   N=249
In your work or business, do you have any partners or other
self-employed colleagues?
   %
40.2   Yes, has partner(s)
59.3   No
-    (Don't know)
0.4   (Refusal/Not answered)
NOTE: DOES NOT INCLUDE EMPLOYEES

Q250   **ASK ALL SELF-EMPLOYED IN CURRENT OR LAST JOB**
[SEmpNum]   N=354
In your work or business, (do/did) you have any employees, or
not?
IF YES: How many?
IF 'NO EMPLOYEES', CODE 0.
FOR 500+ EMPLOYEES, CODE 500.
NOTE: FAMILY MEMBERS MAY BE EMPLOYEES ONLY IF THEY RECEIVE A
REGULAR WAGE OR SALARY.
Range: 0 ... 500
Median: 0
   %
0.5   (Don't know)
-    (Refusal/Not answered)

ASK ALL WHO HAVE EVER WORKED
(for self-employed: coded from [SEmpNum])   N=3070

Q251 [REmpWork]
      Including yourself, how many people (are/were) employed at the
      place where you usually (work/will work/worked)(from)?
      PROBE FOR CORRECT PRECODE.
      %
7.3   None
17.9 Under 10
15.4 10-24
22.7 25-99
22.0 100-499
13.8 500 or more
0.7   (Don't know)
0.0   (Refusal/Not answered)

ASK ALL IN PAID WORK   N=1748

Q254 [WkJbTim]
      In your present job, are you working ... READ OUT ...
      RESPONDENT'S OWN DEFINITION
      %
77.9 ... full-time,
22.0 or, part-time?
0.1   (Don't know)
-     (Refusal/Not answered)

Q257 [WkJbHrsI]
      How many hours do you normally work a week in your main job -
      including any paid or unpaid overtime?
      ROUND TO NEAREST HOUR.
      IF RESPONDENT CANNOT ANSWER, ASK ABOUT LAST WEEK.
      IF RESPONDENT DOES NOT KNOW EXACTLY, ACCEPT AN ESTIMATE.
      FOR 95+ HOURS, CODE 95.
      FOR 'VARIES TOO MUCH TO SAY', CODE 96.
      Median : 40 hours
1.3   Varies too much to say
0.3   (Don't know)0.0   (Refusal/Don't know)

ASK ALL CURRENT EMPLOYEES   N=1499

Q258 [EJbHrsX]
      What are your **basic or contractual hours** each
      week in your main job - **excluding** any paid and unpaid overtime?
      ROUND TO NEAREST HOUR.
      IF RESPONDENT CANNOT ANSWER, ASK ABOUT LAST WEEK.
      IF RESPONDENT DOES NOT KNOW EXACTLY, ACCEPT AN ESTIMATE.
      FOR 95+ HOURS, CODE 95.
      FOR 'VARIES TOO MUCH TO SAY', CODE 96.
      Median 37.0 hours
      %
3.0   Varies too much to say
1.3   (Don't know)
-     (Refusal/Not answered)

ASK ALL WAITING TO TAKE UP PAID WORK OR NOT
WORKING BUT HAD A JOB IN THE PAST   N=1322

Q259 [ExPrtFul]
      (Was the job/will the job be) ... READ OUT ...
      %
72.5 ... full-time - that is, 30 or more hours per week,
27.3 or, part-time?
-     (Don't know)
0.2   (Refusal/Not answered)

ASK ALL WHO HAVE EVER WORKED   N=3070

Q289 [UnionSA]
      (May I just check) are you **now** a member of a trade union or
      staff association?
      CODE FIRST TO APPLY
      %
18.5 Yes, trade union
78.0 Yes, staff association
0.1   No
0.1   (Don't know)
      (Refusal/Not answered)

IF 'No/DK' AT [UnionSA]
Q290 [TUSAEver]
      Have you **ever** been a member of a trade union or staff
      association?
      CODE FIRST TO APPLY
      %
26.9 Yes, trade union
2.7   Yes, staff association
48.3 No
0.2   (Don't know)
0.1   (Refusal/Not answered)

ASK ALL CURRENT EMPLOYEES   N=1499
[Employdt]
Q291 For how long have you been continuously employed by your
      present employer?
      Median : 48 months
      %
0.1   (Don't know)

ASK ALL NOT IN PAID WORK   N=1395
Q294 [NPWork10]
      In the seven days ending last Sunday, did you have any paid
      work of less than 10 hours a week?
      %
4.2   Yes
95.8 No
-     (Don't know)
-     (Refusal/Not answered)

ASK ALL CURRENT EMPLOYEES   N=1499

Q295 [WageNow]
How would you describe the wages or salary you are paid for the job you do - on the low side, reasonable, or on the high side?
IF LOW: Very low or a bit low?

%
10.6 Very low
24.4 A bit low
57.4 Reasonable
7.4 On the high side
0.0 Other answer (WRITE IN)
-    (Don't know)
-    (Refusal/Not answered)

Q297 [PayGap]
CARD
Thinking of the **highest** and the **lowest** paid people at your place of work, how would you describe the **gap** between their pay, as far as you know?
Please choose a phrase from this card.

%
17.4 Much too big a gap
29.7 Too big
43.3 About right
2.9 Too small
0.4 Much too small a gap
6.2 (Don't know)
0.1 (Refusal/Not answered)

Q298 [WageXpct]
If you stay in this job, would you expect your wages or salary over the coming year to ..READ OUT...

%
23.8 ..rise by **more** than the cost of living,
47.5 rise by the **same** as the cost of living,
15.9 rise by **less** than the cost of living,
10.3 or, **not** to rise at all?
1.5 (Will not stay in job)
1.0 (Don't know)
0.0 (Refusal/Not answered)

IF 'not to rise at all' AT [WageXpct]
Q299 [WageDrop]
Would you expect your wages or salary to stay the same, or in fact to go down?

%
9.7 Stay the same
0.7 Go down
-    (Don't know)
2.5 (Refusal/Not answered)

ASK ALL CURRENT EMPLOYEES   N=1499

Q300 [NumEmp]
Over the coming year do you expect your workplace to be .. READ OUT ...

%
27.0 .. increasing its number of employees,
16.2 reducing its number of employees,
54.1 or, will the number of employees stay about the same?
0.6 Other answer (WRITE IN)
2.1 (Don't know)
-    (Refusal/Not answered)

Q302 [LeaveJob]
Thinking now about your own job.
How likely or unlikely is it that you will leave this employer over the next year for any reason?
Is it .. READ OUT ...

%
10.7 .. very likely,
13.8 quite likely,
32.2 not very likely,
42.3 or, not at all likely?
1.0 (Don't know)
-    (Refusal/Not answered)

IF 'Very likely' OR 'Quite likely' AT [LeaveJob]
Q303 CARD
-Q311 Why do you think you will leave? Please choose a phrase from this card or tell me what other reason there is.
CODE ALL THAT APPLY
Multicoded (Maximum of 9 codes)

%
1.3 Firm will close down [WhyGo1]
2.2 I will be declared redundant [WhyGo2]
0.7 I will reach normal retirement age [WhyGo3]
1.4 My contract of employment will expire [WhyGo4]
0.9 I will take early retirement [WhyGo5]
15.3 I will decide to leave and work for another employer [WhyGo6]
1.7 I will decide to leave and work for myself, as self-employed [WhyGo7]
0.9 I will leave to look after home/children/relative [WhyGo8]
0.7 Return to education [WhyGo11]
2.3 Other answer (WRITE IN) [WhyGo8]
1.0 (Don't know)
0.1 (Refusal/Not answered)

ASK ALL CURRENT EMPLOYEES   N=1499
[ELookJob]
Suppose you lost your job for one reason or another
- would you start looking for another job, would you
wait for several months or longer before you started looking,
or would you decide not to look for another job?

Q323
%
Start looking   89.6
Wait several months or longer   3.1
Decide not to look   6.3
(Don't know)   1.0
(Refusal/Not answered)   -

IF 'Start looking' AT [ELookJob]
[EFindJob]
How long do you think it would take you to find an acceptable
replacement job?
IF LESS THAN ONE MONTH, CODE AS ONE MONTH
IF 'NEVER' PLEASE CODE 96
ENTER NUMBER. THEN SPECIFY MONTHS OR YEARS
Median: 2 months

Q326
%
(Don't know)   -
(Refusal/Not answered)   1.1

IF '3 Months or more/never/Don't know' AT [EFindJob]
[ERetrain]
How willing do you think you would be in these circumstances to
retrain for a different job ... READ OUT ...
...very willing,
quite willing,
or - not very willing?

Q327
%
...very willing,   20.4
quite willing,   9.7
or - not very willing?   5.0
(Don't know)   -
(Refusal/Not answered)   1.0

ASK ALL CURRENT EMPLOYEES
[ESelfEm]
For any period during the last five years, have you worked
as a **self-employed** person as your main job?
Yes
No

Q328
%
Yes   6.2
No   93.7
(Don't know)   0.1
(Refusal/Not answered)   -

**ASK ALL NOT UNEMPLOYED, PERMANENTLY SICK OR
RETIRED**   N=2218
[NwUnemp]
During the last **five years** - that is since May 1994 - have
you been unemployed and seeking work for any period?
Yes
No

Q330
%
Yes   20.0
No   80.0
(Don't know)   -
(Refusal/Not answered)   -

**ASK ALL WHO ARE CURRENTLY UNEMMPLOYED OR
'Yes' AT [NwUnemp]**   N=576
[NwUnempT]
For how many **months** in total during the last five years, that
is, since May 1994, have you been unemployed and seeking work?
INTERVIEWER: IF LESS THAN ONE MONTH, CODE AS 1.
Median: 6 months

Q332
%
(Don't know)   1.4
(Refusal/Not answered)   0.3

ASK ALL UNEMPLOYED   N=132
[CurUnemp]
How long has this **present** period of unemployment and seeking
work lasted so far?
ENTER NUMBER. THEN SPECIFY MONTHS OR YEARS
Median: 6 months

Q335
%
(Don't know)   1.7
(Refusal/Not answered)   1.3

[JobQual]
How confident are you that you will find a job to match your
qualifications ... READ OUT ...
... very confident,
quite confident,
not very confident,
or, not at all confident?

Q336
%
... very confident,   13.9
quite confident,   39.3
not very confident,   22.0
or, not at all confident?   24.4
(Don't know)   -
(Refusal/Not answered)   0.4

[UFindjob]
Although it may be difficult to judge, how long **from now** do you
think it will be before you find an acceptable job?
ENTER NUMBER. THEN SPECIFY MONTHS OR YEARS
CODE 96 FOR NEVER
Median: 3 months

Q339
%
(Never)   16.4
(Don't know)   18.2
(Refusal/Not answered)   0.4

Q340   **IF 3 MONTHS OR MORE OR DK AT [UFindJOB]**   N=132
[URetrain]*
How willing do you think you would be in these circumstances to retrain for a different job ... READ OUT ...

Q341   [UJobMove]*
How willing would you be to move to a different area to find an acceptable job ... READ OUT ...

Q342   [UBadJob]*
And how willing do you think you would be in these circumstances to take what you would now consider to be an unacceptable job ... READ OUT ...

	[URetrain]	[UJobMove]	[UBadJob]
	%	%	%
very willing,	20.4	9.3	5.4
quite willing,	9.7	13.9	15.1
or, not very willing?	5.0	45.7	46.3
(Don't know)	-	2.5	4.6
(Refusal/Not answered)	1.0	0.4	0.4

ASK ALL UNEMPLOYED

Q343   [ConMove]
Have you ever **actually** considered moving to a different area - an area other than the one you live in now - to try to find work?
%
Yes   35.2
No   64.4
(Don't know)   -
(Refusal/Not answered)   0.4

Q344   [UJobChnc]
Do you think that there is a real chance nowadays that you will get a job in this area, or is there **no** real chance nowadays?
%
Real chance   55.0
No real chance   40.0
(Don't know)   4.6
(Refusal/Not answered)   0.4

Q345   [FPtWork]
Would you prefer full- or part-time work, if you had the choice?
%
Full-time   70.6
Part-time   20.2
Not looking for work   8.8
(Don't know)   -
(Refusal/Not answered)   0.4

Q346   **IF 'Part-time' AT [FPtWork]**   N=132
[Parttime]
About how many hours per week would you like to work?
PROBE FOR BEST ESTIMATE
Range: 1 ... 30
Median : 21.5 hours
%
(Don't know)   -
(Refusal/Not answered)   0.4

ASK ALL LOOKING AFTER HOME

Q347   [EverJob]
Have you, during **the last five years**, ever had a full- or part-time job of 10 hours or more a week?   N=360
Yes   34.2
No   65.6
(Don't know)   -
(Refusal/Not answered)   0.2

Q348   **IF 'No' AT [EverJob]**
[FtJobSer]
How seriously in the past five years have you considered getting a **full-time job**
PROMPT, IF NECESSARY: Full-time is 30 or more hours a week ... READ OUT ...
%
... very seriously,   2.0
quite seriously,   3.4
not very seriously,   7.0
or, not at all seriously?   53.3
(Don't know)   -
(Refusal/Not answered)   0.2

Q349   **IF 'Not very seriously', 'Not at all seriously' OR 'DK' AT [FtJobSer]**
[PtJobSer]
How seriously, in the past five years, have you considered getting a **part-time** job ... READ OUT ...
%
... very seriously,   2.3
quite seriously,   4.3
not very seriously,   8.2
or, not at all seriously?   44.9
(Don't know)   0.5
(Refusal/Not answered)   0.2

ASK ALL CURRENTLY SELF-EMPLOYED   N=249

Q350 [SEmplee]
Have you, for any period in the last five years, worked as an employee as your main job rather than as self-employed?

%
25.9   Yes
73.6   No
-   (Don't know)
0.4   (Refusal/Not answered)

Q351 **IF 'Yes' AT [SEmplee]**
[SEmpleeT]
In total for how many months during the last five years have you been an employee?
ENTER NUMBER OF MONTHS
Range: 1 ... 60
Median: 24 months

%
0.2   (Don't know)
0.4   (Refusal/Not answered)

Q352 **IF 'No/DK' AT [SEmplee]**
[SEmplSer]
How seriously in the last five years have you considered getting a job as an **employee** ... READ OUT ...

%
4.7   ... very seriously,
5.1   quite seriously,
9.8   not very seriously,
53.1   or, not at all seriously?
0.9   (Don't know)
0.4   (Refusal/Not answered)

Q353 **ASK ALL CURRENTLY SELF-EMPLOYED**
[BnslOK]
Compared with **a year ago**, would you say your business is doing ... READ OUT ...

%
13.8   ... very well,
23.8   quite well,
40.0   about the same,
12.3   not very well,
1.6   or, not at all well?
7.1   (Business not in existence then)
0.9   (Don't know)
0.4   (Refusal/Not answered)

Q354 [BuslFut]
And over **the coming year**, do you think your business will do ... READ OUT ...

%
34.8   ... better,
51.8   about the same,
8.9   or, worse than this year?
2.2   Other answer (WRITE IN)
1.8   (Don't know)
0.4   (Refusal/Not answered)

ASK ALL CURRENT EMPLOYEES   N=1499

Q356 [WpUnions]
At your place of work are there unions, staff associations, or groups of unions recognised by the management for negotiating pay and conditions of employment?
IF YES, PROBE FOR UNION OR STAFF ASSOCIATION
IF 'BOTH', CODE '1'

%
42.7   Yes : trade union(s)
4.5   Yes : staff association
49.3   No, none
3.4   (Don't know)
0.0   (Refusal/Not answered)

Q357 **IF 'Yes: trade unions/staff association/both' AT [WpUnion2]**
[WpUnsure]
Can I just check: does management **recognise** these unions or staff associations for the purposes of negotiating **pay and conditions of employment?**

%
44.8   Yes
1.6   No
0.7   (Don't know)
3.4   (Refusal/Not answered)

Q358 [WpUnionW]
On the whole, do you think *(these trade unions do their / this staff association does its)* job well or not?

%
29.0   Yes
15.3   No
2.9   (Don't know)
3.4   (Refusal/Not answered)

Q359 [TUShould]
CARD   N=1499
Listed on the card are a number of things trade unions or staff associations can do. Which, if any, do you think is the **most important** thing they should try to do **at your workplace**?
UNIONS OR STAFF ASSOCIATIONS SHOULD TRY TO:
Improve working conditions
Improve pay
Protect existing jobs
Have more say over how work is done day-to-day
Have more say over management's long-term plans
Work for equal opportunities for women
Work for equal opportunities for ethnic minorities
Reduce pay differences at the workplace
(None of these)
(Don't know)
(Refusal/Not answered)

%
14.6
9.2
14.6
1.9
3.7
0.4
0.4
1.3
0.6
0.5
3.4

ASK ALL CURRENT EMPLOYEES
Q360 [IndRel]
In general how would you describe relations between management and other employees at your workplace ... READ OUT ...
... very good,
quite good,
not very good,
or, not at all good?
(Don't know)
(Refusal/Not answered)

%
34.0
48.4
13.3
4.0
-
-

Q361 [WorkRun]
And in general, would you say your workplace was ... READ OUT ...
... very well managed,
quite well managed,
or, not well managed?
(Don't know)
(Refusal/Not answered)

%
26.2
52.9
20.6
0.3
-

ASK ALL EXCEPT THOSE WHO ARE WHOLLY RETIRED OR PERMANENLTY SICK OR DISABLED   N=2350
Q362 [NwEmpErn]
IF IN PAID WORK: Now for some more general questions about your work. For some people their job is simply something they do in order to earn a living. For others it means much more than that. On balance, is your present job ... READ OUT ...
IF NOT IN PAID WORK: For some people work is simply something they do in order to earn a living. For others it means much more than that. In general, do you think of work as ... READ OUT ...
...just a means of earning a living,
or, does it mean much more to you than that?
(Don't know)
(Refusal/Not answered)

%
35.8
63.1
1.1
-

Q363 [NwEmpLiv]
IF 'Just a means of earning a living' AT [NwEmpErn]
Is that because ... READ OUT ...
there are no (better/good) jobs around here,
you don't have the right skills to get a (better/good) job
or, because you would feel the same about **any** job you had?
(Don't know)
(Refusal/Not answered)

%
7.9
9.9
15.4
2.4
1.3

ASK ALL IN PAID WORK   N=1748
Q364-Q372
CARD
Now I'd like you to look at the statements on the card and tell me which ones best describe **your own** reasons for working at present.
PROBE: Which others? CODE ALL THAT APPLY
Multicoded (Maximum of 9 codes)
Working is the normal thing to do [WkWork1]
Need money for basic essentials such as food, rent or mortgage [WkWork2]
To earn money to buy extras [WkWork3]
To earn money of my own [WkWork4]
For the company of other people [WkWork5]
I enjoy working [WkWork6]
To follow my career [WkWork7]
For a change from my children or housework [WkWork8]
Other answer (WRITE IN) [WkWork9]
(Don't know)
(Refusal/Not answered)

%
36.6
69.6
50.7
34.7
27.4
55.1
31.8
9.0
2.8
-
0.1

IF MORE THAN ONE ANSWER GIVEN AT [WkWork] N=1748

Q384 [WkWkMain]
CARD AGAIN
And which one of these would you say is your **main** reason for working?

%	
5.1	Working is the normal thing to do
50.1	Need money for basic essentials such as food, rent or mortgage
6.8	To earn money to buy extras
6.8	To earn money of my own
1.3	For the company of other people
8.8	I enjoy working
5.3	To follow my career
0.9	For a change from my children or housework
0.6	Other answer (WRITE IN)
0.2	(Don't know)
0.1	(Refusal/Not answered)

ASK ALL CURRENT EMPLOYEES N=1499

Q385 [SayJob]
Suppose there was going to be some decision made at your place of work that changed the way you do your job. Do you think that **you personally** would have any say in the decision about the change, or not?
IF `DEPENDS': Code as `Don't know'

%	
54.3	Yes
42.8	No
2.9	(Don't know)
-	(Refusal/Not answered)

IF 'Yes' AT [SayJob]

Q386 [MuchSay]
How much say or chance to influence the decision do you think you would have ... READ OUT ...

%	
11.8	...a great deal,
22.3	quite a lot,
20.2	or, just a little?
-	(Don't know)
2.9	(Refusal/Not answered)

ASK ALL CURRENT EMPLOYEES

Q387 [MoreSay]
Do you think you should have **more** say in decisions affecting your work, or are you satisfied with the way things are?

%	
45.4	Should have more say
54.2	Satisfied with way things are
0.4	(Don't know)
-	(Refusal/Not answered)

ASK ALL IN PAID WORK N=1748

Q388 [WkPrefJb]
If without having to work, you had what you would regard as a reasonable living income, do you think you would still prefer to *(have a paid job/ do paid work)* or wouldn't you bother?

%	
69.2	Still prefer paid (job/work)
28.9	Wouldn't bother
1.5	Other answer (WRITE IN)
0.3	(Don't know)
-	(Refusal/Not answered)

ASK ALL CURRENT EMPLOYEES N=1499

Q390 [PrefHour]
Thinking about the number of hours you work each week including regular overtime, would you prefer a job where you worked ... READ OUT ...

%	
5.0	...more hours per week,
38.4	fewer hours per week,
56.3	or, are you happy with the number of hours you work at present?
0.3	(Don't know)
-	(Refusal/Not answered)

IF 'More hours' AT [PrefHour]

Q391 [MoreHour]
Is the reason why you don't work more hours because ... READ OUT ...

%	
3.8	your employer can't offer you more hours,
0.7	or, your personal circumstances don't allow it?
0.5	(Both)
-	(Don't know)
0.3	(Refusal/Not answered)

IF 'Fewer hours' AT [PrefHour]

Q393 [FewHour]
In which of these ways would you like your working hours to be shortened ... READ OUT ...

%	
12.4	shorter hours each day,
25.2	or, fewer days each week?
0.7	Other answer (WRITE IN)
0.1	(Don't know)
0.3	(Refusal/Not answered)

IF 'Fewer hours' AT [PrefHour]

Q395 [EarnHour]
Would you still like to work fewer hours, if it meant earning less money as a result?

%	
9.1	Yes
26.4	No
2.8	It depends
-	(Don't know)
0.3	(Refusal/Not answered)

Q396 **ASK ALL IN PAID WORK**
[WkWorkHd]   N=1748
CARD
Which of these statements best describes your feelings about your job?
In my job :

%	
8.6	I only work as hard as I have to
43.6	I work hard, but not so that it interferes with the rest of my life
47.4	I make a point of doing the best I can, even if it sometimes does interfere with the rest of my life
0.3	(Don't know)
-	(Refusal/Not answered)

ASK ALL CURRENT EMPLOYEES

Q397 [EWrkArrA]*
CARD
Please use this card to say whether any of the following arrangements are available to you, at your workplace ...
... Part-time working, allowing you to work less than the full working day?

Q398 [EWrkArrB]*
CARD AGAIN
(Is this available to you at your workplace?)
... flexible hours, so that you can adjust your own daily working hours?

Q399 [EWrkArrC]*
CARD AGAIN
(Is this available to you at your workplace?)
... job-sharing schemes, where part-timers share one full-time job?

Q400 [EWrkArrD]*
CARD AGAIN
(Is this available to you at your workplace?)
... working from home at least some of the time?

Q401 [EWrkArrE]*
CARD AGAIN
(Is this available to you at your workplace?)
... term-time contracts, allowing parents special time off during school holidays?

Q402 [EWrkArrF]*
CARD AGAIN
(Is this available to you at your workplace?)
... nurseries provided by your employer for the young children of employees?

Q403 [EWrkArrG]*   N=1499
CARD AGAIN
(Is this available to you at your workplace?)
... arrangements by your employer for the care of children during school holidays?

Q404 [EWrkArrH]*
CARD AGAIN
(Is this available to you at your workplace?)
... childcare allowances towards the cost of child care?

Q405 [EWrkArrI2]*
CARD AGAIN
(Is this available to you at your workplace?)
... 'career breaks', that is keeping jobs open for a few years so that people can return to work after caring for young children?

	[EWrkArrA]	[EWrkArrB]	[EWrkArrC]
	%	%	%
Not avail. & I wd not use it	33.8	21.2	53.9
Not avail. but I wd use it	11.0	38.2	17.1
Avail. but I do not use it	31.7	13.1	20.4
Avail. & I do use it	21.8	26.5	5.2
(Don't know)	1.8	1.0	3.4
(Refusal/Not answered)	-	-	-

	[EWrkArrD]	[EWrkArrE]	[EWrkArrF]
	%	%	%
Not avail. & I wd not use it	52.5	51.5	65.8
Not avail. but I wd use it	28.3	25.8	24.0
Avail. but I do not use it	5.8	11.4	7.0
Avail. & I do use it	11.8	6.4	0.7
(Don't know)	1.4	4.9	2.6
(Refusal/Not answered)	0.1	-	-

	[EWrkArrG]	[EWrkArrH]	[EWrkArrI2]
	%	%	%
Not avail. & I wd not use it	64.6	60.3	45.0
Not avail. but I wd use it	25.5	31.0	21.1
Avail. but I do not use it	5.2	2.8	22.8
Avail. & I do use it	0.8	0.4	2.9
(Don't know)	3.9	5.5	8.2
(Refusal/Not answered)	-	-	-

ASK ALL CURRENT MALE EMPLOYEES   N=762

Q406   [EWrkArrJW] *
        CARD AGAIN
        (Is this available to you at your workplace?)
        ... paternity leave, allowing fathers extra leave, when
        their children are born? *
        %
29.1   Not avail. & I wd not use it
18.5   Not avail. but I wd use it
29.4   Avail. but I do not use it
13.8   Avail. & I do use it
9.1   (Don't know)
-       (Refusal/Not answered)

ASK ALL CURRENT FEMALE EMPLOYEES   N=737

Q407   [EWrkArrJW]
        Is this available at your workplace?
        ... paternity leave, allowing fathers extra leave, when their
        children are born?
        %
47.1   Not available
35.5   Available
17.4   (Don't know)
-       (Refusal/Not answered)

ASK ALL CURRENT EMPLOYEES   N=1499

	[EWrkArrL]	[EWrkArrM]	[EWrkArrN]

Q408   [EWrkArrL] *
        CARD AGAIN
        (Is this available to you at your workplace?)
        ... time off, either paid or unpaid, to care for sick children?

Q409   [EWrkArrM] *
        CARD AGAIN
        (Is this available to you at your workplace?)
        ... time off, either paid or unpaid, to care for children for
        reasons other than their sickness?

Q410   [EWrkArrN] *
        CARD AGAIN
        (Is this available to you at your workplace?)
        ... time off, either paid or unpaid, to care for people other
        than children? *

	[EWrkArrL]	[EWrkArrM]	[EWrkArrN]
	%	%	%
Not avail. & I wd not use it	19.8	29.3	25.1
Not avail. but I wd use it	19.6	22.4	24.5
Avail. but I do not use it	34.5	24.3	25.2
Avail. & I do use it	15.3	10.1	13.3
(Don't know)	10.8	14.0	12.0
(Refusal/Not answered)	-	-	-

Q411   [EWrkArK2]
        (Is this available to you at your workplace?)
        ... Any other arrangement to help people combine
        jobs and childcare?
        %
2.4   Yes
92.1   No
5.4   (Don't know)
0.1   (Refusal/Not answered)

ASK ALL IN PAID WORK FOR ANY NUMBER OF HOURS
PER WEEK (AT [REconAct] OR AT [NPWork10])

Q413   [WChdLt5]
        Can I just check, do you have any children under five living
        at home? *
        %
16.1   yes
83.7   No
0.2   (Don't know)
-       (Refusal/Not answered)

IF 'no' AT [WChdLt5]

Q414   [WChd512]
        Do you have any children aged five to eleven living at
        home? *
        %
14.6   Yes
69.0   No
-       (Don't know)
0.2   (Refusal/Not answered)

IF 'no' AT [WCh512]

Q415   [WChd1214]
        Do you have any children aged twelve to fourteen
        living at home? *
        %
4.9   Yes
64.1   No
-       (Don't know)
0.2   (Refusal/Not answered)

ASK ALL IN PAID WORK FOR ANY NUMBER OF HOURS PER WEEK

Q416   [ESOlRsp2]
        Some people have responsibilities for looking after a disabled,
        sick, or elderly friend or relative. Is there anyone like this
        who depends on you to provide some regular care for them?
        %
11.7   Yes
88.2   No
0.1   (Don't know)
0.8   (Refusal/Not answered)

N=1499

N=1779

Q417

IF 'Yes' AT [ESO1Rsp2]   N=1779
[ESO1AfH2]
Does this responsibility ...READ OUT...
prevent you from working longer hours in your job,
or does it make no difference to your working hours?

%	
2.5	(Don't know)
9.2	(Refusal/Not answered)
-	
0.1	

ASK ALL LOOKING AFTER THE HOME AND NO WORK AT
ALL   N=328

Q418
[HChdLt5]
Can I just check, do you have any children under five living
at home? *

%	
28.2	yes
71.1	No
0.7	(Don't know)
-	(Refusal/Not answered)

IF 'no' AT [HChdLt5]

Q419
[HChd512]
Do you have any children aged five to eleven living at
home? *

%	
14.3	Yes
56.9	No
-	(Don't know)
0.7	(Refusal/Not answered)

IF 'no' AT [HChd512]

Q420
[HChd1214]
Do you have any children aged twelve to fourteen
living at home?

%	
3.2	Yes
53.7	No
-	(Don't know)
0.7	Refusal/Not answered)

ASK ALL LOOKING AFTER THE HOME WITH NO WORK AT ALL

Q421
[HoldResp]
Some people have responsibilities for looking after a disabled,
sick or elderly friend or relative. Is there anyone like this
who depends on you to provide some regular
care for them?

%	
14.3	Yes
85.4	No
0.3	(Don't know)
-	(Refusal/Not answered)

Q422

IF 'Yes' AT [HoldResp]   N=328
[HoldAfHr]
Does this responsibility ... READ OUT ...
... prevent you from getting a paid job,
or, would you not want a paid job anyway?

%	
6.3	(Don't know)
6.8	(Refusal/Not answered)
1.2	
0.3	

ASK ALL 'WHOLLY RETIRED   N=652

Q423
[REmplPen]
Do you receive a pension from any past employer?

%	
53.2	Yes
46.5	No
0.1	(Don't know)
0.2	(Refusal/Not answered)

IF WHOLLY RETIRED AND MARRIED

Q424
[SEmplPen]
Does your (husband/wife/partner) receive a pension from any
past employer?

%	
23.7	Yes
32.6	No
0.5	(Don't know)
0.4	(Refusal/Not answered)

ASK ALL WHOLLY RETIRED

Q425
[PrPenGet]
And do you receive a pension from any **private**
arrangements you have made in the past, that is **apart**
from the state pension or one arranged through an employer?

%	
12.8	Yes
86.9	No
0.1	(Don't know)
0.3	(Refusal/Not answered)

Q426

IF WHOLLY RETIRED AND MARRIED   N=652

[SPrPnGet]
And does your (husband/wife/partner) receive a pension from any private arrangements he/she has made in the past, that is apart from the state pension or one arranged through an employer?

%
5.5 Yes
51.1 No
0.4 (Don't know)
0.3 (Refusal/Not answered)

Q428

ASK ALL WHOLLY RETIRED AND MALE AGED 66 OR FEMALE AGED 61 OR OVER   N=544

[RPension]
On the whole would you say the present state pension is on the low side, reasonable, or on the high side?
IF 'ON THE LOW SIDE': Very low or a bit low?

%
39.3 Very low
37.6 A bit low
21.8 Reasonable
0.6 On the high side
0.5 (Don't know)
0.1 (Refusal/Not answered)

Q429

[RPenInYr]
Do you expect your state pension in a year's time to purchase more than it does now, less, or about the same?

%
5.8 More
60.2 Less
32.9 About the same
0.9 (Don't know)
0.1 (Refusal/Not answered)

Q430

ASK ALL WHOLLY RETIRED   N=652

[RetirAg2]
At what age did you retire from work?
NEVER WORKED, CODE: 00
Median: 60 years

%
0.4 (Don't know)
0.3 (Refusal/Not answered)

ENGLISH NATIONALISM (ENGLAND ONLY)   N=2722

Q431

IN ENGLAND: ASK ALL

[RLvElsE]
Have you ever lived anywhere other than England for more than a year?
IF YES: Where was that? PROBE TO IDENTIFY CORRECT CODE
ELSEWHERE IN UK = SCOTLAND, WALES, N. IRELAND, CHANNEL ISLANDS, ISLE OF MAN

%
77.6 No - have never lived anywhere outside England for more than a year
4.8 Yes - elsewhere in UK
15.1 Yes - outside UK
2.5 Yes - elsewhere in UK and outside UK
- (Don't know)
0.1 (Refusal/Not answered)

Q432

[NatID]
CARD
Some people think of themselves first as British. Others may think of themselves first as English. Which, if any, of the following best describes how you see yourself?

%
17.3 English, not British
14.5 More English than British
36.8 Equally English and British
11.1 More British than English
13.5 British, not English
3.3 Other answer (WRITE IN)
3.2 (None of these)
0.3 (Don't know)
- (Refusal/Not answered)

Q434

[GBPride]*
CARD
How proud are you of being British or do you not see yourself as British at all?

Q435

[NatPride]*
CARD AGAIN
And how proud are you of being English, or do you not see yourself as English at all?

N=2722

	[GBPride]	[NATPride]
	%	%
Very proud	42.9	43.6
Somewhat proud	38.5	32.8
Not very proud	8.6	7.1
Not at all proud	2.3	2.2
(Not English)	6.2	13.1
(Don't know)	1.4	1.0
(Refusal/Not answered)	0.2	0.1

Q436 [PatrEng1]*
CARD
People have different views about what it means to be truly English. Some would say a person needs to be **born** in England to be truly English.
How much do **you** think this matters?

Q437 [PatrEng3]*
CARD AGAIN
How much do **you** think it matters to being truly English that a person has lived in England for most of their life?

Q438 [PatrEng4]*
CARD AGAIN
How much do **you** think it matters to being truly English that a person has English parents?

Q439 [PatrEng6]*
CARD AGAIN
And how much do **you** think it matters to being truly English that a person is white?

	[PatrEng1]	[PatrEng3]
	%	%
Great deal	29.4	23.2
Quite a bit	28.4	39.1
Not very much	27.3	24.5
Not at all	14.3	11.9
(Don't know)	0.6	1.2
(Refusal/Not answered)	-	0.1

N=2722

	[PatrEng4]	[Patrtrng6]
	%	%
Great deal	24.8	12.0
Quite a bit	31.2	12.4
Not very much	27.4	28.1
Not at all	15.4	46.0
(Don't know)	1.2	1.3
(Refusal/Not answered)	0.1	0.1

Q440 -Q443
CARD
Which, if any, of the three categories on this card applies to you?
PROBE: Any others?
Multicoded (Maximum of 4 codes)

	%
Born in England [PatEnBrn]	87.2
Lived in England most of my life [PatEnLiv]	85.0
Have English parents [PatEnPar]	73.5
None of these [PatEnNon]	3.9
(Don't know)	0.0
(Refusal/Not answered)	0.1

Q444 [EngLearn]*
CARD
Please say from this card how much you agree or disagree with each of these statements.
England has a lot to learn from the rest of Britain in running its affairs

Q445 [EngCitzn]*
CARD AGAIN
(Please say from this card how much you agree or disagree with each of these statements.)
I would rather live in England than in any other part of Britain

Q446 [EngAshmd]*
CARD AGAIN
(Please say from this card how much you agree or disagree with each of these statements.)
There are some things about England today that make me ashamed to be English
IF RESPONDENT SAYS HE/SHE IS NOT ENGLISH: CODE AS 'NEITHER AGREE NOR DISAGREE'

N=2722

Q447 [EngCrit]*
CARD AGAIN
(Please say from this card how much you agree
or disagree with each of these statements.)
People in England are too ready to criticise their country

Q448 [EngProud]*
CARD AGAIN
(Please say from this card how much you agree or disagree with
each of these statements.)
England can only really feel proud of itself if it becomes
independent from the rest of Britain

	[EngLearn]	[EngCitzn]
	%	%
Strongly agree	5.0	20.8
Agree	23.3	39.1
Neither agree nor disagree	33.0	22.1
Disagree	30.8	15.3
Strongly disagree	5.3	1.8
(Don't know)	2.4	0.8
(Refusal/Not answered)	0.1	-

	[EngAshmd]	[EngCrit]	[EngProud]
	%	%	%
Strongly agree	12.2	9.6	1.8
Agree	45.7	50.5	8.6
Neither agree nor disagree	20.4	20.5	17.0
Disagree	17.9	17.1	53.9
Strongly disagree	2.8	1.0	16.5
(Don't know)	0.8	1.0	2.2
(Refusal/Not answered)	0.1	0.1	-

Q449 [EngSpor1]
CARD
Some people - even those who do not follow sport very closely -
always back English teams or athletes when they are competing
against another country. Others do not. How about you?
Please choose an answer from this card.
IF 'DEPENDS ON SPORT/COUNTRY' PROBE: Generally speaking ...?
IF 'NOT INTERESTED IN SPORT' CODE DON'T KNOW

%
63.4 I always back the English team/athlete against others
23.2 I sometimes back the English team/athlete
3.3 I rarely back the English team/athlete
4.2 I never back the English team/athlete
3.3 (It depends)
2.6 (Don't know)
0.1 (Refusal/Not answered)

N=2722

Q450 [EngSpor2]
CARD
Some English people will also back Scottish teams
or athletes if they are competing abroad.
Others will not. How about you?
Please choose an answer from this card.
IF 'DEPENDS ON SPORT/COUNTRY' PROBE: Generally speaking ...?
IF 'NOT INTERESTED IN SPORT' CODE DON'T KNOW (CTRL K)
%
42.3 I always back the Scottish team/athlete against foreign teams/athletes
30.3 I sometimes back the Scottish team/athlete
8.4 I rarely back the Scottish team/athlete
12.1 I never back the Scottish team/athlete
3.7 (It depends)
3.1 (Don't know)
0.1 (Refusal/Not answered)

Q451 [EngParl]
CARD
With all the changes going on in the way the different parts of
Great Britain are run, which of the following do you think
would
be best for England ...READ OUT...
%
62.3 ..for England to be governed as it is now, with laws made by
the UK parliament,
15.2 for each region of England to have its own assembly that runs
services like health,
17.9 or, for England as a whole to have its own new parliament with
law-making powers?
1.4 (None of these)
3.2 (Don't know)
0.1 (Refusal/Not answered)

Q452 [ChngMin]
In the last few years, some groups have been getting ahead
while others have been losing out.
Firstly, ethnic minority groups in England.
Do you think they have been getting ahead, losing out, or have
things stayed much the same for them?
%
45.8 Getting ahead
39.0 Stayed much the same
8.9 Losing out
6.3 (Don't know)
0.1 (Refusal/Not answered)

Q453 **IF 'Getting ahead' OR 'Losing out' AT [ChngMin]**   N=2722
[MinGood]
On the whole, do you think this is a good thing
or a bad thing?
%
21.3 A good thing
23.6 A bad thing
9.0 Neither a good thing nor a bad thing
0.6 (Don't know)
6.4 (Refusal/Not answered)

Q454 **IN ENGLAND: ASK ALL**
[ChngRich]
And what about well-off people in England?
(In the last few years)Do you think they have been getting
ahead, losing out, or have things stayed much the same for
them?
%
65.0 Getting ahead
27.7 Stayed much the same
3.6 Losing out
3.8 (Don't know)
- (Refusal/Not answered)

Q455 **IF 'Getting ahead' OR 'Losing out' AT [ChngMin]**
[RchGood]
On the whole, do you think this is a good thing or a bad thing?
%
14.5 A good thing
40.6 A bad thing
12.8 Neither a good thing nor a bad thing
0.7 (Don't know)
3.8 (Refusal/Not answered)

Q456 **IN ENGLAND: ASK ALL**
[ChngWrkC]
And what about ordinary working people in England?
Do you think they have been getting ahead, losing out, or have
things stayed much the same for them?
%
17.7 Getting ahead
44.4 Stayed much the same
36.2 Losing out
1.8 (Don't know)
- (Refusal/Not answered)

Q457 **IF 'Getting ahead' OR 'Losing out' AT [ChngMin]**
[WrkCGood]
On the whole, do you think this is a good thing or a bad thing?
%
16.6 A good thing
35.9 A bad thing
1.2 Neither a good thing nor a bad thing
- (Don't know)
1.8 (Refusal/Not answered)

Q458 **IN ENGLAND: ASK ALL**   N=2722
[NatLearn] *
CARD
Now turning to think about **Britain** rather than England.
Please say from this card how much you agree or disagree with
each of these statements.
Britain has a lot to learn from other countries in running its
affairs

Q459 [NatCitzE] *
CARD AGAIN
(Please say from this card how much you agree or disagree with
each of these statements.)
I would rather be a citizen of Britain than of any other
country in the world

Q460 [NatAshmE] *
CARD AGAIN
(Please say from this card how much you agree or disagree with
each of these statements.)
There are some things about Britain today that make me ashamed
to be British

Q461 [NatCrit] *
CARD AGAIN
(Please say from this card how much you agree or disagree with
each of these statements.)
People in Britain are too ready to criticise their country

Q462 [NatState] *
CARD AGAIN
(Please say from this card how much you agree or disagree with
each of these statements.)
The government should do everything it can to keep all parts of
Britain together in a single state

Q463 [NatCoop] *
CARD AGAIN
(Please say from this card how much you agree or disagree with
each of these statements.)
Britain should co-operate with other countries, even if it
means giving up some independence

N=2722

	[NatLearn] %	[NatCitzE] %	[NatAshmE] %
Strongly agree	8.8	29.0	7.8
Agree	36.5	45.8	51.1
Neither agree nor disagree	21.3	15.0	16.4
Disagree	28.1	7.9	21.2
Strongly disagree	3.7	1.2	2.4
(Don't know)	1.6	1.0	1.0
(Refusal/Not answered)	0.1	0.1	0.1

	[NatCrit] %	[NatState] %	[NatCoop] %
Strongly agree	7.7	19.7	3.4
Agree	55.2	44.9	31.4
Neither agree nor disagree	19.0	17.9	17.1
Disagree	15.9	14.8	36.1
Strongly disagree	0.7	1.4	9.6
(Don't know)	1.5	1.3	2.3
(Refusal/Not answered)	0.1	0.1	0.1

Q464 [EngSym1]*
CARD
When some people think of the Union Jack they see it as more British than English. Others think of it as more English than British. Please choose a phrase from this card to show how you think of the Union Jack.

Q465 [EngSym2]*
CARD AGAIN
And what about the Royal Navy? Please choose a phrase from this card to show how you think of the Royal Navy.

Q466 [EngSym3]*
CARD AGAIN
And what about the Houses of Parliament?

Q467 [EngSym4]*
CARD AGAIN
And what about pubs?
(When some people think of pubs they see them as more British than English. Others think of them as more English than British. Please choose a phrase from this card to show how you think of pubs.)

Q468 [EngSym5]*
CARD AGAIN
What about Guy Fawkes night?
(Please choose a phrase from this card to show how you think of Guy Fawkes night.)

Q469 [EngSym6]*
CARD AGAIN
And what about fox-hunting?

Q470 [EngSym7]*
CARD AGAIN
And the Labour party?

Q471 [EngSym8]*
CARD AGAIN
And the Conservative party?

N=2722

	[EngSym1] %	[EngSym2] %	[EngSym3] %
English, not British	7.5	6.9	11.1
More English than British	10.9	7.6	18.5
Equally English and British	31.5	31.8	27.1
More British than English	24.8	22.4	17.6
British, not English	22.4	27.3	21.6
Neither English nor British	1.5	1.5	1.6
(Don't know)	1.3	2.5	2.4
(Refusal/Not answered)	0.1	0.1	0.1

	[EngSym4] %	[EngSym5] %	[EngSym6] %
English, not British	13.9	29.0	31.1
More English than British	15.5	24.4	26.3
Equally English and British	33.7	20.7	16.0
More British than English	12.4	7.8	7.9
British, not English	14.5	10.5	9.5
Neither English nor British	6.3	3.5	5.0
(Don't know)	3.5	3.9	4.0
(Refusal/Not answered)	0.1	0.1	0.2

N=2722

	[EngSym7]	[EngSym8]
	%	%
English, not British	9.2	14.0
More English than British	10.0	21.6
Equally English and British	34.5	27.7
More British than English	16.4	12.1
British, not English	20.3	15.8
Neither English nor British	5.3	3.9
(Don't know)	3.9	4.6
(Refusal/Not answered)	0.3	0.3

Q472 [ScotGo]
If in the future Scotland were to become
independent and leave the UK, would you be sorry,
pleased, or neither pleased nor sorry?

	%
Sorry	40.4
Pleased	7.1
Neither pleased nor sorry	51.8
(Don't know)	0.6
(Refusal/Not answered)	0.1

Q473 [PrejNowE]
Do you think there is generally more racial prejudice in
Britain
now than there was 5 years ago, less, or about the same amount?

	%
More now	32.7
Less now	21.6
About the same	43.2
Other (WRITE IN)	0.1
(Don't know)	2.1
(Refusal/Not answered)	0.2

IN ENGLAND: ASK ALL
Q475 [PrejFutE]
Do you think there will be more, less, or about the same amount
of racial prejudice in Britain in 5 years time compared with
now?

	%
More in 5 years	35.5
Less	24.3
About the same	36.7
Other (WRITE IN)	0.3
(Don't know)	2.9
(Refusal/Not answered)	0.2

N=2722

Q477 [SRPrejE]
How would you describe yourself
... READ OUT ...
... as very prejudiced against people of other races,
a little prejudiced,
or, not prejudiced at all?
Other (WRITE IN)
(Don't know)
(Refusal/Not answered)

	%
	2.0
	26.2
	70.5
	0.6
	0.4
	0.4

IN ENGLAND: ASK ALL
Q479 [ChOppMiE]
CARD
Please use this card to say whether you think attempts to give
equal opportunities to black people and Asians in Britain have
gone too far or not gone far enough?

	%
Gone much too far	8.1
Gone too far	26.1
About right	36.5
Not gone far enough	23.5
Not gone nearly far enough	1.8
(Don't know)	3.7
(Refusal/Not answered)	0.3

Q480 [Immigr3E] *
CARD
There are different opinions about immigrants from other
countries living in Britain.
(By 'immigrants' we mean people who come to settle in Britain.)
How much do you agree or disagree with each of the following
statements
... READ OUT ... immigrants take jobs away from people who were
born in Britain?
Please choose an answer from this card.

Q481 [Immigr4E] *
CARD AGAIN
(How much do you agree or disagree with the following statement
... READ OUT ...
..immigrants make Britain more open to new ideas and cultures?

	[ImmigSc3]	[ImmigSc4]
	%	%
Strongly agree	10.7	8.5
Agree	33.5	61.2
Neither agree nor disagree	20.5	14.0
Disagree	29.3	13.7
Strongly disagree	4.7	1.2
(Don't know)	1.0	1.1
(Refusal/Not answered)	0.2	0.2

CONSTITUTIONAL ISSUES (MAINLY VERSION A)

N=1066

Q483

VERSION A: ASK ALL

[GovtWork]

CARD

Which of these statements best describes your opinion on the present system of governing in Britain?

%

Works extremely well and could not be improved	2.5
Could be improved in small ways but mainly works well	45.4
Could be improved quite a lot	38.4
Needs a great deal of improvement	11.4
(Don't know)	2.0
(Refusal/Not answered)	0.2

Q484

[Lords]

Do you think that the House of Lords should remain as it is or is some change needed?

%

Remain as it is	27.2
Change needed	64.2
(Don't know)	8.4
(Refusal/Not answered)	0.2

Q485

IF 'Change needed' AT [Lords]

[LordAbol]

of Lords? Should it be . . . READ OUT . . .

%

. . . abolished altogether,	13.9
or, reformed in some other way?	49.5
(Don't know)	0.8
(Refusal/Not answered)	8.6

Q486

IF 'reformed' AT [LordAbol]

[Heredit]

Should there be any place in this reformed body for **hereditary peers**, that is, people who are there by birth?

Yes	11.7
No	35.6
(Don't know)	2.2
(Refusal/Not answered)	9.4

Q487

VERSION A: ASK ALL

[Monarchy]

How important or unimportant do you think it is for Britain to continue to have a monarchy ... READ OUT ...

%

...very important	33.9
quite important	34.5
not very important	16.7
not at all important	5.5
or, do you think the monarchy should be abolished?	8.6
(Don't know)	0.7
(Refusal/Not answered)	0.2

Q488

[VoteSyst]

Some people say that we should change the voting system to allow smaller political parties to get a fairer share of MPs. Others say we should keep the voting system as it is, to produce more effective government.

Which view comes closest to your own . . . READ OUT . . .

IF ASKED, REFERS TO 'PROPORTIONAL REPRESENTATION'

%

...that we should change the voting system	34.5
or, keep it as it is?	62.5
(Don't know)	2.7
(Refusal/Not answered)	0.2

Q489

[WelshAss]

CARD

An issue in Wales is the question of an elected assembly - a special parliament for Wales dealing with Welsh affairs. Which of these statements comes closest to your view?

%

Wales should become independent, separate from the UK and the European Union	5.6
Wales should become independent, separate from the UK but part of the European Union	12.6
Wales should remain part of the UK, with its own elected parliament which has law-making **and** taxation powers	35.2
Wales should remain part of the UK, with its own elected assembly which has limited law-making powers **only**	22.8
Wales should remain part of the UK **without** an elected assembly	14.6
(Don't know)	9.0
(Refusal/Not answered)	0.2

Q490

VERSION A: ASK ALL (ALSO ASKED ON VERSIONS B AND C OF ALL IN ENGLAND)

[ScotPar2]

CARD

An issue in Scotland is the question of an elected parliament - a special parliament for Scotland dealing with Scottish affairs.

Which of these statements comes closest to your view?

%

Scotland should become independent, separate from the UK and the European Union	6.9
Scotland should become independent, separate from the UK but part of the European Union	13.1
Scotland should remain part of the UK, with its own elected parliament which has **some** taxation powers	45.1
Scotland should remain part of the UK, with its own elected parliament which has **no** taxation powers	13.3
Scotland should remain part of the UK **without** an elected parliament	13.6
(Don't know)	7.8
(Refusal/Not answered)	0.2

N=1066

Q491 [NIreland]
Do you think the long-term policy for Northern Ireland should be for it
... READ OUT ...

%	
26.8	...to remain part of the United Kingdom
54.5	or, to unify with the rest of Ireland?
1.4	**EDIT ONLY:** NORTHERN IRELAND SHOULD BE AN INDEPENDENT STATE
-	**EDIT ONLY:** NORTHERN IRELAND SHOULD BE SPLIT UP INTO TWO
4.1	**EDIT ONLY:** IT SHOULD BE UP TO THE IRISH TO DECIDE
2.1	Other answer (WRITE IN)
10.7	(Don't know)
0.4	(Refusal/Not answered)

Q493 **VERSION A: ASK ALL**
[VotedEU]
A lot of people did not vote in the European election. How about you? Did you vote in the elections on the 10th of June or didn't you manage to?

%	
34.0	Yes: voted
65.3	No
0.6	(Refused to say)
0.1	(Don't know)
-	(Refusal/Not answered)

Q494 **IF 'Yes' AT [VotedEU]**
[VotedEU]
Which party did you vote for in the European election?
DO NOT PROMPT

%	
10.3	Conservative
11.5	Labour
4.7	Liberal Democrat
0.9	Scottish National Party (SNP)
1.3	Plaid Cymru
1.4	Green Party
0.6	Other (WRITE IN)
1.7	UK Independence Party
	Pro-Euro Conservative Party
1.3	Refused to disclose voting
0.4	(Don't know)
0.7	(Refusal/Not answered)

Q496 **VERSION A: ASK ALL** (ALSO ASKED OF ALL ON VERSIONS B AND C IN ENGLAND)
[ECPolicy]
CARD
Do you think Britain's long-term policy should be . . .READ OUT

%	
13.5	...to leave the European Union,
42.6	to stay in the EU and try to **reduce** the EU's powers,
20.3	to leave things as they are,
10.6	to stay in the EU and try to **increase** the EU's powers,
6.1	or, to work for the formation of a single European government?
6.6	(Don't know)
0.3	(Refusal/Not answered)

Q497 **VERSION A: ASK ALL**
[EcuView]
CARD
And here are three statements about the future of the pound in the European Union. Which **one** comes closest to your view?

%	
16.5	**Replace** the pound by the single currency
22.4	Use **both** the pound and a new European currency in Britain
58.0	Keep the pound as the **only** currency for Britain
2.9	(Don't know)
0.2	(Refusal/Not answered)

Q498 **VERSION A: ASK ALL** (ALSO ASKED OF ALL ON VERSIONS B AND C IN ENGLAND)
[EuroRef]
If there were a referendum on whether Britain should join the single European currency, the Euro, how do you think you would vote? Would you vote to joint the Euro, or not to join the Euro?
IF 'would not vote', PROBE: If you **did** vote, how would you vote?
IF RESPONDENT INSISTS THEY WOULD NOT VOTE, CODE DON'T KNOW

%	
28.3	To join the Euro
64.8	Not to join the Euro
6.6	(Don't know)
0.2	(Refusal/Not answered)

Q499 **VERSION A: ASK ALL**
[EURfLike]
(Can I just check,) how likely do you think that you would be to vote in such a referendum? Would you be
. . . READ OUT . . .

%	
57.4	. . . very likely,
23.4	fairly likely,
10.2	not very likely,
7.9	or, not at all likely?
0.8	(Don't know)
0.2	(Refusal/Not answered)

Q500 [EffecLaw]
In your view, how effective are the present laws against racial discrimination? Are they .. READ OUT ...
%
8.3 ... very effective,
44.2 fairly effective,
33.2 not very effective,
5.6 or, not at all effective?
8.4 (Don't know)
0.2 (Refusal/Not answered)

IF 'Not very effective' OR 'Not at all effective' AT [EffecLaw]
Q501 [AnyLaw]
Do you think that any law against racial discrimination can really work?
%
11.1 Yes
26.5 No
1.3 (Don't know)
8.6 (Refusal/Not answered)

VERSION A: ASK ALL
Q502 [RaceViiw]
CARD
Some people say there should be a special law against attacks on people because of their race. Others say these attacks should be treated by the law just like any other attacks. Do you think there should be a special law against racial violence or not?
%
21.6 Definitely should
24.5 Probably should
24.3 Probably should not
26.7 Definitely should not
2.7 (Don't know)
0.2 (Refusal/Not answered)

N=1066

BEGGING (MAINLY VERSION A)

N=3143

ASK ALL
Q503 [Begging]
Now some questions about people who beg, that is, who ask for money for themselves without offering anything in return. In the last four weeks have you yourself come across anyone in Britain begging?
NOTE: THIS INCLUDES PEOPLE USING A SIGN TO BEG
IT DOES not INCLUDE PEOPLE SELLING SOMETHING, PERFORMING IN THE STREET, OR COLLECTING FOR CHARITY.
%
48.0 Yes
51.8 No
0.1 (Don't know)
0.2 (Refusal/Not answered)

Q504 [BegOft]
CARD
Generally speaking, how often do you come across people begging? Remember, by begging I mean someone asking for money for themselves without offering anything in return.
NOTE: IF RESPONDENT SAYS 'When I go shopping/to town' PROBE FOR HOW OFTEN THIS HAPPENS.
%
10.6 Most days
19.0 At least once a week
16.0 At least once a month
21.9 At least once every few months
11.6 At least once a year
8.8 Less often than once a year
11.7 Never
- (Don't know)
- (Refusal/Not answered)

IF NOT 'never' AT [BegOft]
Q505 [GiveBeg]
CARD
Thinking now of when you do come across people begging. How often, if at all, do you give them money?
%
44.3 Never
18.6 Seldom
20.3 Some of the time
2.8 A lot of the time
1.9 Always or most of the time
0.2 (Don't know)
0.2 (Refusal/Not answered)

Q506
IF NOT 'never' AT [GiveBeg]
[GiveMuch]
CARD
And when you do give money, how much, on average, do you give?

N=3143

%	
20.0	50p or less
20.5	51p-£1
2.2	£1.01-£2.50
0.2	£2.51-£5.00
0.1	More than £5
0.5	(Varies too much to say)
0.2	(Don't know)
0.2	(Refusal/Not answered)

Q507
VERSION A: ASK ALL
[BuskOft]
CARD
Generally speaking, how often do you come across people busking for money - that is singing, playing instruments or performing in a public place?

N=1066

%	
8.2	Most days
28.5	At least once a week
22.7	At least once a month
20.4	At least once every few months
8.8	At least once a year
3.9	Less often than once a year
7.1	Never
0.2	(Don't know)
0.2	(Refusal/Not answered)

Q508
IF NOT 'never' AT [BuskOft]
[GiveBusk]
CARD
And how often, if at all, do you give money when you come across people busking?

%	
34.3	Never
23.6	Seldom
27.8	Some of the time
3.8	A lot of the time
3.1	Always or most of the time
0.2	(Don't know)
0.2	(Refusal/Not answered)

Q509
VERSION A: ASK ALL
[BigOft]
CARD
Generally speaking, how often do you come across people selling 'The Big Issue' - the magazine sold by homeless people?

N=1066

%	
16.8	Most days
28.5	At least once a week
19.2	At least once a month
12.0	At least once every few months
4.8	At least once a year
3.3	Less often than once a year
14.6	Never
0.5	(Don't know)
0.2	(Refusal/Not answered)

Q510
IF NOT 'never' AT [BigOft]
[GiveBig]
CARD
And how often, if at all, do you buy a copy when you come across people selling 'The Big Issue'?

%	
52.9	Never
12.5	Seldom
12.1	Some of the time
2.7	A lot of the time
4.4	Always or most of the time
0.5	(Don't know)
0.2	(Refusal/Not answered)

Q511
VERSION A: ASK ALL
[BegLuck]
Which of these statements comes closest to your view?
Generally speaking, ... READ OUT ...

%	
44.1	...most people who beg have been unlucky in their lives,
42.6	or, most people who beg have only themselves to blame for their situation?
12.9	(Don't know)
0.3	(Refusal/Not answered)

Q512
[BegTrFam]
(And which of these statements comes closest to your view?)
Generally speaking, ... READ OUT ...

%	
41.4	...most people who beg come from very troubled family backgrounds,
46.7	or, most people who beg come from no more troubled family backgrounds than the rest of us?
11.6	(Don't know)
0.3	(Refusal/Not answered)

N=1066

Q513 [BegLazy]
(And which of these statements comes closest to your view?) Generally speaking, ... READ OUT ...
%
41.0 ...most people who beg are too lazy to find a job,
44.9 or, most people who beg would work if they could find a job?
13.8 (Don't know)
0.4   (Refusal/Not answered)

Q514 [BegGen]
(And which of these statements comes closest to your view?) Generally speaking, ... READ OUT ...
%
55.0 ...most people who beg genuinely need help,
35.0 or, most people who beg do not genuinely need help?
9.7   (Don't know)
0.3   (Refusal/Not answered)

Q515 [BegBen]
(And which of these statements comes closest to your view?) Generally speaking, ..READ OUT...
%
55.2 most people who beg also get state benefits,
27.7 or, most people who beg do not also get state benefits?
21.7 (Don't know)
0.3   (Refusal/Not answered)

Q516 [WelfBeg]*
CARD
How much do you agree or disagree with each of the following statements?
In today's Welfare State there is no excuse for anyone to beg.

Q517 [SelfBeg]*
CARD AGAIN
(And how much do you agree or disagree...)
I could never be so desperate that I needed to beg for money.

Q518 [NeverBeg]*
CARD AGAIN
(And how much do you agree or disagree...)
People should never give to beggars.

Q519 [DespBeg]*
CARD AGAIN
(And how much do you agree or disagree...)
No one begs for money unless they are really desperate.

Q520 [AngryBeg]*
CARD AGAIN
(And how much do you agree or disagree...)
I feel angry that more is not done to help people who beg.

N=1066

Q521 [GuiltBeg]*
CARD AGAIN
(And how much do you agree or disagree...)
I generally feel guilty if I do not give anything to someone who is begging.

Q522 [EasyBeg]*
CARD AGAIN
(And how much do you agree or disagree...)
Begging is just an easy way of making a living.

Q523 [RespBeg]*
CARD AGAIN
(And how much do you agree or disagree...)
People who beg don't deserve to be treated with the same respect as the rest of us.

Q524 [HelpBeg]*
CARD AGAIN
(And how much do you agree or disagree...)
It is everyone's responsibility to help people less fortunate than themselves.

Q525 [RealBeg]*
CARD AGAIN
(And how much do you agree or disagree...)
I can usually tell whether someone begging really needs help.

Q526 [BigBeg]*
CARD AGAIN
(And how much do you agree or disagree...)
People who sell 'The Big Issue' are no different to beggars.

Q527 IF NOT 'never' AT [GiveBeg]
[FoodBeg]*
CARD AGAIN
(And how much do you agree or disagree...)
I am more likely to give money to someone begging if I feel sure they will spend it on food or shelter.

N=1066

	[WelfBeg]	[SelfBeg]	[NeverBeg]
	%	%	%
Agree strongly	18.1	31.7	8.8
Agree	42.0	33.4	17.1
Neither agree nor disagree	12.2	13.1	25.9
Disagree	24.0	15.8	41.9
Disagree strongly	2.0	3.1	5.2
(Don't know)	1.5	2.5	0.7
(Refusal/Not answered)	0.3	0.5	0.3

	[DesPBeg]	[AngryBeg]	[GuiltBeg]
	%	%	%
Agree strongly	5.4	4.9	2.9
Agree	29.5	29.1	26.5
Neither agree nor disagree	15.7	24.2	11.6
Disagree	41.4	35.6	43.6
Disagree strongly	6.0	4.4	14.4
(Don't know)	1.7	1.5	0.6
(Refusal/Not answered)	0.3	0.3	0.4

	[EasyBeg]	[RespBeg]	[HelpBeg]
	%	%	%
Agree strongly	9.1	3.6	9.5
Agree	34.5	15.5	51.6
Neither agree nor disagree	18.3	19.3	18.0
Disagree	33.1	48.2	19.0
Disagree strongly	4.1	11.8	1.1
(Don't know)	0.5	1.3	0.5
(Refusal/Not answered)	0.4	0.4	0.3

	[RealBeg]	[BigBeg]	[FoodBeg]
	%	%	%
Agree strongly	4.8	2.1	9.0
Agree	33.1	17.4	34.8
Neither agree nor disagree	23.0	14.9	4.3
Disagree	32.4	51.2	4.8
Disagree strongly	3.8	6.7	0.5
(Don't know)	2.6	0.7	0.7
(Refusal/Not answered)	0.4	0.4	0.3

N=1066

VERSION A: ASK ALL

[MoreBeg]
Do you think there are more, less, or about
the same number of people begging in Britian now
as there were five years ago?

Q528
%
More than 5 years ago   61.5
Less   7.3
About the same   19.9
(Don't know)   11.0
(Refusal/Not answered)   0.4

IF NOT DK/REFUSAL AT [MoreBeg]
[ReasBeg]
Do you think this is ... READ OUT ...
...the result of government policies,
or, for some other reason?

Q529
%
                              26.3
                              56.1
(Don't know)   6.2
(Refusal/Not answered)   -

RELIGION AND CLASSIFICATION

N=3143

ASK ALL
[Religion]
Do you regard yourself as belonging to any particular religion?
IF YES: Which?
CODE ONE ONLY - DO NOT PROMPT

Q657

	%
No religion	43.8
Christian - no denomination	6.2
Roman Catholic	8.9
Church of England/Anglican	27.1
Baptist	1.2
Methodist	2.4
Presbyterian/Church of Scotland	3.5
Other Christian	0.2
Hindu	0.5
Jewish	0.3
Islam/Muslim	1.5
Sikh	0.5
Buddhist	-
Other non-Christian	0.3
Free Presbyterian	0.2
Brethren	-
United Reform Church (URC)/Congregational	0.3
Other Protestant	1.9
(Refusal)	0.4
(Don't know)	0.1
(Not answered)	0.7

Q660

IF NOT 'Refusal/NA AT [RelRFW]
[FamRelig]
In what religion, if any, were you brought up?
PROBE IF NECESSARY: What was your family's religion?
CODE ONE ONLY - DO NOT PROMPT

	%
No religion	11.2
Christian - no denomination	6.1
Roman Catholic	13.3
Church of England/Anglican	49.6
Baptist	1.4
Methodist	5.4
Presbyterian/Church of Scotland	5.7
Other Christian	0.3
Hindu	0.5
Jewish	0.4
Islam/Muslim	1.6
Sikh	0.5
Buddhist	-
Other non-Christian	0.1
Free Presbyterian	0.2
Brethren	0.1
United Reform Church (URC)/Congregational	-
Other Protestant	1.6
(Refusal)	0.1
(Don't know)	0.2
(Not answered)	1.1

Q665

IF RELIGION GIVEN AT EITHER [Religion] OR [FamRelig]
[ChAttend]
Apart from such special occasions as weddings, funerals and baptisms, how often nowadays do you attend services or meetings connected with your religion?
PROBE AS NECESSARY.

	%
Once a week or more	11.1
Less often but at least once in two weeks	1.8
Less often but at least once a month	5.3
Less often but at least twice a year	8.9
Less often but at least once a year	6.8
Less often	4.9
Never or practically never	48.6
Varies too much to say	0.5
(Don't know)	-
(Refusal/Not answered)	1.3

Q666
-Q673

ASK ALL
CARD
Please say which, if any, of the words on this
card describes the way **you** think of **yourself**.
Please choose as many or as few as apply.
PROBE: Any other?
Multicoded (Maximum of 8 codes)

%
69.5   British *[NatBrit]*
57.3   English *[NatEng]*
16.9   European *[NatEuro]*
2.6   Irish *[NatIrish]*
0.4   Northern Irish *[NatNI]*
10.0   Scottish *[NatScot]*
5.2   Welsh *[NatWelsh]*
2.1   Other answer (WRITE IN) *[NatOth]*
0.5   (None of these) *[NatNone]*
0.7   **EDIT ONLY:** OTHER - ASIAN MENTIONED *[NatAsia]*
0.1   **EDIT ONLY:** OTHER - AFRICAN /CARIBBEAN MENTIONED *[NatAfric]*
  (Don't know)
1.0   (Refusal/Not answered)

Q686

IF MORE THAN ONE ANSWER GIVEN AT [National]
[BNation]
CARD AGAIN
And if you had to choose, which one **best** describes the way
you think of yourself?

Q689

ASK ALL
[RaceOri2]
CARD
To which of these groups do you consider you belong?

%
0.6   BLACK: of African origin
0.7   BLACK: of Caribbean origin
0.1   BLACK: of other origin (WRITE IN)
1.2   ASIAN: of Indian origin
0.6   ASIAN: of Pakistani origin
0.5   ASIAN: of Bangladeshi origin
0.2   ASIAN: of Chinese origin
0.1   ASIAN: of other origin (WRITE IN)
93.3   WHITE: of any European origin
0.5   WHITE: of other origin (WRITE IN)
0.7   MIXED ORIGIN (WRITE IN)
0.3   OTHER (WRITE IN)
0.1   (Don't know)
1.0   (Refusal/Not answered)

Q695

ASK ALL
[RPrivEd]
Have you ever attended a fee-paying, **private**
primary or secondary school in the United Kingdom?
'PRIVATE' PRIMARY OR SECONDARY SCHOOLS INCLUDE:
INDEPENDENT SCHOOLS
SCHOLARSHIPS AND ASSISTED PLACES AT FEE-PAYING SCHOOLS
THEY EXCLUDE:
DIRECT GRANT SCHOOLS (UNLESS FEE-PAYING)
VOLUNTARY-AIDED SCHOOLS
GRANT-MAINTAINED ('OPTED OUT') SCHOOLS
NURSERY SCHOOLS

%
10.5   Yes
88.5   No
-   (Don't know)
1.0   (Refusal/Not answered)

Q696

IF 'Married' OR 'Living as married' AT [MarStat2]
[SPrivEd]
Has your *(husband/wife/partner)* ever attended a fee-paying,
private primary or secondary school in the United Kingdom?
'PRIVATE' PRIMARY OR SECONDARY SCHOOLS INCLUDE:
INDEPENDENT SCHOOLS
SCHOLARSHIPS AND ASSISTED PLACES AT FEE-PAYING SCHOOLS
THEY EXCLUDE:
DIRECT GRANT SCHOOLS (UNLESS FEE-PAYING)
VOLUNTARY-AIDED SCHOOLS
GRANT-MAINTAINED ('OPTED OUT') SCHOOLS
NURSERY SCHOOLS

%
4.8   Yes
59.6   No
0.1   (Don't know)
0.7   (Refusal/Not answered)

Q698

IF NO CHILDREN IN HOUSEHOLD (AS GIVEN IN HOUSEHOLD GRID)
[OthChld3] *
Have you ever been responsible for bringing up any children of
school age, including stepchildren?

%
34.4   Yes
32.3   No
0.7   (Don't know)
  (Refusal/Not answered)

N=3143

Q697 **IF CHILDREN IN HOUSEHOLD (AS GIVEN IN HOUSEHOLD GRID) OR 'yes' AT [othChld3]** N=3143
[ChPrivEd]
And (have any of your children/ has your child) ever attended a fee-paying, **private** primary or secondary school in the United Kingdom?
'PRIVATE' PRIMARY OR SECONDARY SCHOOLS INCLUDE:
INDEPENDENT SCHOOLS
SCHOLARSHIPS AND ASSISTED PLACES AT FEE-PAYING SCHOOLS
THEY EXCLUDE:
DIRECT GRANT SCHOOLS (UNLESS FEE-PAYING)
VOLUNTARY-AIDED SCHOOLS
GRANT-MAINTAINED ('OPTED OUT') SCHOOLS
NURSERY SCHOOLS
%
7.6   Yes
59.0 No
-     (Don't know)
1.0   (Refusal/Not answered)

ASK ALL
Q700 [Tea2]
How old were you when you completed your continuous full-time education?
PROBE IF NECESSARY
'STILL AT SCHOOL' - CODE 95
'STILL AT COLLEGE OR UNIVERSITY' - CODE 96
'OTHER ANSWER' - CODE 97 AND WRITE IN
Range: 1 ... 97
Median: 16 years old
%
0.2   Still at school
1.7   Still at college/university
0.2   Other answer
0.2   (Don't know)
1.0   (Refusal/Not answered)

ASK ALL
Q703 [SchQual]
CARD
Have you passed any of the examinations on this card?
%
58.6 Yes
40.3 No
-     (Don't know)
1.0   (Refusal/Not answered)

Q704 **IF 'Yes' AT [SchQual]**
-Q722 CARD AGAIN Which ones?
      PROBE: Any others?
%   Multicoded (Maximum of 19 codes)
      GCSE Grades D-G
      GCSE Grades 2-5
27.9 CSE 'O'-level Grades D-E or 7-9   [EdQual1]
      Scottish (SCE) Ordinary Bands D-E
      Scottish Standard Grades 4-7

      CSE Grades A-C
      CSE Grade 1
      GCE 'O'-level A-C or 1-6
      School Certificate or Matriculation
46.5 Scottish (SCE) Ordinary Bands A-C   [EdQual2]
      Scottish Standard Grades 1-3 or Pass
      Scottish School Leaving Certificate Lower Grade
      SUPE Ordinary
      Northern Ireland Junior Certificate

      GCE 'A'-level/ 'S'-level/ 'AS'-level
19.2 Higher School Certificate   [EdQual3]
      Scottish SCE/SLC/SUPE at Higher Grade
      Northern Ireland Senior Certificate

1.8   Overseas school leaving exam or certificate   [EdQual4]
0.0   (Don't know)
1.1   (Refusal/Not answered)

ASK ALL
Q727 [PschQual]
CARD
And have you passed any of the exams or got any of the qualifications on **this** card?
%
53.3 Yes
45.7 No
-     (Don't know)
1.0   (Refusal/Not answered)

Q728
-Q745

IF 'Yes' AT [PachQual]
CARD AGAIN Which ones? PROBE: Any others?
Multicoded (Maximum of 18 codes)   N=3143

%
4.9   Recognised trade apprenticeship **completed** [EdQual5]
8.6   RSA/other clerical, commercial qualification [EdQual6]
8.1   City&Guilds Certif - Part I [EdQual22]
6.9   City&Guilds Certif - Craft/ Intermediate/ ordinary/ Part II [EdQual23]
4.1   ity&Guilds Certif - Advanced/ Final/ Part III [EdQual24]
1.7   City&Guilds Certif - Full Technological/ Part IV [EdQual25]
4.7   BEC/TEC General/Ordinary National Certif (ONC) or Diploma (OND) [EdQual10]
5.2   BEC/TEC Higher/Higher National Certif (HNC) or Diploma (HND) [EdQual11]
3.3   NVQ/SVQ Lev 1/GNVQ Foundation lev [EdQual17]
4.8   NVQ/SVQ Lev 2/GNVQ Intermediate lev [EdQual18]
3.1   NVQ/SVQ Lev 3/GNVQ Advanced lev [EdQual19]
0.7   NVQ/SVQ Lev 4 [EdQual20]
0.1   NVQ/SVQ Lev 5 [EdQual21]
1.3   Teacher training qualification [EdQual12]
2.7   Nursing qualification [EdQual13]
6.7   Other technical or business qualification/certificate [EdQual14]
11.4 Univ/CNAA degree/diploma [EdQual15]
5.3   Other recognised academic or vocational qual (WRITE IN) [EdQual16]
-     (Don't know)
1.0   (Refusal/Not answered)

Q766
-Q774

VERSION A: ASK ALL
CARD   N=1066
On this card are ways in which people are asked to give to charity. Some people are not able to give. How about you: in which, if any, of these ways have you given money to charity in the last year.
Any others?
PROBE UNTIL NO
CODE ALL THAT APPLY
Multicoded (Maximum of 9 codes)

%
82.0 Buying raffle tickets [CharRaff]
48.9 Buying goods in a sale or fete [CharFete]
44.7 Buying goods in a charity shop [CharShop]
54.7 Giving in a door-to-door collection [CharDoor]
52.4 Giving in a street collection [CharSt]
34.6 Giving in a church collection [CharChch]
15.0 Giving to a TV or radio appeal [CharTVRd]
64.7 Sponsoring someone in a fundraising event [CharSpon]
31.6 Sponsoring an event in aid of charity [CharEvnt]
3.0   (None of these) [charNone]
0.1   (Don't know)
0.5   (Refusal/Not answered)

Q775

ASK ALL
[PastVot]   N=3143
Thinking back to the last (UK) **general election** in 1997 - do you remember which party you voted for then, or perhaps you didn't vote in that election?
IF NECESSARY SAY: The one where Tony Blair won against John Major.
DO NOT PROMPT. FOR 'CAN'T REMEMBER', CODE DON'T KNOW

%
23.7 Did not vote/ not eligible
21.3 Yes, voted: - Conservative
39.3 - Labour
9.2   - Liberal Democrat
1.1   - Scottish National Party
0.3   - Plaid Cymru
0.2   - Green Party
0.4   - Other (WRITE IN)
3.3   - Referendum Party
1.0   Refused to say
-     (Don't know)
-     (Refusal/Not answered)

Q789

ASK ALL WHO ARE MARRIED OR LIVING AS MARRIED
[SEconAct]   N=2047
CARD (PERCENTAGES REFER TO THE HIGHEST ANSWER ON THE LIST)
Which of these descriptions applied to what your partner was doing last week, that is the seven days ending last Sunday?
PROBE: Which others? CODE ALL THAT APPLY
Multicoded (Maximum of 11 codes)

%
0.6   In full-time education (not paid for by employer, including on vacation)
0.1   On government training/employment programme (eg. Youth Training, Training for Work etc)
62.2 In paid work (or away temporarily) for at least 10 hours in week
0.2   Waiting to take up paid work already accepted
1.2   Unemployed and registered at a benefit office
0.6   Unemployed, **not** registered, but actively looking for a job (of at least 10 hrs a week)
0.2   Unemployed, wanting a job (of at least 10 hrs per week) but **not** actively looking for a job
3.2   Permanently sick or disabled
18.6 Wholly retired from work
11.5 Looking after the home
10.3 (Doing something else) (WRITE IN)
-     (Don't know)
1.3   (Refusal/Not answered)

Q790 **ASK ALL WHO ARE MARRIED/LIVING AS MARRIED AND PARTNER IS NOT WORKING.** [N=771]
[SLastJob]
How long ago did your partner last have a paid job of at least 10 hours a week?
GOVERNMENT PROGRAMS/SCHEMES DO NOT COUNT AS 'PAID JOBS'

%
12.6 Within past 12 months
20.7 Over 1, up to 5 years ago
20.9 Over 5, up to 10 years ago
24.3 Over 10, up to 20 years ago
13.0 Over 20 years ago
5.1 Never had a paid job of 10+ hours a week
0.1 (Don't know)
3.3 (Refusal/Not answered)

ASK WHERE PARTNERS JOB DETAILS ARE BEING COLLECTED * [N=295]

Q791 [PTitle] **(NOT ON THE DATAFILE)**
Now I want to ask you about your (husband/wife/partner)'s present job. What is (his/her) job?
PROBE IF NECESSARY: What is the name or title of the job?
IF NECESSARY: What was the name or title of the job?

Q792 [PTypeWk] **(NOT ON THE DATAFILE)**
What kind of work does (he/she) do most of the time?
IF RELEVANT: What materials/machinery does (he/she) use?

Q793 [PTrain] **(NOT ON THE DATAFILE)**
What training or qualifications are needed for that job?

Q794 [PSuper2]
Does your (husband/wife/partner) directly supervise or is (he/she) directly responsible for the work of any other people?

%
34.4 Yes
56.3 No
9.3 (Refusal/Not answered)

Q795 **IF 'Yes' AT [PSuper2]**
[PSuper2]
How many?
Median: 5 (of those supervising any)
7.4 (Don't know)
21.2 (Refusal/Not answered)

Q797 **ASK WHERE PARTNERS JOB DETAILS ARE BEING COLLECTED** [N=295]
[PEmplyee]
In (his/her) (main) job is (he/she) ... READ OUT ...
%
69.8 ... an employee,
20.6 or self-employed?
0.4 (Don't know)
9.3 (Refusal/Not answered)

Q799 **ASK ALL WHERE PARTNER'S JOB DETAILS ARE BEING COLLECTED AND PARTNER IS/WAS EMPLOYEE IN CURRENT/LAST JOB** [N=234]
[PSupman2]
Can I just check, is (he/she) ... READ OUT ...
%
20.2 ...a manager,
11.4 a foreman or supervisor,
56.2 or not?
 -    (Don't know)
12.1 (Refusal/Not answered)

Q800 [POcSect2]
CARD
Which of the types of organisation on this card does (he/she) work for?
%
65.7 PRIVATE SECTOR FIRM OR COMPANY Including, for example, limited companies and PLCs
1.2 NATIONALISED INDUSTRY OR PUBLIC CORPORATION Including, for example, the Post Office and the BBC
18.6 OTHER PUBLIC SECTOR EMPLOYER
      Incl eg: - Central govt/ Civil Service/ Govt Agency
      Local authority/ Local Educ Auth (incl 'opted out' schools)
      Universities
      Health Authority / NHS hospitals / NHS Trusts/ GP surgeries
      Police / Armed forces
1.0 CHARITY/ VOLUNTARY SECTOR Including, for example, charitable companies, churches, trade unions
1.0 Other answer (WRITE IN)
 -   (Don't know)
12.6 (Refusal/Not answered)

Q802 **ASK ALL WHERE PARTNERS JOB DETAILS ARE BEING COLLECTED** [N=295]
[PEmpMake] **[NOT ON THE DATAFILE]**
IF EMPLOYEE: What does (his/her) employer make or do at the place where (he/she) works (from)?
IF SELF-EMPLOYED: What does (he/she) make or do at the place where (he/she) works (from)?

* Details of partner's job were collected only if the respondent was neither working nor retired and the partner was working or retired.

Q807 [PEmpWork]
IF **EMPLOYEE**: Including (himself/herself), how many people are employed at the place where (he/she) usually works from?
IF **SELF-EMPLOYED**: Does (he/she) have any employees?
IF YES: PROBE FOR CORRECT PRECODE.   N=295

%	
12.9	(No employees/DO NOT USE IF EMPLOYEE)
21.2	Under 10
10.0	10-24
16.4	25-99
11.7	100-499
11.5	500 or more
7.0	(Don't know)
9.3	(Refusal/Not answered)

Q818 [PPartFull]
Is job ...READ OUT...

%	
77.7	... full-time - that is, 30 or more hours per week,
13.0	or, part-time?
-	(Don't know)
9.3	(Refusal/Not answered)

ASK ALL
Q847 [AnyBN2]
CARD   N=3143
Do you (or your wife/husband/partner) receive any of the state benefits on this card at present?

%	
60.7	Yes
38.2	No
-	(Don't know)
1.1	(Refusal/Not answered)

Q848 -Q865
IF 'Yes' AT [AnyBN2]
CARD AGAIN Which ones? PROBE:
Multicoded (Maximum of 18 codes)   N=3143

%	
23.2	State retirement pension (National Insurance) [BenefOAP]
0.9	War Pension (War Disablement Pension or War Widows Pension) [BenefWar]
1.3	Widow's Benefits (Widow's Pension and Widowed Mother's Allowance) [BenefWid]
2.6	Jobseeker's Allowance/ Unemployment Benefit / Income Support for the Unemployed [BenefUB]
6.1	Income Support (other than for unemployment) [BenefIS]
27.0	Child Benefit (formerly Family Allowance) [BenefCB]
1.6	One Parent Benefit [BenefOP]
2.8	Family Credit [BenefFC]
7.9	Housing Benefit (Rent Rebate) [BenefHB]
8.6	Council Tax Benefit (or Rebate) [BenefCT]
5.4	Incapacity Benefit / Sickness Benefit / Invalidity Benefit [BenefInc]
0.4	Disability Working Allowance [BenefDWA]
4.3	Disability Living Allowance (for people under 65) [BenefDLA]
2.1	Attendance Allowance (for people aged 65+) [BenefAtA]
0.5	Severe Disablement Allowance [BenefSev]
1.4	Invalid Care Allowance [BenefICA]
0.5	Industrial Injuries Disablement Benefit [BenefInd]
-	(Don't know)
1.2	(Refusal/Not answered)

Q886
ASK ALL
[MainInc]
CARD
Which of these is the **main** source of income for you (and your husband/wife/partner) at present?

%	
61.6	Earnings from employment (own or spouse / partner's)
8.6	Occupational pension(s) - from previous employer(s)
14.5	State retirement or widow's pension(s)
1.9	Jobseeker's Allowance/ Unemployment benefit
3.9	Income Support
0.6	Family Credit
3.7	Invalidity, sickness or disabled pension or benefit(s)
0.3	Other state benefit (WRITE IN)
1.1	Interest from savings or investments
0.4	Student grant
1.0	Dependent on parents/other relatives
0.9	Other main source (WRITE IN)
0.2	(Don't know)
1.3	(Refusal/Not answered)

N=2087

VERSION A & B: ASK ALL
[FagsNow]
Do you yourself ever smoke cigarettes?

	Q892
	%
Yes	29.9
No	69.4
(Don't know)	0.1
(Refusal/Not answered)	0.6

IF 'Yes' AT [FagsNow]
[SmokDay]
About how many cigarettes a day do you usually smoke?
IF 'CAN'T SAY', CODE 997
Median: 15 cigarettes

	Q893
	%
(Don't know/Can't say)	3.7
(Refusal/Not answered)	2.6

Q889

ASK ALL *
[HHincome]
CARD
Which of the letters on this card represents the total income
of your household from **all** sources **before tax**?
Please just tell me the letter.
NOTE: INCLUDES INCOME FROM BENEFITS, SAVINGS, ETC.

N=3143

Q890

ASK ALL IN PAID WORK
[REarn] *
CARD AGAIN
Which of the letters on this card represents your own gross or
total earnings, before deduction of income tax and national
insurance?

N=1748

	[HHincome]	[REarn]
	%	%
Q (Less than £4,000)	4.0	7.0
T (£4,000- £5,000)	8.1	6.5
O (£6,000- £7,000)	7.2	7.6
K (£8,000- £9,999)	5.1	7.8
L (£10,000-£11,999)	5.9	9.6
B (£12,000-£14,999)	6.0	11.0
Z (£15,000-£17,999)	7.2	9.8
M (£18,000-£19,000)	4.2	6.5
F (£20,000-£22,999)	4.9	5.7
J (£23,000-£25,999)	5.7	5.8
D (£26,000-£28,999)	4.7	4.7
H (£29,000-£31,999)	3.9	2.0
C (£32,000-£34,999)	3.7	1.3
G (£35,000-£37,999)	2.9	1.2
P (£38,000-£40,999)	2.0	1.1
N (£41,000-£43,999)	1.7	0.5
Y (£44,000-£46,999)	1.5	0.9
S (£47,000 or more)	7.6	3.9
(Don't know)	8.0	2.1
(Refusal/Not answered)	5.8	5.0

Q891

ASK ALL
[Ownshare]
Do you (or does your wife/husband/partner)own any shares quoted
on the Stock Exchange, including unit trusts and PEPs?
(PEP = PERSONAL EQUITY PLAN)

N=3143

	%
Yes	35.0
No	62.9
(Don't know)	0.1
(Refusal/Not answered)	0.6

ADMINISTRATION

N=3143

Q895 **ASK ALL**
[PhoneX]
Is there a telephone in (your part of) this accommodation?
%
94.5 Yes
4.4 No
- (Don't know)
1.1 (Refusal/Not answered)

Q896 **IF 'Yes' AT [PhoneX]**
[PhoneBck]
A few interviews on any survey are checked by a supervisor to make sure that people are satisfied with the way the interview was carried out. In case my supervisor needs to contact you, it would be helpful if we could have your telephone number.
ADD IF NECESSARY: Your 'phone number will **not** be passed to anyone outside SCPR.
IF NUMBER GIVEN, WRITE ON THE ARF
NOTE: YOU WILL BE ASKED TO KEY IN THE NUMBER IN THE ADMIN BLOCK
%
87.9 Number given
6.6 Number refused
- (Don't know)
1.1 (Refusal/Not answered)

Q897 **ASK ALL**
[ComeBac2]
Sometime in the next year, we may be doing a follow up survey and may wish to contact you again. Could you give us the address or phone number of someone who knows you well, just in case we have difficulty in getting in touch with you.
IF NECESSARY, PROMPT: Perhaps a relative or friend who is unlikely to move?
WRITE IN DETAILS ON ARF
%
45.5 Information given
46.4 Information not given (other than code 3)
6.9 DO NOT PROMPT: Outright refusal ever to take part again
0.1 (Don't know)
1.1 (Refusal/Not answered)

VERSIONS B AND C QUESTIONNAIRE

COUNTRYSIDE (MAINLY VERSIONS B AND C)

N=2077

Q551 **VERSIONS B & C: ASK ALL**
[CtryConc]
Now some questions about the countryside.
Are you personally concerned about things that may happen to the countryside, or does it not concern you particularly?
IF CONCERNED: Are you very concerned, or just a bit concerned?

%
51.3 Very concerned
32.4 A bit concerned
15.3 Does not concern me particularly
0.2 (Don't know)
0.8 (Refusal/Not answered)

Q552 [SetAsid1]*
CARD
Modern methods of farming mean it now takes less land to produce the same amount of food. Please say how much you are in favour of or against each of these ways of paying farmers to use their spare land. Remember that if this happened on a large scale, income tax or VAT might have to go up to meet the costs.
First, how much are you in favour of or against paying farmers to change to organic farming which takes up more land?

Q553 [SetAsid2]*
CARD AGAIN
(And how much are you in favour of or against...)
paying farmers to 'set aside' spare land and not use it at all?

Q554 [SetAsid3]*
CARD AGAIN
(And how much are you in favour of or against...)
paying farmers to 'set aside' spare land for woodland, to encourage wildlife?

Q555 [SetAsid4]*
CARD AGAIN
(And how much are you in favour of or against...)
paying farmers to 'set aside' spare land for forestry and timber?

	[SetAsid1]	[SetAsid2]
	%	%
Strongly in favour	12.9	2.0
In favour	36.1	16.3
Neither in favour nor against	27.2	20.9
Against	17.8	42.9
Strongly against	3.1	14.7
(Don't know)	1.9	2.3
(Refusal/Not answered)	0.9	1.0

	[SetAsid3]	[SetAsid4]
	%	%
Strongly in favour	15.0	8.4
In favour	64.2	57.4
Neither in favour nor against	10.7	18.8
Against	6.7	11.4
Strongly against	1.3	1.7
(Don't know)	1.1	1.4
(Refusal/Not answered)	1.0	1.0

N=3143

ASK ALL
Q556 [ResPres]
Can I just check, would you describe the place where you live as ... READ OUT ...

%
8.0 ...a big city,
23.7 the suburbs or outskirts of a big city,
48.9 a small city or town,
16.6 a country village,
1.7 or, a farm or home in the country?
0.2 (Other answer (WRITE IN))
0.1 (Don't know)
0.8 (Refusal/Not answered)

N=2077

Q558 **VERSIONS B & C: IF 'big city', 'suburbs', 'small town' OR 'other' AT [ResPres]**
[CntryLiv]
Have you **ever** lived in the countryside, or in a country village or town - for instance when you were a child or at some time before now?

%
32.6 Yes
47.8 No
- (Don't know)
1.0 (Refusal/Not answered)

Q559
VERSIONS B & C: IF 'big city', 'suburbs', 'small town', 'village' OR 'other' AT [ResPres]　[N=2077]
[CntryDis]
About how far do you live from the nearest **open countryside** that you can visit or walk in? Please do not include city parks.
IF NOT SURE, PROBE FOR ESTIMATE

%	
35.8	Less than ¼ mile (15 mins walk)
14.2	¼ up to 1 mile (15-30 mins walk)
18.6	Over 1 mile, up to 3 miles
18.3	Over 3 miles, up to 10 miles
7.4	Over 10 miles
2.9	(Don't know)
1.0	(Refusal/Not answered)

Q560
VERSION B & C :IF 'small town', 'village', 'country', 'other', DK OR REFUSAL AT [ResPres]
[CityLiv]
Have you **ever** lived in a big city or the suburbs or outskirts of a big city - for instance when you were a child or at some time before now?

%	
27.8	Yes
39.1	No
-	(Don't know)
1.0	(Refusal/Not answered)

Q561
VERSION B & C: ASK ALL
[ResChoos]
If you had a **free** choice would you choose to live in ...
READ OUT ...

%	
4.9	...a big city,
14.9	the suburbs or outskirts of a big city,
28.8	a small city or town,
36.0	a **country** village,
13.4	or, a farm or home in the country?
0.7	(Other answer (WRITE IN))
0.2	(Don't know)
1.0	(Refusal/Not answered)

Q563
-Q568
CARD
Taking your answer from the card, which of these facilities, if any, are there within about fifteen minute walk of here?
Multicoded (Maximum of 6 codes)

%	
82.9	An NHS doctor [NrDoctor]
92.1	A small shop/or corner shop selling basic groceries [NrShop]
71.8	A medium:large supermarket or store [NrSuperm]
89.7	A primary school [NrSchool]
94.4	A bus/tram stop,rail,tube or metro stations [NrTransp]
91.7	A pub/bar/restaurant [NrPubRes]
1.3	(None of these) [NearNone]
0.3	(Don't know)
6.4	(Refusal/Not answered)

[N=2077]

Q569
[NearDoc]*
CARD
Please use this card to tell me how important it is for **you and your household** to have, within about fifteen minutes **walk** ...an NHS doctor?

Q570
[NearShop]*
CARD AGAIN
...a small shop or corner shop selling basic groceries?

Q571
[NearSupM]*
CARD AGAIN
...a medium to large supermarket or store?

Q572
[NearSchl]*
CARD AGAIN
And how important is it for **you and your household** to have, within about fifteen minutes **walk** ...a primary school?

Q573
[NearTran]*
CARD AGAIN
...a bus or tram stop, rail, tube or metro station?

Q574
[NearPub]*
CARD AGAIN
...a pub, bar or restaurant?

	[NearDoc]	[NearShop]	[NearSchl]
	%	%	%
Very important	55.2	35.5	30.5
Fairly important	23.9	43.2	16.7
Not very important	15.3	16.8	14.4
Not at all important	4.4	3.4	37.3
(Don't know)	0.1	0.1	-
(Refusal/Not answered)	1.1	1.1	1.1

	[NearTran]	[NearPub]	[NearSupm]
	%	%	%
Very important	45.1	17.8	24.1
Fairly important	30.0	22.7	37.1
Not very important	15.7	34.9	30.8
Not at all important	8.1	23.5	7.1
(Don't know)	-	-	-
(Refusal/Not answered)	1.1	1.1	1.0

VERSION B QUESTIONNAIRE

TRANSPORT (VERSION B)

N=1022

Q576 VERSION B: ASK ALL
[TransCar]
(May I just check...) ... do you, or does anyone in your household, own or have the regular use of a car or a van?
IF 'YES' PROBE FOR WHETHER RESPONDENT, OR OTHER PERSON(S) ONLY, OR BOTH

%
29.0 Yes, respondent only
19.3 Yes, other(s) only
33.1 Yes, both
18.2 No
- (Don't know)
0.4 (Refusal/Not answered)

Q577 IF 'Yes' AT [TransCar]
[NumbCars]
How many vehicles in all?

%
48.0 One
26.6 Two
5.4 Three
1.2 Four
0.1 Five or more
- (Don't know)
0.4 (Refusal/Not answered)

Q578 VERSION B: ASK ALL
[TrfPb6U]*
CARD
Now thinking about traffic and transport problems, how serious a problem **for you** is congestion on motorways?

Q579 [TrfPb7U]*
CARD AGAIN
(And how serious a problem **for you** is ...)
...increased traffic on country roads and lanes?

Q580 [TrfPb8U]*
CARD AGAIN
(And how serious a problem **for you** is ...)
...traffic congestion at popular places in the countryside?

Q581 [TrfPb9U]*
CARD AGAIN
(And how serious a problem **for you** is ...)
...traffic congestion in towns and cities?

Q582 [TrfPb10U]*
CARD AGAIN
(And how serious a problem **for you** are ...)
...exhaust fumes from traffic in towns and cities?

	[TrfPrb6]	[TrfPrb7]	[TrfPrb8]
	%	%	%
A very serious problem	15.1	11.7	10.6
A serious problem	20.6	31.2	32.7
Not a very serious problem	35.3	36.6	35.5
Not a problem at all	28.1	19.4	19.7
(Don't know)	0.4	0.7	1.0
(Refusal/Not answered)	0.4	0.4	0.4

	[TrfP9U]	[TrfB10U]
	%	%
A very serious problem	33.4	40.5
A serious problem	37.7	34.5
Not a very serious problem	18.9	16.4
Not a problem at all	9.4	7.5
(Don't know)	0.3	0.7
(Refusal/Not answered)	0.4	0.4

Q583 IF 'yes,respondent', 'yes, both' OR DK/REFUSAL AT [TransCar]
[GetAbB1]*
CARD
I am going to read out some of the things that might get people to **cut down** on the number of car journeys they take.
For each one, please tell me what effect, if any, this might have on how much **you yourself** use the car to get about.
...gradually doubling the cost of petrol over the next ten years?

Q584 [GetAbB2]*
CARD AGAIN
(What effect, if any, might this have on how much you yourself use the car?)
...greatly improving **long distance** rail and coach services?

Q585 [GetAbB3]*
CARD AGAIN
(What effect, if any, might this have on how much you yourself use the car?)
...greatly improving the reliability of **local** public transport?

N=1022

	[GetAbB1] %	[GetAbB2] %	[GetAbB3] %
Might use car even more	0.4	0.3	0.2
Might use car a little less	18.1	17.3	18.6
Might use car quite a bit less	14.7	13.5	15.5
Might give up using car	5.2	2.3	5.2
It would make no difference	23.7	28.4	22.4
(Don't know)	0.1	0.3	0.2
(Refusal/Not answered)	0.4	0.4	0.4

	[GetAbB4] %	[GetAbB5] %	[GetAbB6] %
Might use a car even more	0.4	0.1	0.1
Might use a car a little less	16.0	12.5	12.8
Might use car quite a bit less	12.9	7.9	10.7
Might give up using car	5.7	4.5	3.6
It would make no difference	26.4	36.7	34.5
(Don't know)	0.4	0.4	0.3
(Refusal/Not answered)	0.4	0.4	0.4

	[GetAbB7] %	[GetAbB8] %	[GetAbB9] %
Might use a car even more	0.1	0.1	0.4
Might use a car a little less	7.7	1.7	16.0
Might use car quite a bit less	7.2	3.5	14.4
Might give up using car	1.7	1.4	4.6
It would make no difference	45.0	9.9	26.6
(Don't know)	0.3	0.1	0.1
(Refusal/Not answered)	0.4	0.2	0.4

	[GetAbB10] %
Might use a car even more	0.2
Might use a car a little less	13.0
Might use car quite a bit less	16.5
Might give up using car	5.4
It would make no difference	26.8
(Don't know)	0.2
(Refusal/Not answered)	0.4

N=1022

Q586 [GetAbB4] *
CARD AGAIN
(What effect, if any, might this have on how much you yourself use the car?)
...charging all motorists around £2 each time they enter or drive through a city or town centre at peak times?

Q587 [GetAbB5] *
CARD AGAIN
(What effect, if any, might this have on how much you yourself use the car?)
...charging £1 for every 50 miles motorists travel on motorways?

Q588 [GetAbB6] *
CARD AGAIN
(What effect, if any, might this have on how much you yourself use the car?)
...making parking penalties and restrictions much more severe?

Q589 [GetAbB7] *
CARD AGAIN
(What effect, if any, might this have on how much you yourself use the car?)
...special cycle lanes on roads around here?

IF 'yes, respondent', 'yes, both' OR DK/REFUSAL AT [TransCar]
AND CHILDREN AGED 3-18 IN THE HOUSEHOLD
Q590 [GetAbB8]
CARD AGAIN
(What effect, if any, might this have on how much you yourself use the car?)
...a free school bus service for your children?

IF 'yes, respondent', 'yes, both' OR DK/REFUSAL AT [TransCar]
Q591 [GetAbB9] *
CARD AGAIN
(What effect, if any, might this have on how much you yourself use the car?)
...cutting in half local public transport fares?

Q592 [GetAbB10] *
CARD AGAIN
(What effect, if any, might this have on how much you yourself use the car?)
...cutting in half long distance rail and coach fares?

Q593

VERSION B: ASK ALL   N=1022

[Drive]

May I just check, do you **yourself drive** a car at all these days?

	%
Yes	67.9
No	31.6
(Don't know)	-
(Refusal/Not answered)	0.4

Q594

IF 'Yes' AT [Drive]

[Travel1]*

CARD

How often nowadays do you **usually** travel

...by car as a driver?

Q595

VERSION B: ASK ALL

[Travel2]*

CARD AGAIN

(How often nowadays do you **usually**...)

...travel by car as a passenger?

Q596

[Travel3]*

CARD AGAIN

(How often nowadays do you **usually**...)

...travel by local bus?

	[Travel1] %	[Travel2] %	[Travel3] %
			N=1022
Every day or nearly every day	43.5	11.1	6.5
2-5 days a week	16.4	24.1	12.3
Once a week	4.1	24.3	7.6
Less often but at least once a month	1.6	15.2	10.8
Less often than that	1.1	11.9	16.2
Never nowadays	1.1	12.9	46.2
(Don't know)	-	-	-
(Refusal/Not answered)	0.4	0.4	0.4

Q597

[Travel4]*

CARD AGAIN (How often nowadays do you **usually**...)

...travel by train?

Q598

[Travel6]*

CARD AGAIN

(How often nowadays do you **usually**...)

...travel by bicycle?

	[Travel4] %	[Travel6] %
Every day or nearly every day	3.1	4.2
2-5 days a week	1.9	3.6
Once a week	2.3	4.8
Less often but at least once a month	4.8	5.9
Less often than that	34.7	6.8
Never nowadays	42.8	74.4
(Don't know)	-	-
(Refusal/Not answered)	0.4	0.4

Q599

[Travel9]*

CARD AGAIN

(How often nowadays do you **usually**...)

...go somewhere on foot at least 15 minutes' walk away?

Q600

IF 'Yes' AT [TransCar] AND CHILDREN AGED 3-18 IN HOUSEHOLD

[Travel10]*

CARD AGAIN

How often nowadays *(is your child / are any of your children)* **usually** driven to school by a member of your household?

	[Travel9] %	[Travel10] %
		N=210
Every day or nearly every day	33.2	4.1
2-5 days a week	24.0	3.0
Once a week	18.0	0.8
Less often but at least once a month	7.3	1.2
Less often than that	5.9	0.8
Never nowadays	11.1	8.8
(Don't know)	-	-
(Refusal/Not answered)	0.4	0.4

Q601

ASK THOSE WHO HAVE CAR AND TRAVEL EVERYDAY BY CAR AND ODD SERIAL NUMBERS

[CutQrt1] *

CARD

Suppose you were forced for some reason to cut around **a quarter** of your regular car trips?

How inconvenient would you find it?

Please choose your answer from this card

Q602 [CutHalf1] *
CARD AGAIN   N=210
Suppose you were forced for some reason to cut
as many as a half of your regular car trips.
How inconvenient would you find it?
Please choose your answer from this card

Q603 ASK THOSE WHO HAVE A CAR AND TRAVEL BY EVERY
DAY BY CAR AND EVEN SERIAL NUMBERS
[CutHalf2] *
CARD   N=232
Suppose you were forced for some reason to cut half of your
regular car trips.
How inconvenient would you find it?
Please choose your answer from this card

Q604 [CutQrt2] *
CARD AGAIN
Suppose you were forced for some reason to cut only around a
quarter of your regular car trips.
How inconvenient would you find it?
Please choose your answer from this card

	[CutQrt1] %	[CutHalf1] %
Not at all inconvenient	2.7	1.6
Not very inconvenient	10.1	4.2
Fairly inconvenient	32.1	16.7
Very inconvenient	54.1	76.4
(Don't know)	-	-
(Refusal/Not answered)	1.1	1.1

	[CutHalf2] %	[CutQrt2] %
Not at all inconvenient	1.9	4.8
Not very inconvenient	9.4	15.1
Fairly inconvenient	23.0	35.0
Very inconvenient	62.8	42.2
(Don't know)	0.5	0.5
(Refusal/Not answered)	2.4	2.4

VERSION C QUESTIONNAIRE

EDUCATION (VERSION C)

N=1056

Q530 **VERSION C: ASK ALL**
[EdSpend1]
CARD
Now some questions about education.
Which of the groups on this card, if any, would be your highest priority for **extra** government spending on education?

%
13.6 Nursery or pre-school children
21.1 Primary school children
24.2 Secondary school children
24.7 Less able children with special needs
12.1 Students at colleges or universities
1.5 (None of these)
2.0 (Don't know)
0.8 (Refusal/Not answered)

Q531 **IF RESPONSE GIVEN AT [EdSpend1]**
[EdSpend2]
CARD AGAIN
And which is your next highest priority?

%
13.2 Nursery or pre-school children
25.6 Primary school children
23.5 Secondary school children
21.6 Less able children with special needs
11.0 Students at colleges or universities
0.6 (None of these)
0.3 (Don't know)
2.8 (Refusal/Not answered)

N=1056

Q532 **VERSION C: ASK ALL**
[PrimImp1]
CARD
Here are a number of things that some people think would improve education in our schools.
Which do you think would be the **most** useful one for improving the education of children in **primary** schools - aged (5-11/5-12) years? Please look at the whole list before deciding.

%
1.5 More information available about individual schools
8.4 More links between parents and schools
18.8 More resources for buildings, books and equipment
15.7 Better quality teachers
36.1 Smaller class sizes
1.1 More emphasis on exams and tests
13.3 More emphasis on developing the child's skills and interests
1.6 Better leadership within individual schools
0.8 Other (WRITE IN)
2.0 (Don't know)
0.8 (Refusal/Not answered)

Q534 **IF RESPONSE GIVEN AT [PrimImp1]**
[PrimImp2]
CARD AGAIN
And which do you think would be the **next** most useful one for children in **primary** schools?

%
1.2 More information available about individual schools
8.4 More links between parents and schools
24.2 More resources for buildings, books and equipment
14.5 Better quality teachers
20.9 Smaller class sizes
3.6 More emphasis on exams and tests
20.7 More emphasis on developing the child's skills and interests
2.5 Better leadership within individual schools
0.6 Other (WRITE IN)
0.4 (Don't know)
2.9 (Refusal/Not answered)

Q536 | **VERSION C: ASK ALL** N=1056
[SecImp1]
CARD
And which do you think would be the **most** useful thing for improving the education of children in **secondary** schools - aged (11-18/12-18) years?

%
1.5 More information available about individual schools
5.0 More links between parents and schools
17.9 More resources for buildings, books and equipment
20.4 Better quality teachers
21.9 Smaller class sizes
4.0 More emphasis on exams and tests
11.3 More emphasis on developing the child's skills and interests
12.1 More training and preparation for jobs
2.0 Better leadership within individual schools
0.7 Other (WRITE IN)
2.4 (Don't know)
0.9 (Refusal/Not answered)

Q538 | **IF RESPONSE GIVEN AT [SecImp1]**
[SecImp2]
CARD AGAIN
And which do you think would be the **next** most useful one for children in **secondary** schools?

%
1.2 More information available about individual schools
5.9 More links between parents and schools
17.9 More resources for buildings, books and equipment
14.7 Better quality teachers
14.5 Smaller class sizes
6.9 More emphasis on exams and tests
15.1 More emphasis on developing the child's skills and interests
17.0 More training and preparation for jobs
3.6 Better leadership within individual schools
0.1 Other (WRITE IN)
0.1 (Don't know)
3.3 (Refusal/Not answered)

Q540 | **VERSION C: ASK ALL**
[SchSelec]
CARD
Which of the following statements comes closest to your views about what kind of **secondary** school children should go to?

%
45.6 Children should go to a different kind of secondary school, according to how well they do at primary school
50.8 All children should go to the same kind of secondary school, no matter how well or badly they do at primary school
2.5 (Don't know)
1.1 (Refusal/Not answered)

Q541 | N=1056
[HEdOpp]
Do you feel that opportunities for young people in Britain to go on to **higher education** - to a university or college - should be increased or reduced, or are they at about the right level now?
IF INCREASED OR REDUCED: a lot or a little?
%
25.0 Increased a lot
18.6 Increased a little
47.5 About right
3.7 Reduced a little
0.6 Reduced a lot
3.7 (Don't know)
1.0 (Refusal/Not answered)

Q542 | [HEFees2]
At present, some full-time university students have to pay a £1,000 **tuition fee**. Others have all or part of the fee paid by the government. Whether they have to pay or not depends upon the student's circumstances and those of their family. Do you think that ... READ OUT ...
%
40.3 ... **all** students should get their tuition fees paid,
50.8 **some** students, depending on their circumstances, should get their tuition fees paid, as now,
4.3 or, **no** students should get their tuition fees paid by the government?
2.5 (It depends)
1.2 (Don't know)
1.0 (Refusal/Not answered)

Q543 | [HEGrant]
And, at present, some full-time British university students get grants to help cover their **living** costs. Getting a grant depends upon the student's circumstances and those of their family. Do you think that ... READ OUT ...
%
28.7 ... **all** students should get grants to help cover their living costs,
64.2 **some** students should get grants to help cover their living costs, as now,
2.8 or, that no grants should be given to help cover students' living costs?
2.0 (It depends)
1.3 (Don't know)
1.0 (Refusal/Not answered)

Q544 [HELoan]   N=1056

Many full-time university students are now taking out government loans to help cover their living costs. They have to start repaying these loans when they begin working.
Generally speaking, do you think that ...
READ OUT ...

	%
...students **should** be expected to take out loans to help cover their living costs,	29.5
or, students **should not** be expected to take out loans to help cover living costs?	58.0
(It depends)	9.1
(Don't know)	2.4
(Refusal/Not answered)	1.0

Q545 [SexEdSc1]

Some people think that **all** schools should teach sex education to children before they are 11. Others say that **parents** should be allowed to choose whether or not their young child has sex education. What about you? Do you think that ... READ OUT ...

	%
... **all** children aged 11 and under should have sex education at school,	41.5
or, should parents be allowed to choose?	55.9
(Don't know)	1.5
(Refusal/Not answered)	1.1

IF 'parental choice'/DK AT [SexEdSc1]

Q546 [SexEdSc2]

What about children aged 12 to 16? Do you think that ...
READ OUT ...

	%
... **all** children aged 12 to 16 should have sex education at school,	41.2
or, should parents be allowed to choose?	15.1
(Don't know)	1.2
(Refusal/Not answered)	1.1

VERSION C: ASK ALL

Q547 [PMS] *

CARD

Now I would like to ask you some questions about sexual relationships.
If a man and woman have sexual relations before marriage, what would your general opinion be?

Q548 [ExMS] *

CARD AGAIN

What about a **married person** having sexual relations with someone other than his or her partner?

Q549 [HomoSex] *   N=1056

CARD AGAIN

What about sexual relations between two adults of the same sex?

	[PMS] %	[ExMS] %	[HomoSex] %
Always wrong	8.4	59.9	37.9
Mostly wrong	6.0	25.1	10.6
Sometimes wrong	16.6	9.0	8.9
Rarely wrong	10.1	0.7	7.4
Not wrong at all	51.8	1.8	27.1
(Depends/varies)	4.7	1.4	5.1
(Don't know)	0.8	0.5	1.2
(Refusal/Not answered)	1.5	1.5	1.8

TASTE AND DECENCY (VERSION C)   N=1056

VERSION C: ASK ALL

Q608
[SexCine]
CARD *
I am now going to ask what you think should be allowed or not allowed to be shown on television or at the cinema.
Thinking first about a frank scene in a film showing **a man and a woman character having sex.**
Using this card, please say what you feel about **a film at the cinema** which includes a scene like that?

Q609
IF 'special adult cinema' AT [SexCine]
[SexCin2] *
CARD AGAIN
And what would be your second option (for a film at the cinema including a scene like this)?

	[SexCine]	[SexCin2]
	%	%
Should not be allowed to be shown at all	14.4	4.1
Only at special adult cinemas	16.7	-
At ord. cinemas but only to people aged 18+	45.1	11.9
At ord. cinemas but only to people aged 15+	16.6	0.4
At ord. cinemas but only to people aged 12+	2.8	-
Allowed to be shown to anyone	1.2	0.1
(Don't know)	1.1	0.2
(Refusal/Not allowed)	2.2	3.3

VERSION C: ASK ALL

Q610
[SexRegTV] *
CARD
How about the **same** scene in a film on one of the **regular television channels**, that is BBC1 and 2, ITV, (Channel4/S4C) and Channel 5?
Using this card, please say what you would feel about that?

Q611
[SexSubAd] *
CARD AGAIN
Thinking now of a **subscription channel** for which people pay a regular amount, and which regularly shows **adult films**.
How would you feel about a film with this same scene of a man and a woman character having sex being shown on this channel?

Q612
[SexSubGn] *
CARD AGAIN
And how would you feel about this same scene being shown on a different subscription channel which does **not** normally show this sort of film?

Q613
[SexDigit] *
CARD AGAIN
Thinking now of the new **digital channels** some people have, which need a special piece of equipment but no regular subscription.
How do you feel about this same scene in a film being shown on one of these channels?
IF 'never heard of digital TV', CODE AS DON'T KNOW

N=1056

	[SexRegTV]	[SexSubAd]
	%	%
Not allowed to be shown at all	23.2	17.4
Only after midnight	17.5	19.6
Only after 10 o'clock in the evening	35.2	28.2
Only after 9 o'clock in the evening	18.1	10.1
Only after 8 o'clock in the evening	1.5	2.3
Allowed to be shown at any time	1.6	18.2
(Don't know)	0.7	1.8
(Refusal/Not answered)	2.2	2.3

	[SexSubGn]	[SexDigit]
	%	%
Not allowed to be shown at all	35.0	22.2
Only after midnight	15.2	18.7
Only after 10 o'clock in the evening	26.4	31.5
Only after 9 o'clock in the evening	12.2	13.3
Only after 8 o'clock in the evening	1.5	1.2
Allowed to be shown at any time	5.0	5.4
(Don't know)	2.4	5.5
(Refusal/Not answered)	2.3	2.2

Q614
[SexVideo]
CARD
Now suppose the **same** film, including the frank scene of a man and woman character having sex, was available on a **video for sale or rent**.
Using this card, please say how widely you think the video should be available.

%	
13.4	Should be banned altogether
23.7	Only in special adult shops
45.5	In any shop but available only to people aged 18 or over
10.9	In any shop but available only to people aged 15 or over
2.2	In any shop but available only to people aged 12 or over
1.1	In any shop and available to anyone
1.0	(Don't know)
2.2	(Refusal/Not answered)

N=1056

Q615 [SexInter]
CARD
And what if this same scene was in a film available through the internet or World Wide Web. Using this card, please say what you would feel about that.
%
38.3 Should not be available at all
50.8 Access should be available only to authorised subscribers aged 18+
5.4 Should be available to anyone with Internet access
3.3 (Don't know)
2.2 (Refusal/Not answered)

Q616 [HSexCin] *
GO BACK TO CARD
Now I want to ask you about a different kind of scene that may appear in a film. This time, instead of a male and a female character, there is a frank scene with two adult male characters having sex.
Using this card again, what would your opinion be of a film at the cinema including a scene like that?

IF 'special adult cinema' AT [HSexCin]
Q617 [HSexCin2] *
CARD AGAIN
And what would be your second option?
(for a film at the cinema including a scene like this)

	[HSexCin]	[HSexCin2]
	%	%
Should not be allowed to be shown at all	36.0	9.9
Only at special adult cinemas	23.7	-
At ordinary cin. but only to people aged 18+	29.2	12.6
At ordinary cin. but only to people aged 15+	6.6	-
At ordinary cin. but only to people aged 12+	1.0	0.1
Allowed to be shown to anyone	0.5	-
(Don't know)	0.8	1.1
(Refusal/Not answered)	2.2	3.1

Q618 [HSexRgTV] *
CARD
How about the same scene in a film on one of the regular television channels?
(Using this card, please say what you would feel about that.)
REGULAR TELEVISION CHANNELS = BBC1 AND 2, ITV, (CHANNEL4/S4C) AND CHANNEL 5.

N=1056

Q619 [HSexSbAd] *
CARD AGAIN
And how about a subscription channel for which people pay a regular amount, and which regularly shows adult films.

How would you feel about a film with this same scene of two adult male characters having sex being shown on this channel?

Q620 [HSexSbGn] *
CARD AGAIN
And how would you feel about this same scene being shown on a different subscription channel which does not normally show this sort of film?

Q621 [HSexDigi] *
CARD AGAIN
And how about the new digital channels some people have, which need a special piece of equipment but no regular subscription. (How do you feel about this same scene in a film being shown on one of these channels?)
IF 'never heard of digital TV', CODE AS DON'T KNOW

	[HSexRegTV]	[HSexSbAd]
	%	%
Not be allowed to be shown at all	48.3	34.5
Only after midnight	18.1	21.7
Only after 10 o'clock in the evening	19.8	19.6
Only after 9 o'clock in the evening	9.5	8.0
Only after 8 o'clock in the evening	0.5	0.6
Allowed to be shown at any time	0.7	12.0
(Don't know)	0.8	1.4
(Refusal/Not answered)	2.2	2.2

	[HSexSbGn]	[HSexDigi]
	%	%
Not be allowed to be shown at all	52.1	41.6
Only after midnight	14.9	19.2
Only after 10 o'clock in the evening	17.4	20.3
Only after 9 o'clock in the evening	8.1	8.9
Only after 8 o'clock in the evening	3.1	0.5
Shown at any time	1.6	2.9
(Don't know)		4.1
(Refusal/Not answered)	2.5	2.5

Q622 [HSexVide]
CARD
Now suppose the **same** film, including the frank scene of two adult male characters having sex, was available on a **video for sale or rent**. Using this card, please say how widely you think the video should be available.

	%
Should be banned altogether	31.7
Only in special adult shops	28.2
In any shop but available only to people aged 18 or over	29.1
In any shop but available only to people aged 15 or over	5.1
In any shop but available only to people aged 12 or over	1.3
In any shop and available to anyone	0.9
(Don't know)	1.1-
(Refusal/Not answered)	2.5

Q623 [HSexInte]
CARD
And what if this same scene was in a film available through the **internet** or **World Wide Web**. Using this card, please say what you would feel about that.

	%
Should not be available at all	51.3
Access should be available only to authorised subscribers aged 18+	39.7
Should be available to anyone with Internet access	4.4

Q624 [LesCine] *
GO BACK TO CARD
What if the film showed a frank scene of two adult **female** characters having sex.
Using this card again, what would your opinion be of a film at the **cinema** including a scene like that?

Q625 IF 'special adult cinema' AT [LesCine]
[LesCin2] *
CARD AGAIN
And what would be your second option?
(for a film at the cinema including a scene like this)

	[LesCine]	[LesCin2]
	%	%
Should not be allowed to be shown at all	35.4	8.0
Only at special adult cinemas	20.7	11.8
At ordinary cin. but only to people aged 18+	31.7	0.1
At ordinary cin. but only to people aged 15+	7.3	0.1
At ordinary cin. but only to people aged 12+	0.9	-
Allowed to be shown to anyone	0.7	0.1
(Don't know)	0.8	0.7
(Refusal/Not answered)	2.5	3.3

N=1056

VERSION C: ASK ALL

Q626 [LesRegTV] *
CARD
How about the **same** scene in a film on one of the regular television channels?
(Using this card, please say what you would feel about that.)
REGULAR TELEVISON CHANNELS = BBC1 AND 2, ITV, (CHANNEL 4/S4C) AND CHANNEL 5.

Q627 [LesSubAd] *
CARD AGAIN
And how about a **subscription channel** for which people pay a regular amount, and which regularly shows **adult films**.
How would you feel about a film with this same scene of two adult female characters having sex being shown on this channel?

Q628 [LesSubGn] *
CARD AGAIN
And how would you feel about this same scene being shown on a different subscription channel which does **not** normally show this sort of film?

Q629 [LesDigit] *
CARD AGAIN
And how about the new **digital channels** some people have, which need a special piece of equipment but no regular subscription.
(How do you feel about this same scene in a film being shown on one of these channels?)
IF 'never heard of digital TV', CODE AS DON'T KNOW

	[LesRegTV]	[LesSubAd]
	%	%
Not be allowed to be shown at all	42.5	32.9
Only after midnight	20.8	21.6
Only after 10 o'clock in the evening	22.2	21.8
Only after 9 o'clock in the evening	9.5	7.9
Only after 8 o'clock in the evening	0.7	0.7
Allowed to be shown at any time	0.8	11.4
(Don't know)	0.9	1.1
(Refusal/Not answered)	2.6	2.6

	[LesSubGn]	[LesDigit]
	%	%
Not allowed to be shown at all	47.8	39.2
Only after midnight	17.3	19.4
Only after 100'clock in the evening	19.9	22.6
Only after 9 o'clock in the evening	8.0	9.1
Only after 8 o'clock in the evening	0.7	0.5
Allowed to be shown at any time	0.7	3.4
(Don't know)	1.2	3.3
(Refusal/Not answered)	2.6	2.6

N=1056

N=1056

Q630 [LesVideo]
CARD
Now suppose the **same** film, including the frank sex scene of two adult female characters having sex, was available on a **video for sale or rent**. Using this card, please say how widely you think the video should be available.

%
32.5 Should be banned altogether
24.6 Only in special adult shops
32.0 In any shop but available only to people aged 18 or over
5.9 In any shop but available only to people aged 15 or over
0.9 In any shop but available only to people aged 12 or over
0.7 In any shop and available to anyone
0.8 (Don't know)
2.6 (Refusal/Not answered)

Q631 [LesInter]
CARD
And what if this same scene was in a film available through the **internet** or **World Wide Web**. Using this card, please say what you would feel about that.

%
50.9 Should not be available at all
40.8 Access should be available only to authorised subscribers aged 18+
3.8 Should be available to anyone with Internet access
2.0 (Don't know)
2.6 (Refusal/Not answered)

Q632 [SexGra12]
We have been talking about films and videos in general, but there are, of course, different types of film. Some contain sex scenes which are part of a developing relationship between the main characters. Others show sex scenes which don't seem to be essential to the plot.
Think first of films in which a frank sex scene between a man and a woman character does **not** seem to be essential to the plot. Should they **ever**, in your view, be allowed to be seen...
... by **12** year olds?

%
5.7 Yes
90.8 No
1.1 (Don't know)
2.4 (Refusal/Not answered)

Q633 IF 'NO/DK' AT **[SexGra12]**
[SexGra15]
[Thinking of films in which a frank sex scene between a man and a woman character does **not** seem to be essential to the plot. Should they **ever**, in your view, be allowed to be seen ...)
... by **15** year olds?

%
22.4 Yes
68.2 No
1.3 (Don't know)
2.4 (Refusal/Not answered)

Q634 IF 'NO/DK' AT **[SexGra15]**
[SexGra18]
(Thinking of films in which a frank sex scene between a man and a woman character does **not** seem to be essential to the plot. Should they **ever**, in your view, be allowed to be seen ...)
... by **18** year olds?

%
51.6 Yes
16.7 No
1.0 (Don't know)
2.5 (Refusal/Not answered)

Q635 IF 'NO/DK' AT **[SexGra18]**
[SexGraAn]
(Thinking of films in which a frank sex scene between a man and a woman character does **not** seem to be essential to the plot. Should they **ever**, in your view, be allowed to be seen ...)
... by **anyone at all**?

%
1.7 Yes
15.1 No
0.9 (Don't know)
2.5 (Refusal/Not answered)

Q636 VERSION C:ASK ALL
[SexRel12]
And how about films in which a frank sex scene between a man and a woman character **is** part of a developing relationship between the main characters. Should they **ever**, in your view be allowed to be seen ...
... by **12** year olds?

%
13.7 Yes
82.7 No
1.2 (Don't know)
2.4 (Refusal/Not answered)

Q637 **IF 'NO/DK' AT [SexRel12]**　　　N=1056
[SexEdV15]
(Thinking of films in which a frank sex scene
between a man and a woman character **is** part of a
developing relationship between the main characters. Should
they **ever**, in your view, be allowed to be seen ...)
.... by **15** year olds?
%
33.8　Yes
49.0　No
1.1　(Don't know)
2.4　(Refusal/Not answered)

Q638 **IF 'NO/DK' AT [SexRel15]**
[SexRel18]
(Thinking of films in which a frank sex scene between a man and
a woman character **is** part of a developing relationship between
the main characters.
Should they **ever**, in your view, be allowed to be seen ...)
.... by **18** year olds?
%
38.2　Yes
11.5　No
0.5　(Don't know)
2.4　(Refusal/Not answered)

Q639 **IF 'NO/DK' AT [SexRel18]**
[SexRelAn]
(Thinking of films in which a frank sex scene between a man and
a woman character **is** part of a developing relationship between
the main characters.
Should they **ever**, in your view, be allowed to be seen ...)
.... by **anyone at all?**
%
1.2　Yes
10.3　No
0.5　(Don't know)
2.4　(Refusal/Not answered)

Q640 **VERSION C: ASK ALL**
[SexEdV12]
Now how about **educational videos** containing a frank scene of a
man and a woman character having sex.
Should they **ever**, in your view be allowed to be seen ...
.... by **12** year olds?
%
38.4　Yes
57.7　No
1.5　(Don't know)
2.4　(Refusal/Not answered)

Q641 **IF 'NO/DK' AT [SexEdV12]**　　　N=1056
[SexEdV15]
(And how about **educational videos** containing a
frank scene of a man and a woman character having sex.
Should they **ever**, in your view, be allowed to be seen ...)
.... by **15** year olds?
%
31.5　Yes
26.2　No
1.4　(Don't know)
2.4　(Refusal/Not answered)

Q642 **IF 'NO/DK' AT [SexEdV15]**
[SexEdV18]
(And how about **educational videos** containing a frank scene of a
man and a woman character having sex.
Should they **ever**, in your view, be allowed to be seen ...)
.... by **18** year olds?
%
18.4　Yes
8.6　No
0.6　(Don't know)
2.4　(Refusal/Not answered)

Q643 **IF 'NO/DK' AT [SexEdV18]**
[SexEdVAn]
(And how about **educational videos** containing a frank scene of a
man and a woman character having sex.
Should they **ever**, in your view, be allowed to be seen ...)
.... by **anyone at all?**
%
0.5　Yes
8.2　No
0.6　(Don't know)
2.4　(Refusal/Not answered)

Q644 **VERSION C: ASK ALL**
[Erotic12]
Now think of films made for entertainment rather than education
in which showing frank sex scenes between a man and a woman
character is the **main purpose** of the film.
Should they **ever**, in your view be allowed to be seen ...
.... by **12** year olds?
%
6.6　Yes
89.9　No
1.1　(Don't know)
2.4　(Refusal/Not answered)

Q645 IF 'NO/DK' AT [Erotic12]   N=1056
[Erotic15]
(And how about films made for entertainment rather than education in which showing frank sex scenes between a man and a woman character is the **main purpose** of the film.
Should they **ever**, in your view be allowed to be seen ...)
.... by **15** year olds?

	%
Yes	22.8
No	67.4
(Don't know)	0.8
(Refusal/Not answered)	2.4

Q646 IF 'NO/DK' AT [Erotic15]
[Erotic18]
(And how about films made for entertainment rather than education in which showing frank sex scenes between a man and a woman character is the **main purpose** of the film.
Should they **ever**, in your view be allowed to be seen ...)
.... by **18** year olds?

	%
Yes	50.1
No	7.5
(Don't know)	0.6
(Refusal/Not answered)	2.4

Q647 IF 'NO/DK' AT [Erotic18]
[EroticAn]
(And how about films made for entertainment rather than education in which showing frank sex scenes between a man and a woman character is the **main purpose** of the film.
Should they **ever**, in your view be allowed to be seen ...)
.... by **anyone at all**?

	%
Yes	3.2
No	14.4
(Don't know)	0.6
(Refusal/Not answered)	2.4

Q648 VERSION C: ASK ALL
[Porn12]
Of course, most films shown on television and at the cinema do **not** show the **actual sex act in detail**.
How about films that do show that.
Should they **ever**, in your view be allowed to be seen ...
.... by **12** year olds?

	%
Yes	4.9
No	91.7
(Don't know)	0.9
(Refusal/Not answered)	2.4

Q649 IF 'NO/DK' AT [Porn12]   N=1056
[Porn15]
(And how about films that show the actual sex act in detail..
Should they **ever**, in your view be allowed to be seen ...)
.... by **15** year olds?

	%
Yes	16.9
No	74.7
(Don't know)	1.1
(Refusal/Not answered)	2.4

Q650 IF 'NO/DK' AT [Porn15]
[Porn18]
(And how about films that show the actual sex act in detail..
Should they **ever**, in your view be allowed to be seen ...)
.... by **18** year olds?

	%
Yes	53.7
No	21.5
(Don't know)	0.6
(Refusal/Not answered)	2.4

Q651 IF 'NO/DK' AT [Porn18]
[PornAn]
(And how about films that show the actual sex act in detail..
Should they **ever**, in your view be allowed to be seen ...)
.... by **anyone at all**?

	%
Yes	3.0
No	18.5
(Don't know)	0.6
(Refusal/Not answered)	2.4

National Centre *for* **Social Research**

Formerly SCPR

Charity No. 258538

Head Office	**Operations Department**
35 Northampton Square	100 Kings Road, Brentwood
London EC1V 0AX	Essex CM14 4LX
Telephone 0171 250 1866	Telephone 01277 200 600
Fax 0171 250 1524	Fax 01277 214 117

A

P.1850   Green team

BRITISH SOCIAL ATTITUDES 1999

Summer 1999

SELF-COMPLETION QUESTIONNAIRE

INTERVIEWER TO ENTER

2001-6 | 1 | 1 | Serial number

2009-11   Sampling point

2012-15   Interviewer number

OFFICE USE ONLY

2007-8 | 2 | 0 | Card number

2016-20   Batch Number

2021 | A | Version

SPARE 2022-34

To the selected respondent:

Thank you very much for agreeing to take part in this important study - the fifteenth in this annual series. The study consists of this self-completion questionnaire, and the interview you have already completed. The results of the survey are published in a book each autumn; some of the questions are also being asked in thirty other countries, as part of an international survey.

Completing the questionnaire:

The questions inside cover a wide range of subjects, but most can be answered simply by placing a tick (✓) in one or more of the boxes. No special knowledge is required: we are confident that everyone will be able to take part, not just those with strong views or particular viewpoints. The questionnaire should not take very long to complete, and we hope you will find it interesting and enjoyable. **Only you should fill it in, and not anyone else at your address.** The answers you give will be treated as confidential and anonymous.

Returning the questionnaire:

Your interviewer will arrange with you the most convenient way of returning the questionnaire. If the interviewer has arranged to call back for it, please fill it in and keep it safely until then. If not, please complete it and post it back in the pre-paid, addressed envelope, AS SOON AS YOU POSSIBLY CAN.

THANK YOU AGAIN FOR YOUR HELP.

The National Centre for Social Research is an independent social research institute registered as a charitable trust. Its projects are funded by government departments, local authorities, universities and foundations to provide information on social issues in Britain. The British Social Attitudes survey series is funded mainly by one of the Sainsbury Family Charitable Trusts, with contributions also from other grant-giving bodies and government departments. Please contact us if you would like further information.

1

N=819

To begin, we have some questions about opportunities for getting ahead ...

Please tick one box for each of these to show how important you think it is for getting ahead in life ...

[AHEAD1]
1a. First, how important is coming from a wealthy family?
PLEASE TICK ONE BOX ONLY

	%
Essential	3.3
Very important	15.4
Fairly important	30.6
Not very important	30.0
Not important at all	17.1
Can't choose	2.2
(NA)	1.4

[AHEAD7]
b. Knowing the right people?
PLEASE TICK ONE BOX

	%
Essential	11.2
Very important	29.7
Fairly important	41.3
Not very important	12.1
Not important at all	3.1
Can't choose	0.6
(NA)	2.0

2. How much do you agree or disagree with each of the following statements?
PLEASE TICK ONE BOX ON EACH LINE

	Strongly agree	Agree	Neither agree nor disagree	Disagree	Strongly disagree	Can't choose	(NA)
[GETON1] a. In Britain people get rewarded for their effort	% 2.0	30.5	33.4	27.0	3.4	1.8	1.9
[GETON2] b. In Britain people get rewarded for their intelligence and skills	% 3.7	44.3	25.0	21.8	2.2	1.0	2.0
[GETON3] c. To get all the way to the top in Britain today, you have to be corrupt	% 4.1	13.0	25.7	38.9	12.8	2.9	2.6

2

N=819

3. Do you agree or disagree with each of these statements?
PLEASE TICK ONE BOX ON EACH LINE

	Strongly agree	Agree	Neither agree nor disagree	Disagree	Strongly disagree	Can't choose	(NA)
[INEQRICH] a. Inequality continues to exist because it benefits the rich and powerful	% 12.1	45.8	23.2	12.1	1.6	3.3	2.0
[PAYSTUDY] b. No one would study for years to become a lawyer or unless they expected to earn a lot more than ordinary workers	% 12.7	53.6	12.1	17.5	1.6	1.1	1.5
[DIFFSNEC] c. Large differences in income are necessary for Britain's prosperity	% 1.4	15.6	23.2	45.7	9.5	2.1	2.4
[INEQJOIN] d. Inequality continues to exist because ordinary people don't join together to get rid of it	% 4.6	29.8	26.2	29.1	4.4	3.4	2.5

[EARNDESV]
4. Please think now about the amount of money you earn. Would you say that you earn ...
If you are not working now, please think about your last job.
PLEASE TICK ONE BOX ONLY

	%
Much less than I deserve	12.2
Less than I deserve	43.7
What I deserve	36.8
More than I deserve	1.6
Much more than I deserve	0.1
I have never worked	0.5
Can't choose	3.3
(NA)	1.8

3

5. We would like to know what you think people in these jobs actually earn.

Please write in how much you think they usually earn each year before taxes.

(Many people are not exactly sure about this, but your best guess will be close enough. This may be difficult, but it is very important, so please try.)

Please write in how much they actually earn each year, before tax

		(Don't know)	(NA)
[JOBPAY6] a. First, about how much do you think a skilled worker in a factory earns. [JOBPAY2]	median: £ 15,000	2.9	12.2
b. A doctor in general practice? [JOBPAY5]	median: £ 35,000	3.0	12.4
c. The chairman of a large national corporation? [JOBPAY13]	median: £ 125,000	3.6	12.0
d. A solicitor? [JOBPY12B]	median: £ 50,000	3.2	11.8
e. A shop assistant? [JOBPAY14]	median: £ 9,000	2.9	12.2
f. The owner-manager of a large factory? [JOBPAY15]	median: £ 60,000	3.2	12.5
g. An Appeal Court judge? [JOBPAY10]	median: £ 80,000	3.6	12.5
h. An unskilled worker in a factory? [JOBPAY11]	median: £ 10,000	2.9	12.6
i. A cabinet minister in the UK government? [JOBPAYME]	median: £ 60,000	3.5	12.4
j. Someone in your occupation - about how much do they actually earn?	median: £ 15,000	3.2	13.6

If you are not working now, please think about your last occupation.

If you have never worked, please tick here →

6. Next, what do you think people in these jobs ought to be paid - how much do you think they should earn each year before taxes, regardless of what they actually get?

Please write in how much they should earn each year, before tax

		(Don't know)	(NA)
[SHDPAY66] a. First, about how much do you think a skilled worker in a factory should earn. [SHDPAY2]	median: £ 18,000	3.3	16.4
b. A doctor in general practice? [SHDPAY5]	median: £ 40,000	3.3	15.7
c. The chairman of a large national corporation? [SHDPAY13]	median: £ 75,000	3.6	16.1
d. A solicitor? [SHDPY12B]	median: £ 40,000	3.4	16.0
e. A shop assistant? [SHDPAY14]	median: £ 12,000	3.3	15.8
f. The owner-manager of a large factory? [SHDPAY14]	median: £ 50,000	4.2	16.6
g. An Appeal Court judge? [SHDPAY10]	median: £ 50,000	3.7	16.2
h. An unskilled worker in a factory? [SHDPAY10]	median: £ 12,000	3.3	15.8
i. A cabinet minister in the UK government? [SHDPAYME]	median: £ 45,000	3.6	16.9
j. Someone in your occupation - about how much ought they to earn? [SHDPAYME]	median: £ 18,000	3.2	17.2

If you are not working now, please think about your last occupation.

If you have never worked, please tick here →

4

7. Please show how much you agree or disagree with each of these statements.

PLEASE TICK ONE BOX ON EACH LINE

	Strongly agree	Agree	Neither agree nor disagree	Disagree	Strongly disagree	Can't choose	(NA)
[INCDIFFS] a. Differences in income in Britain are too large.	% 30.7	49.0	11.2	5.2	0.6	1.2	2.0
[INCDIFF] b. It is the responsibility of the government to reduce the differences in income between people with high incomes and those with low incomes	% 18.0	47.0	15.3	12.2	2.1	1.8	3.7

[HILOWTAX]

8. Do you think people with high incomes should pay a larger share of their income in taxes than those with low incomes, the same share, or a smaller share?

PLEASE TICK ONE BOX ONLY

	%
Much larger share	21.2
Larger	55.2
The same share	20.4
Smaller	0.3
Much smaller share	-
Can't choose	1.6
(NA)	1.4

9. Turning now to international differences, how much do you agree or disagree with each of these statements?

PLEASE TICK ONE BOX ON EACH LINE

	Strongly agree	Agree	Neither agree nor disagree	Disagree	Strongly disagree	Can't choose	(NA)
[WRLDDIFF] a. Present economic differences between rich and poor countries are too large [HELPPOOR]	% 22.8	55.3	14.1	2.6	-	3.3	2.0
b. People in wealthy countries should make an additional tax contribution to help people in poor countries	% 10.9	33.9	21.8	23.8	4.0	2.9	2.6

10. Is it right or wrong that people with higher incomes can …

PLEASE TICK ONE BOX ON EACH LINE

	Definitely right	Somewhat right	Neither right nor wrong, mixed feelings	Somewhat wrong	Very wrong	Can't choose	(NA)
[BUYHLTH] a. Buy better health care than people with lower incomes [BUYEDUCN]	% 21.3	19.8	19.4	17.0	20.5	0.3	1.6
b. Buy better education for their children than people with lower incomes	% 24.5	19.6	16.7	16.3	20.7	0.3	1.9

5

N=819

11. In all countries, there are differences or even conflicts between different social groups. In your opinion, in Britain how much conflict is there between ...

PLEASE TICK ONE BOX ON EACH LINE

		Very strong conflicts	Strong conflicts	Not very strong conflicts	There are no conflicts	Can't choose	(NA)
[CONFLICT1] a.	Poor people and rich people?	% 7.0	37.9	43.0	3.8	6.0	2.2
[CONFLICT2] b.	The working class and the middle class?	% 2.5	20.7	58.3	10.0	4.7	3.7
[CONFLICT4] c.	Management and workers?	% 6.3	37.1	44.6	3.3	4.6	4.1
[CONFLICT7] d.	People at the top of society and people at the bottom?	% 16.3	43.0	29.8	3.5	4.4	3.0
[CONFLICT6] e.	Young people and older people?	% 5.1	27.4	50.1	10.0	4.6	2.9

[SOCSCALE]

12. In our society there are groups which tend to be towards the top and groups which tend to be towards the bottom. Below is a scale that runs from top to bottom. Where would you put yourself on this scale?

PLEASE TICK ONE BOX ONLY

		%
Top	1	0.4
	2	1.5
	3	4.0
	4	10.5
	5	31.8
	6	18.1
	7	14.5
	8	8.8
	9	5.1
Bottom	10	2.0
(Don't know)		-
(NA)		3.3

[SOCSCL10]

13. And ten years ago, where did you fit in then?

PLEASE TICK ONE BOX ONLY

		%
Top	1	0.5
	2	2.0
	3	5.7
	4	9.2
	5	29.1
	6	17.3
	7	14.1
	8	10.2
	9	5.2
Bottom	10	2.8
(Don't know)		-
(NA)		3.8

6

N=819

[RJOBFJOB]

14. Please think of your present job (or your last one if you don't have one now).

If you compare this job with the job your father had when you were 16, would you say that the level or status of your job is (or was) ...

PLEASE TICK ONE BOX ONLY

	%
Much higher than your father's	14.3
Higher	25.6
About equal	27.1
Lower	15.2
Much lower than your father's	7.0
I have never had a job	0.7
(Father has never had a job)	8.4
Can't choose or does not apply	-
(NA)	1.8

[DPAYRESP]

15. In deciding how much people ought to earn, how important should each of these things be, in your opinion?

a. First, the amount of responsibility that goes with the job - how important do you think that ought to be in deciding pay?

PLEASE TICK ONE BOX ONLY

	%
Essential	22.6
Very important	51.8
Fairly important	22.1
Not very important	1.4
Not important at all	0.2
Can't choose	0.5
(NA)	1.4

[DPAYEDUC]

b. The number of years spent in education and training?

PLEASE TICK ONE BOX ONLY

	%
Essential	12.6
Very important	42.4
Fairly important	35.2
Not very important	6.7
Not important at all	1.6
Can't choose	0.5
(NA)	1.0

[DAYSUPR]

c. Whether the job requires supervising others - how important should that be in deciding pay?

PLEASE TICK ONE BOX ONLY

	%
Essential	10.9
Very important	46.2
Fairly important	36.9
Not very important	4.2
Not important at all	0.3
Can't choose	0.4
(NA)	1.1

7

[DPAYFAM]
d. What is needed to support a family?

PLEASE TICK ONE BOX ONLY

	%
Essential	15.4
Very important	39.3
Fairly important	25.6
Not very important	8.7
Not important at all	5.4
Can't choose	2.7
(NA)	2.8

[DPAYCHLD]
e. Whether the person has children to support - how important should that be in deciding pay?

PLEASE TICK ONE BOX ONLY

	%
Essential	9.3
Very important	25.2
Fairly important	30.0
Not very important	19.9
Not important at all	12.2
Can't choose	2.2
(NA)	1.2

[DPAYWELL]
f. How well he or she does the job - how important should that be in deciding pay?

PLEASE TICK ONE BOX ONLY

	%
Essential	21.1
Very important	55.8
Fairly important	19.4
Not very important	1.2
Not important at all	0.7
Can't choose	0.5
(NA)	1.3

[DPAYHARD]
g. How hard he or she works at the job?

PLEASE TICK ONE BOX ONLY

	%
Essential	20.1
Very important	54.8
Fairly important	21.0
Not very important	1.8
Not important at all	0.5
Can't choose	0.5
(NA)	1.3

OFFICE USE ONLY

N=819

8

[EARNFAIR]
16. Is your pay fair? We are not asking about what you <u>do</u> earn, nor what you would <u>like</u> to earn - but what you feel is fair given your skills and effort. Is your pay ....

IF NOT WORKING NOW, PLEASE TELL ABOUT YOUR LAST JOB.

PLEASE TICK ONE BOX ONLY

	%
Much less than is fair	13.1
A little less than is fair	36.6
About fair for me	38.6
A little more than is fair	4.8
Much more than is fair	0.5
I have never had a job	0.8
Can't choose	3.6
(NA)	2.0

17. Which of the following statements do you think are generally true and which false?

PLEASE TICK ONE BOX ON EACH LINE

N=2478

	True	False	(NA)
	%		
[COUNCIL1]			
a. Council tenants pay low rents	47.1	45.8	7.1
[COUNCIL2]			
b. Councils give a low standard of repairs and maintenance	47.6	45.2	7.1
[COUNCIL3]			
c. Council estates are generally pleasant places to live	32.3	60.6	7.1

[RENTBUY]
18. Suppose a newly-married young couple, both with steady jobs, asked your advice about whether to buy or rent a home. If they had the choice, what would you advise them to do?

PLEASE TICK ONE BOX ONLY

	%
To buy a home as soon as possible	65.1
To wait a bit, then try to buy a home	28.5
Not to plan to buy a home at all	1.7
Can't choose	3.5
(NA)	1.2

OFFICE USE ONLY

N=819

9

19. Still thinking of what you might say to this young couple, please tick one box for each statement below to show how much you agree or disagree with it.

PLEASE TICK ONE BOX ON EACH LINE

N=2478

		Agree strongly	Just agree	Neither agree nor disagree	Just disagree	Disagree strongly	(NA)
[HOMERISK]		%					
a. Owning your home can be a risky investment		8.4	31.3	22.1	21.5	14.5	2.2
[BUYCHEAP]		%					
b. Over time, buying a home works out less expensive than paying rent		46.7	37.4	8.0	4.2	2.1	1.4
[MOVEHOME]		%					
c. Owning your home makes it easier to move when you want to		18.5	27.1	26.5	18.7	7.4	1.8
[MONEYTIE]		%					
d. Owning a home ties up money you may need urgently for other things		5.9	23.2	23.9	30.0	9.8	2.1
[FREEDOM]		%					
e. Owning a home gives you the freedom to do what you want to it		35.6	39.3	13.6	7.3	2.2	2.1
[FINBURDN]		%					
f. Owning a home is a big financial burden to repair and maintain		13.8	36.3	27.1	16.3	4.3	2.2
[LEAVEFAM]		%					
g. Your own home will be something to leave your family		35.8	42.0	14.5	3.7	1.6	2.5
[HOMERESP]		%					
h. Owning a home is just too much of a responsibility		2.7	5.9	21.1	39.0	29.0	2.3
[RISKJOB]		%					
i. Owning a home is too much of a risk for couples without secure jobs		24.5	36.9	18.8	14.3	3.7	1.8
[WAITFAM]		%					
j. Couples who buy their own homes would be wise to wait before starting a family		16.1	32.4	30.6	13.5	5.6	1.8

[PREFLIV]
20. In your opinion, would you rather live in an area where most people own their homes, or where most people rent, or where there is a mixture?

PLEASE TICK ONE BOX ONLY

%
Where most people own 55.0
Where most people rent 1.2
Mixture 25.6
Don't mind either way 16.5
Can't choose 1.1
(NA) 0.7

[OWNRENT]
21. Do most people around here own their homes, or do most people rent, or is it about equal?

PLEASE TICK ONE BOX ONLY

%
Most people own 60.1
Most people rent 10.8
About equal 25.0
Can't choose 3.5
(NA) 0.7

10

[DISTSPND]
22. In your opinion, should your local council spend ...

PLEASE TICK ONE BOX ONLY

%
... more money in the poorer parts of the district compared to other parts 39.5
... more money in the better off parts of the district compared to other parts 1.0
... or should it spend its budget equally across the district? 55.5
Can't choose 3.4
(NA) 0.6

[DISTINC]
23. Do you think most people would describe this area as a poorer part of the district, a better off part of the district, or is it more or less equally mixed?

PLEASE TICK ONE BOX ONLY

%
A poorer part of the district 9.5
A better off part of the district 37.8
More or less equally mixed 49.2
Can't choose 2.9
(NA) 0.7

24. Thinking now about renting from the council and renting from a private landlord. From what you know or have heard, which type of landlord do you think is generally better at ...

PLEASE TICK ONE BOX ON EACH LINE

		Council much better	Council a bit better	Same	Private landlords a bit better	Private landlords much better	Can't choose	(NA)
[QUALHOUS]		%						
a. ... providing a good quality of housing?		19.0	27.0	15.6	17.6	6.0	13.4	1.5
[REPAIRS]		%						
b. ... providing a good standard of repairs and maintenance?		17.6	32.7	19.1	11.7	4.0	12.7	2.3
[GOODNEIG]		%						
c. ... providing housing in good neighbourhoods?		5.6	9.7	24.0	29.6	15.2	13.1	2.8
[REASRENT]		%						
d. ... charging reasonable rents?		24.9	41.7	15.2	2.6	1.3	12.0	2.4
[SECURITY]		%						
e. ... giving their tenants long-term security?		39.3	34.6	10.9	1.9	1.8	9.2	2.3
[VALUEMON]		%						
f. ... giving good value for money?		21.1	32.6	18.8	6.4	2.3	16.3	2.5

OFFICE USE ONLY

N=2478

11

N=2478

25 Please tick one box for each statement below to show how much you agree or disagree with it.

PLEASE TICK ONE BOX ON EACH LINE

	Agree strongly	Agree	Neither agree nor disagree	Disagree	Disagree strongly	Can't choose	(NA)
[IMPAREA1] a. It is just too difficult for someone like me to do much about improving my local area %	10.0	31.4	29.8	20.2	3.3	3.5	1.8
[IMPAREA2] b. There is no point in doing my best to improve my local area unless others do the same %	10.3	40.6	16.8	24.3	3.8	2.3	1.8
[IMPAREA3] c. It's a disgrace that people around here don't do more to improve the local area %	8.5	24.7	35.7	21.7	3.9	3.5	2.0

26 Please tick one box for each of the following statements to show how much you agree or disagree with each of these statements.

PLEASE TICK ONE BOX ON EACH LINE

	Agree strongly	Agree	Neither agree nor disagree	Disagree	Disagree strongly	Can't choose	(NA)
[MINWAG2] a. It is right that the law should set a minimum wage so that no employer can pay their workers too little %	53.3	34.5	4.1	5.0	1.4	0.8	0.9
[MWDOWN] b. A minimum wage will mean wage levels will go down, because employers won't pay workers any more than this minimum level %	6.1	20.4	26.9	36.5	5.1	3.0	2.0
[MWLOSJOB] c. There should be no minimum wage set by law because it will mean too many low paid workers will lose their jobs %	4.6	11.6	17.1	44.0	16.6	4.1	2.0

27 How much do you agree or disagree with each of these statements?

PLEASE TICK ONE BOX ON EACH LINE

	Agree strongly	Agree	Neither agree nor disagree	Disagree	Disagree strongly	Can't choose	(NA)
[FALSCONF] a. A lot of false benefit claims are a result of confusion rather than dishonesty %	4.5	15.6	17.6	42.7	15.3	3.4	1.0
[CHEATPOR] b. The reason that some people on benefit cheat the system is that they don't get enough to live on %	8.4	27.4	15.2	33.0	11.6	3.1	1.3

12

N=2478

[BEN500]
28a. Consider this situation:

An unemployed person on benefit takes a casual job and is paid in cash. He does not report it to the benefit office and is £500 in pocket. Do you feel this is wrong or not wrong?

PLEASE TICK ONE BOX ONLY

	%
Not wrong	3.0
A bit wrong	18.3
Wrong	45.8
Seriously wrong	28.6
Can't choose	3.6
(NA)	0.6

[BEN500DO]
b. And how likely do you think it is that you would do this, if you found yourself in this situation?

PLEASE TICK ONE BOX ONLY

	%
Very likely	7.3
Fairly likely	16.2
Not very likely	31.8
Not at all likely	38.0
Can't choose	5.7
(NA)	1.0

[PAY500]
29a. Now consider this situation:

A person in paid work takes on an extra weekend job and is paid in cash. He does not declare it for tax and so is £500 in pocket. Do you feel this is wrong or not wrong?

PLEASE TICK ONE BOX ONLY

	%
Not wrong	12.6
A bit wrong	29.7
Wrong	41.1
Seriously wrong	11.8
Can't choose	4.2
(NA)	0.6

[PAY500DO]
b. And how likely do you think it is that you would do this, if you found yourself in this situation?

PLEASE TICK ONE BOX ONLY

	%
Very likely	11.5
Fairly likely	22.5
Not very likely	31.0
Not at all likely	28.5
Can't choose	5.7
(NA)	0.7

OFFICE USE ONLY

13

N=2478

[D/SAB500]

30. And now consider this situation:

A person has been receiving extra benefit since a back injury stopped him working. Even though he is now well enough to do some types of full-time work, he does not tell the benefit office and is £500 in pocket. Do you feel this is wrong or not wrong?

PLEASE TICK ONE BOX ONLY

	%
Not wrong	1.4
A bit wrong	10.8
Wrong	56.9
Seriously wrong	28.3
Can't choose	2.0
(NA)	0.7

[GOVBEN]

31. Which is it more important for the government to do?

	%
PLEASE TICK ONE BOX ONLY To get people to claim benefits to which they are entitled	32.2
OR	
To stop people claiming benefits to which they are not entitled	55.0
Can't choose	12.3
(NA)	0.5

[JOBWORK]

32. Nowadays some people on benefit are asked to visit the job centre every six months to talk about ways in which they might find work. Which of these statements comes closest to what you think should happen to their benefits if they do not go?

PLEASE TICK ONE BOX ONLY

	%
Their benefits should not be affected	12.5
Their benefits should be reduced a little	26.3
Their benefits should be reduced a lot	18.0
Their benefits should be stopped	33.9
Can't choose	8.6
(NA)	0.7

14

N=2478

33. From what you know or have heard, please tick a box for each of the items below to show whether you think the National Health Service in your area is, on the whole, satisfactory or in need of improvement.

PLEASE TICK ONE BOX ON EACH LINE

		In need of a lot of improvement	In need of some improvement	Satis-factory	Very good	(NA)
a.	[HSAREA1] GPs' appointment systems	% 13.5	31.6	42.3	11.5	1.1
b.	[HSAREA2] Amount of time GP gives to each patient	% 7.3	21.8	56.3	13.1	1.5
c.	[HSAREA3] Being able to choose which GP to see	% 7.5	19.5	55.5	15.7	1.8
d.	[HSAREA4] Quality of medical treatment by GPs	% 5.5	15.7	53.4	22.9	2.4
e.	[HSAREA5] Hospital waiting lists for non-emergency operations	% 34.7	42.9	18.3	1.9	2.3
f.	[HSAREA6] Waiting time before getting appointments with hospital consultants	% 40.9	39.8	14.7	1.9	2.7
g.	[HSAREA7] General condition of hospital buildings	% 13.2	31.7	42.5	10.0	2.6
h.	[HSAREA9] Staffing level of nurses in hospitals	% 29.2	40.3	24.0	4.2	2.3
i.	[HSAREA10] Staffing level of doctors in hospitals	% 28.0	41.8	23.3	4.1	2.9
j.	[HSAREA11] Quality of medical treatment in hospitals	% 6.8	24.9	50.6	15.3	2.3
k.	[HSAREA12] Quality of nursing care in hospitals	% 7.0	21.2	45.0	24.3	2.5
l.	[HSAREA13] Waiting areas in accident and emergency departments in hospitals	% 19.3	36.1	37.2	4.7	2.7
m.	[HSAREA14] Waiting areas for out-patients in hospitals	% 12.4	34.2	45.1	5.8	2.6
n.	[HSAREA15] Waiting areas at GPs' surgeries	% 4.1	15.8	62.3	15.8	2.1
o.	[HSAREA16] Time spent waiting in out-patient departments	% 21.6	47.9	26.2	1.7	2.5
p.	[HSAREA17] Time spent waiting in accident and emergency departments before being seen by a doctor	% 34.2	43.0	18.1	1.9	2.8
q.	[HSAREA18] Time spent waiting for an ambulance after a 999 call	% 7.0	28.5	48.3	11.2	5.0

15

34. In the last twelve months, have you or a close family member ...

PLEASE TICK ONE BOX ON EACH LINE

N=2478

		Yes, just me	Yes, not me but close family member	Yes, both	No, neither	(NA)
[GPUSESC]						
a.	... visited an NHS GP?	% 21.9	16.2	54.9	5.5	1.5
[OUTPUSSC]						
b.	... been an out-patient in an NHS hospital?	% 21.6	26.7	14.2	34.3	3.3
[INPUSSC]						
c.	... been an in-patient in an NHS hospital?	% 11.0	21.0	3.6	59.6	4.7
[VISTUSSC]						
d.	... visited a patient in an NHS hospital?	% 18.3	14.5	25.6	37.1	4.5
[PRIVUSSC]						
e.	... had any medical treatment as a private patient?	% 4.4	5.7	2.2	84.5	3.1
[PRDNUSSC]						
f.	... had any dental treatment as a private patient?	% 10.2	5.9	9.1	72.0	2.8
[NHDNUSSC]						
g.	... had any dental treatment as an NHS patient?	% 15.9	13.6	28.0	40.4	2.0

N=819

35. [NHSCATER] How well would you say the National Health Service nowadays caters for everyone's medical needs?

PLEASE TICK ONE BOX ONLY

%
Very well 7.4
Adequately 48.9
Not very well 33.1
Not at all well 7.0
Can't choose 2.0
(NA) 1.6

36. [NHSSPEND] If the government had to choose between the three options below, which do you think it should choose?

PLEASE TICK ONE BOX ONLY

%
Spend more on the NHS, even if this means an increase in taxes 66.7
Keep spending on the NHS at about the same level as now 26.2
Spend less on the NHS and reduce taxes 1.0
Can't choose 4.7
(NA) 1.4

37. [HEALSAME] Which of these views comes closest to your own?

PLEASE TICK ONE BOX ONLY

%
Health care should be the same for everyone 70.8
People who can afford it should be able to pay for better health care 24.2
Can't choose 3.5
(NA) 1.6

16

N=819

38. [RATIONSHI] Which of these two statements comes closest to your view?

PLEASE TICK ONE BOX ONLY

%
With people living longer, the NHS will always have too many demands on it and should cut down or cut out certain types of treatment 11.6

OR

Everybody has a right to health care, so the NHS should never cut down or cut out any types of treatment 81.7
Can't choose 4.6
(NA) 2.0

39. [RATIONWIL] And which of the following two statements best describes what you think will actually happen in the future?

PLEASE TICK ONE BOX ONLY

%
The NHS will have enough money and resources to provide everyone with the treatment they need when they need it 17.6

OR

The NHS will not have enough money and resources for everyone and will have to cut out certain types of treatment 70.4
Can't choose 9.9
(NA) 2.1

40a. [SMOKEWIL] Suppose two equally sick people in the same area go on a waiting list at the same time for the same heart operation. One is a heavy smoker, the other does not smoke. Which one do you think would be likely to get the operation first ....

PLEASE TICK ONE BOX ONLY

%
... the non-smoker, 58.7
the smoker, 3.2
or, would their smoking habits make no difference? 27.3
Can't choose 9.2
(NA) 1.7

b. [SMOKESHD] And in your opinion which one should get the operation first?

PLEASE TICK ONE BOX ONLY

%
... the non-smoker, 41.0
the smoker, 1.6
or, should their smoking habits make no difference? 47.5
Can't choose 8.2
(NA) 1.7

17

[AGEWIL]

41a. Now, suppose two other equally sick people in the same area go on a waiting list for the same heart operation. In this case one is aged 70, the other 30. Which one do you think would be likely to get the operation first?

PLEASE TICK ONE BOX ONLY

	%
... the 30 year old,	56.2
the 70 year old,	5.1
or, would their ages make no difference?	29.0
Can't choose	7.7
(NA)	2.0

[AGESHD]

b. And in your opinion which one should get the operation first?

PLEASE TICK ONE BOX ONLY

	%
... the 30 year old,	33.9
the 70 year old,	4.6
or, should their ages make no difference?	51.3
Can't choose	8.2
(NA)	2.0

[COSTSHD]

42. Please say how much you agree or disagree with the following

a. If the NHS had to choose, it should give lower priority to expensive treatments so that more money is available to treat a larger number of sick people whose treatment costs less.

PLEASE TICK ONE BOX ONLY

	%
Agree strongly	4.7
Agree	19.6
Neither agree nor disagree	29.4
Disagree	24.3
Disagree strongly	8.5
Can't choose	11.4
(NA)	2.2

[COSTWIL]

b. And do you think the NHS does this now?

PLEASE TICK ONE BOX ONLY

	%
Always or most of the time	6.0
Some of the time	59.0
Hardly ever	7.1
Never	1.8
Can't choose	24.2
(NA)	1.9

18

[SEVERSHD]

43. Please say how much you agree or disagree with the following.

a. If the NHS had to choose, the seriousness of their condition should be the only basis for choosing between patients.

PLEASE TICK ONE BOX ONLY

	%
Agree strongly	22.2
Agree	46.4
Neither agree nor disagree	11.3
Disagree	9.2
Disagree strongly	1.7
Can't choose	7.8
(NA)	1.4

[SEVERWIL]

b. And do you think the NHS does this now?

PLEASE TICK ONE BOX ONLY

	%
Always or most of the time	17.4
Some of the time	54.9
Hardly ever	4.7
Never	1.7
Can't choose	19.2
(NA)	2.0

44. Suppose that the NHS did have to make these sorts of choices about who to treat, or the order in which they should be treated. Please tick one box on each line below to show how much say you think each of these groups should have.

PLEASE TICK ONE BOX ON EACH LINE

		All or most of the say	Some of the say	None of the say	Can't choose	(NA)
[SHDSAY1] a. The government?	%	4.1	29.1	55.0	6.5	5.3
[SHDSAY2] b. GPs?	%	28.6	61.5	2.0	3.9	4.0
[SHDSAY3] c. Hospital or health service managers?	%	10.2	43.2	33.7	6.6	6.3
[SHDSAY4] d. Hospital doctors?	%	56.2	35.0	1.0	3.6	4.3
[SHDSAY5] e. The general public?	%	7.1	35.0	43.9	9.1	5.0
[SHDSAY6] f. Independent health experts?	%	11.3	55.3	17.9	10.6	4.9

19

N=819

45. And how much say do you think each of these groups does have nowadays in these sorts of decisions?

PLEASE TICK ONE BOX ON EACH LINE

		All or most of the say	Some of the say	None of the say	Can't choose	(NA)
a.	The government? *[DOESSAY1]*	% 29.6	45.2	10.9	9.2	5.1
b.	GPs? *[DOESSAY2]*	% 6.7	68.1	12.7	7.0	5.6
c.	Hospital or health service managers? *[DOESSAY3]*	% 35.1	46.8	5.2	7.6	5.4
d.	Hospital doctors? *[DOESSAY4]*	% 19.0	63.1	6.3	6.1	5.6
e.	The general public? *[DOESSAY5]*	% 0.8	11.8	72.7	9.3	5.4
f.	Independent health experts? *[DOESSAY6]*	% 6.0	47.0	24.7	16.5	5.8

46. *[GUIDELIN]* If these sorts of difficult decisions need to be made, which do you think is the better way of making them?

PLEASE TICK ONE BOX ONLY

	%
There should be publicly available guidelines about who should get priority for health care	25.0
Medical experts should be allowed to make these sorts of decisions as they see best	59.5
Can't choose	13.1
(NA)	2.3

47. Some people say the NHS should cut down on very expensive treatments or services and use the savings to provide less expensive treatments or services for more people. With this aim, how much would you be in favour of, or against, the NHS cutting down on ...

PLEASE TICK ONE BOX ON EACH LINE

		Strongly in favour	In favour	Neither in favour nor against	Against	Strongly against	Can't choose	(NA)
	Cutting down on ...							
a.	heart transplants *[NHSCUT1]*	% 2.3	5.1	15.6	41.3	26.5	6.2	3.0
b.	long term nursing care of the elderly *[NHSCUT2]*	% 3.1	6.8	14.8	39.2	27.1	6.1	3.0
c.	intensive care for very premature babies whose survival is in doubt *[NHSCUT3]*	% 4.8	8.6	12.7	32.0	32.0	6.7	3.1

20

N=819

48. Other people say the NHS should cut down on certain treatments or services that should be provided instead by private medicine or charities. With this aim, how much would you be in favour of, or against, the NHS cutting down on ...

PLEASE TICK ONE BOX ON EACH LINE

		Strongly in favour	In favour	Neither in favour nor against	Against	Strongly against	Can't choose	(NA)
	Cutting down on ...							
a.	fertility treatment *[NHSPRIV1]*	% 13.0	24.9	26.3	20.7	7.3	4.8	3.0
b.	hospice care for the terminally ill *[NHSPRIV2]*	% 3.3	6.7	12.3	42.9	28.8	2.7	3.3
c.	cosmetic surgery *[NHSPRIV3]*	% 31.3	29.0	18.1	8.4	6.7	3.6	3.0

49. One way of getting more money into the NHS is to charge people for certain things. How much would you be in favour of or against introducing charges for ...

PLEASE TICK ONE BOX ON EACH LINE

		Strongly in favour	In favour	Neither in favour nor against	Against	Strongly against	Can't choose	(NA)
	Charges for ...							
a.	visiting your GP? *[NHSCHAR1]*	% 1.3	7.1	8.0	43.7	35.5	0.8	3.5
b.	your GP visiting you at home? *[NHSCHAR2]*	% 3.0	14.3	11.7	40.0	27.3	0.7	3.1
c.	the cost of your hospital meals when you are an inpatient? *[NHSCHAR3]*	% 3.9	20.9	18.0	31.5	21.8	1.3	2.6

50. *[IMPOTENT]* Which of these statements comes closest to your view about the treatment of male sexual impotence?

PLEASE TICK ONE BOX ONLY

	%
Treatment of male sexual impotence should not be available on the NHS	13.5
Treatment of male sexual impotence should be available on the NHS - but only when it is caused by particular medical conditions	50.9
Treatment of male sexual impotence should be available on the NHS - whatever its cause	22.7
Can't choose	10.1
(NA)	2.9

21

51. How much do you agree or disagree with each of the following statements?

PLEASE TICK ONE BOX ON EACH LINE

N=819   OFFICE USE ONLY

	Agree strongly	Agree	Neither agree nor disagree	Disagree	Disagree strongly	Can't choose	(NA)
[ANYCOST] a. No medical treatment, no matter what it costs, is too expensive to save a life	% 38.4	33.9	9.9	8.9	2.9	3.1	2.9
[RATIONFT] b. As demand on the NHS grows, it will have to ration some treatments	% 4.0	36.9	19.0	25.1	8.4	3.5	3.3
[NHSSCOR] c. There should be a national scoring system for particular medical treatments that decides how quickly a person goes up the waiting list	% 3.9	32.1	23.4	21.6	8.7	7.0	3.3

[GIVECHNG]
52. Suppose you saw someone begging in the street. Would you be ....

PLEASE TICK ONE BOX ONLY

   %

.... more likely to give money if you had some spare change easily to hand, 32.2

or would this make no difference to whether you gave money or not? 64.4

(NA) 3.5

[GIVEGEN]
53a. Now suppose you saw someone in their late teens begging in the street. Would you be ....

PLEASE TICK ONE BOX ONLY

   %

.... more likely to give if the person was a man, 0.6

more likely to give if the person was a woman, 3.9

or would this make no difference? 92.8

(NA) 2.6

[GIVEAGE]
b. Now suppose you saw a man begging in the street. Would you be ....

PLEASE TICK ONE BOX ONLY

   %

.... more likely to give if he was in his late teens, 1.5

more likely to give if he was in his late 50s, 10.5

or would this make no difference? 85.2

(NA) 2.9

[GIVEDIR]
c. Now suppose you saw a man in his late teens begging in the street. Would you be ....

PLEASE TICK ONE BOX ONLY

   %

.... more likely to give if he was asking for money directly, 3.3

more likely to give if he was not asking for money directly, 26.3

or would this make no difference? 67.5

(NA) 2.9

22

N=819   OFFICE USE ONLY

[GIVEDOG]
d. Now suppose you saw a man, again in his late teens, begging in the street. Would you be ....

PLEASE TICK ONE BOX ONLY

   %

.... more likely to give if he had a <u>dog</u> with him, 10.2

<u>less</u> likely to give if he had a dog, 9.4

or would this make no difference? 77.2

(NA) 3.2

[GIVEBABY]
e. Now suppose you saw a <u>woman</u> in her late teens begging in the street. Would you be ....

PLEASE TICK ONE BOX ONLY

   %

.... <u>more</u> likely to give if she had a <u>baby</u> with her, 32.1

<u>less</u> likely to give if she had a baby with her, 5.7

or would this make no difference? 58.7

(NA) 3.5

54. Please tick one box for each statement below to show how much you agree or disagree with it.

PLEASE TICK ONE BOX ON EACH LINE

	Agree strongly	Agree	Neither agree nor disagree	Disagree	Disagree strongly	Can't choose	(NA)
[SORRBEGR] a. If I saw a man in his late teens begging in the street I would feel sorry for him	% 5.4	28.9	21.5	28.1	10.1	2.9	3.0
[ANGBEGR] b. If I saw a man in his late teens begging in the street I would feel angry with him	% 3.0	16.2	30.9	35.4	7.4	3.9	3.3
[ALCOBEG] c. Most people who beg spend what they are given on alcohol or drugs	% 9.7	36.2	30.4	11.8	2.4	5.9	3.7
[HOMEBEG] d. Most people who beg are homeless	% 4.1	31.9	26.8	25.6	2.7	5.6	3.3

55. Please tick one box for each statement below to show how much you are in favour of, or against, each of these things that could be done about begging.

PLEASE TICK ONE BOX ON EACH LINE

	Strongly in favour	In favour	Neither in favour nor against	Against	Strongly against	(NA)
[TRAINBEG] a. Providing training to help people who beg get work, even if this means an increase in taxes	% 9.4	43.3	26.0	15.6	2.7	3.0
[ACCMBEG] b. Providing accommodation so that people who beg can get off the street, even if this means an increase in taxes	% 9.3	43.4	24.5	16.6	3.3	2.9
[CLAIMBEG] c. Making it easier for people who beg to claim benefits	% 6.1	31.1	29.5	24.9	5.0	3.4
[MOVEBEG] d. Allowing the police to 'move on' beggars from particular areas in towns and cities	% 8.5	41.7	26.8	16.8	3.0	3.3
[ARRESBEG] e. Arresting people for begging in public	% 6.3	17.5	31.9	32.9	8.3	3.1

Page 23

[PROPREP]
56. How much do you agree or disagree with this statement?
"Britain should introduce proportional representation, so that the number of MPs each party gets matches more closely the number of votes each party gets?"

PLEASE TICK ONE BOX ONLY

N=819

	%
Strongly agree	15.1
Agree	35.0
Neither agree nor disagree	17.9
Disagree	11.5
Strongly disagree	4.2
Can't choose	13.1
(NA)	3.3

57. Please tick one box for each statement to show how much you agree or disagree with it.

PLEASE TICK ONE BOX ON EACH LINE

N=2478

		Agree strongly	Agree	Neither agree nor disagree	Disagree	Disagree strongly	(NA)
a.	The welfare state makes people nowadays less willing to look after themselves [WELFRESP]	% 9.2	37.0	26.9	22.6	2.4	1.8
b.	People receiving social security are made to feel like second class citizens [WELFSTIG]	% 5.7	35.4	28.0	27.4	1.8	1.6
c.	The welfare state encourages people to stop helping each other [WELFHELP]	% 3.7	28.1	34.3	30.1	1.6	2.2
d.	The government should spend more money on welfare benefits for the poor, even if it leads to higher taxes [MOREWELF]	% 6.1	33.8	29.9	25.1	3.2	1.8
e.	Around here, most unemployed people could find a job if they really wanted one [UNEMPJOB]	% 11.8	44.6	21.9	17.6	2.1	1.9
f.	Many people who get social security don't really deserve any help [SOCHELP]	% 4.7	22.1	31.4	35.7	3.9	2.2
g.	Most people on the dole are fiddling in one way or another [DOLEFIDL]	% 7.7	27.8	34.6	24.7	3.2	1.9
h.	If welfare benefits weren't so generous, people would learn to stand on their own two feet [WELFEET]	% 7.4	30.2	26.7	28.9	4.9	1.9

58. Please tick one box for each statement below to show how much you agree or disagree with it.

PLEASE TICK ONE BOX ON EACH LINE

		Agree strongly	Agree	Neither agree nor disagree	Disagree	Disagree strongly	(NA)
a.	Government should redistribute income from the better-off to those who are less well off [REDSTRB]	% 8.1	28.0	26.8	29.8	5.3	2.0
b.	Big business benefits owners at the expense of workers [BIGBUSNN]	% 11.2	41.5	27.7	15.8	1.4	2.4
c.	Ordinary working people do not get their fair share of the nation's wealth [WEALTH]	% 12.3	48.0	24.7	11.9	1.1	2.0
d.	There is one law for the rich and one for the poor [RICHLAW]	% 20.4	41.2	19.8	14.7	2.1	1.8
e.	Management will always try to get the better of employees if it gets the chance [INDUST4]	% 16.7	43.7	22.2	14.0	1.7	1.8

Page 24

59. Please tick one box for each statement below to show how much you agree or disagree with it.

PLEASE TICK ONE BOX ON EACH LINE

N=2478

		Agree strongly	Agree	Neither agree nor disagree	Disagree	Disagree strongly	(NA)
a.	Young people today don't have enough respect for traditional British values [TRADVALS]	% 18.5	47.1	23.7	8.1	0.9	1.7
b.	People who break the law should be given stiffer sentences [STIFSENT]	% 30.0	47.2	15.8	5.0	0.6	1.4
c.	For some crimes, the death penalty is the most appropriate sentence [DEATHAPP]	% 28.4	28.5	14.1	17.4	10.0	1.6
d.	Schools should teach children to obey authority [OBEY]	% 29.6	53.6	10.7	4.2	0.5	1.3
e.	Censorship of films and magazines is necessary to uphold moral standards [CENSOR]	% 24.0	45.0	14.9	11.1	3.3	1.7

[QTIME]
60a. To help us plan better in future, please tell us about how long it took you to complete this questionnaire.

PLEASE TICK ONE BOX ONLY

	%
Less than 15 minutes	13.2
Between 15 and 20 minutes	30.2
Between 21 and 30 minutes	26.7
Between 31 and 45 minutes	16.5
Between 46 and 60 minutes	6.6
Over one hour	4.9
(NA)	1.7

[SQDATES]
b. And on what date did you fill in the questionnaire?

PLEASE WRITE IN: DATE [ ]   [0] 1999
                              MONTH

Thank you very much for your help

Please keep the completed questionnaire for the interviewer if he or she has arranged to call for it. Otherwise, please post it as soon as possible in the pre-paid envelope provided.

OFFICE USE ONLY

National Centre *for* Social Research

Formerly SCPR
Charity No. 258538

Head Office
35 Northampton Square
London EC1V 0AX
Telephone 0171 250 1866
Fax 0171 250 1524

Operations Department
100 Kings Road, Brentwood
Essex CM14 4LX
Telephone 01277 200 600
Fax 01277 214 117

B

P.1850   Green team

BRITISH SOCIAL ATTITUDES 1999

SELF-COMPLETION QUESTIONNAIRE

Summer 1999

INTERVIEWER TO ENTER

2401-6	1 1		Serial number
2409-11			Sampling point
2412-15			Interviewer number

OFFICE USE ONLY

2407-8	2 4		Card number
2416-20			Batch Number
2421	B		Version
SPARE 2422-34			

To the selected respondent:

Thank you very much for agreeing to take part in this important study - the fifteenth in this annual series. The study consists of this self-completion questionnaire, and the interview you have already completed. The results of the survey are published in a book each autumn; some of the questions are also being asked in thirty other countries, as part of an international survey.

Completing the questionnaire:

The questions inside cover a wide range of subjects, but most can be answered simply by placing a tick (√) in one or more of the boxes. No special knowledge is required: we are confident that everyone will be able to take part, not just those with strong views or particular viewpoints. The questionnaire should not take very long to complete, and we hope you will find it interesting and enjoyable. **Only you should fill it in, and not anyone else at your address.** The answers you give will be treated as confidential and anonymous.

Returning the questionnaire:

Your interviewer will arrange with you the most convenient way of returning the questionnaire. If the interviewer has arranged to call back for it, please fill it in and keep it safely until then. If not, please complete it and post it back in the pre-paid, addressed envelope, AS SOON AS YOU POSSIBLY CAN.

THANK YOU AGAIN FOR YOUR HELP.

The National Centre for Social Research is an independent social research institute registered as a charitable trust. Its projects are funded by government departments, local authorities, universities and foundations to provide information on social issues in Britain. The British Social Attitudes survey series is funded mainly by one of the Sainsbury Family Charitable Trusts, with contributions also from other grant-giving bodies and government departments. Please contact us if you would like further information.

7

Note: Questions 1-18 on version B of the questionnaire are the same as Q17-34 on Version A.

N=1658

Now some questions about the countryside.

[DAMAGE]

19a. Which one of these two statements comes closest to your own views?

PLEASE TICK ONE BOX ONLY

%

Industry should be prevented from causing damage to the countryside, even if this sometimes leads to higher prices   88.0

OR

Industry should keep prices down, even if this sometimes causes damage to the countryside   10.1

(NA)   1.9

[CTRYJOBS]

b. And which of these two statements comes closest to your own views?

PLEASE TICK ONE BOX ONLY

%

The countryside should be protected from development, even if this sometimes leads to fewer new jobs   75.2

OR

New jobs should be created, even if this sometimes causes damage to the countryside   22.3

(NA)   2.5

8

20. Please tick one box on each line to show whether you agree or disagree with each of the following statements.

PLEASE TICK ONE BOX ON EACH LINE

		Agree strongly	Agree	Neither agree nor disagree	Disagree	Disagree strongly	(NA)
a.	[HOUSBUIL] New housing should be built in cities, towns and villages rather than in the countryside	% 29.4	43.6	20.3	5.1	0.7	0.9
b.	[KEEPBELT] It is more important to keep green-belt areas than to build new homes there	% 36.4	43.8	12.6	5.2	0.6	1.4
c.	[PLANLAWS] Planning laws should be relaxed so that people who want to live in the countryside may do so	% 5.1	26.0	28.1	30.2	9.3	1.4
d.	[FARMRSAY] Compared with other users of the countryside farmers have too much say	% 6.5	22.2	41.8	23.9	3.9	1.7
e.	[LESSVIST] The beauty of the countryside depends on stopping too many people from visiting it	% 2.0	10.9	27.2	51.8	6.8	1.3
f.	[CNTRPEO] People should worry less about protecting the countryside, and more about those who have to make their living there	% 3.5	18.1	35.0	35.5	6.4	1.5
g.	[CNTRPOP] Some parts of the countryside are now so popular that it's no longer a pleasure to visit them	% 7.8	35.3	29.0	24.7	2.1	1.2

21. Here are some statements about the countryside. Please tick one box for each to show whether you agree or disagree with it.

PLEASE TICK ONE BOX ON EACH LINE

		Agree strongly	Agree	Disagree	Disagree strongly	(NA)
a.	[COUNTRY1] Modern methods of farming have caused damage to the countryside	% 17.1	52.2	27.6	0.5	2.7
b.	[COUNTRY2] If farmers have to choose between producing more food and looking after the countryside, they should produce more food	% 3.2	27.3	60.6	5.7	3.2
c.	[COUNTRY3] All things considered, farmers do a good job in looking after the countryside	% 6.2	70.4	19.0	1.5	2.8
d.	[COUNTRY4] Government should withhold some subsidies from farmers and use them to protect the countryside, even if this leads to higher prices	% 6.1	49.8	37.7	2.8	3.6

OFFICE USE ONLY

N=1658

9

N=1658

22. The following are some things people have said about living in the countryside or a country village, compared to living in a town or city. Please tick one box for each statement below to show how much you agree or disagree with it.

PLEASE TICK ONE BOX ON EACH LINE

	Agree strongly	Agree	Neither agree nor disagree	Disagree	Disagree strongly	Can't choose	(NA)
[CTRYCRIM] a. There is less crime in the countryside	% 8.2	51.9	20.2	14.7	1.2	3.0	0.8
[CTRYWORK] b. It is harder to get a good job if you live in the countryside	% 7.5	53.2	18.9	16.5	1.1	1.8	0.9
[CTRYKIDS] c. The countryside is a better place to bring up children	% 16.5	55.4	18.3	7.0	0.2	1.3	1.3
[CTRYBORE] d. Living in the countryside is very boring	% 2.0	8.1	21.7	49.6	15.9	1.5	1.2
[CTRYSCHO] e. The schools in the countryside tend to be better	% 4.4	28.6	42.5	16.8	1.3	5.3	1.2
[CTRYENVR] f. The countryside provides a healthier environment to live in	% 24.7	65.8	6.4	1.1	0.3	0.6	0.9
[CTRYCAR] g. If you live in the countryside, you are more likely to need a car to get around	% 35.9	56.8	4.4	1.5	0.2	0.2	1.0
[CTRYCOST] h. It is more expensive to live in the countryside	% 14.9	36.7	27.5	15.2	1.2	3.4	1.0
[CTRYCOMM] i. There is more community spirit in the countryside	% 14.7	50.0	24.3	7.3	0.3	2.4	0.9

N=1658

23. [ACTOUTS] Do you work or study outside the home?
PLEASE TICK ONE BOX ONLY

%
Yes 52.7 → ANSWER Q24
No 45.3 → GO TO Q25a
(NA) 2.0

24. [WAYTRAVL] What is the main form of transport you normally use for your journey to your workplace or place of study? (By 'main form' of transport, we mean the form you use for the longest distance.)
PLEASE TICK ONE BOX ONLY

%
I travel by car on my own 28.3
I travel by car with at least one other person 8.5
I travel by motorbike, moped or motor scooter 0.5
I travel by public transport (train, bus, underground, tram) 7.5
I travel by bicycle 1.6
I walk 4.8
Other (PLEASE SAY WHAT) 0.4
(NA) 3.2

10

N=818

EVERYONE PLEASE ANSWER
Now some questions on roads and public transport.

25a. [TOWNTRAN] Thinking first about towns and cities. If the government had to choose ...
PLEASE TICK ONE BOX ONLY

%
... it should improve roads 35.3
... it should improve public transport 62.2
(NA) 2.6

b. [CTRYTRAN] And in country areas, if the government had to choose ...
PLEASE TICK ONE BOX ONLY

%
... it should improve roads 29.4
... it should improve public transport 67.5
(NA) 3.1

26a. [CARWALK] How much do you agree or disagree with this statement? "Many of the short journeys I now make by car I could just as easily walk."
PLEASE TICK ONE BOX ONLY

%
Agree strongly 11.1
Agree 30.4
Neither agree nor disagree 12.0
Disagree 26.4
Disagree strongly 10.9
I never travel by car 4.9
Can't choose 2.5
(NA) 1.8

b. [CARBUS] And how much do you agree or disagree with this statement? "Many of the short journeys I now make by car I could just as easily go by bus."
PLEASE TICK ONE BOX ONLY

%
Agree strongly 6.1
Agree 23.7
Neither agree nor disagree 11.8
Disagree 36.7
Disagree strongly 12.7
I never travel by car 4.2
Can't choose 2.8
(NA) 1.9

OFFICE USE ONLY

11

N=818

[CARTAXHI]
27. Please tick one box to show how much you agree or disagree with this statement.
"For the sake of the environment, car users should pay higher taxes."

PLEASE TICK ONE BOX ONLY

	%
Agree strongly	2.7
Agree	8.1
Neither agree nor disagree	16.5
Disagree	42.9
Disagree strongly	26.3
Can't choose	2.3
(NA)	1.2

[CUTCARS]
28a. How important do you think it is to cut down the number of cars on Britain's roads?

PLEASE TICK ONE BOX ONLY

	%
Very important	26.1
Fairly important	47.9
Not very important	14.3
Not at all important	3.8
Can't choose	6.7
(NA)	1.2

[PTIMPRIM]
b. And how important is it to improve public transport in Britain?

PLEASE TICK ONE BOX ONLY

	%
Very important	65.0
Fairly important	28.9
Not very important	2.7
Not at all important	0.8
Can't choose	1.5
(NA)	1.1

12

N=818

29. Many people feel that public transport should be improved. Here are some ways of finding the money to do it. How much would you support or oppose each one, as a way of raising money to improve public transport?

PLEASE TICK ONE BOX ON EACH LINE

		Strongly support	Support	Neither support nor oppose	Oppose	Strongly oppose	Can't choose	(NA)
[PTIMPR1]	a. Gradually doubling the cost of petrol over the next ten years	% 1.3	6.7	12.1	37.6	37.6	2.9	1.7
[PTIMPR2]	b. Charging all motorists around £2 each time they enter or drive through a city or town centre at peak times	% 5.1	20.3	12.5	32.5	25.3	3.2	1.6
[PTIMPR3]	c. Cutting in half spending on new roads	% 4.4	16.3	19.6	30.0	23.7	4.0	2.0
[PTIMPR4]	d. Cutting in half spending on maintenance of the roads we have already	% 1.0	6.2	13.1	43.4	31.5	2.7	2.0
[PTIMPR5]	e. Charging £1 for every 50 miles	% 3.5	20.6	15.4	30.2	24.6	3.9	1.8
[PTIMPR6]	f. Increasing taxes like VAT that we all pay on goods and services	% 0.5	8.3	15.0	36.0	34.8	3.3	2.1
[PTIMPR7]	g. Increasing road tax for all vehicles	% 1.5	12.5	12.7	35.1	34.0	2.5	1.8
[PTIMPR8]	h. Taxing employers for each car parking space they provide for their employees	% 4.9	20.9	18.1	26.4	23.2	4.4	2.1

13

OFFICE
USE
ONLY

[TRAFFPRBN]

30a. Please tick one box for each statement to show which is closest to your views about the following statement.

"The amount of traffic on the roads is one of the most serious problems for Britain."

PLEASE TICK **ONE** BOX ONLY

	%
Definitely true	27.4
Probably true	45.5
Probably not true	17.2
Definitely not true	4.8
Can't choose	3.9
(NA)	1.2

[TRAFCONG]

b. How true do you think the following statement is?

"Within the next twenty years or so, traffic congestion will be one of the most serious problems for Britain."

PLEASE TICK **ONE** BOX ONLY

	%
Definitely true	39.2
Probably true	46.8
Probably not true	9.0
Definitely not true	1.3
Can't choose	2.4
(NA)	1.4

31. Please tick one box for each of these statements below to show how much you agree or disagree with it.

PLEASE TICK ONE
BOX ON EACH LINE

	Agree strongly	Agree	Neither agree nor disagree	Disagree	Disagree strongly	Can't choose	(NA)
[BUSPRIOR] a. Buses should be given more priority in towns and cities, even if this makes things more difficult for car drivers	% 19.4	44.1	17.2	13.2	3.3	1.7	1.1
[CYCPEDPR] b. Cyclists and pedestrians should be given more priority in towns and cities even if this makes things more difficult for other road users	% 21.7	43.9	17.9	11.5	2.0	1.8	1.2

National Centre *for* Social Research

Formerly SCPR
Charity No. 258538

Head Office
35 Northampton Square
London EC1V 0AX
Telephone 0171 250 1866
Fax 0171 250 1524

Operations Department
100 Kings Road, Brentwood
Essex CM14 4LX
Telephone 01277 200 600
Fax 01277 214 117

C

P.1850   Green team

BRITISH SOCIAL ATTITUDES 1999   Summer 1999

SELF-COMPLETION QUESTIONNAIRE

INTERVIEWER TO ENTER

2401-6 | 1 | 1 | Serial number

2409-11   Sampling point

2412-15   Interviewer number

OFFICE USE ONLY

2407-8 | 2 | 4 | Card number

2416-20   Batch Number

2421 | C | Version

SPARE 2422-34

To the selected respondent:

Thank you very much for agreeing to take part in this important study - the fifteenth in this annual series. The study consists of this self-completion questionnaire, and the interview you have already completed. The results of the survey are published in a book each autumn; some of the questions are also being asked in thirty other countries, as part of an international survey.

Completing the questionnaire:

The questions inside cover a wide range of subjects, but most can be answered simply by placing a tick (✓) in one or more of the boxes. No special knowledge is required: we are confident that everyone will be able to take part, not just those with strong views or particular viewpoints. The questionnaire should not take very long to complete, and we hope you will find it interesting and enjoyable. **Only you should fill it in, and not anyone else at your address.** The answers you give will be treated as confidential and anonymous.

Returning the questionnaire:

Your interviewer will arrange with you the most convenient way of returning the questionnaire. If the interviewer has arranged to call back for it, please fill it in and keep it safely until then. If not, please complete it and post it back in the pre-paid, addressed envelope, AS SOON AS YOU POSSIBLY CAN.

THANK YOU AGAIN FOR YOUR HELP.

The National Centre for Social Research is an independent social research institute registered as a charitable trust. Its projects are funded by government departments, local authorities, universities and foundations to provide information on social issues in Britain. The British Social Attitudes survey series is funded mainly by one of the Sainsbury Family Charitable Trusts, with contributions also from other grant-giving bodies and government departments. Please contact us if you would like further information.

7

Note: Q1-18 of Version C of the questionnaire are the same as Q17-34 of Version A of the questionnaire.

19. From what you know or have heard, please tick one box on each line to show how well you think <u>state</u> secondary schools nowadays ...

PLEASE TICK ONE BOX ON EACH LINE

	Very well	Quite well	Not very well	Not at all well	(NA)
a. ... prepare young people for work? [STATSEC1]	% 5.6	43.1	41.2	7.1	3.0
b. ... teach young people basic skills such as reading, writing and maths? [STATSEC2]	% 13.2	54.5	23.6	6.6	2.1
c. ... bring out young people's natural abilities? [STATSEC3]	% 6.6	42.4	38.4	9.7	3.0

20. And from what you know or have heard, please tick one box for each statement about <u>universities and colleges</u> now compared with 10 years ago.

PLEASE TICK ONE BOX ON EACH LINE

	Much better now than 10 years ago	A little better	About the same	A little worse	Much worse now than 10 years ago	(NA)
a. [UNIQUAL] On the whole, do you think that students leaving university are <u>better</u> qualified or <u>worse</u> qualified nowadays than they were 10 years ago? [UNITEACH]	% 11.9	22.7	42.6	15.8	4.1	2.9
b. And do you think that the standard of teaching in universities is better or worse nowadays than it was 10 years ago? [UNIJOBS]	% 9.1	20.1	49.8	13.7	3.9	3.4
c. And do you think that students leaving university have better or worse job prospects nowadays than they had 10 years ago?	% 4.3	14.7	23.4	34.4	20.4	2.8

10

Note: Q21-24 of Version C of the questionnaire are the same as Q19-22 of Version B.

N=840

25. You may have heard of genetically modified or 'GM' foods. These are made from plants which have had their genes altered. Some people say that growing these plants may damage other plants and wildlife and that food made from them may not be safe to eat. Other people say that growing these plants may mean lower food prices and less use of pesticides and weedkillers.

Please say how much you agree or disagree with each of these statements about genetically modified (GM) foods.

PLEASE TICK ONE BOX ON EACH LINE

	Agree strongly	Agree	Neither agree nor disagree	Disagree	Disagree strongly	Can't choose	(NA)
a. In order to compete with the rest of the world, Britain should grow genetically modified (GM) foods [GMGROW]	% 3.2	6.8	17.8	37.2	27.9	5.6	1.5
b. Genetically modified (GM) foods should be banned, even if food prices suffer as a result [GMBAN]	% 20.6	31.4	21.9	14.3	5.3	5.4	1.2
c. On balance, the advantages of genetically modified (GM) foods outweigh any dangers [GMDANGER]	% 2.1	9.4	22.3	34.0	22.5	8.2	1.4
d. We should never interfere with the genes of plants and animals [GMGENES]	% 29.0	33.5	17.6	10.4	4.7	4.0	0.7

26. [GMWILDLF] In general, do you think that growing genetically modified (GM) foods poses a danger to other plants and wildlife?

PLEASE TICK ONE BOX ONLY

	%
Definitely	33.5
Probably	39.4
Probably not	12.3
Definitely not	1.2
Can't choose	12.9
(NA)	0.7

27. [GMSAFE] Do you think that all genetically modified (GM) foods already available in the shops are safe to eat?

PLEASE TICK ONE BOX ONLY

	%
Definitely	4.1
Probably	29.9
Probably not	36.4
Definitely not	12.0
Can't choose	16.8
(NA)	0.7

Note: Q28-31 of Version C of the questionnaire are the same as Q57-60 of Version A of the questionnaire.

OFFICE USE ONLY

14

N=818

32. Here are some things that might be done about Britain's traffic problems. Please tick one box for each to say how strongly you would be in favour or against it.

PLEASE TICK ONE BOX ON EACH LINE		Strongly in favour	In favour	Neither in favour nor against	Against	Strongly against	Can't choose	(NA)
a. Many more streets in cities and towns reserved for pedestrians only [PEDESTR]	%	16.9	52.7	17.4	7.8	2.0	1.7	1.6
b. Increasing parking charges [PARKCHRG]	%	3.5	16.4	22.7	41.7	11.3	1.9	2.5
c. Increasing road tax for large cars only [ROADTAX]	%	8.9	27.9	16.9	31.9	10.1	2.5	1.8
d. Increasing the number of speed bumps on roads [SPEEDBMP]	%	7.4	27.5	20.3	27.0	14.4	2.2	1.4
e. Reducing the number of parking spaces [PARKSPCE]	%	1.5	5.5	19.8	49.6	19.1	2.8	1.7
f. Having more road-narrowing schemes [ROADNRRW]	%	4.6	16.8	27.0	32.7	14.0	3.4	1.6

Note: Questions 33–36 on Version B of the questionnaire are the same as Q57-60 on Version A of the questionnaire.

Subject index